THE REMINISCENCES OF
Rear Admiral Albert G. Mumma
U.S. Navy (Retired)

INTERVIEWED BY
Paul Stillwell

U.S. Naval Institute • Annapolis, Maryland

Copyright © 2001

Preface

A great deal of the history of the U.S. Navy focuses on the operational aspects and just sort of takes for granted that the ships were there to be operated. This oral history of the late Rear Admiral Albert G. Mumma demonstrates that the reality requires a great deal of dedicated effort to produce those ships. It deals primarily with the technical aspects of the U.S. fleet: ship design, engineering, model testing, construction, sea trials, repairs, and conversion. Added to this are the political aspects of determining how many ships are to be built and in which shipyards. But there was more to Albert Mumma than that. He grew up in a service family, and for the first dozen years or so of his commissioned service he was a seagoing line officer. He enhanced his professional knowledge with overseas postgraduate work in France and thus was well qualified to branch off into the engineering duty specialty when the opportunity arose.

This memoir originated in 1986 from a suggestion made by Rear Admiral Brooks Harral, brother-in-law of Admiral Mumma. In the ensuing years we completed the interviews. I found Mumma to be a forceful, energetic, can-do individual who was not at all hesitant about expressing his opinions. And I found him to be understandably quite proud of his achievements, which he capped in the late 1950s by serving as Chief of the Bureau of Ships. He had truly risen to the top of his profession as a naval engineer.

Along the way, as a line officer, Mumma served in the commissioning crew of the aircraft carrier Saratoga and later in the destroyers Waters and Clark. He made important contributions at the David Taylor Model Basin, both as a mid-grade officer and as the commanding officer of the facility. In World War II he specialized in propellers at a time when hundreds of new warships were being fitted with them. Near the end of the war he had an extraordinary assignment as a member of the small group of naval officers who went to Europe to assess German progress in developing atomic weapons and various shipboard propulsion systems. In the years immediately after the war he was on the ground floor of the U.S. Navy's nuclear power program. He expressed in this memoir the view that Hyman G. Rickover was not his choice to run the program, nor did he believe Rickover was a sufficiently broad-gauged individual to serve as a flag officer. The name "Rickover" emerges time and again throughout this history.

In the 1950s Mumma served in the San Francisco Bay-area naval shipyards at Hunters Point and Mare Island, commanding the latter during its centennial. He believed that shipyard duty was vital as a means of applying the professional education that he had received in engineering matters. As the Chief of BuShips in the late 1950s Mumma worked closely with the Navy's top leaders during a period of profound technological innovation: surface warships armed with guided missiles, nuclear submarines with teardrop-shaped hulls that maximized underwater performance, and the Polaris ballistic missile submarines. Along with the technology, the reader also gets a picture of the political prowess needed to accomplish change. An added fillip is a discussion of William Francis Gibbs, the flinty ship designer who oversaw the design and construction of the nation's last great passenger liner, the SS United States.

In the course of moving from the raw transcript to this final version, Admiral Mumma made a number of handwritten changes to the original version. I have done further editing in the interests of accuracy, smoothness, and clarity. At times various sections of the text have been moved from one place to another in order to improve the continuity of the narrative. In addition, I have inserted footnotes to provide further information for readers who use the volume. My biggest regret is that understaffing of the oral history program prevented the completion of this transcript during Admiral Mumma's lifetime. Had he had an opportunity to review the edited version one more time, he would likely have enhanced the quality of the finished product even further.

Ms. Ann Hassinger of the Naval Institute's history division has made a significant contribution through her diligence in the overall process of printing, proofreading, and overseeing the binding of the completed volumes.

Finally, the Naval Institute expresses its gratitude to the McMullen Family Foundation of Secaucus, New Jersey, for its generous financial support to facilitate completion of this memoir. Admiral Mumma was a mentor to John J. McMullen and helped facilitate his postgraduate education.

Paul Stillwell
Director, History Division
U.S. Naval Institute
May 2001

ALBERT GIRARD MUMMA
REAR ADMIRAL, U.S. NAVY (RETIRED)

Albert Girard Mumma was a son of the Midwest, having been born in Findlay, Ohio, on 2 June 1906 as a member of a family with an outstanding military tradition. His father, Colonel Morton C. Mumma, USA, was a graduate of the U.S. Military Academy, class of 1900. His two brothers, Rear Admiral Morton C. Mumma, Jr., USN (Ret.), and Major George E. Mumma, USA (Ret.), both graduated from the U.S. Naval Academy.

Albert Mumma received his early education at Army posts in Iowa, Texas, the Philippines, Georgia, and Washington, D.C. He graduated from Iowa City High School in 1922 and received a congressional appointment to the Naval Academy. While a midshipman he was a member of the rifle team and the Masqueraders drama group. He graduated with distinction, standing 18th in his class of 456. He received the award established by the class of 1924 for standing highest in the graduating class for the course in the Department of Engineering and Aeronautics. He was commissioned an ensign upon graduation, to date from 3 June 1926. Subsequent dates of rank were as follows: lieutenant (junior grade), 3 June 1929; lieutenant, 29 June 1936; lieutenant commander, 26 June 1940; commander, 15 August 1942; captain, 1 August 1943; rear admiral, 1 July 1954.

Sea duty during his early career as a commissioned officer included service on board the light cruiser Richmond (CL-9) in 1926; the armored cruiser Seattle, flagship of the United States Fleet, in 1927; and on board the aircraft carrier Saratoga (CV-3) during her fitting-out period and from the time of her commissioning, 16 November 1927, until June 1931. After duty on board the destroyer Waters (DD-115), he attended the Navy's Postgraduate School in Annapolis, Maryland, from 1932 to 1934. From 1934 to 1936 he completed his postgraduate work at l'Ecole Nationale Superieure du Génie Maritime in Paris, France. In 1936, upon finishing his studies, Lieutenant Mumma was ordered as chief engineer of a new destroyer leader, the USS Clark (DD-361).

As a lieutenant commander he served as propeller officer at the David Taylor Model Basin, Carderock, Maryland, doing special propeller and shaft design research at the time the United States entered World War II. In January 1943, when he was a commander, he was assigned to the propeller desk in the Bureau of Ships with additional duty at the Model Basin. He received a letter of commendation from the Secretary of the Navy for his outstanding services as head of that section. He was one of four naval members of the top secret Alsos Mission of the Manhattan District, which investigated German progress on the atomic bomb in late 1944 and early 1945. Later he also frequently had additional duty with the successor Naval Technical Mission in France, Germany, and other parts of Europe. It was in connection with this work that he headed the technical group that visited the headquarters of Admiral Karl Doenitz at Flensburg and Glucksburg, Germany, just prior to V-E Day. This group secured Dr. Helmuth Walter and his group that had done development work on U-boats, V-1 and V-2 rockets, and torpedoes for the Germans. On the staff of Commander Naval Forces Europe, Mumma was head of the Naval Technical Intelligence Division that evaluated the research work of German naval scientists. During this last portion of the war he also served as assistant naval attaché in London and as naval member of the U.S.-London Munitions Board.

After returning to the United States, on 20 December 1945 Captain Mumma became Deputy Director of Ship Design in charge of the design of machinery in the Bureau of Ships. In early 1946 the Bureau of Ships established an internal organization for the handling of nuclear matters, including studies of the possible application of nuclear power to ship propulsion. This organization was later formalized in May 1947, naming three new sections: Radiological Safety Section, Atomic Warfare Defense Section, and Nuclear Power Section. In 1949 he was assigned as production officer at San Francisco Naval Shipyard (Hunters Point). Then in 1951 he was ordered as commanding officer of the David Taylor Model Basin. In 1954 he was promoted to rear admiral and became shipyard commander at Mare Island Naval Shipyard, Vallejo, California. He participated in the Mare Island Centennial in 1954 and during his tenure converted the yard to nuclear submarine construction. In 1955 he was appointed by the President as Chief of the Bureau of Ships, Navy Department, Washington, D.C. During his time in the billet, the Navy acquired a nuclear-powered destroyer, cruiser, and aircraft carrier, guided missile ships, high-speed nuclear attack submarines, and Polaris ballistic missile submarines. Upon completion of this duty, Admiral Mumma voluntarily retired on 1 May 1959.

Following his retirement from active naval service, Admiral Mumma joined the Worthington Corporation in June 1959 as vice president of engineering. In 1961 he was elected vice president, group executive. He was elected a director in 1962, executive vice president in 1964, and president on 20 April 1967. He was elected chairman on 27 November 1967 and retired from the corporation in that position on 1 July 1971. In 1971 he was appointed by President Richard Nixon as chairman of the American Shipbuilding Commission, which studied and reported to the President and Congress on measures to improve the shipbuilding posture of the U.S. merchant marine. He spent his retirement years in Florida, New Hampshire, and Pennsylvania. Admiral Mumma died on 15 July 1997 in Gladwyne, Pennsylvania.

He held the following awards: Commendation Ribbon, American Defense Service Medal, American Campaign Medal, European-African-Middle Eastern Campaign Medal; World War II Victory Medal, and the National Defense Service Medal, as well as the Expert Rifleman and Expert Pistol Shot medals.

Admiral Mumma married Miss Carmen Evelyn Braley of Iowa on 1 October 1927. They were the parents of three sons: Albert Girard Mumma, Jr., John Stanton Mumma, and David Braley Mumma.

He was a member of the American Society of Naval Engineers and in 1957 he served a one-year term as president of the organization. He was also a member of the Society of Naval Architects and Marine Engineers and served as its president in 1959-1960.

Authorization

The U.S. Naval Institute is hereby authorized to make available to individuals, libraries, and other repositories of its choosing the transcripts of five oral history interviews concerning the life and naval career of the undersigned. The interviews were recorded on 3 October 1986, 20 April 1987, 3 March 1988, 4 March 1988, and 3 September 1988 in collaboration with Paul Stillwell for the U.S. Naval Institute.

The undersigned does hereby release and assign to the U.S. Naval Institute the rights and title to these interviews, with the exception that the undersigned retains the right to use the material for his own purposes, as he sees fit. The copyright in both the oral and transcribed versions shall be the sole property of the U.S. Naval Institute. The tape recordings of the interviews are and will remain the property of the U.S. Naval Institute.

Signed and sealed this 1st day of Oct. 1996.

Albert G. Mumma
Rear Admiral, U.S. Navy (Retired)

Thank you
P.S. we are now in
Villa 25- A.G.M.

Interview Number 1 with Rear Admiral Albert G. Mumma, U.S. Navy (Retired)

Place: U.S. Naval Institute, Annapolis, Maryland

Date: Friday, 3 October 1986

Interviewer: Paul Stillwell

Paul Stillwell: Admiral, to begin at the beginning, could you tell me something about your family background and your earliest memories of your own life?

Admiral Mumma: My dad was regular Army, class of 1900.[*] So we, as a family, moved to many, many Army posts all over the United States and the Philippines and other parts of the world. When I was a young fellow, about age nine, in the Philippines I went aboard a Navy destroyer as a guest with my family, and was extremely interested in the USS Barry (DD-2).[†] I told my father I wanted to go to the Naval Academy. I didn't really want to go to West Point. In spite of some lack of enthusiasm on his part, he admitted that that might be a good idea. He had served various times in ROTC duties.[‡] The first one was when he was a young assistant professor of military science and tactics at the University of Iowa. He went back there as the professor of military science and tactics in 1919, after World War I.

Paul Stillwell: Had he served overseas in France during the war?

Admiral Mumma: No. His story was a very strange one, because he had been one of the top rifle shots in the Army. He had been a member of the Palma International Team

---

[*] The interviewee's father was Morton Claire Mumma, a graduate of the U.S. Military Academy class of 1900. His father was a cavalry officer who retired from active duty as a lieutenant colonel in 1928 and was promoted to colonel on the retired list in 1930. He then worked for 14 years for Sears and Roebuck. The senior Mumma died on 30 May 1945 at the age of 67.
[†] USS Barry (DD-2) was commissioned 24 November 1902. She had a standard displacement of 420 tons, was 250 feet long, and 24 feet in the beam. Her top speed was 28 knots. She was armed with two 3-inch guns and two torpedo tubes.
[‡] ROTC—Reserve Officer Training Corps.

twice, had captained the cavalry rifle team, wherein he was a specialist in cavalry. And he had attended the national matches many, many times up at Camp Perry, Ohio. So as a result, he knew almost all of the major riflemen in the United States, including Newton D. Baker, who was the Secretary of War in World War I. When the war broke out in 1917, we were stationed at Fort D. A. Russell, Wyoming, with a cavalry regiment.

Word came from Washington that that cavalry regiment was going to be reassigned to field artillery. They were not going to use cavalry; they needed field artillery in World War I. So dad was ordered to Washington on Newton D. Baker's staff, on the general staff. At that time the whole State, War, and Navy departments were in the old State-War-Navy Building, which is now the office of the President's building. Newton D. Baker told him, "Morton, you are not going to go overseas. Your job in this war is to teach every single rifleman in the United States and pistol shot, how to shoot. The way in which you're going to do this is we're going to set up a small arms firing school at Camp Perry, Ohio, and you will have command of it. We will send there one officer from every regiment in the United States. He will then go back to his own unit and teach them to shoot after you have taught him how to shoot—both pistol and rifle, movable targets, fixed targets, etc."

They even had two aircraft there in early 1918 when this was started. One of them was a de Havilland IV. It was flown by then Major Smith, who was one of the three original Army fliers taught by Wilbur and Orville Wright. So I met him early in my life and had an interest in aviation. I flew in that airplane—first flight I ever had.

Paul Stillwell: What year would that have been?

Admiral Mumma: At that time I was 12. My brother Mort also flew in that same plane.[*]

At any rate, the winter of 1918 came, and Newton D. Baker said, "You've got to set up a winter small arms firing school." So Dad was ordered to Columbus, Georgia. They dug out of the woods an area that was then called Camp Benning—now Fort Benning—I believe the largest army post in the world. That was our small arms firing school for winter quarters, when you could not use Camp Perry because of the weather.

---

[*] Morton C. Mumma, Jr., who later graduated from the Naval Academy in the class of 1925.

Then came the armistice and the end of the necessity for that activity.* Dad was ordered back to the University of Iowa as professor of military science and tactics, and I went through Iowa City High School there. So the beginning of my preparation for the Naval Academy was Iowa City High School. I graduated from high school in three and a half years. I took all the extra courses that were needed to enter Naval Academy. I graduated sufficiently high in my class that I entered on certificate. In those days if you had an adequate certificate, you didn't have to take the substantiating exams. So my brother and I both entered that way.

I was appointed by Congressman Harry Hull of that district. My dad was with me at the academy when I entered; I think it was the third of July of 1922. At that time Sinclair Gannon was commandant of midshipmen.† He was class of 1900 at the Naval Academy, and he and my Dad had played football against each other in the Army-Navy game. So I was introduced to Sinclair Gannon rather early. Henry B. Wilson was the superintendent.‡

Paul Stillwell: How had your older brother gotten interested in coming to the Naval Academy?

Admiral Mumma: He had planned to go to West Point. In 1921, when an appointment came due for him, he had graduated from that same high school. He had adequate grades and so forth to get in on a certificate. They didn't have an appointment available for West Point, but they did have one for the class of '25 at the Naval Academy. In those days, starting with the class of—oh, I guess, 1915—they started switching back from the Naval Academy to the Army. Quite a number of officers did so. When my brother's class entered, that was possible, and he planned to do that. But at the end of four years, he had the Navy pretty well indoctrinated in his thoughts.

---

* The armistice ending World War I was on 11 November 1918.
† Captain Sinclair Gannon, USN, served from 1925 to 1928 as the Naval Academy's commandant of midshipmen.
‡ Rear Admiral Henry B. Wilson, USN, served as superintendent of the Naval Academy from July 1921 to February 1925.

In addition, he had learned—I think during his second class year—that such a switch was no longer contemplated. They didn't need any additional officers from the Naval Academy to supplement West Point; all West Point graduates were able to fill the requirement. So he then stayed in the Navy, and he went to a battleship. He then went to destroyers and submarines and finally commanded all PTs in the Southwest Pacific during World War II.

When I graduated a year later, my first interest, of course, was engineering—had been from the beginning.

Paul Stillwell: How had that interest developed?

Admiral Mumma: Well, I just was mechanically inclined. As a kid I'd always worked on the automobiles—changed the spark plugs, set the timing. The fact that my father allowed me to do it on our family car is a surprise to me now. I doubt if I would be equally enthusiastic about one of my sons doing that on our family car. I took mechanical drawing in high school; I took trigonometry in high school. I did things that would prepare me for the Naval Academy.

Paul Stillwell: Did you go to a preparatory school as such—one of the cram schools?

Admiral Mumma: No, I just went through high school. But the net result of that was that I had a sort of a burning interest. And I did well, because I suppose I was one of the few in my class that had taken mechanical drawing before coming to the Naval Academy. So I immediately began getting very high marks in what we then called ME & NC—marine engineering and naval construction. Well, by the time I had gone through three years of engineering at ME & NC, it was changed to the department of engineering and aeronautics. My class was the first class to get aeronautical engineering training at the Naval Academy—both in studies as well as practical. We were also the first class where half the class missed one summer cruise in order to take this aviation training. So it wasn't by accident that we had such a high percentage of naval aviators in the class of '26.

One of the young officers that was here at that time was a Lieutenant Radford.* I got to know him. I flew in his flying boats—the H-16s and the F-5Ls—and he was one of the first to sign my flight log.

I was doing well enough my first class year in aviation, and so forth, to bolster my work that I'd been doing the first three years, that I won the then just brand newly established Class of 1924 gold watch for standing first in the class in engineering and aeronautics, which I thought really was quite an honor.

Paul Stillwell: Did you have any trouble adjusting to the naval discipline, given your background?

Admiral Mumma: No, I'd had quite adequate discipline during my time with Dad in the Army. It was a little different life, but I enjoyed every bit of it, really. And I stood well. I had a little trouble overcoming the lead that these guys had in academics. We had one or two members at the Naval Academy who had already graduated from colleges. And, of course, they had a very great head start, in the first two or three years at least. But, oh, I think I stood about 70-something my first year, which was in the upper 10%. Because we started at about 780-some in my class.† Then I stood about 60-some the next year; and then I stood about 20-some; and then my first class year, I stood about eight.

Paul Stillwell: You moved up every year.

Admiral Mumma: So, and by the time I graduated, that composite, I ended up number 18, which was a star man. So that was heading toward my goal of becoming an engineer in the Navy.

Paul Stillwell: The top people in the classes then typically went into that branch.

---

* Lieutenant Arthur W. Radford, USN, later a four-star admiral. He served as Chairman of the Joint Chiefs of Staff, 1953-57.
† The Naval Academy class of 1926 began with 683 midshipmen; 456 graduated.

Albert G. Mumma, Interview #1 (10/3/86) – Page 6

Admiral Mumma: Yes, almost all the people going into marine engineering and naval construction, and getting the postgraduates, were all within about the top 10% of the class.

Paul Stillwell: Had you given any thought to going into aviation yourself?

Admiral Mumma: Oh, yes. Well, my class had this automatic aviation training. Only half the class did the first-class midshipmen's cruise. The other half of the class stayed here and took aviation training. I then took the aviation training the summer after graduation. I was in the class group that took the first class cruise. So we had three of the most wonderful cruises. Our first class cruise was from Annapolis all the way through the Panama Canal, all the way up the West Coast to Seattle—Bremerton—and all the way back.

Paul Stillwell: Which ship was that in?

Admiral Mumma: I was at that time in the New York.* My second class cruise was in the Wyoming.† That was a European cruise. My youngster cruise, I was in the Arkansas, and that was also a European cruise. So in those two cruises we saw the Scandinavian countries; we saw England, Scotland; we saw France; we saw Spain; we saw Portugal, Gibraltar, the Azores, back to the States.

These ships were all coal burners, you must remember. So we had to coal ship at a lot of those ports. Of course, in those days, the starboard half of the ship was all midshipmen. And the port half of the ship was all regular crew. So they removed half the crew of each of those ships during the time the midshipmen were aboard, and the midshipmen manned all aspects of the starboard half of the ship. We manned those boilers; we manned those engine rooms, and so forth. And, of course, depending upon how lowly a young seaman you were, you scrubbed decks, you cleaned out the heads, you did everything that was required in those ships.

---

* USS New York (BB-34) was commissioned 15 April 1914.
† USS Wyoming (BB-32) was commissioned as a battleship in 1912 and served in that role until being demilitarized as a result of the 1930 London Treaty on the limitation of naval armaments.

This was the big deal, because every single person on the ship coaled ship, except the captain and the band. Even the executive officer was down there shoveling coal with the black gang. You'd pile the coal on deck from a damn dirty old Welsh coal collier, and you would end up blacker than the ace of spades when you came out of that barge. And you coaled ship until you finished. Sometimes it was 10 hours; sometimes it was 24 hours; sometimes it was more hours, depending upon how much striking down you had to do. Well, with three coaling ships for cruises, you were pretty well toughened up by the time you graduated. And each year aboard ship you moved up a scale. You became a sub-petty officer as a second classman. You became a first class petty officer as a first classman.

Paul Stillwell: You said everybody coaled except the captain and the band. Why was the band exempt?

Admiral Mumma: The band was exempt because they had to play the whole time during the coaling to keep up the morale and the spirits of this crowd. It was a discouraging process. [Laughter] At any rate, they'd bring sandwiches down, and you'd eat sandwiches on the job—coffee, and so on. You'd eat on the job.

Well, in 1923 I was a youngster. In other words, I'd just finished plebe year. These three battleships went to Europe. I was assigned to the Arkansas, which was a pretty ancient battleship even in those days.[*] I was in the deck force the first half of the cruise and of course, the last half of the cruise went into the black gang and shoveled coal.

I don't know that everybody realizes that in those days half the crew was put ashore, and the whole starboard half of the ship was turned over to the midshipmen to operate. The first classmen were the senior petty officers, the second classmen were middle petty officers, and the third classmen were—in other words, youngsters—were

---

[*] USS Arkansas (BB-33) was commissioned 17 September 1912. Following modernization in 1925-26 she had a standard displacement of 26,100 tons, was 562 feet long and 106 feet in the beam. Her top speed was 21 knots. She was armed with 12 12-inch guns and 16 5-inch guns. She was the oldest U.S. battleship in active service during World War II, eventually being decommissioned in 1946.

the ordinary seamen. So we did all the routine work on board ship that had to do with scrubbing decks; with having to do with all sorts of menial tasks that happened.

The skipper of this USS Arkansas was Captain Ridley McLean, who had a reputation of being something of a sundowner—in other words, a tough man to work for.* For example, when we were out scrubbing the decks in the morning before breakfast with swabs and with holystoning in some occasions, we would suddenly look up and find that the skipper would be standing up on the upper platform deck just above us, watching to see that we holystoned athwartships to ensure that we did not wear down the grain of the wood unevenly by holystoning fore and aft.† This holystoning athwartships was supposed to keep the deck wear uniform and reduce the graininess of the deck.

Well, this used to, shall we say, annoy us midshipmen somewhat. We were in Copenhagen for several days, and we had a very interesting time visiting the Tivoli Gardens, etc. The skipper took a walk into town one day, and he was run over by a whole flotilla of bicycles and sprained his ankle pretty badly. Then he was confined to his room for several days while his ankle healed, which removed him from his platform view of our work. We felt that things were going much better when the skipper was laid up. So that was a first experience with a very tough taskmaster. Of course, we all learned sooner or later at the Naval Academy that you did the best you could under all circumstances, particularly if you had a tough taskmaster.

Paul Stillwell: You mentioned before we started the tape that when he'd come out to watch you in the morning he was still in his pajamas.

Admiral Mumma: That's right. He would step out in his pajamas to make sure that we were on the job early.

Paul Stillwell: Do you remember any other eccentricities from Captain McLean?

---
* Captain Ridley McLean, USN, commanded the battleship Arkansas (BB-33) from 1922 to 1924.
† Holystoning refers to the practice of cleaning a ship's wooden decks by scraping them with bricks pushed back and forth across the planks by means of wooden handles. It is a laborious operation.

Admiral Mumma: Well, he actually was, I think a pretty reasonable skipper under the circumstances, because we had to coal ship every single place we stopped. I already mentioned to you that when you coaled ship, everybody coaled ship except the captain and the band, including the executive officer and all the officers. So that it had a very humanizing effect on all of us, this coaling ship process. Of course, he had had his experience as a coaling officer when he was a younger officer himself, because all ships were coal-burners in those days.

Paul Stillwell: I think he was something of a disciple of Admiral Sims, wasn't he?*

Admiral Mumma: Yes, I think he had served with him, and I think he, you know, was an old-time Navy sea dog, so to speak.

Moving ahead, I was in the group that then, after I graduated, took aviation training here at the Naval Academy. We got flight pay. My classmates who took the training previously did not get flight pay, because there was no provision for midshipmen to get flight pay. But there was a provision for ensigns to get flight pay, so we got flight pay during this summer, which caused a little consternation. Plus the fact that we had the benefit of that first class cruise, which I thought was tremendous. So I thought I was just lucky to be in that half of the class.

The second thing was that we didn't get any leave after graduation. We went directly into aviation training. So we got our leave at the end of the aviation training—the month of September. At the end of that leave, when I went back to Iowa to visit the family, I was ordered to the Richmond, a four-stack light cruiser.

Paul Stillwell: Before you get to that, I'd like you to discuss your rifle team activities while you were at the Naval Academy, because you were obviously following your father's example.

---

* Vice Admiral/Admiral William S. Sims, USN, served as Commander U.S. Naval Forces Operating in European Waters from 1917 to 1919.

Admiral Mumma: Well, my brother and I both had been shooters ever since we were kids. We used to go hunting with Dad. Because I was the youngest, I would get a chance to shoot first with my Winchester automatic .22. If I missed, my brother would use his 410 shotgun. If he missed, then Dad would get the rabbit, or the squirrel, or the bird, or whatever we were hunting, with his 10-gauge or 12-gauge shotgun. So we not only hunted, but we also did a lot of shooting along with Dad.

I remember going with my Dad in 1919, when he did not have command of the national matches. It was commanded that time by a Marine officer, and it was at Caldwell, New Jersey. We were up there after a flood that spring in 1919. It was terrible. We were all quartered in the camp. That was the occasion that my father took to take us up to West Point, from camp. My brother and I participated in the matches as tyros—youngsters, you know—and we didn't win anything much. But later, in 1920, my brother and my Dad shot on a Leach Cup team—800, 900, and 1,000 yards, all prone. My brother broke the world's record with a 215 out of 215. It has been tied since, but, of course, never has been beaten. My Dad was on the team. It was a pickup team, and they won the Leach Cup. But it was not an official group, and the Leach Cup was supposed to be for an organization. I don't know that we should say this out loud, but when they decided that they wouldn't accredit them as an organization, they called it the KMA Team, which was "kiss my ass." But they won the match.

Paul Stillwell: Nineteen twenty was the year that the Navy team did a great deal to contribute to the Olympic team—Carl Osburn and Willis Lee.[*] Did you know them?

Admiral Mumma: Yes, all of those fellows came to the national matches. In 1920 and '21, when those fellows were at the national matches, the midshipmen gave a very good account of themselves at Camp Perry. I met almost all of them: class of '22, '23, '24. Armand Morgan was in '24.[†] So when I entered in 1922, I knew quite a number of them, even though '22 had already graduated.

---

[*] Commander Carl T. Osburn, USN, and Lieutenant Commander Willis A. Lee, Jr., USN, were members of the U.S. team for the 1920 Olympic Games in Antwerp, Belgium. Lee won five gold medals as part of the team.
[†] Midshipman Armand M. Morgan, USN, finished first in his class in the final overall standings.

Paul Stillwell: Do you have any specific recollections of Osburn or Lee from your encounters with them?

Admiral Mumma: Well, Lee was called Chink Lee, and he was a terrific, terrific rifleman. My brother was absolutely one of the best, however. I don't remember anyone really besting him in the long run. Because he became, like my Dad, a distinguished rifleman. He was also a distinguished pistol shot, which means that you have won three major events at the national matches in each event, pistol and rifle. My brother also became a distinguished shooter. I was too heavily engaged in engineering to follow up on it the way my brother did. But it worked in with his ordnance interest, and so forth, so he followed that line all his life. I was a little less enthusiastic about rifle shooting, and I never achieved the excellence that he did. I was a member of the Navy rifle team in 1927, the year after I graduated, and we went to Camp Perry. But after that I was ordered to the Saratoga, brand-new ship. I was in heaven in that brand-new aircraft carrier.

Paul Stillwell: You said Lee was an expert rifleman. What qualities made him so good?

Admiral Mumma: Well, he was patient; he was kind; he was considerate of others; he was a good leader. He did these things that—you have to have steady nerves if you're going to be a good rifleman. And most riflemen did have good steady nerves.

Paul Stillwell: He had bad eyes, which were certainly a handicap.

Admiral Mumma: Well, in those days they used shooting glasses. I never did use shooting glasses, even though I had a little myopia. But in pistol I was better than I was in rifle. As a matter of fact, in those days we had a competition here in Bancroft Hall.* I remember having a possible score in pistol—a score matched by only one other fellow in the class of '28, who also had a possible. But I don't know that they have that same kind

---

* Bancroft Hall is the large multi-wing dormitory that houses Naval Academy midshipmen. It also contains the offices of members of the executive department, including the commandant, executive officer, and battalion and company officers.

of competition anymore. I've never heard of anyone, other than the two of us, having possible scores in pistol.

Paul Stillwell: You mean you got as high as was possible?

Admiral Mumma: Yes. But he did that after I did. So for a while I was pistol champ. But I never followed up on it professionally the way my brother did. I wanted to stick to engineering.

Paul Stillwell: Did these shooting glasses differ from regular spectacles in any way?

Admiral Mumma: Well, they were usually only half specs on the right side, which was ordinarily the shooting eye, to keep the bolt from hitting the glass and breaking it. Other than that, they would look like ordinary glasses.

Paul Stillwell: Did they confer any magnification?

Admiral Mumma: No, they restored your eyesight to normal and that was all. However, in some matches you could use a telescope mounted right on the rifle. In many, many instances, the use of a telescope was mandatory if you were going to do well to dope the wind. You'd look through the scope and see the heat waves going this way and that way, which would tell you what the wind down range was doing. So that you could then adjust your windage and allow for the bullet to be carried a little bit by the wind, which got to be quite scientific among real good riflemen and pistol shots. Pistol not so much because much shorter range. But at 800, 900, 1,000 yards, doping the wind was really an art.

Paul Stillwell: I'm sure it would be.

Admiral Mumma: So that was the reason my brother was so strongly involved with the rifle team here at the Naval Academy and the ordnance department. Then his son also has carried on after him in rifle work.* Up until very recently he was the executive director of the National Rifle Association. My brother was also the executive director of the National Rifle Association, which I never was. I was a member but not active in it.

Paul Stillwell: Did your younger brother also join that interest in shooting?

Admiral Mumma: Not to the same degree, no. He was a Johnny-come-lately from that point of view. He was eight years behind me at the Naval Academy.† We had both graduated, so he was interested in other things—particularly football—more than in rifle shooting.

Paul Stillwell: And he probably hadn't shared these hunting trips with your father.

Admiral Mumma: No, he hadn't. We older two sons used to go to camp with Dad. I remember we went to Camp Perry when he was captain of the cavalry team and slept in the tent with him. We'd go out and shoot as kids. We'd have a .22 match, and we'd have all kinds of fun.

Paul Stillwell: Was there a friendly Army-Navy rivalry within the family?

Admiral Mumma: Oh, yes. Mother was always praying for a tie.

Paul Stillwell: At Army-Navy football games?

Admiral Mumma: Yes. Ah, that was terrible.

---

* The interviewee's nephew, referred to here, is Morton C. Mumma III, who graduated from the U.S. Military Academy in the class of 1948 and eventually retired as an Air Force colonel in 1978.
† Midshipman George E. Mumma, USN, graduated from the Naval Academy in 1934 and resigned that same year. He later served as an Army officer during World War II and retired in 1945 as a major.

Albert G. Mumma, Interview #1 (10/3/86) – Page 14

Paul Stillwell: Do you have recollections of going up to the Polo Grounds to see those games?[*]

Admiral Mumma: Oh, yes. You know, my class was the one that never saw a Navy victory. Army beat us all four years.[†] One year we were playing at Memorial Stadium in Baltimore. Garbisch was Army's kicker, and he beat us 12-0.[‡] The score was Garbisch 12, Navy 0. He kicked four field goals. Well, thereafter, whenever we went through Baltimore, we always pulled down the shades.

Paul Stillwell: Well, you should have stayed one year longer because the '26 Navy team was a very good one.

Admiral Mumma: I later saw the '26 game at Soldier Field in Chicago.[§]

After I had graduated and gone through the period of aviation training, I then reported to the Richmond.[**] She and three other ships—one division of light cruisers—were headed for Guantanamo from New York. We were third ship in column. The Detroit was the flagship. When we were, I'd say, about 100 miles east of Jacksonville we noticed a reddish glow in the far east. In those days there was no warning of hurricanes. This was late September. The only warning you'd ever get was in case a ship happened to be in the path of a hurricane. There was no aviation warning of any kind. So we decided this was a hurricane. Everybody came to that conclusion pretty quickly. So we steamed due east, supposedly to avoid it. But we didn't avoid this one. This was the hurricane that demolished Miami in 1926. We four ships opened to triple distance, and we battened everything down. And those ships had tripod masts.

---

[*] In the early 1920s the annual Army-Navy game was at the Polo Grounds, a ballpark in New York City.
[†] The scores: 1922, Army 17, Navy 14; 1923, Army 0, Navy 0; 1924, Army 12, Navy 0; 1925, Army 10, Navy 3.
[‡] Cadet Edgar W. Garbisch was in the class of 1925 at the Military Academy.
[§] The 1926 game ended in a 21-21 tie.
[**] USS Richmond (CL-9), an Omaha-class light cruiser, was commissioned 2 July 1923. She had a standard displacement of 7,050 tons, was 555 feet long, and 55 feet in the beam. Her top speed was 34 knots. She was armed with twelve 6-inch guns, four 3-inch guns, and ten 21-inch torpedo tubes. She was eventually decommissioned in 1945 after service in World War II.

Paul Stillwell: Very tall ones.

Admiral Mumma: They had no covered access to the bridge. So we had to climb those ladders to the bridge during that hurricane. I've never been through a hurricane since then, and I don't ever want to be. We had about 130 miles an hour in the dangerous semicircle. In the so-called safer semicircle, it was down to something of the order of about 90, which gave the progress of the hurricane at about 20 miles an hour. We were very definitely ensconced in the upper semicircle, because we had turned east and the hurricane was going just a little below us. We saw the center go by just a little bit to the starboard of us.

We had to slow to steerageway, about six knots. We couldn't make any more speed against the waves. You would look at the ship ahead of you, and the whole stern would come out of the water with four propellers fanning the breeze. The rudder was going like this—wiggle-waggle. Then you look at the ship astern, and you see her bow come out of the water. You see all the way down the keel to under the bridge. Then you know that you are rolling about 45 to 50 degrees on each side—rolling over 90 degrees total. And wallowing in this, we were very fortunate to keep steerageway and to keep into the waves without broaching.

Paul Stillwell: That class of ship was a particularly bad roller, wasn't it?

Admiral Mumma: Well, they were a flush-deck ship. We took solid water actually splashing against the bridge, which was a high bridge. But it would hit the forward turrets. It would hit everything and spray all over the ship. That ship was so tightly battened down that we were actually getting water down the stacks. Nobody went on deck unless they were going on watch to the bridge. It was so tightly battened down that it was a funkhole down below. Almost everybody in the ship was sick at one time or another during that storm. I was a pretty good sailor. I didn't ordinarily get seasick, but, boy, I was on that ship that time.

Paul Stillwell: It would be tough to eat and sleep in that kind of circumstance.

Admiral Mumma: We didn't sleep. You thought you were sleeping, but all you were doing was hanging on.

Paul Stillwell: And you had foul air on top of that.

Admiral Mumma: Yes. So that was an experience that I didn't ever want to go through again. Secondly, we got down to Guantanamo, and I met up with my ship, which was the Seattle.* When I reported aboard, Handle Bars Hughes was commander in chief of the fleet.† The Seattle was the oldest ship in the Navy practically. The Rochester was the only other one that was in service at the time down in the Panama's area.

Paul Stillwell: Special Service Squadron.

Admiral Mumma: Yes. The USS Seattle, incidentally, was also a coal burner.

Paul Stillwell: One of the old armored cruisers.

Admiral Mumma: Yes, she was an armored cruiser of the armored cruiser squadron. She previously was called the Washington, and then became the Seattle. "The Washington and the Tennessee, the finest ships that sail the sea." Well, the Tennessee was the Memphis later, and the Memphis was impaled on the rocks at Santo Domingo.‡ When we went into Santo Domingo Harbor in 1927, here was our sister ship high and dry on the rocks. It wasn't until World War II that that ship was completely dismantled for the scrap iron. It was quite a monument when we were there in 1927.

---

* USS Seattle (armored cruiser number 11) was commissioned 7 August 1906 as the Washington; she was renamed in 1916. The ship was 504 feet long, 72 feet in the beam, and displaced 15,700 tons. She was armed with four 10-inch guns and 16 6-inch.
† Admiral Charles F. Hughes, USN, served as Commander in Chief U.S. Fleet in 1926-27, then was Chief of Naval Operations, 1927-30. The Seattle served as flagship of the U.S. Fleet from 1923 to 1927.
‡ USS Memphis (armored cruiser number 10) was washed ashore by a tidal wave at Santo Domingo on 29 August 1916. For details see Captain Edward L. Beach, USN (Ret.), "Sentimental Mission to Memphis, Naval History, October 1993, pages 16-20.

Paul Stillwell: Captain Ned Beach has written about that because his dad was the skipper of the Memphis when she went aground.*

Admiral Mumma: All right, well, anyhow, when I was standing watches in the Seattle, old Handle Bars Hughes couldn't sleep very well. He would come up, and he would stand the 4:00 to 8:00 watch with me, and he would tell me how he remembered my father. They were both riflemen, and he'd shot on the Navy team against my Dad on the Army team. So the admiral was a very, very pleasant fellow, although he looked forbidding. They called him "Handle Bars" because he had these two enormous flowing mustachios. He had the reputation of being a pretty sour old puss. But he really was a fine gentleman. Then later when we'd be at anchor at, say, Guantanamo, or somewhere, I'd have the midwatch, or the 4:00 to 8:00 watch, why, the old boy would come up and you'd pace the deck—down and up. You learned how to pace the deck properly and keep a good watch out for everything that was going on. So I enjoyed that extra little instruction I used to get from Admiral Hughes.

Paul Stillwell: Was he a storyteller at all during these walks?

Admiral Mumma: To some degree, yes. He wasn't very voluble in his stories. But occasionally he'd tell a story and they were, usually, in the really olden days and the coal burners and the sailing days, because he was in the sailing ships as well.† Many of these ships had been originally rigged for sail, many of the old coal burners.

Paul Stillwell: With your contact with the fleet staff, did you get any extra insight into fleet operations that you might not have had in another ship?

Admiral Mumma: Oh, indirectly as officer of the deck, and maneuvering and handling

---

* Edward Latimer "Ned" Beach, Jr., Naval Academy class of 1939, has written a number of books, most notably the submarine novel Run Silent, Run Deep. His father, also named Edward Latimer Beach, was an 1888 Naval Academy graduate who wrote popular fiction for boys. For a profile of Ned Beach, see Naval History, Summer 1988, pages 62-64.
† Hughes graduated from the Naval Academy in 1888, the same year as did Edward L. Beach.

the ship. I qualified for top watch at anchor almost immediately. That meant that you rendered honors to all visiting dignitaries. That first year at sea, we left New York in January, and we didn't get back north until about June. The reason for it was that the commander in chief made a goodwill tour of the Caribbean. That itinerary after Guantanamo consisted of Kingston, Jamaica, and we went to Colon, Panama, on the Atlantic side. Then we went to Caracas, Venezuela, Santo Domingo, Haiti, and then back north. And we fired battle practice while we were south.

Paul Stillwell: Are there any of those ports that particularly stand out in your mind?

Admiral Mumma: Venezuela was one that stood out in my mind because there we moored at La Guaira and took the train up to Caracas.

The most amazing thing was that at every port, the whole ship's officer company was entertained everywhere. It wasn't a very large ship, and it didn't have a very large officer staff—even including the staff of the commander in chief—so we all had to go. If you didn't have the watch, you went out on the party. We all had to go to the parties ashore. Then they'd invite all the bigwigs from local areas to the party aboard ship, and we had to go to that party. So after about five or six of these ports, we all were hankering to get the watch. [Laughter] Our laundry was working overtime, because we were in mess jackets the whole time, whether ashore or aboard ship.

Paul Stillwell: You were being killed with kindness.

Admiral Mumma: I'll say. Well, I can remember in Santo Domingo, that was notable because of our sister ship, the <u>Memphis</u>, being on the rocks there. And they had a very nice shindig for us at the country club there, a beautiful orchestra, and music, and dinner, and so forth. I remember I was dancing with one of the Santo Domingan gals; they spoke Spanish in Santo Domingo, whereas in Haiti, they spoke French. But suddenly came some guards with rifles marching one of my shipmates in the junior officers' mess in to the dance floor. He apparently had been strolling in the garden with one of the young ladies. They were preserving her integrity by ensuring that they didn't get too far away.

So they marched him in, and turned him over to some of the senior officers. He was an ensign. I will not mention his name.

Paul Stillwell: Did all the girls have duennas with them?

Admiral Mumma: In those days they were very carefully protected, particularly in Spanish-speaking areas.

Paul Stillwell: How comfortable were the living conditions on board the Seattle?

Admiral Mumma: There were only 11 of us in the junior officers' mess: three classmates of mine, and the classes of '24, '25, and '26 were all in the junior officers' mess in those days. In the big ships, they moved up to the wardroom when they became senior ensigns, but we were all in JO mess. There were only 11 of us, and none of us were married at that time.

Well, at any rate, we'd been south, you see, in September, October, and November. We came up in early November and went into the navy yard for overhaul at Brooklyn. I was in the deck force, so I wasn't very heavily engaged in the real overhaul. So I got leave and went back to Iowa, to go to the Army-Navy game in Chicago. I blew into Iowa City at about 4:00 in the morning. Dad met me at the station. I went back home and went to bed. I was informed by my sister that I had a date—a blind date—with a very, very nice girl named Carmey Braley that I had known of but had never met.

Paul Stillwell: Your present wife.

Admiral Mumma: My present wife. So that was a most eventful weekend. I arrived on the Wednesday before Thanksgiving, and I had an extra ticket. Took her in to the Army-Navy game in Chicago. All the girls in the Kappa house, "Oh, you're going to the Army-Navy game." So my sister went to the Army-Navy game too. They came in on the train, because they had to go to classes on Friday after Thanksgiving. Dad said he'd go down to the station and meet my sister. I said, "I'll go, Dad; I'll go along."

So when Dad saw that my bride-to-be and my sister both got off, he turned and looked at me. He said, "Now I know why you wanted to come." Because I didn't know whether she was going to be able to come or not. But, anyhow, in those days we called it "pitching woo," and I pitched all the woo I could in that very short time. But we wrote each other all the time thereafter. We were engaged the following Fourth of July, and we were married the following October 1 in 1927.

Paul Stillwell: Sounds as if you were a very successful pitcher.

Admiral Mumma: Okay. Well, having successfully managed to get to Chicago and also to get my girl there that I had hopes of marrying someday, why, my dad and mother sat on the Army side. Of course, I had Navy tickets, so we sat on the Navy side. We had a very interesting game, because it ended up a 21-21 tie. Navy were national champs that year, and Army wasn't expected to do as well as they did. But they had some breaks, and good breaks. Afterward, the girls went back by train because of the time schedules they had, but I drove back with Mother and Dad.

I found that my father was very silent all the way back. He had played football at West Point and, in addition to that, had officiated many, many, many times in many games—sometimes including Navy. One time was the Michigan-Navy game just the year before, when Michigan took us apart. Dad was head linesman at that game, and he said the Navy line was a sieve. Well, I was a midshipman at that time, and I had to admit that it was performing a little bit like that. This time, we were halfway back to Iowa City from Chicago in the car before my father finally said, "Albert, you know, Navy should have won that game. They had a better team, better coached, and they had just some bad breaks." So after that, we could discuss that game thoroughly. There wasn't any problem. But until he let down the bars that far, I would have had trouble making any comment.

Paul Stillwell: He was controlling the situation.

Admiral Mumma: So that was that. At any rate, to go back a bit, now the funny thing was when I was detached from the ship in Annapolis. The ship was going on to Brooklyn to be decommissioned, and the flag was going to transfer to the Texas.* So I had a rather interesting thing ahead of me, which was to report to the Navy Rifle Team. I was to report at Curtis Guild Rifle Range in Wakefield, Massachusetts.

Well, I had a little money saved up by then. So I went ashore in Annapolis, and I bought a little Essex coupe. I put my luggage and stuff in the trunk, and I started driving up to Boston. I got as far as Philadelphia. My brother Mort was in destroyers there, so I drove to his address in Philadelphia. I found them sitting on a trunk in the middle of an empty apartment. They were all packed up with a little baby, who was Mort III, in Virginia's lap. I said, "Mort, where in the hell are you going?"

He said, "I'm going to the rifle team. Where're you going?"

I said, "I'm going to the rifle team." I said, "Well, my God, isn't that something? How are you planning to get there?"

He said, "We've got train tickets, and we're waiting for the taxi right now."

I said, "All right, call off the taxi. Load your stuff in my car, and we'll all drive up together." So we did. The three of us sat across in this little coupe, with the baby on our laps, and we drove up through New York. Went up the Boston Post Road, and so forth, and then they found a house in Wakefield. I lived with them and shared the expense during the rifle team training.

Now, the reason the Curtis Guild Rifle Range was chosen was that it was noted for very severe fishtail winds. If you could dope wind at Curtis Guild, you could dope wind anywhere, and so that was our training. We went to the toughest place they could find for us to train before Camp Perry.

Well, that was a very interesting time. My brother's wife Virginia said, "You've done nothing but talk about this girl back in Iowa. Why don't we have Martha and Carmen visit us here." (My sister was Martha.) We telephoned, we wired, we did everything, and finally we got them to come. That's how come I got engaged on the Fourth of July in Wakefield, Massachusetts, and managed to sew up the plan to be married before reporting to the new ship. I didn't know then which ship it was going to

---

* Admiral Hughes shifted his flag to the battleship Texas (BB-35) on 1 September 1927.

be. But, as it later turned out, it was the Saratoga. So I went from the oldest ship in the Navy to the newest.

Paul Stillwell: Did the woo pitching interfere or distract from your shooting at all?

Admiral Mumma: Well, I taught her how to shoot a pistol in case of necessity. All the naval officers' wives in those days pretty much were trained to shoot a pistol. Because they were alone an awful lot of the time when we were at sea. We'd go on a six-month cruise, and if it was that long, the girls would get together and live together with the kids. But if it was only six weeks or three months, why, then they wouldn't go to that trouble.

We were at sea one time, and one of my shipmate's wives was in Long Beach. A guy stole into her room and apparently was about to attack her. She pulled out a .45 from under her pillow and shot him. He got to the window and collapsed before he died. If he'd gotten out the window he had come in, it might have been a more difficult thing for her, because she might have had a little trouble proving that he was inside the window. But he died inside her apartment. I can name names there, but I don't think it's necessary.

Paul Stillwell: I'm interested in your reflections on serving in that old ship, the Seattle. What kind of shape was she in?

Admiral Mumma: Well, she was in pretty good shape. She had a four-cylinder, quadruple-expansion engine, and she had 10-inch turrets. We had full-power runs there, and being a young engineer, I was down there taking the indicator cards. I computed the horsepower. So I always got that kind of extra duties because of my interest in engineering. That I enjoyed.

Paul Stillwell: Why was the fleet staff in such an old, smaller ship?

Admiral Mumma: Well, they didn't want to use a ship of the line as a flagship in those days, because they felt that a ship of the line would have to be right in the thick of things, whereas, the commander in chief probably should be a little more detached and able to handle the fleet as such, rather than be a real participant in the firing of the battle.

In those days we had two forces we called the Battle Force and the Scouting Force, and they had largely different assignments. It still dated from the old days of the old battle line and so on. This gradually disappeared as the aircraft carriers began coming into operation. I particularly enjoyed the aircraft carrier assignment, because the Saratoga was a very technically challenging ship. She was an electric drive ship with 180,000 horsepower, and on trials we developed 217,000 horsepower at 35 knots.

Paul Stillwell: Why such a difference between her rated horsepower and what you got out of her?

Admiral Mumma: Well, that's the margin that the designers put in. Sometimes you get it out, and sometimes you don't. But they always like to have some margin there for foul bottom and a few other things. But under the circumstances, she made the highest speed that had ever been made by any large ship. In those days it was 35 knots.[*]

Paul Stillwell: Which is still impressive for a ship today.

Admiral Mumma: Still pretty good. But, of course, she was light at the time we were running the trials. She didn't have her aircraft on board. And she was sort of a half-breed between the old engineering design and the new engineering design, because those turbine generators—she was electric drive, and she had four shafts with two induction motors of 22,500 horsepower each, on each shaft. She had an electric drive switchboard in the main control room that looked like a Christmas tree—red and green lights all over the place for which motors were in operation and which were not, the generators, the auxiliary generators. All that were on the switchboard. It took a great deal of indoctrination to train an officer to handle that control system. I was a plank owner; I reported to the ship a month and a half before she was commissioned on November 16,

---

[*] On 25 June 1928 the Saratoga made five runs over a measured mile course near San Vicente Island off the coast of Southern California. The ship averaged 33 knots for the five runs and was labeled the "fastest ship afloat."

1927.* Our first skipper was Captain Yarnell, and we had a succession of very fine skippers.†

Paul Stillwell: What impressions do you have of Yarnell specifically?

Admiral Mumma: Oh, he was one of the foremost gentlemen I've ever served with—tremendous man. And very kind, considerate of younger officers. I was extremely fond of him. We had three other skippers. We had Halligan; we had McCrary; and the last one was Horne, who was later Vice Chief to Ernie King.‡ I served with all four of them.

Paul Stillwell: Any recollections of the latter three that you've mentioned?

Admiral Mumma: Yes, they were all excellent and very fine officers—in contrast to the Lexington. The Lexington had a skipper and an exec, both of which had reputations of being sundowners.§ Ernie King and Hoover.**

We had a happy ship. Ken Whiting was our first exec, and Albert Read was our next exec.†† We seemed to have the cream of the crop of the aviation people too.

Paul Stillwell: Mitscher was on board.

---

* USS Saratoga (CV-3), a Lexington-class aircraft carrier, had a standard displacement of 33,000 tons, was 888 feet long, 106 feet in the beam, an extreme width of 130 feet on the flight deck, and had a draft of 24 feet. She had a top speed of 33.5 knots and could accommodate approximately 60-70 aircraft. She was originally armed with eight 8-inch guns that were later removed in World War II.
† Captain Harry E. Yarnell, USN, commanded the Saratoga from 16 November 1927 to 15 September 1928. He later became a four-star admiral and Commander in Chief Asiatic Fleet.
‡ Captain John Halligan, Jr., USN, commanded the ship from 15 September 1928 to 20 April 1929; Captain Frank R. McCrary, USN, from 5 September 1930 to 1 June 1932; Captain Frederick J. Horne, USN, from 20 April 1929 to 5 September 1930. As a four-star admiral, Horne was Vice Chief of Naval Operations during World War II.
§ "Sundowner" is a Navy slang term for a very strict officer. In sailing ship days, officers were required to be back aboard ship before sundown. The term came to be applied to a captain who insisted on observing the regulation even after it had outlived its usefulness.
** Captain Ernest J. King, USN, commanded the USS Lexington (CV-2) from 1930 to 1932. His executive officer was Commander John H. Hoover, USN. Later, as a captain, Hoover commanded the Lexington from June 1938 to June 1939.
†† Commander Kenneth Whiting, USN; Commander Albert C. Read, USN.

Admiral Mumma: Mitscher was our first air officer.* So that we were very, very lucky with the officers that we had in that ship. We beat the "Lex" in everything. We beat her in battle practice. We beat her at short range. We beat her in football. I was in the ship for the first 25,000 landings. When I left that ship, I was the oldest officer plank owner on that ship, not in age, but in service. I went from there to destroyers. Ordinarily you'd serve a couple of years with the ship, then go to destroyers. But I really enjoyed serving four years in that ship.

Paul Stillwell: Did you give any thought during those years of taking flight training?

Admiral Mumma: Well, yes. They started with our class with what they called indoctrinal flight training after graduation. You've had this probably with some others. But indoctrinal flight training meant that you spent three months on indoctrinal flight training at Norfolk, or at San Diego, taking flight training, as such. If you were physically qualified, you were continued and would go on to Pensacola. If you weren't, at least you'd been indoctrinated. I was detached from the Saratoga for that temporary duty to take the indoctrinal flight training in San Diego. You had to take it within the first three years while you were supposed to be an ensign.

In those days the ship was at Long Beach almost all the time, whereas the squadrons are operating out of Coronado at North Island.† I had an instructor by the name of Dutch Greber, a lieutenant.‡ Dutch said to me any number of times, "You fly the airplane all right. Go take another physical exam." Because I had been considered "not qualified" because I had a little myopia. It wasn't serious. I was about 15-16/20, instead of being 20/20. So he said, "You fly the airplane okay. Go take another exam."

So I'd come back, "No, I'm sorry. I can't pass the exam."

So I would fly some more. He'd say, "Go take another exam."

So I never passed that doggone eye exam. Now, I don't own any glasses.

---

* Lieutenant Commander Marc A. Mitscher, USN. As a vice admiral in World War II, Mitscher was a noted carrier task force commander in the Pacific.
† North Island Naval Air Station is on the end of the Coronado peninsula, across the harbor from San Diego.
‡ Lieutenant Charles F. Greber, USN.

Because as you grow older, you know, myopia becomes a little bit farsighted. So now I have 20/20 vision, and all my aviators friends, classmates, all go around with big, thick glasses on. At any rate, I'm lucky in that respect. But I sure miss being in aviation, because aviation was in my blood—engineering and aviation both.

So my potential career in aviation was doomed. But my interest in aviation did not wane in any way, even though I started out in that ship as assistant to the assistant engineer for doing the form H, which was efficiency officer. So I did all the computations and so forth to submit on the efficiency performance of the ship—the fuel burned. I was fueling officer and so forth, had to do all that sort of thing, which was a good flunky job for a young fellow.

Paul Stillwell: Was there very stringent competition for fuel efficiency at that time?

Admiral Mumma: Well, the only other ship that got in competition with us was the "Lex," and we always beat the "Lex."

So then the next job, I was assistant in the main drive division. That gave me responsibility for taking care of the maintenance on the turbines and the generators and the motors. Then I went to the deck force, and I became number two turret officer, had the second division and the forecastle.

Paul Stillwell: The 8-inch turret.

Admiral Mumma: Eight-inch turrets, yes. I had that for about a year.

Paul Stillwell: Were there regular magazines and barbettes below those turrets?

Admiral Mumma: Oh, yes, yes, there was room enough for them there. Of course, the ship was heavily loaded starboard side because of all the armament and so forth were on that side.

Paul Stillwell: The uptakes and the bridge.

Admiral Mumma: But we had compensating ballast tanks on the other side that we didn't touch, because they compensated for that starboard side weight. Well, being refueling officer, I had to be sure we didn't put a heel on the ship. At any rate, I was no longer refueling officer, of course, when I had the second division, but I had the forecastle, anchoring, all that sort of thing. And I stood deck watches. Later I stood main drive watches in the main control room.

Then my last job there, as a junior grade lieutenant, I was boiler division officer. That boiler division was something. They had 16 boilers—up and over. There were no passageways through that lower deck, and that was a very, very important aspect of the survivability of those ships. As a matter of fact, I think it can be proved that the "Lex" really did not have to be abandoned, that she probably could have gotten back to Pearl when she took that licking down in the South Pacific.[*] Because those ships were so beautifully protected with those boiler rooms outboard, that even if you'd flooded half the boiler rooms, she would stay afloat under almost any conditions. She would heel, but you could counterflood. So in my book, that's one reason why the Saratoga came through the war unscathed, except for damage. She did not ever get in danger of sinking.

Paul Stillwell: She was torpedoed several times.

Admiral Mumma: Yes.

Paul Stillwell: How did the Saratoga handle when you had the bridge watches?

Admiral Mumma: Oh, she handled like a destroyer. Oh, she was fabulous. If you didn't alert your destroyers, the first thing you know they'd be running into you, because you could turn just about as fast as they could. When you'd turn to go into the wind, you'd sometimes turn very quickly, because here comes a lame duck wants to get aboard. And you turn damn quickly into the wind to get him aboard before he goes into the water.

---

[*] USS Lexington (CV-2) was sunk 8 May 1942 during the Battle of the Coral Sea.

Let me tell you a very interesting experience in the <u>Saratoga</u>. A classmate of mine had the deck. This was very early on. I was not on duty, but I was on the ship. We were doing a lot of experimentation in the ship, primarily consisting of trying out everything. This particular time we were trying landing and takeoff at anchor in Long Beach Harbor. Well, Theda Combs was landing signal officer, very good friend of mine at the time, and so on.* Dick Whitehead was one of the ship's pilots—later Admiral Whitehead.† And Tomlinson was also one of the ship's pilots.‡

Anyhow, this landing at anchor—nobody'd ever done this before except on the <u>Pennsylvania</u> when they ran a plane down the ramp over the gun turrets.§ We had motor launches hooked onto the stern, and we towed the ship, because the ship used to sashay on the anchor like this—sometimes into the wind, and sometimes not. So you'd have to tow the stern around so the stern would be downwind, and these motor launches on the stern would tow her around to keep her headed into the wind. They had fellows up on the deck telling them what to do.

Well, John Fitzsimmons, my classmate, had the deck, and he was operating on the deck level.** Dick Whitehead was one of the first ones to make this try. He took off in this O2U, which was in those days the scouting plane and belonged to the ship, not the squadrons. He flew around up there a while, and then he started in. I was up on deck watching this. Theda Combs was giving him the high signal—too high, too high, too high. Then he was waving—too high, too high. Dick Whitehead was still not getting down enough to come in, because he'd been used to landing on a moving target, and here was a stationary target and he wasn't down far enough. Finally, Theda Combs decided that he was going to crash if he didn't take off, so he waved him off. Dick Whitehead gave it the gun, but he forgot to pull up the tailhook.

The tailhook caught the top wire of the barrier, yanked him out of the air, slammed him on the deck. The wheels came up through the lower wing, completely

---

* Lieutenant Thomas S. Combs, USN.
† Lieutenant Richard F. Whitehead, USN.
‡ Lieutenant Daniel W. Tomlinson, USN. The oral history of Tomlinson, who retired as a captain, is in the Naval Institute collection.
§ On 18 January 1911, civilian Eugene B. Ely became the first man to land an airplane on a U.S. Navy ship when he brought his Curtiss pusher down onto a wooden platform jury-rigged on board the armored cruiser <u>Pennsylvania</u> in San Francisco Bay.
** Ensign John P. Fitzsimmons, USN.

collapsed the landing gear. The propeller dug into the deck, bent, and curved right up through. There he was, flopped on the deck with this bent propeller just holding him into the deck. And no landing gear, slammed onto the deck. The fortunate thing was, it was right on the after elevator. So they unhooked the top wire of the barrier, and by this time Fitzsimmons was running over to see if Whitehead was all right. The siren had sounded, and everybody thought he'd be in terrible shape. But Dick Whitehead stepped out of the airplane like this, and he said, "Say, Fitz, did those girls come down from Hollywood that were coming this afternoon?"

Paul Stillwell: Mr. Casual.

Admiral Mumma: God, this is a classic in the Navy. I don't know whether you've ever heard this before or not.

Paul Stillwell: No, I hadn't.

Admiral Mumma: But this was really something. Well, of course, what they did—they just unhooked all the wires, and down the damaged plane went into the after elevator space, down on the hangar, and they finally dug her off the elevator and sent that airplane for rebuilding.

I had a very bad experience when, among others, we were on the Saratoga at Long Beach Harbor. At one stage of the game, they had been transferring some gasoline from one tank to another and, apparently, the piping arrangement was improperly valved by the guy in charge and spilled a large amount of gasoline over the side in an overflow. This happened on the starboard side of the ship, and that was where the captain's gig side was moored to the boom alongside. The officer of the deck soon realized what had happened. He put out the smoking lamp all over the ship, but apparently somebody must have thrown a cigarette over the side.

All that gasoline on the water went up in flames, and the flames were higher than the stack of the ship with all that burning. The captain's gig had been called away, and one of the gig crew was on the boom, one of them was down in the boat, and one of them was on the way. We lost two men in that, and I lost the gig. The gig was part of my division. There was an investigation and a court-martial, but it was found that the officer of the deck had done everything he could, but that the air officer in charge had not inspected the piping alignment properly, to ensure that it did not overflow. It burned the paint work off the side. She had one whole blackened side of the ship. They said that you could see the flames from way inland. Some people said as far as Los Angeles, but I don't believe that.

Paul Stillwell: What year did that happen? Do you recall?

Admiral Mumma: That was fairly soon after we arrived out there. It was probably in late '28.

Paul Stillwell: What do you remember of Theda Combs as a shipmate?

Admiral Mumma: Oh, he was a wonderful man; a very, very good friend; a very thorough officer in aviation.

We went through 25,000 landings without a single fatality in the Saratoga. In that same period, the Lexington had seven fatalities out of 25,000 landings. A lot of that credit goes to Admiral Combs. He set up that landing signal outfit from the very beginning, the way it should have been operated, and it was perfect. He was a friend of mine all my life until he died.

Paul Stillwell: Did you ever encounter Mel Pride who worked on the arresting gear?[*]

Admiral Mumma: Yes.

Paul Stillwell: What do you recall about him?

---

[*] Lieutenant Alfred M. Pride, USN. The oral history of Pride, who retired as a tombstone four-star admiral, is in the Naval Institute collection.

Admiral Mumma: Well, he was, shall I say, a little more formal—a little less approachable. Theda was always just such a terrific shipmate, as well as a very fine example to younger officers.

Paul Stillwell: Both of those men wound up as fleet commanders in the 1950s.*

Admiral Mumma: Well, the term shipmate is really a big one, you know. When you've been at sea with people for a long time, you get to know them pretty well. I didn't have anything against Mel Pride. I thought he was a fine officer. I thought Ken Whiting was a terrific exec.

Paul Stillwell: I'd be interested in your memories of him too.

Admiral Mumma: Well, you see, he was one of the originals.

Paul Stillwell: He was the man who devised the landing signal officer concept.

Admiral Mumma: Yes. Ken was a very kind officer, very dedicated to teaching younger officers in the right ways of doing things. He was very helpful to all of us. You know, in later years when I was at the Model Basin and had the aeronautical engineering part of the Model Basin under my command, I appreciated more and more the contribution that Ken Whiting had made. Because he was one of the originals trained—as was Major Smith—by the Wright Brothers. The Army trained three of them, and the Navy trained three of them. I think eventually it totaled about six on each service.

We had another rather peculiar and interesting experience. This was Tomlinson, and, of course, he was very famous for his work in connection with fast aircraft.

Paul Stillwell: Precision flying.

---

* Combs commanded the Sixth Fleet, and Pride commanded the Seventh Fleet.

Admiral Mumma: Yes, precision flying—everything of that kind. He had the world's record several times and so on.

Paul Stillwell: A rough-and-ready sort of guy.

Admiral Mumma: Yes. At any rate, one time we were in San Diego, and he was flying a floatplane—not one of the ship's. He had been up to Miramar. He was coming from that lake back to the bay, and he was going to land there. But he found that he was very low on fuel, and he didn't know whether he was really going to make that bay. As he came down, he was stretching that glide because he was running out of fuel. He was right over the heart of San Diego when the engine quit—no more gas. He had enough altitude that he hoped he might make the bay

He was headed for the pier right at the end of Broad Street there, coming right down. He was going to land just alongside that pier if he made it, but he wasn't going to make it. So as he got down, he gradually eased the tail of this floatplane down, until the tail end of the pontoon was hitting the street. He skidded along like that with his maximum up angle stopping the airplane. Then at the last minute, he eased it off so that it just went on over on the front of the whole skeg of the pontoon. Then the plane stopped, and it tilted over on one wing float. The plane wasn't even severely damaged. They brought the truck with the crane; they picked it up and put it on the truck and drove it away. They had to do hardly any repair work. That shows the kind of aviator he was.[*]

Paul Stillwell: That must have been quite a spectacle for the people on the street to have an airplane coming in.

Admiral Mumma: Oh, they scattered like flies. Oh, boy. And the word got around that he was coming in, sirens and everything going. Well, that's the kind of experiences that we had in the Saratoga with this pioneering of aviation. After all, she was CV-3, you know. The Lexington was CV-2, but we beat her into commission by a month and a

---

[*] Tomlinson discussed this incident in his own oral history. In Tomlinson's version, he was flying a Curtiss Jenny, an airplane with wheels rather than a pontoon, when the engine quit. He landed on Olive Street in Coronado after having to hop over a milk truck that he encountered near the end of the flight.

half.* So that's the reason why we were doing all the pioneering work. We went through the Panama Canal. They were built to go through the canal by putting up the side rails and sponsons and all that sort of thing, so that we could get through. We had about a foot and a half on each side. We went through without major damage. When the "Lex" came through—I don't know whether you ever heard this or not.

Paul Stillwell: I heard she snapped off the concrete light posts.

Admiral Mumma: Well, she swung around, and the overhanging bow just clipped off the lights as she went down the center mole in the Panama Canal.

Paul Stillwell: You hadn't done that, I take it.

Admiral Mumma: Boy, I'll say we hadn't. We thought, oh, there's the old "Lex."

Paul Stillwell: Was there great rivalry between the two ships?

Admiral Mumma: Oh, yes, there was a great rivalry between the two ships, and that's why we were such a happy ship in all respects—that it wasn't very difficult to beat the "Lex."

Paul Stillwell: What do you remember about the caliber of the enlisted men on board?

Admiral Mumma: We're now talking about the early '20s when the ship was going to be commissioned and they had people coming into the Navy right after World War I. They had to pretty well skim the cream of the crop to put them in a ship like this, the Saratoga, because there were not all the best people that stayed in the service. Right after World War I was boom period, and the roaring '20s were going on fine. Then came the crash in '29, then hard times.† It was during those hard times, during the '30s, that we got the real

---

*USS Lexington was commissioned 14 December 1927, four weeks after the Saratoga.
†The Great Depression started with the stock market crash in October 1929.

cream of the crop into the services. Because those were the times when some of the kids off the farms, and all those other guys, couldn't find anything to do. There was no work, no area of contribution, so they'd get in the service. That was the basic, fundamental groundwork on which we built the Navy just before World War II, and we were very fortunate in that respect.

Paul Stillwell: You probably had college graduates who hadn't been able to find jobs.

Admiral Mumma: We had college graduates joining as enlisted men, yes. Well, I kept track of things like that occasionally. Shortly before the war, I was chief engineer of what they called a destroyer leader—gold-plated destroyer, the Clark. During that time we had these men that had come in from all over the United States, very highly qualified people and almost every one of them at least a high school graduate.

Paul Stillwell: Were you involved in any fleet problems in the Saratoga?

Admiral Mumma: Oh, yes, yes, of course. They made up fleet problems that involved the "Lex" and the Saratoga on opposite sides, trying to evaluate the aircraft carrier situation. As was usual, we came out pretty well. Because we really had a pretty sharp bunch of skippers. On this one occasion when the "Lex" and some other ships were supposed to defend the Panama Canal and we were in the attacking force, we went all the way south, well away from the canal, and came up the coast of Peru and Colombia with a very interesting plan of attack, to attack the Panama Canal from that very unexpected direction. Of course, in those days you didn't have active enough surveillance from anything other than aircraft to be able to know that we were doing this.

Paul Stillwell: No radar.

Admiral Mumma: No radar. And no satellites.

Paul Stillwell: Certainly not.

Admiral Mumma: So under the circumstances, nobody knew that we were doing this, and we came up hugging that coast and launched aircraft, and made a complete destruction of the Panama Canal, ostensibly. So that was, I think, a little beginning of the fact that aircraft carriers could pull off things of this kind that you could completely catch people unexpectedly and unprepared for that kind of an attack.[*]

So this began to percolate, and some of the old battleship mentality began to evaporate in the face of this carrier success. And the inability of the "Lex" to prevent it was another interesting point. Because you had to not only locate your enemy, but you had to be able to attack him before he launched his attack. That was evident when our carriers were at sea at Pearl Harbor and were unable to find the Japanese fleet, which was an indication that they're not all that effective defensively unless you've got additional scouting capability.[†] Whereas offensively, the Japs proved how terrifically effective it could be. We had succeeded in proving that in 1929, but the Japs tore a page out of our book. Every time we made any progress, they knew about it, and they did something about it.

Paul Stillwell: What do you recall about shipyard periods?

Admiral Mumma: When we were based in the old days in Long Beach, the Saratoga had to go to Bremerton every time it went in for overhaul.[‡] We transported our families up to Bremerton, got local quarters for them for two to three months, and then we'd move back to Long Beach when the ship would move back, because the yard period was about the only time we had any real time to be with our families.

Along this line was an interesting thing. The Saratoga and the "Lex" used to go up to Bremerton together, sometimes overlapping a little bit. On one occasion, 1929, both ships were scheduled in Bremerton in the fall. We were scheduled first, in the

---

[*] This mock attack took place on 26 January 1929. For another first-person account, see Eugene E. Wilson, "The Navy's First Carrier Task Force," U.S. Naval Institute Proceedings, February 1950, pages 159-169.
[†] When the Japanese carrier force was approaching Hawaii for the attack on Pearl Harbor in December 1941, it took a northern route to avoid detection. The American carriers had gone to the west to deliver aircraft to Wake and Midway islands.
[‡] Puget Sound Navy Yard, Bremerton, Washington.

Saratoga. And along to Bremerton a little bit later, was the Lexington. That fall in 1929 there was a tremendous drought in the Northwest—very, very little rain, which is very unusual in that area.

Paul Stillwell: It certainly is.

Admiral Mumma: The drought was so bad that the fish, the salmon, could not get up to their spawning ground. They passed a law that it would be absolutely illegal for anyone to take a salmon out of any stream or creek for any purpose whatsoever. Then they mobilized every game warden they could get all over the Northwest to spawn salmon in the little pools part way up the creeks where they were dying. They hand-spawned the salmon, hand-spawned the males and the females both to fertilize the eggs, and that was really what saved the industry.

But also the Northwest depended so heavily on hydroelectric power that all the reservoirs were low; the rivers were low; everything was low. So there was going to be a big question as to which one of the naval ships was supposed to stick around and provide electric power to the Northwest. We were lucky; we got away. But the "Lex" had to stay up there, and she hooked up at Tacoma.[*] She went alongside a great big barge that had some special transformers on the barge, which hiked the voltage up. Those electric-drive ships had 5,500-volt generators, and we had direct motors at 5,500 volts, so we had high voltage in those ships compared to other electric-drive ships. So they hooked up these transformers to our 5,500 volt on the primary side, then the secondary hiked it up to line voltage for the transmission. But the strange thing was that in spite of the so-called emergency, the Lexington never had to provide more than one 45,000 unit's worth of power. They never ran more than one unit anywhere near full power. They alternated various units one to another, but the load never got over 45,000 horsepower.

Paul Stillwell: Remarkable use for a Navy ship.

---

[*] In December 1929 and January 1930, because of a severe drought in the Pacific Northwest, the turbo generators of the USS Lexington (CV-2) supplied electrical power to the city of Tacoma, Washington. For details see Steven A. Payne, "The Carrier That Lit Up Tacoma," Naval History, Fall 1990, pages 23-25.

Admiral Mumma: Yes, it was an unusual one, but it got quite a bit of recognition for the Navy in the area, even though it wasn't all that really essential in the long run because it began to rain shortly thereafter. They were there the month of November and we had left in early November.

Paul Stillwell: Was there any contention within the ship between the aviators and the non-aviators?

Admiral Mumma: Not a serious amount. I was basically a black-shoe sailor.[*] But I flew an awful lot. All my friends, the aviators, would allow me to fly the aircraft—any two-seater aircraft, they'd allow me to fly it because they knew I'd had a lot of flight training experience. But not on a carrier, either landing or taking off—ashore, yes, but not on a carrier. So I did a lot of flying that was unofficial. I got a tremendous feel for aviation by osmosis, even though my regular job was not that.

Well then, after the four years in the Saratoga with deck, and engineering experience, and a small amount of communications experience, I was ordered to destroyers, and I went to an old four-piper. That was the DD-115, the Waters.[†] I'd been aboard the Barry (DD-2) out in the Philippines when I was a kid. This ship was not a forecastle ship like the Barry. She was a flush-deck destroyer. The oldest ship we had in the Navy at the time that I went to these destroyers was the Manley, number 74. But we were one of the older ones. They were pretty good ships, but they were not very dry forward, because they were flush deckers, no forecastle. I was a devotee of a forecastle deck for destroyers, because I've had a feeling that you've got to keep the bow out of the water if you really want to make any speed in a small ship. Because the minute you plunge that bow, you're lifting an awful lot of water. So I felt that in many respects those ships were limited in their ability to perform in rough weather.

---

[*] In the early days of naval aviation, the aviators wore brown shoes with their khaki uniforms and green uniforms. They thus acquired the nickname "brown shoes" to distinguish them from the traditional surface ship officers, who were known as "black shoes."
[†] USS Waters (DD-115), a Wickes-class destroyer, was commissioned 8 August 1918. Displacement was 1,154 tons, length 314 feet, beam of 31 feet, and draft of 10 feet. Top speed was 35 knots. She was armed with four 4-inch guns, two 3-inch guns, and 12 21-inch torpedo tubes. The Waters, which operated in both World Wars, was finally decommissioned on 12 October 1945.

I remember one time in 1932 we went to Hawaii for maneuvers. We were so tight on fuel oil in those days that we could not steam at anything except most economical speed from San Diego to Hawaii. No maneuvers en route at all. All the maneuvers were after we got there. In other words, we got on a steady course and headed for Hawaii at most economical speed, which was usually between 10 and 15 knots, and rolled all the way. Of course, those ships were not particularly designed against rolling. But we didn't sit down in the wardroom for meals. We stood up—had an arm around a stanchion, and the mess boys passed us finger food. That's what we had, and that's the way we ate. When you got in your bunk, you propped yourself in with about three or four pillows on either side of you so you wouldn't roll out of your bunk, and that was the way we slept. There was one member of that crew, one officer in that group, that took a bucket with him every time he went up on watch. He just couldn't take it. But that was the worst rolling I've ever seen; I think we were under way about seven days, rolling every minute.

Paul Stillwell: What was your job in the Waters?

Admiral Mumma: I was gunnery officer in that ship. Howard Orem, who was an ordnance specialist, was chief engineer.[*] So my engineering and ordnance duties were exchanged with Howard Orem. We talked about that many years later as we were good friends. I was basically an engineer, but I had enough topside duty in the Saratoga and in the destroyer, that I had a feeling that I was also a regular naval officer, not just an engineer. I enjoyed all aspects of that. We fired a very good, very good battle practice in that ship, and we did well. And here was another leadership point. The skipper of that ship was C. Julian Wheeler.[†] I think he was class of '16, if I'm not mistaken.

Paul Stillwell: Yes, he was.

Admiral Mumma: C. Julian was the youngest skipper in the bay, without any question. Being junior, we had to do all the dirty work. We'd pick up the buoy. We'd always go in

---

[*] Lieutenant Howard E. Orem, USN.
[†] Lieutenant Commander C. Julian Wheeler, USN, commanded the Waters from 1931 to 1934. The oral history or Wheeler, who retired as a rear admiral, is in the Naval Institute collection.

and do any of the errands. When he reported on board, the first thing he did was get all the officers together. He said, "Now, gentlemen, I intend to have you operate this ship. I will stand the first watch with each of you, your first watch that you stand." We'd almost all been on the ship before he reported. We'd had a skipper before him. He said, "If I'm satisfied with your performance, thereafter you will handle the ship whether I'm on the bridge or not."

Well, that sounded pretty good. I just wondered how good it was going to turn out. Well, it turned out that after he stood a watch with each of us, we all handled the ship. We took the ship away from the buoy; we picked up the buoy; we took her alongside the dock; we took her alongside the tender; we left the tender; we took the ship into formation; we took the ship out of formation; we went into maneuvers. The officer of the deck did all this. The captain would occasionally take it to keep his hand in. But I tell you, that was a fabulous experience. And do you know, not a single one of us ever bunged up anything on that ship for him.

Paul Stillwell: Well, that was a way of repaying his confidence in you.

Admiral Mumma: Yes. We weren't overly cautious. We were pretty high, wide, and handsome ship handlers. So was he; he was fabulous in that respect. In other words, he trained officers. He just wasn't skipper of a ship. That was his job. Now, in other words, he and his wife have been life-long ideals of ours from many points of view. We knew them very, very well. But, I tell you, we've lost track. I don't know what's happened to him.

Paul Stillwell: He died, and I have heard from his widow.[*] We have his oral history here.

Admiral Mumma: I'd like to look him up in the book and see, because he was a great skipper. I was so lucky. I served with so many great skippers: in the Saratoga, in the destroyer, and then, honest to goodness, two destroyers. Well, it makes all the difference

---

[*] Admiral Wheeler died 12 June 1981 at Menlo Park, California.

in the world in the way you respond and perform, I think. And that's true with everybody, I think. If they have good leadership and confidence in the junior people, the junior people perform.

Paul Stillwell: Now, you mentioned this formation operations. What did that involve? What sort of operations did you use those for?

Admiral Mumma: Well, in those days they were trying to evolve various methods of scouting for destroyers, in combination with an aircraft and without aircraft. They were attempting to get strategy and tactics evolved, which had to do with this kind of search and develop kind of an attack procedure

Paul Stillwell: Was there an offensive role for the old four-stackers when you were in the Waters? Did you have torpedo practice in formation, for example?

Admiral Mumma: Oh yes, we had. We did that. As a matter of fact, by that time it had become, instead of a gang torpedo attack, it was pretty much individual attack, which would eventually later be coordinated, I presume, by some commander. But each ship had its own torpedo exercises.

Incidentally, on the Waters we had just finished doing roller path data.[*] I was gunnery officer on the Waters and was all set for short range, when suddenly—we had picked up the buoy—and suddenly along came the Rathburne, the DD-113. I had the deck, and I looked, and I said, "My gosh, he's coming right at us." So I passed the word, "Stand by for a ram." Sure enough, his bow came in, and it hit our waist gun foundation on the left side of the deckhouse, and boom-boom-boom-boom-boom as his billboard just clipped off my stanchions underneath my port gun. And boom-boom-boom-boom—down went the gun like this. This is just after I had finished the roller path; we were going to fire next week. So I said, "Captain, we've got a problem." We had to go alongside the tender right away, put new stanchions in, and then we had to go and do a roller path all over again. And we had to swing ship in addition to all that additional

---

[*] The roller path is a circle of cylindrical bearings upon which a gun mount or gun turret rotates.

work. So we did all right, but it wasn't as well as it would have been if we'd had a little more time.

Paul Stillwell: Did those ships exercise at night very much?

Admiral Mumma: Yes, we had night battle. We used to have a great deal of night ship operation. We all did plane guarding in those days, and we got quite good at following night maneuvers of aircraft carriers and things of that kind. We all had our crack at that, not only in the old four-piper, but also in the destroyer leader Clark later. So that was a lot of very good experience for all of us younger officers.

In 1932 we were in Hawaii, supposedly for six weeks' maneuvers. The whole fleet wound up staying for a total of three months. The reason for that was Japanese activity in Manchuria, and so we stayed.

Paul Stillwell: When you were in the Waters, you mentioned she was one of the older ships. What kind of material condition was she in?

Admiral Mumma: She wasn't bad. As a matter of fact, those destroyers had been pretty well maintained. They'd been in and out of commission a few times, so that even though we didn't have the same methods of laying ships up in the old days—didn't dehumidify them and everything—why, we found those ships were in pretty good condition and position to do a job.

Paul Stillwell: What methods were used to preserve them when they weren't being operated?

Admiral Mumma: In the old days, they just closed them up pretty much and prevented access. And they used desiccants and changed the desiccants every so often. It wasn't active dehumidification the way we did it after World War II.

Paul Stillwell: Was there any special preservative used, such as Cosmolene was later?

Admiral Mumma: I don't think it was anything more than a coat of preservative. They used to call them buckets of rust, because they were almost all mostly red-leaded, not gray painted.* They looked like buckets of rust.

Paul Stillwell: Sure.

Admiral Mumma: But, actually, they just didn't bother painting them gray. They just red-leaded them and let them look that way.

Paul Stillwell: Well, there was a group down in San Diego known as red-lead row for that reason.

Admiral Mumma: Yes. Sure.

Paul Stillwell: Was anything done to the machinery or the weaponry during those periods?

Admiral Mumma: Well, ordinarily, you know, there was something done in the way of preserving the machinery with Cosmolene. That was the magic material in those days. Everything had to be gunked with Cosmolene to prevent it from rusting, and it usually was pretty successful.

Paul Stillwell: Did your family live with you there ashore in southern California. The carrier had been up at Long Beach. Now you were in San Diego. Where did you live?

Admiral Mumma: Well, in Long Beach in the aircraft carrier duty, we lived in courts. Most of them were these little apartment house courts, and they probably had one or two stories. With a little court, they usually had a washing machine section to them. They

---

* Red lead is the term for an orange-colored preservative that is used as an undercoat for the usual gray paint.

were $35.00 to $50.00 a month, and that was it. Then when the ships went to sea for long cruises—like we went to the East Coast in '30 for six months—why, then a lot of them went home. Families went home or doubled up. It was pretty rough in some respects, but the girls and the families managed pretty well, and they operated on the basis, "Well, this is the life I got myself into, and that's the way it's going to be."

Paul Stillwell: Well, I would think that just being together with other Navy wives had a positive effect too.

Admiral Mumma: Oh, it had a very beneficial effect for them to gang up together. And that's where Claudia and Smeddy, and Carmey and I—we were in San Diego together in years past.* And then in Coronado another time together. We were good friends at the Naval Academy, but, my gosh, we became very close friends later, after retirement.

Paul Stillwell: Did the Navy do anything to support the families?

Admiral Mumma: No, absolutely nothing. As a matter of fact, all three of our sons were born in civilian hospitals and with civilian doctors, and at my expense. Every time we had a baby, why, I had to either go to the bank or use some money I'd saved. It wasn't until World War II, of course, when benefits came along so the dependents began to get some kind of medical attention.

Paul Stillwell: At least you had the advantage over many civilians of having a steady job, so that helped.

Admiral Mumma: We took a pay cut too.

Paul Stillwell: That's true.

---

* This is a reference to Lieutenant (junior grade) William R. Smedberg III, USN, and his wife Claudia. Smedberg, who was a Naval Academy classmate of Mumma, eventually retired as a vice admiral. His oral history is in the Naval Institute collection.

Admiral Mumma: I had a very strange experience. I was detached in 1932 from the Waters and ordered to PG School.* When I got to the PG school, I found that a law had been passed in the meantime that said if you took a month's leave, you were supposed to lose your pay during the month's leave. You could take it in spurts, and, therefore, distribute your loss of pay. I got to Annapolis, and I found I had already lost a month's pay. I also found that they put a hold on transportation payments for travel in 1932. So I had to go to the man at the bank in order to live. I just didn't have any money at all. I had made the trip across the continent with the family and had gotten there—at that time we had two boys—and reported to the PG School. I had no money coming, even though I had a month's pay on the books, I thought. I was supposed to get my transportation money when I got there, but I didn't get that either.

Paul Stillwell: Did the latter eventually catch up with you?

Admiral Mumma: Well, I finally got that when they finally passed that supplemental appropriation. But I never got the month's pay back.

In 1934—about January, I guess it was—I was at the Postgraduate School. I happened to be leading my PG group in engineering. I'd already had a year and a half at the PG School here in Annapolis, and I would normally have gone to the University of California to finish my third year of postgraduate. Suddenly was called down to the office of Captain Sadler, who was in command of the PG school.† Captain Sadler said, "Mumma, would you like to go to Paris to study and finish your postgraduate?"

I said, "Yes, sir, I certainly would."

He said, "Well, I tell you what you do. You go up to Washington, and you go see Admiral Land who is Chief of the Bureau of Construction and Repair—Jerry Land. And you go see Admiral Mike Robinson, who is Chief of the Bureau of Engineering."‡ From

---

* Originally established at Annapolis, Maryland, on 9 June 1909, the Naval Postgraduate School was later moved to the grounds of the former Hotel Del Monte in Monterey, California, in June 1951.
† Captain Frank H. Sadler, USN.
‡ Rear Admiral Emory S. Land, USN, served as Chief of the Bureau of Construction and Repair from 1933 to 1937. Rear Admiral Samuel M. Robinson, USN, served as Chief of the Bureau of Engineering from 1931 to 1935 and again in 1939-40.

subsequent information I know that they were very good friends and cooperated beautifully in the two bureaus—C&R and Engineering.

In 1933, the Normandie had made a transatlantic crossing, breaking the world's record for transatlantic travel by two knots over the records previously set by the Queens. And this was done on approximately the same size ship with 40,000 less horsepower. If this is a duplication of what was in there in the past, it could be eliminated. But this so intrigued Admiral and Admiral Land that they, in mutual discussion, decided that the Normandie must have some hydrodynamic advantages, due to theoretical considerations or actual practice, that must have resulted in this very fine performance of the Normandie relative to the Queens.[*] The French had done some rather amazing things with speed of destroyers recently also. They decided that one way of attacking this problem of finding out what was going on over there was to send a student over there. So that was why I had been suddenly called down to Captain Sadler's office and sent to meet the admirals.

So I came back and I reported to Captain Sadler, "Yes, I would like very much to go."

He said, "Well, of course, you took French at the Naval Academy, didn't you?"

I said, "No, sir, unfortunately, I took Spanish." I recoiled and I thought, "My God, here goes my chance." But I said, "I'll tell you what I'll do, Captain. If you let me drop one half of that machine design course that I'm taking, I can keep up that course all right, and I can pass that course without any problem. Let me put that additional time, both in the PG school during some class hours, as well as tutoring outside with one of the French profs here at the Academy. I'll be ready to speak French by the time I finish the PG course here in June."

He said, "That's a good idea." So he talked to the people over here at the language department. He got Professor Bluestone assigned to me for this task.[†] So I took a lot of additional French instruction from Bluestone, both during and after working

---

[*] This information must have come from advance reports on the ship's design rather than demonstrated performance. The French passenger liner Normandie did not make her maiden voyage until May 1935, when she won the Blue Riband with a transatlantic run at a speed of 29.98 knots. The British liner Queen Mary made her first transatlantic crossing in May-June 1936 and in August of that year captured the Blue Riband with a speed of 30.63 knots. The still-unfinished Queen Elizabeth went from Britain to New York in early 1940 because of the uncertainties resulting from the recently started World War II.

[†] Professor Henry Bluestone taught for many years at the Naval Academy; in the mid-1930s he was on special duty with the Navy's Postgraduate School.

hours. By the end of June I was doing fairly well with French, and some technical French. Most of the Spanish had evaporated.

Then I went up and had a very interesting talk because I'd been told, "Now look, there are only about two people that have done this foreign education in recent years. One was Ben Moreell, who went to the Ecole des Ponts et Chausées—bridges and roads—in France some years ago. The other one was Lieutenant Commander Schade, Packy Schade, class of '23, who went to the University of Berlin and studied structures. Why don't you talk to those fellows?"[*]

So I went and I talked to Ben Moreell. He was a lieutenant commander at the time. I said, "They're talking about sending me to France."

He said, "Okay, whatever you do, when you're trying to learn the language, go over as soon as you can before the course starts, and live in the country and speak the language three months or so if you can. And then you don't stay in Paris. Everybody in Paris speaks English. Don't go to Grenoble, and don't go to Tours. That's where all the American teachers that are trying to learn French—professors and instructors want to go, those two places, because they have a good French language instruction course. But there're so damn many Americans there that you'll spend 80% of your time talking English. Go to Nancy in Lorraine. There are no Americans there, and you'll be forced to speak French." And he said, "Incidentally, I stayed with a Madame Couroux. She was the sister of the French hero General Mangan during World War I. Her husband has died, and she runs a pension there. There are only French people in this pension. It's a beautiful mansion with tennis courts and everything. She runs a gorgeous place there where you can learn French. You go to the University of Nancy and take the course."

I said, "Okay." So I did exactly that.

We packed up all our kids. By this time number three had just arrived; the older boys were six and two. We sailed on the Fourth of July from New York. A rather interesting part of the story was the fact that we had been assigned originally down in C deck, which is minimum first class for military people traveling. Gradually they had sold out the less expensive area, and we were moved up to B deck. So when we checked in at

---

[*] Lieutenant Commander Ben Moreell, Civil Engineer Corps, USN, studied in Paris in 1932-33. He was later a flag officer and served as Chief of the Bureau of Yards and Docks in World War II. Lieutenant Henry A. Schade, Construction Corps, USN.

the pier, we were told we were in B62. We went aboard, went back to B62, and here was a big champagne party going on there. Apparently, a couple had been very recently married and were taking a European trip for their honeymoon. I came in, walking in with the baby in the bassinet, and they said, "Oh, and now, here comes the baby."

Well, of course, we beat a hasty exit. We found out from the purser that we had been moved up to A14, which was a far nicer room, bigger, much more roomy. We enjoyed it very much.

Paul Stillwell: What ship was that?

Admiral Mumma: That was the SS Washington. She was the flagship of the United States Lines at that time.

The strange thing was that for the first half of that cruise, everybody thought we were the bride and groom because the stewardesses fed our three boys up in the children's dining room most of the time. But on about the third day out, we brought the two older boys down for lunch with us. The people then began to socialize with us a bit, realizing that we had been married for some time. And the bride and groom were finally identified as to who they were.

When we arrived in Paris, I reported in to the embassy there. Then-Commander Thebaud was the naval attaché.[*] He was a most kind and very helpful individual. At that time there were only about three U.S. naval officers in all of Europe. They were naval attachés in various places. The naval attaché in Paris was also naval attaché in Spain. In other words, we didn't have enough naval officers in Europe to have one in each of those countries. Imagine. There were no American ships in Europe, not a one in the European theater. So we were kind of isolated over there. But this was in '34, in July. We got there about the tenth of July. Went up to Nancy.

I enrolled in the university and took French. With my car driving around, I talked to the people in the gas station. I talked to the people in the garages, all that sort of thing. I began to develop technical knowledge as well as conversational French. We didn't speak a single word of English at dinner, lunch, or breakfast. Only time I could speak in

---

[*] Commander Leo H. Thebaud, USN.

English was to my wife in the privacy of my bedroom. The kids learned French instantly. Our oldest at that time was six, and the next one was two, and the youngest was a baby—all boys. Then Madame Couroux knew a place in Paris where there was a pension also. So we were the only family in this other pension, and, again, we had a fine if we spoke any words in English. So that helped both of us to learn the language.

I met the genius behind the <u>Normandie</u>, who was a Professor Barrillon.[*] Of course, I had studied David Taylor's books when I was a postgraduate. I knew that David Taylor had invented the bulbous bow and knew that David Taylor had done many other outstanding things in the development of hydrodynamics.[†] But Barrillon put them together in the first transatlantic ship that carried most of those principles.

Barrillon was an engineer-in-chief in the French Navy. He was the head of the Paris Model Basin, and he was an instructor in the Génie Maritime, the school I was attending. In other words, here was a man of that caliber, was still teaching students, and head of the model basin, and an engineer-in-chief. He was one of the most fabulous men I have ever met. He was the first, I think, in the world to do mathematical computation of the resistance of ships—theoretically, equations, integration, and all that sort of thing of a phenomenon that is basically experimental. That's what the model basins are for, is to experimentally produce the information from which you can scale up to the full scale. So I sat at his knees, literally, in many respects, and learned as much as I could about hydrodynamics and ship design.

So instead of just being an engineer, I became also a naval constructor, you see, not having gone through naval construction at MIT.[‡] But there's a point here. When the Navy's postgraduate instruction was started, it wasn't started in the Naval Academy. Postgraduate instruction was started in the Navy in about 1870. They used to go to the University of Glasgow, the Royal Naval College at Greenwich, the University of Berlin, and the Ecole d'Application de Génie Maritime, the school of applying maritime engineering. You see, that's what that means. Well, the school is now called the Ecole

---

[*] Engineer General Second Class Emile-Georges Barrillon, French Navy.
[†] David W. Taylor was a pioneer in warship design in the U.S. Navy. He received his postgraduate education at the Royal Naval College in Britain in the late 1880s. He was Chief of the Bureau of Construction and Repair, 1914-22. The Navy model basin at Carderock, Maryland, is named for him, as was the destroyer <u>David W. Taylor</u> (DD-551), which was commissioned in 1943.
[‡] MIT—Massachusetts Institute of Technology.

Superior Nationale de Génie Maritime—in other words, the national top school for marine engineering.

Then in 1901 it was felt that we had an adequate capability for our own postgraduate work here in the United States. They began sending most of them to MIT and to other colleges. But with a background of that engineering education in Europe, you see, many of our earliest engineers, including David W. Taylor, had taken their postgraduate overseas—almost all of them—and brought back that knowledge to the United States. The French were extremely theoretical in most of their approach and not too practical. But in the case of the Normandie, they had done a pretty damn good job of hydrodynamic design. But they had made some mistakes.

I visited the Normandie in 1935 in Le Havre when she went into dry dock after her first year in service.* I examined her underwater body thoroughly from a theoretical point of view, which was, you know, new stuff to me, but I grabbed onto it. Then, in digging deeper and deeper into her story, I had found out that she had very severe vibration, in addition to her high performance and speed. In talking to Professor Barrillon about that, he agreed, yes, the vibration was caused by propellers being too close to the bossings which held the propeller shafts outboard. They didn't have struts out there; they had bossings. The bossings were not cut away enough so that the pressure pulse of each blade going by would not impact on the hull of the ship. The tips had a pulse also that impacted the hull of the ship and would cause vibration at a propeller blade frequency.

Well, I also discovered, by doing a little calculation, that the shaft would spring longitudinally with these pulses. And, being built into a thrust bearing at the other end, that the shaft itself was acting as a spring, and that you could actually approach longitudinal resonance, in which it would get so severe that the vibration would be just a continuous hammering against the thrust blocks in that ship as each blade went by, on all four propellers. Well, I soon realized that that was a fundamental phenomenon. They had the ship in dry dock. She was electric drive. They changed the number of RPM in that ship in order to lower the speed of the propellers. They changed the propellers; they

---

* The Normandie went into service in 1935.

changed the bossings in order to get rid of the vibrations. They never succeeded completely in getting rid of the vibration.

When I came back in 1936, the North Carolina and the Washington were the first two of our new battleships being designed at that time. I spent about six weeks in Washington being debriefed about what I'd learned in Europe, including armor plate, placements, and so forth that we'd been trying to find out for years. We found out the French ministry knew all about the British inclined armor and all that sort of thing. I told this to the guys up in design, and one of them said, "Oh, we've been trying to find out that for years." So I went all through my notebooks and got debriefed on all this stuff.

Paul Stillwell: Did you think Europe was superior technologically then?

Admiral Mumma: Theoretically. Not so much practically. Theoretically, the British and the French, both of them—and the Germans—have been really quite excellent because their educational systems have been fabulous. Practically, they don't apply it as well as we do. But then when you get right down to it, when you combine the two—the top theory and the top practice—you get the top performance of everything. That's what we were trying to do.

I mentioned earlier the loss of a month's pay when I was on leave. I had another experience like that. Roscoe Hillenkoetter and I were on duty in Europe at the same time.* He was a courier there in '33-34, and he came back in '35. I went over in '34 and came back in '36. So we overlapped a year there, during which time he had been already selected from lieutenant to lieutenant commander. I had already been selected from lieutenant (j.g.) to lieutenant. I previously told you that there wasn't a single ship in the European theater. There were no U.S. doctors; there were no dentists; there were no medical men in the European theater. Here we were, over there, and we couldn't take the examinations that were required in those days for promotion. We couldn't take our physicals; we couldn't get a dental exam. So he and I both wrote a letter to the Bureau of Navigation, "Examine us on our record so that we can draw our pay."† I was at that time

---

* Lieutenant Roscoe H. Hillenkoetter, USN, assistant naval attaché in Paris.
† Prior to World War II, assignments of naval officers were made by the Bureau of Navigation. On 13 May 1942, it became the Bureau of Naval Personnel (BuPers), a title that better described its function.

one year already into the next pay grade, and we were supposed to be getting exchange relief.

And no, absolutely no. They came back, "You will not be promoted on your record. No, you will be promoted when you get back and take your exams." Well, in other words, when I got back to the United States in '36, all my classmates had already been promoted from jaygee to lieutenant.* They had already drawn their money for that year. I got back, and I not only did not draw my money right away, I had to take my exams and then wait a period of time until they were approved, and then draw my money—my back pay—for over a year, but no exchange relief.

Paul Stillwell: Now, what do you mean by exchange relief?

Admiral Mumma: Exchange relief was supposed to compensate you for devaluation of the dollar overseas. I never got the exchange relief. I lost over a year's worth of extra pay.

Those were some of the things that they have done to the military over the years that nobody realizes or appreciates. They did another one. The Congress passed a law in '59—the year I retired from the Navy—that your retired pay would no longer be computed based on active duty pay. What that resulted in was that we stagnated in our flat retired pay, after I retired as a rear admiral upper half, flat for years and years, while the others got increases in pay and ours stayed flat. That was called recomputation. I don't know whether you've ever heard of it or not.

Paul Stillwell: Yes, I have.

Admiral Mumma: It never has been recomputed. Secondly, when we did get, shall we say, a cost of living increase along with civilian employees that had gotten it for years ahead of us, we still had this gap. And it's still there. In other words, my retired pay is nowhere near where it would have been if my father had been retired at the same grade, same rank, and so forth. He would have been computed at three-quarters of base pay of

---

* Jaygee—lieutenant (junior grade).

active duty people the rest of his life. I'm stuck with a—not only the cost of living has now been knocked off this past year—but this whole scale has been escalated downward. This is one way they're not playing fair with the military. That was an agreement with the Congress; it had survived 150 years of operation that way with the military. Then the Congress did away with it in '58 and '59. These are the kinds of things that are discouraging to some of these younger people when they see this happening. And now they're complaining bitterly about the retired pay of the military, you know.

Paul Stillwell: Probably people more recent than you that are the subject of the complaints.

Admiral Mumma: Yes. Okay, that's enough on that subject.

Paul Stillwell: You mentioned Admiral Hillenkoetter. He became something of an intelligence specialist. He was the first head of the CIA.[*] Did he have an intelligence role over in Europe then when you were there?

Admiral Mumma: Yes, he was a courier at the time that I was going to school there. And, of course, he being one of the few officers in Europe, we knew them very well. He and his wife Jane were very, very good friends of ours. She's still alive and living up in Weehawken, New Jersey.[†] Hilly, of course, had visited all over Europe, all the embassies, as a courier. They carried the diplomatic pouches from one diplomatic office to another, and they covered everything. They even went down to Addis Ababa and places of that type; they'd cover the Balkans. They'd cover Russia, Germany, U.K., Spain, Italy. He was the Navy courier.

There was an Army courier who was out of the class of '20 at West Point. His name was Hayden Sears.[‡] He's dead now, and so is Hilly. But Hayden Sears and he used

---

[*] Rear Admiral Roscoe H. Hillenkoetter, USN, served as Director of Central Intelligence from 30 April 1947 to 7 October 1950. On 18 September 1947, as a result of the new National Security Act, the Central Intelligence Agency replaced the previous Central Intelligence Group on 18 September 1947.
[†] Hillenkoetter, who retired as a tombstone vice admiral in 1957, died 18 June 1982 in New York City.
[‡] Captain Hayden A. Sears, USA, was an assistant military attaché in the U.S. embassy in Paris in 1933-34 and then a diplomatic courier for the European Information Center, 1934-36.

to alternate which trip they would take. They would cover all of Europe. About the only good thing that we would get out of it would be that occasionally, coming back from Moscow, they'd bring back a gallon of fresh caviar. Then we'd have a champagne and caviar party on that gallon of caviar. I think they paid about $10.00 then for a gallon of caviar.

Paul Stillwell: How did they travel, by train?

Admiral Mumma: Train always. Always by train. They always had a locked compartment, so that they supposedly could not be approached, or attacked, or the diplomatic pouch touched in any way. So he had a pretty good basic experience in Europe. So it wasn't by accident that he was appointed naval attaché to the Vichy government in France when France fell.[*] Then, of course, when the invasion started, why, all this changed, and in many respects this subterfuge of operating with the Vichy government disappeared. But Hilly had a very good basic broad knowledge of Europe and was an ideal man to be the first CIA director.

Paul Stillwell: He also had the advantage that he came from Harry Truman's home state. He had been captain of the Missouri, and that's when Truman got to know him.[†]

Admiral Mumma: Oh, yes. Well, he was a great guy. Didn't you think so?

Paul Stillwell: Yes.

Admiral Mumma: He sure was.

---

[*] Vichy, a resort town in south-central France, became the site of a French government on 1 July 1940 after most of the nation had been occupied by Germans shortly before. The new state of Vichy France governed the one-third of the country the Germans did not occupy. The new government existed officially until the summer of 1944 but actually had little power after November 1942, when Germans occupied the remainder of France.

[†] As a captain, Hillenkoetter commanded the battleship Missouri (BB-63) from 6 November 1945 to 31 May 1946. President Harry S. Truman, a Missourian, visited the ship while Hillenkoetter was skipper.

Paul Stillwell: Do you have any specific incidents that you recall regarding Hillenkoetter?

Admiral Mumma: Oh, gosh.

Paul Stillwell: Did your families live near each other?

Admiral Mumma: I don't think I know any specific anecdotes about it, except that we sure felt kind of isolated. There weren't many U.S. military over there in Europe in those days. But Hilly and I and the others in the attaché groups kind of stuck together, because there weren't very many American civilians in Europe either. All the young people had come back to the U.S. because of the Depression. There were very few tourists, except a few teachers would come over to Tours or Grenoble. The small group of Americans in Paris all became very good friends.

A rather amusing little incident, though. We all had a little alliance with the American church in Paris. There were a few young boys of Americans living there, and one of the young officers there was in the Army Air Corps, a Captain Boatner.* He had a son who was about 16 years old. The pastor of the American church asked me, would I form a chapter of sea scouts because there were some teenage Americans there that needed to be kept out of trouble. So, not that I wasn't adequately busy with my postgraduate work, I went to work on forming this sea scout chapter, and Mark Boatner's son was one of them. Well, at this time we're talking about, 1934 and '35, this young man came back and went to college. He became an Air Force officer, and by the middle of the war, my sea scout student was a general.

Paul Stillwell: And you were a captain in the Navy during that part of the war.

Admiral Mumma: Oh, incidentally, there was another interesting experience there. This Major Smith, that had been my father's pilot for the aircraft operation of small arms firing during World War I, was the head of the Battle of Monuments Commission in Paris

---

* Captain Mark J. Boatner, Jr., USA, was a civil engineer rather than an aviator.

at the time that we were there. The U.S. ambassador to France at that time was Mr. Straus of the Macy Company.* Because there were so few people there of any military character, he called me one day, and he said, "Lieutenant, I need someone for the Memorial Day ceremony at Chateau-Thierry. We have to make a speech at that cemetery."† And, do you know, I think this Colonel Smith is the one that put him up to it. So I had to go out to Chateau-Thierry and represent the ambassador and make a speech in French about the heroic operation of the Americans and the French, and the British, together in the battle of Chateau-Thierry, and especially the Marine Corps. Well, a junior grade lieutenant making this speech as the representative of the ambassador. That was something.

Paul Stillwell: Did you get any special living allowance to cope with French prices?

Admiral Mumma: No, no. As a matter of fact, I was just given travel orders. And in between the two years of instruction at the Génie Maritime, we had what is called a "stage." The "stage" was a trip around all the French industrial establishments that had anything to do with military marine business of that type, including the French navy yards at Cherbourg, Le Havre, and at Brest, and at Toulon, and into Switzerland, and in France, in Sulzer Brothers, and Esherfiche, and those industrial companies. So that I became quite familiar with the industrial capacity of Europe and particularly the French Navy. So that was why I was later selected—not only for language speaking, but also for industrial knowledge of the area—to be a member of the Alsos Mission, which we're not at that point to talk about yet.

Paul Stillwell: Well, I'd like to hear about it when we get to it. Did you file any intelligence reports with the ONI when you were over in France on these things?‡

---

* Jesse Isidor Straus was U.S. ambassador to France from 1933 to 1936.
† In the spring of 1918 American troops blocked an enemy offensive at Chateau-Thierry and helped prevent the Germans from crossing the Marne River to reach Paris.
‡ ONI—Office of Naval Intelligence.

Admiral Mumma: Not as such. I got debriefed when I got back, and we went over my notebooks, but I did not act as an intelligence officer, no.

Paul Stillwell: Did you get to Germany at all?

Admiral Mumma: Not on that trip. No, I was in England; I was in France; I was in Spain. I did get to northern Italy, but that was on a vacation. I didn't get anything official in those areas. In later years, after World War II, I got into all those areas very officially.

Paul Stillwell: After you came back from Europe, then you were assigned to the USS Chicago, a new heavy cruiser.

Admiral Mumma: Actually, before leaving Europe in 1936 in July, I had been informed, of course, that I had been selected for promotion from junior grade lieutenant to lieutenant, as I told you. My class was the first class to have selection from every grade, ensign on up. Since I was not able to take my exams physical or mental, therefore I sat in Europe for over a year as a junior grade lieutenant after making my number. When I returned to the States, I was thrown in with the rest of the class of '26 and '27, all of whom were full lieutenants, and I was still a junior grade lieutenant. I went to the Bureau of Navigation, as it was called in those days, in Washington and arranged for my exams to be sent to the ship a month after I reported to give me a little chance to get reoriented before taking my exams. And they said, sure, that would be fine.

I spent six weeks of being debriefed in Washington from my experience in France and observation of the Normandie, and all those other aspects. Among other things that I'd made notes of was the inner-armor arrangement of the Nelson and Rodney, British battleships. We had never known how that armor had been arranged, but the French knew all about it. It was a point of the discussion how to design armor for big ships at the Génie Maritime. So I thumbed through my notebook of the whole period with both the Bureau of Construction and Repair and the Bureau of Engineering, debriefing all items that were of interest to both design sections. So I sat in Commander Solberg's office.* He was at that time head of design in the Bureau of Engineering. In the Bureau of Construction and Repair I talked to Captain Chantry at that time was head of design, and John Niedermair was the senior design engineer, and Les Kniskern was in charge of preliminary hull design.†

After the six-week period during which I was debriefed in Washington, I reported to Long Beach, to the Chicago.‡ And we lived in Long Beach. There I was assistant engineer.

Paul Stillwell: Had you still not taken your promotion exams?

Admiral Mumma: No, I hadn't taken them yet. I was in the wardroom as a jaygee, but the Filipino boys never did promote me. I was always sitting down at the end of the lieutenants, no matter how junior they were relative to me.

The strange thing was that when I reported to the Chicago, I found that my exams were already on board with the requirement that they had to be taken within two weeks. So I had only two weeks to get ready and get out of my French thinking into strategy and tactics and everything else that a naval officer is supposed to know. Most of it is a little remote from engineering. But I did it and managed to pass the exam all right, so I got promoted. Well, by about Christmastime, I guess, I got my two stripes. I bounced, really, from one of the juniors to beyond the middle of the lieutenants on the ship.

The engineering department there was quite standard, prewar design, and the Chicago was a ship that carried one of the flags.

Paul Stillwell: Didn't she have commander cruisers?

---

* Commander Thorwald A. Solberg, USN.
† Captain Allan J. Chantry, Jr., Construction Corps, USN; John Niedermair, a civilian whose oral history is in the Naval Institute collection; Lieutenant Commander Leslie A. Kniskern, Construction Corps, USN.
‡ USS Chicago (CA-29) was commissioned 9 March 1931. She had a standard displacement of 9,300 tons, was 600 feet long and 66 feet in the beam. Her top speed was 32 knots. She was armed with nine 8-inch guns, and eight 5-inch guns. The Chicago sank in the Rennell Islands on 30 January 1943 as a result of attacks by Japanese aircraft.

Albert G. Mumma, Interview #1 (10/3/86) -- Page 58

Admiral Mumma: Yes, we had Commander Cruisers Scouting Force.*

Paul Stillwell: Was the Chicago in the yard throughout your time on board?

Admiral Mumma: Very little. No, we were most of that time at sea, and we were operating with the fleet.

Paul Stillwell: What do you remember about those operations, any specifics?

Admiral Mumma: Well, I guess I would remember better the operations that immediately followed that, because in the mid-'30s it became fairly obvious that the Japs were getting active in Manchuria area, and so on. It wasn't really until '37 that it got heated up a bit as far as the fleet was concerned.

The Chicago was scheduled to go in the summer of '37 to Alaska, but less than a year after I joined that ship, I was suddenly detached and ordered to the Clark, one of the brand-new destroyers being built in Boston.† It happened that the skipper was Hewlett Thebaud, who had been the naval attaché when I reported to France for duty. He apparently had asked for me as his chief engineer, which I was happy to do because he was a fabulous man.

Paul Stillwell: Mr. Leadership.

Admiral Mumma: Terrific guy. The guy that wrote the leadership book and all that sort of thing.‡ Well, he practiced it. I had the most happy time for two years in that ship with him as skipper. We did a lot of things, and we got a lot accomplished, so forth and so on.

---

* Rear Admiral Edward B. Fenner, USN, Commander Cruisers Scouting Force and Commander Cruiser Division Five.

† USS Clark (DD-360) was a Porter-class destroyer, commissioned 20 May 1936. She had a standard displacement of 1,805 tons, was 381 feet long, 36 feet in the beam, and had a draft of 10 feet. Her design speed was 35 knots. She was armed with eight 5-inch guns and eight 21-inch torpedo tubes. She later operated throughout World War II and was eventually decommissioned 23 October 1945.

‡ Leo H. Thebaud, Naval Leadership, With Some Hints to Junior Officers and Others; a Compilation by and for the Navy, First Edition (Annapolis: U.S. Naval Institute, 1924).

When I was detached from the Chicago, I went overland to the Boston Navy Yard, where the Clark had been built at Fore River and was in the outfitting period at Boston.

Paul Stillwell: She was one of the gold-platers.*

Admiral Mumma: She was a gold-plater and a destroyer leader, so-called in those days, an 1,850-ton destroyer with a forecastle, good size forecastle on them—very, very fine ships in many, many ways.

Alan McCracken, of the class of '22, was exec.† I went as engineer. I was third in seniority in the ship then, and one of the first things the skipper did was recalling our having been shipmates together in France. He said, "Now, Al, you're going to volunteer to run for mess treasurer."‡

I said, "Thank you very much, Captain." So I ran for mess treasurer and for the succeeding two years on the ship, I never got rid of the job. The reason being that we had been having pork chops, lamb chops, veal chops, and we wanted to have roasts and nice things like that. And we wanted to mix the salads at the table, a la France, and so, as a net result, I won hands down on the election.

We did another thing while in Boston. The captain was convinced that if we kept the black boys that we were being assigned in those days—this is in '37—that we would soon be eaten out of house and home in the wardroom, because if you fed them the regular food that we ate, they ate twice as much as we did. So he said that the most reasonable thing that we could possibly do would be to swap off two black boys for one Filipino. The Filipinos would fish and get their own food, and it would be a very economical wardroom. He also sent each steward and cook to the Ritz-Carlton while in the yard, giving the hotel their services free in exchange for teaching them many fine points of the culinary art.

---

* The first of the "gold-platers," the modern destroyers designed in the 1930s, was the USS Farragut (DD-348), commissioned 18 June 1934. They replaced the old four-pipers as the front-line destroyers in the U.S. Fleet.
† Lieutenant Alan R. McCracken, USN.
‡ Wardroom mess treasurer is not considered a desirable job for a ship's officer because he is subject to complaints from those who don't like the food being served.

Paul Stillwell: Does that mean the wardroom mess had to pay for the stewards' food?

Admiral Mumma: Oh, yes. We got a ration allowance for their food, but they would eat twice as much. And, of course, then we had to pay the differential, which was around double the ration allowance each month for each of us. On a small ship of that size, why, it made some difference. So he swapped off two for one Filipino boy, and pretty soon we had all Filipino boys. Of course, they didn't eat too much, and they were very good, basically. This was nearing the end of the Filipino boys as wardroom mess attendants. At any rate, we were also going to carry a flag. We knew that. And that would have been helpful, too, to have a better group for this larger group of officers. We were destined to be a squadron leader.

The ship left and went to the West Coast from Boston. After we got there, we found that almost immediately we would have a flotilla inspection, an admiral's inspection, and so on, being one of the first of our class of the new gold-platers to arrive on the West Coast. But we had a very unfortunate circumstance in that a lot of the other gold-platers were having problems in their condensers. They had unexpected and very rapid deterioration of the condenser tubes and condenser heads in some of these ships. At that time I think we had about 16 new ships on the West Coast in San Diego.

Admiral Pye was the flotilla commander, and Lieutenant Commander Mills was his engineer on the staff.[*] I'd known Mills before from my <u>Saratoga</u> days, when he was at the Bremerton yard. He said, "Al, we've got a problem with all these destroyers. We've got a dozen reports of condenser problems, and we don't know how bad it is. They're all being observed by different people, and we can't evaluate one versus the other." He said, "Would you head up a committee [task force, you might call it] of a couple of other people, including a warrant from the repair ship, and so forth, and put in focus how big a problem this is and which ship is first to be taken care of."

I said, "In addition to my regular duties, Earle?"

---

[*] Rear Admiral William S. Pye, USN, was Commander Destroyer Flotilla Two and Commander Destroyers Battle Force. Lieutenant Commander Earle W. Mills, USN.

He said, "Yes, sir." So I had that additional task inspecting those 16 ships. This warrant officer and I went in and inspected 32 condensers, the entering head and the leaving head of those condensers, so we had 64 condenser heads that we inspected.

Paul Stillwell: What was the problem?

Admiral Mumma: They had a corrosion problem. The designers had decided in their wisdom that monel was a very good anti-corrosive metal; therefore, it would be a very good thing to have monel heads on these condensers. Well, admiralty metal tubing is a brass, basically, and so were the condenser tube sheets. So the net result was that the monel would protect itself in sea water beautifully, but there was an electrolyctic action between the condenser heads and tube ends and the monel heads in the presence of sea water that gave an electrolyctic cell that ate away the tube sheets, and ate away the flared tube ends of the condenser tubes.

Paul Stillwell: Sort of like the reason you put zincs underwater on a hull to take up the electrolyctic action.[*]

Admiral Mumma: Absolutely. In other words, it was a mistake of design. So we were able to catalog which were the worst, which ones could be put off a little bit, and you could live with temporarily. In addition, we made a recommendation that the tube sheets be kept the way they were without any further chemical treatment, but that the condenser heads, both entering and exiting heads, should be coated with lead, which was much more inert chemically in sea water, and prevent the direct action across the sea water electrolyte of the monel versus the brass admiralty metal. We ended up, therefore, in having to lead coat all of those heads. In my ship, particularly, we didn't have the problem, because those ships had been designed with copper heads which was pretty well normal electrolytically (also previous practice), and the copper did not have the same effect against the brass as the monel did.

---

[*] The practice is to put small pieces of zinc on the under body of a ship, particularly on our near the rudder. Thus when there is electrolysis, it is the zinc that is consumed, rather than the steel of the ship itself.

Paul Stillwell: It sounds almost like a parallel to the propeller problem. There should have been a seawater test.

Admiral Mumma: Should have been. Exactly. So we learned that one the hard way. So Earle Mills gave me that extra duty, and we successfully completed that, and we got the priority, which ships should get first attention, and so forth. They were all corrected before the war.

Paul Stillwell: You were talking about these black messmen. What was the perception of blacks in the Navy at that era?

Admiral Mumma: Well, there were a few isolated incidences, where they were tremendously accepted. They were promoted to petty officers and chief petty officers. Some of them got Congressional Medals of Honor for heroism, and so on. They were tremendously accepted so that blacks in the Navy never had the difficulty that the Army had, or some of the other services.

Paul Stillwell: That's not how the blacks saw it, of course. They didn't feel that they got the opportunities that they deserved.

Admiral Mumma: Well, that's possible because it is perfectly true that there were no black officers in those days. Secondly, by the time the Depression came—and we were talking about '37 now—they had been in Depression for a long time. These were young people that were getting into the service at the lowest possible point. The reason for that was that before World War II, in the mid-'30s and later '30s, the opportunities in civilian life were so limited that we were able to attract the best possible young people in the world into the Navy as enlisted men. That is the reason why the blacks came last. We had high school graduates coming in as seamen second, and those were terrific men. And those were the basis, really, on which the chief petty officers and petty officers and a high percentage of the younger officers of the Navy were available when we got into World War II.

That shows the quality of the people that we got during the Depression. And that shows why the blacks, who were relatively uneducated, still were at the bottom of the list. They couldn't make it in the same way that the Depression forced tremendously good quality people into the service.

Paul Stillwell: Well, but the fact that they were limited to the mess branch didn't really give them an opportunity to demonstrate whether they could do the job or not.

Admiral Mumma: They were not limited. As a matter of fact, all the better opportunities were being filled by very qualified enlisted men—I mean some of them college graduates, and almost all of them high school graduates.

Paul Stillwell: Well, there must have been some well-educated black people who might have gone in . . .

Admiral Mumma: Nowhere near the proportion in the mid-'30s. Most of them were in conservation camps and things of that kind. They were not getting a very good education, basically. It was a sad thing because that Depression had a depressive effect on the whole United States—there's no question about it—and the blacks didn't get much help out of it. The Depression was not a help to them.

Paul Stillwell: It was not much of a help to anybody.

Admiral Mumma: No.

Paul Stillwell: How did the engineering plant in the gold-platers compare with the four-stackers?

Admiral Mumma: They were, they were very good. They were basically a development of good engineering, and William Francis Gibbs had a fair amount to do with that, because he had specialized in destroyers and destroyer power plants, and he had a very capable old engineering group in New York City that did the design work.[*] Even the yards that didn't use Gibbs's designs had their own pretty good staffs that they were keeping to do this work. This is one thing you can thank Roosevelt for. Having been an Assistant Secretary of the Navy long years before, he was convinced that the Navy needed building up to prepare for what might happen, and he did a job of doing that.[†] As a matter of fact, I don't know how many people know that we built whole destroyers on the WPA program. Did you know that before?

Paul Stillwell: Well, I didn't know it was the WPA. I knew that it was Depression relief.

Admiral Mumma: Yes. It was the WPA program, Works Progress Administration. We built whole destroyers on that program, which was, to our thinking, a very good way of using that money.

Paul Stillwell: Better than raking leaves.

Admiral Mumma: It sure was.

Paul Stillwell: What else do you recall about the engineering plant?

Admiral Mumma: We had a requirement that we not mix oil and water in those days. We were afraid to do it because you get sputtering or something in a burner if you get a sputter of water coming through it with an oil line. We were too afraid of that blending

---

[*] William Francis Gibbs was the key figure in Gibbs & Cox, Inc. a naval architecture and marine engineering firm. It was founded in 1929 as an outgrowth of the Gibbs Brothers organization, which had been established in 1922. An early Gibbs Brothers task was the conversion of the German ocean liner Vaterland to the Leviathan, a transport in World War I and later a U.S.-flag commercial liner. During World War II, more than 70% of the tonnage launched to support the U.S. war effort was built to Gibbs & Cox designs.

[†] Franklin D. Roosevelt was President of the United States from March 1933 to April 1945. He served as Assistant Secretary of the Navy to Josephus Daniels from 1913 to 1921, during the Wilson Administration.

problem. Actually, part of that was due to bunker C originally, because bunker C had such a high viscosity that it would hold water in it, and we didn't really get into Navy special fuel oil until just before World War II. And Navy special was so much lighter.

When we were coming around, we still had this restriction that we could not put water in oil tanks because of the danger of so-called sputtering. I think it was probably in 1937. We were on our way from Guantanamo to Panama and eventually coming up the West Coast when we were restricted from taking more oil than was necessary than to get to Panama. We were supposed to fuel on the Balboa side for the trip north to Long Beach or San Diego, wherever. It ended up that we were so light with lack of oil and we did not ballast with water, that we almost lost the ship in a following sea one time. We heeled over to 72 degrees; the ship slewed and broached, and at the time it happened, I even had a chief quartermaster on the wheel. But, boy, I'll tell you, we dumped the starboard whaleboat, which was the gig, in the water, and when the ship righted itself finally, slowly, the whaleboat was full of water and bent the davits over like this. So we had a heck of a time with that, but that was caused by this restriction.

I pumped as much oil as possible into the stern, but still without trying to lose suction on the main tanks, and I fed the after boiler room from the stern, and the forward from the forward service tanks, trying to keep the stern down when we had this following sea. That was a risky one. We came awful close to losing that ship. That's what happened, of course, later during the war, during that refueling in the Pacific.[*] The ship was too light and had no ballast. You should ballast a ship always to make sure that you have stability; you can always separate the damned oil and water later if you have to. But you certainly don't want to lose the ship for lack of ballast.

Paul Stillwell: Well, I guess it was a holdover from that mind-set then that still prevailed.

Admiral Mumma: Well, you learned an awful lot of things. The sea is a very tough customer to work with.

---

[*] While operating off the Philippines, ships of the Third Fleet ran into a ferocious typhoon on 18 December 1944. In all, three destroyers—Hull (DD-350), Spence (DD-512), and Monaghan (DD-354)—sank, and a number of other ships were damaged. For details, see C. Raymond Calhoun, Typhoon: The Other Enemy; The Third Fleet and the Pacific Storm of December 1944 (Annapolis: Naval Institute Press, 1981).

Paul Stillwell: What operations do you recall in that ship?

Admiral Mumma: Well, of course, the first thing we did was, shakedown at Guantanamo. We had a short-range battle practice, and so on. In 1937—this is a couple of years before any war started—Bull Halsey was down there as a base commander, and the airfield was part of the base, and they had a training area there.* We didn't operate very closely with them from a point of view of air-sea operations, or anything of that kind. But we did do a lot of our own type of experimentation and development while we were there for about a month shaking down. We fired all the battle practices, and so forth, that were necessary for that year, and then we left for the West Coast. And we transited the canal. It happened, my brother Morton was in command of a submarine down in Panama at that time. My uncle—my dad's kid brother, Major Harlan Mumma class of 1916 at West Point—was at Camp Gaillard. I got them both to ride the ship trans-canal with us from Colon to Panama. Then they went back by train.

Paul Stillwell: Did you get in any fleet exercises?

Admiral Mumma: Not on that trip. We didn't join the fleet until we got to San Diego. Again, here was already a beginning of the Japanese problem, because the Japs had been using a large number of trawlers and so-called tuna boats going in and out of San Diego and casing the bay. Every time one entered, one went out. I don't know to what degree they were actually relaying that information on to Japan, but they knew exactly what we were doing, and so on. So our Navy instituted a new system very shortly after we got there. They had enough ships then so they could do it.

They always used to have one ready destroyer in San Diego, even when I was there back in the early '30s. This ready destroyer was supposed to keep steam up, ready to get under way on about a half hour's notice. Then it was doubled after we got there in '37 to have a ready destroyer in the harbor and another ready destroyer at the entrance to

---

* Captain William F. Halsey, Jr., USN, commanded the naval air station at Pensacola, Florida, in 1937-38. During World War II he was one of the U.S. Navy's most noted flag officers.

the harbor. The ready destroyer at the entrance to the harbor was to board every incoming suspicious-looking kind of a ship, and see what it was bringing in in the way of electronics surveillance equipment, radar, anything of that kind. Radar wasn't even well known at that time. It was only a dream in the eyes of several people.

Paul Stillwell: I doubt that the fishing trawlers had it yet.

Admiral Mumma: No, they didn't. Well, the Japs had a lot of pretty sophisticated electronics on board. And they were sophisticated in taking and reading almost everything they got ahold of, so that we began limiting our communications by radio, and so on. They also did a very good job of casing our support capabilities and our fleet operations. Any time we went to sea, there was always somebody shadowing us. They always managed to get over the horizon just where they could watch battle practices and things. So that it was "Wolf, Wolf, Wolf," and had been since '32 to an increasing degree. So my theory is that by the time Pearl Harbor actually came, "Wolf, Wolf, Wolf" was not any longer a warning to the same degree that it had been. Everybody got tired of "Wolf, Wolf, Wolf."

Paul Stillwell: They were anticlimactic by then.

Admiral Mumma: That's right. Because we had been playing wolf for a long time. And the public doesn't know that. I don't think they do.

Paul Stillwell: Well, the bombing of the Panay was certainly an overt act.[*]

Admiral Mumma: Yes. So then in '39, the fleet went to the East Coast. Things seemed to have quieted down enough so that the fleet maneuvered and operated off the East Coast. We had a long six-month cruise to the East Coast and back. In the meantime, then-Lieutenant Commander McCracken had some severe eye problems, and he was sent

---

[*] On 12 December 1937 the Yangtze River gunboat USS Panay (PR-5) was attacked and sunk by Japanese aircraft near Nanking, China. Two crew members were killed and 43 wounded. Japan claimed it had made an error in identification and paid an indemnity for the incident.

to the hospital. So I became exec as well as engineer, which was almost enough to keep me busy.

By this time Commander Thebaud had been detached and Admiral, then Commander, Bates had succeeded him, Rafe Bates. We called him "Reticent Rafe."[*] Rafe fancied himself quite a strategian and tactician and ended his career up at the war college.[†] This was another anecdotal kind of experience. Rafe Bates was a very tough guy. He was, if anything, overbearing. He'd never been married, and he had none of the, shall we say, gentler characteristics that most husbands acquire.

Paul Stillwell: Of necessity.

Admiral Mumma: So he was a rough, tough sundowner. Following on the heels of Hewlett Thebaud, it was like night and day. Well, at any rate, he drove the exec off the ship, practically. He drove the gunnery officer off the ship. I don't know whether he actually asked for the detachment or not, but that's what happened. Whether it was at their own request or not, I don't know. But at that time I was engineer, and he thought I was doing pretty well. Well, since he had driven the exec off the ship, I became exec as well. We had annual military inspection coming by the flotilla flag, Admiral Pye. What happened was that the captain was so insistent upon getting a very high mark in the annual military inspection that he was driving us all crazy.

Rafe Bates is gone himself, rest his soul.[‡] But we were trying to figure out some way in which we could really do well without being harassed the whole time by the skipper. Just about that time, we were out on maneuvers. I was exec, so I was doing the navigating, and I was also chief engineer. We got out in maneuvers, and the fog suddenly set in out near Coronado Roads as we were about to come in. So the order went out and assigned anchorages to all the flag officers, ships in various locations, and then all the other ships in certain other locations contingent to their flags.

---

[*] Commander Richard W. Bates, USN.
[†] As a commodore in the late 1940s, Bates directed a number of analytical studies of World War II combat actions while on the staff of the Naval War College. When he retired in 1949, he received a tombstone promotion to rear admiral on the basis of his wartime service. He then continued his studies following retirement. See the Naval Institute oral history of Vice Admiral David C. Richardson, USN (Ret.).
[‡] Bates died 26 December 1973 at Newport, Rhode Island.

Our commodore didn't like rolling at sea, so he wanted to get as close in behind Point Loma as possible, because we were all going to anchor out between there and Coronado Roads.* So we had this assigned berth that we were going to be in, and this fog had dropped. It was pea soup, absolutely. The only way to navigate was with hydrophone and hand lead. We had no radar to pierce the fog in those days. We had no lights ashore, nothing. You couldn't see a thing. So I was taking soundings from the hand leads and plotting them up on the bridge. I was also getting the hydrophone bearings from Point Loma. We were supposed to be going into this anchorage.

Suddenly loomed the stern of an aircraft carrier. As we went under the stern of this aircraft carrier, I said, "Captain, that aircraft carrier's out of position. He's supposed to be in such-and-such a berth." The captain thought I was crazy. I said, "Thank God we missed him, though." We kept on going, and I didn't change course. I said, "Keep the same course, Captain." The captain wanted to change course. I said, "No, no, no. We're on the right course to our hole." So we were working away at these bearings, and so on. Finally we got fairly close—I'd say several hundred yards from where the hole was to drop the hook.

The captain said, "The commodore wants to go over the side to go over to the flagship, and he wants to go as soon as we anchor." So he had the officer of the deck call away the gig. The gig coxswain didn't show up right away. When he did show up, the captain leaned over the side of the bridge and saw him show up, he said, "Come up here on the bridge." He came up on the bridge, and he was chewing him out something horrible. I couldn't hear my bearings. I couldn't hear the hydrophone or the soundings.

Finally, I said, "Captain, I can't hear a goddamn thing." Silence fell, and I thought, "Oh, oh, here goes my naval career." But I got the bearings and I got the lead soundings, plotted them, and I said, "Stand by, Captain, we're nearing the anchorage." Finally, I said, "Time to let go, Captain."

So he ordered, "Let go." So we dropped the hook. Then the captain said, "I'm going below." By this we put the gig over the side, and so forth.

I said, "Captain, I'm staying on the bridge. When the fog lifts, I'll get a round of bearings and check our position. I'm not securing main engines yet. I'll secure main

---

* The commodore in this case was Commander Destroyer Squadron Three, embarked in the Clark.

engines as soon as I know that we're in the right spot. If not, I'll pick up the anchor and move a little bit. Okay?"

So he said, "Okay." Then he went below. We waited for the fog to lift, because we didn't want the commodore to get lost in the gig. Finally, in about half an hour, the fog just lifted—boom, like it does out there. When it went up, I said, "Captain, I've taken a round of bearings, and we are within 25 feet of our hole. We're in the right spot. I've taken a check on that aircraft carrier that we missed, and do you know, he's 400 yards out of his."

The captain said, "Stop in the cabin on your way down."

I said, "I'm securing main engines now, Captain." So I secured main engines. I went down. I knocked on the door.

He says, "Come in."

I said, "Yes, sir."

He always called me chief because I was chief engineer. He said, "Chief, that's the best goddamn navigation I ever saw."

I said, "Thank you very much, Captain," and I disappeared. Boy, I thought my naval career was gone when I shouted at him like that. But that's the only way you got along with him. That's the way he liked to be treated, actually.

Paul Stillwell: Do you have any impressions of Admiral Pye?

Admiral Mumma: I didn't know Admiral Pye very well. He was a fine gentleman. He was a good ship man and knew destroyers. I didn't have very much detailed business with him. I was detached very soon after that experience.

Paul Stillwell: Pye had a reputation as a strategist also.

Admiral Mumma: Yes. Oh, well now, wait a minute. I'll tell you the rest of that. During this exact period, getting ready for Admiral Pye's inspection, I had received in the exec's office a study on "Combined aircraft and destroyer operations in scouting." It was one of the things to study on how to do it. Ordinarily my predecessor as exec would have taken that thing, and he would have worried himself sick over it. He would have done it himself and turned it over to the skipper. Well, I already had two jobs, so I went up to the captain—this was after this other episode. I said, "Captain, we got this study on strategy and tactics, combined air and destroyer operations in scouting. Quite truthfully, it's due in two weeks, and truthfully, I don't know how in the hell I'm going to get at it. Besides, I think it's exactly the kind of thing that you want to do personally."

He looked at me and he said, "Chief, are you trying to pass the buck to me?"

I said, "Yes, sir."

He said, "Okay, let me see it." And he did a good job on it. He studied it; he worked it out; and he sent it in. That was his contribution. This was part of the beginning of his becoming a strategian, I think.

Paul Stillwell: What action was required on the ship's part?

Admiral Mumma: This was comment on this treatise. Supposed to add and subtract, and make major revisions, if necessary, and so forth, on this write-up that had been evolved by the flotilla staff.

The <u>Clark</u> was the last ship to go into the navy yard in '39. We were going in for three months' overhaul at Mare Island.[*] Earle Mills, the flotilla engineer, said to me, "Al, I'm out of money. All I can give you is $25,000 for your overhaul."

I said, "My God, Earle, that's peanuts." Most of the ships were up around $100,000 to $200,000 for overhaul.

He said, "Well, do you think you can do it?"

I said, "Yes, I think I can do it, but I'll tell you one thing you're going to have to do. You're going to have to allow me to use that whole $25,000 pretty near for assist ship's force. So that when we go in and we get into trouble with anything that we're going to do ourselves with our ship's force, we can call on the navy yard to help us, but not do the whole job."

He said, "Okay, you can use the whole $25,000 that way if you want to."

---

[*] Mare Island Navy Yard, Vallejo, California.

So we went in, and because I'd had all this postgraduate engineering, I was technically competent to conduct the thing myself.

Paul Stillwell: Though you weren't designated in the Construction Corps.

Admiral Mumma: Right. I didn't really need the navy yard, except for material help occasionally. For example, we were going to lift turbines, and we were going to take clearances on the turbines. This was the prescribed length of time; within the first five years you're supposed to do that. We were going to have to report to the Bureau of Engineering that we had lifted turbines and so forth. Ordinarily, the navy yard would have charged you about, oh, I think $75,000 to do that job. All I got the navy yard to do was to send down the big lifting gear. We ran the lifting gear and lifted the turbines ourselves. We took the clearances ourselves. We overhauled all the pumps ourselves. We did everything of that kind ourselves with the ship's force. At the end of that time, why, we finished two weeks early. We had plenty of time to paint the ship and clean it up. Oh, by the time we left, we were gorgeous. We had probably one of the best overhauls that had ever been done, because we did it ourselves and the men had pride in doing it. We got back down in San Diego. Beautiful ship. Earle Mills came aboard. He said, "My God, this is really something."

I said, "Earle, those men that I had are the guys that did this job. All I had to do is instruct them, and train them a little bit and they would do the job." And I kept track of that. Of those 52 men in that engineers' force, 26 of them became officers during World War II. Which only goes to show that if you invest in them, it'll come out. I think my experience doing that with Earle Mills, when he was later deputy chief of bureau, had more to do with my eventual career probably then anything else.[*]

Paul Stillwell: Just a little thing like that.

Admiral Mumma: It didn't hurt anyhow.

---

[*] As a flag officer, Mills was Deputy Chief of the Bureau of Ships during World War II.

Paul Stillwell: Certainly not.

Admiral Mumma: When I finished that overhaul of the Clark in San Francisco, which turned out effectively, I knew I was about to be detached. From there I was sent to the Model Basin as a young officer, a lieutenant. The David Taylor Model Basin was one of my, shall I say, dream experiences that I was hoping to get some day because of my hydrodynamic experience at the PG, and the French school, and so on, and my experience with the Normandie and all that sort of thing. So immediately they put me in charge of the propeller-excited vibration research, which was, I thought, the bailiwick where I could make a contribution. So that's really where I got my teeth into something. We were just building the new Model Basin out at Carderock, Maryland, in '39.* My work at the Model Basin was, I thought, the most fabulous and interesting job I ever had.

Paul Stillwell: What made the Model Basin so special?

Admiral Mumma: Well, having had this hydrodynamic injection in Europe, I felt that that was my area of possible contribution. I had a very serious wrench on my part. I had spent many years at sea. I was considered a good naval officer at sea. And here I was embarking at the model basin in a technical area of research.

Paul Stillwell: It would take you away from being a line officer.

Admiral Mumma: And it soon evolved that I had to make a decision. Here I was, a line officer, had adequate line experience in many different types of ships, and ambitions of command, et cetera, et cetera, and the question arose as to whether I should apply for specialist assignment as an engineering duty officer.

    I went to my friend Earle Mills, who was then in the Bureau of Engineering, and I went to another friend, Ned Cochrane, who was in the Bureau of Construction and

---

* Prior to the opening of the facility at Carderock, the Navy used a smaller model basin on the grounds of the Naval Gun Factory in Washington, D.C.

Repair.* I talked to them about it. I said, "Look, I'm at a crossroads here. I'm a lieutenant, about to be a lieutenant commander, and if I don't make a decision pretty soon of one of the specialty areas, I am either something or nothing. I can't be both really, apparently." I said, "Quite truthfully, I like the technical side of the business extremely well. I love research and development. I love doing things that are different and new. But I hate to give up the possibility of command. And I don't really believe that you can do both well. You know that an awful lot of my friends have made this decision and with the war coming in, anybody can see this war coming, see that command is the thing you should do. Earle, you're a good friend of mine. I've known you for many years. What do you think?"

He said, "Al, there is only one decision for you to make. You must become an engineering duty officer."

I said, "Why do you say that?"

He said, "Because if you're in one ship, you can affect that one ship. If you're in this job, you can affect the whole Navy."

I said, "Well, that's a pretty big way to put it."

He said, "But it's a possibility. I think you should look at it that way. In other words, where are you good? Just handling ships and handling men?"

I said, "Yes, I'm pretty good at that. I think I proved that."

He said, "Well, what about as a specialist? You've already exercised that area pretty effectively with your postgraduate education. Your experience with me out there in destroyers when you solved our condenser problem for us, and things of this kind." And he said, "That overhaul of that destroyer with $25,000. My God, there's no other way but you to go this way. If you later on forward an application to go back into the line and not stay ED, I'm going to decline it and say that this should not be permitted. You've got to become and stay an ED officer, war or no war."

So I put in an application for ED and was selected. Took my promotion exams for lieutenant commander and passed.

---

* Commander Edward L. Cochrane, Construction Corps, USN. As a flag officer he served as Chief of the Bureau of Ships during World War II.

He was twisting my arm every way he could. And I must admit that in the long run, I feel that it was the right decision. After all, I did get promoted to flag rank. I didn't become a four-star admiral. You can't be a technical four-star admiral unless you've got a bunch of congressmen pushing you to be a four-star admiral like Rickover.*

Paul Stillwell: But there were certainly no guarantees that you would have made it as a line officer either.

Admiral Mumma: No, of course not, of course not. But when I see some of my classmates that did, I think I was in a comparable position to do as well. So God knows what would have happened if I stayed in the unrestricted line. I always thought that I brought to the specialist area a view of the unrestricted line officer.

Paul Stillwell: I think that's a very valid point to make, that a number of the Construction Corps people went to PG training virtually right out of the academy, and they didn't have that experience.

Admiral Mumma: Yes, well, I'd had, oh, roughly ten years of sea duty, which was far more than most of them had ever had, even though I had a four-year PG. That was something that I had to thank the Navy for. Why in the hell would they give me a four-year PG? You know, that was something that I appreciated the Navy doing for me.

So I got into it. I found some tremendous areas that really needed doing. For example, the new Model Basin started building in '36 out here at Carderock. Captain Savvy Saunders was the genius behind the design and the building of that Model Basin.† He had had many, many tours of duty down in the old Model Basin at the Washington Navy Yard. He was the man who had the highest academic average in the history of the Naval Academy. Now, Admiral David W. Taylor had a slightly higher average when he

---

* Hyman G. Rickover was considered the father of the nuclear Navy. He ran the U.S. Navy's nuclear-power program for many years, from 1948 until he eventually left active duty in 1982 with the rank of four-star admiral on the retired list. Rickover Hall at the Naval Academy is named in his honor, as is the nuclear-powered attack submarine Hyman G. Rickover (SSN-709), which was commissioned 21 July 1984.
† Captain Harold E. Saunders, Construction Corps, USN. He had stood number one of the 156 graduates in the Naval Academy's class of 1912. The new Model Basin at Carderock opened in 1940.

graduated, but in those days you could get extra credits above 4.0 by doing extra work. When Savvy Saunders was there, the maximum you could get was 4.0, and he graduated with something up in the 3.90s, as I remember, for the whole four years.

When I came in 1939, I reported to the old Model Basin in the navy yard, which was still the only model basin. The new Model Basin wasn't finished. It was under construction. So this was about the time that Bowen and C&R were having their tussles.[*] The Bureau of Engineering was blaming the Bureau of C&R. The Bureau of C&R was blaming the Bureau of Engineering. So there was a beginning of a feeling among some people that those two bureaus really should be combined into a Bureau of Ships. But it hadn't happened yet.[†] So I was an engineer, basically, when I went to the Model Basin. In other words, I was already a half-breed in the job, even though I had graduated in naval architecture at the Génie Maritime, as well as engineering over there. I wasn't just an engineer; I wasn't just a naval constructor; I was both. Well, that impelled me a little bit toward the Model Basin.

The old Model Basin was a historic place where a hell of a lot of wonderful things had been done. I don't think anybody realizes that that Model Basin down there in Washington, D.C., was the birthplace of the National Advisory Committee for Aeronautics, the NACA. They used to gather down there, a few people that called themselves the Advisory Committee for Aeronautics. They would get models made; they would test them; and they would try them out in that wind tunnel. That wind tunnel was built in 1913. It was the first research wind tunnel in the whole world. It had an 8-foot test section; it had a 500-horsepower fan; and it had over 100 miles an hour in the test section.

The airplane, the NC-4—N stands for Navy, C stands for Curtiss—was down there.[‡] Navy people—Admiral Taylor and others—and Curtiss got together and designed that NC-4 that flew the Atlantic. Lieutenant Commander Albert C. Read, later the second

---

[*] Rear Admiral Harold G. Bowen, USN, served as Chief of the Bureau of Engineering from 1935 to 1939. Rear Admiral Alexander H. Van Keuren, Construction Corps, USN, was Chief of the Bureau of Construction and Repair.
[†] The two bureaus were merged on 20 June 1940 to form the new Bureau of Ships.
[‡] In May 1919 three Navy/Curtiss flying boats—the NC-1, NC-3, and NC-4—set out on a transatlantic flight from Trepassy, Newfoundland, to the Azores. Two of the aircraft dropped out, but the NC-4, whose crew was headed by Lieutenant Commander Albert C. Read, USN, became the first plane to fly nonstop across the Atlantic.

executive officer of the Saratoga, was the pilot of when he flew the Atlantic. When I served with him later, he was a commander; he was the exec after Whiting.

Anyhow, around that Model Basin then, and around that wind tunnel, the Bureau of Aeronautics, Moffett, who was so far ahead of anybody else in the business of aeronautics—Moffett Field is another indication of the recognition that he deserves.[*] Billy Mitchell got all the credit for being a pioneer in aviation and said you can sink battleships with air, but it was Moffett that was the guy that worked from within and built the naval aviation capability.[†] Moffett was one of these guys that used to hang around down at the Model Basin. And Jerome Hunsaker, MIT.

Paul Stillwell: Number one man in the class of 1908.

Admiral Mumma: He was a lieutenant down there in those days at the Model Basin.[‡] And, oh, my gosh, W. F. Durand, a graduate of the Naval Academy class of 1880, used to hang around down there.[§] At that time he had become head of the engineering department at Stanford.

Now here, let me deviate just a minute for something that is, I think, relatively important historically. Before the turn of the century, the Congress passed a law in 1880 that permitted ten graduates from the Naval Academy and ten graduates of West Point to go and form engineering schools in land-grant colleges around the United States. I don't know whether you knew this or not. You can find it down in historical sections here.

One of these was Michelson, who formed Cal-Tech.[**] Another one of them was W.F. Durand. He went to Worcester and formed Worcester Polytech. He went from there to Cornell and formed the engineering department at Cornell. He went from

---

[*] Rear Admiral William A. Moffett, USN, was Chief of the Bureau of Aeronautics from 1921 until his death in 1933.
[†] Brigadier General William Mitchell, USA, was Chief of the Army Air Service in the early 1920s. In June 1921 he conducted a controversial series of bombing tests against warships in an effort to demonstrate that air power had made surface warships obsolete. In 1925 he was court-martialed for defiance of his superiors; he resigned from the Army rather than accept a five-year suspension.
[‡] Jerome C. Hunsaker had resigned from the active Navy in 1926 and remained in the Naval Reserve.
[§] William F. Durand resigned from the active Navy in 1887; he lived until August of 1958.
[**] Albert Michelson, a graduate of the Naval Academy's class of 1873, won worldwide recognition in the 1870s for successfully measuring the speed of light. He was commissioned a master in 1879 and resigned from the Navy in 1881 to continue his study of physics. In 1907 he became the first American to receive the Nobel Prize in physics.

Cornell to Purdue and formed the engineering department there. He went from Purdue to Stanford and formed the engineering department there. In other words, he was Mr. Engineering, practically speaking. Most of these engineering departments were formed in that period—between 1880 and 1900 when we were first beginning to come alive to engineering in this country. MIT was not considered an adequate place to take Navy PGs until 1901, and Columbia was no good for engineers until 1909.

All right. Now, W.F. Durand used to come on down here, and he was sort of the leader of this group. So then this so-called Advisory Committee for Aeronautics that was operating informally and advising any person that wanted to find out something about aviation. The Congress suddenly woke up and said, "Why, we'll make it a National Advisory Committee for Aeronautics." And they did. That's one reason why the Navy has had such a close relationship with NACA from the very beginning.

Paul Stillwell: And now it's NASA.

Admiral Mumma: Now it's the National Aeronautics and Space Administration.

In 1953, when I had command of the Model Basin, for the 50th anniversary of flight, I assembled every one of those old-timers that I could get down at the old Model Basin for the decommissioning of that 8-foot wind tunnel, the first research wind tunnel in the world.* The Wright brothers used to come down to that wind tunnel to get basic information, because their little old wind tunnel up there in Dayton wasn't big enough to handle real research. So in the very early days of aviation had its birth right there at the old Model Basin.

So I had all these guys: I had Albert Read holding his model of the NC-4 that was tested in that wind tunnel, on his lap when we took the picture. I had Jerry Hunsaker there, that I had known for many years, and he's now gone, unfortunately—wonderful, wonderful man, tremendously recognized all over the world as one of the greatest men in aviation. And W.F. Durand himself died at the age of about 96 and was the oldest living

---

* On 17 December 1903 the brothers Orville and Wilbur Wright conducted the first powered flight with a small airplane at Kitty Hawk, North Carolina. The initial flight lasted 12 seconds and covered 120 feet.

graduate of the Naval Academy when he died. So that these are the beginnings of some of the basics that have made us great.

I really, I really enjoyed that Model Basin—period—not only for the challenge of the past that was there, but the building on the future. So when I was there at the Model Basin as a young officer, I was the only line officer in the place. All the others were naval constructors. Savvy Saunders was a naval constructor. We had a Marine detachment there, so I had to take charge of the Marine detachment. And I stood officer of the day duties.

During that time at the Model Basin, we did some things that had never been done before. For example, the vibration on those battleships: with the hydrodynamic experience that I had gained and with my electrical knowledge and other mechanical knowledge, we decided that—before those battleships went to sea, I had a feeling that they were going to vibrate, and I knew damn well that we were going to have trouble with them.

Out there at the Model Basin, there was a scientist by the name of Dr. Wesley Curtis, and he was a very fine electronics, electric-design man. He had designed and built the electronic organ that was bought by Hammond to be the first electric organ. He had the patent, and he made money off the patents. So Wes Curtis was an outstanding technical man. So I went to Wes Curtis and I said, "Now look, we've got to make measurements on the shafts of those big ships coming. We want to measure torsion, and we want to measure longitudinal stress." Because I still had a feeling from the Normandie experience that I had seen over in France that we might have longitudinal problems with the battleships.

He said, "Okay we can put—" At that time the Model Basin had three consultants. They had Du Mont, who was the one who had built one of the first televisions.[*] At that time he had built himself a little 4-inch oscilloscope. Dumont was consulting on high-speed reactions of things, things that you couldn't see on an inertial system. You had to record it electronically if you were going to get it at all, and put it on a screen, like the Dumont oscilloscope screen. That was the first thing.

---

[*] Allen B. Du Mont.

The second thing, there were two other consultants. One was a Professor Ruge, and the other was Professor De Forest, both at MIT. De Forest's name was pretty well known; he was an electronics researcher of considerable note up in MIT. Those two had developed what they called strain gauges. A strain gauge was a little wire resistance device; if you pulled it or pushed it from its normal position, it would change its resistance, and you could measure that change. Therefore, if you put it on a piece of steel, and the steel bent, it would change the length of that strain gauge. You could measure how much the steel had moved and calibrate the result in terms of stress. It was first used in aircraft.

The minute I heard of this technique, we started using it at the model basin. And we got Ruge and De Forest down there. And we got Dumont there, and we had huddles with Savvy Saunders and the rest of the crowd there about how we were going to measure some of these phenomena: the twist of the shaft, longitudinal flexure of the shaft, torsional vibrations. We could actually measure pulsing vibrations. So we set up all these kinds of measurements with these top scientists.

One thing that had never been known before was how did an explosion bubble damage a ship. Nobody knew. Did it just blow the side in? Nobody knew. Pictures had never been taken at that speed. We had Dr. Harold Edgerton of MIT, the man who first measured a swinging golf shaft and put it on a photographic film. He's a professor at MIT also. He had developed high-speed photography, and we had him as a consultant. So the thing they had to do then was to get all of these things put together: the strain measurement; the high-speed photography; and the oscilloscope to view it so you could see what was happening, see the vibrations and put it all together.

We managed to put it together, and proved that a bubble—say here's the side of a ship, and here's a bomb explodes off the side of the ship. People in the ship hear multiple explosions. What it is, it's the bubble expanding and contracting, expanding and contracting, expanding and contracting, and migrating all the time toward the ship, until it finally hits the ship. Then it involves the actual ship itself into that expansion and contraction, and blows it in. In other words, this high-speed photography, and the high-speed resolution of it and presentation of it, permitted us to analyze for the first time the physics and phenomenon of an explosion. Wendell Roop was the expert in that field out at the Model Basin.*

So I used all that technology that I could get my hands on and used it on the shafts of the new battleships. I had sat in Commander Solberg's his office when I came back from Europe. He was the head of design in the Bureau of Engineering, so I knew many of the design considerations that were going on in those battleships. One of them was that in an attempt to improve efficiency, they put skegs in front of the propellers on the inboard shafts on the North Carolina and the Washington. And they put skegs on the outboard shafts all the way to the keel on the South Dakota class. So those six ships all had skegs. The idea was that the skegs would feed wake into the propellers and increase the efficiency.†

Theoretically, that sounds very good. Practically, it was not good, the real reason being that that localized wake coming off of the skegs, as each blade went through it, it gave a tremendous pressure pulse—wham—not only to the skeg, but to the ship's hull above it. So at blade frequency, they were inducing additional vibration with these skegs. We couldn't very well take the skegs off, because the whole structure of the ship was built that way. So what we had to do was change the frequency. Being in propeller-excited vibration research, we did the job of trying to figure out how we could do it. We worked first on the Washington, because she went to sea first. And I rode every ship on every trial in those days.‡

Paul Stillwell: She had some bad vibration problems.

Admiral Mumma: Yes. We took the outboard propellers and put them on the inboard shafts. We took the inboard propellers and put them on the outboard shafts. That was a

---

* Lieutenant Wendell P. Roop, Construction Corps, USN.
† For details on the development of the North Carolina (BB-55) and South Dakota (BB-57) classes, see Norman Friedman, U.S. Battleships: An Illustrated Design History (Annapolis: Naval Institute Press, 1985).
‡ The Washington was commissioned 15 May 1941. For an account of her propeller problems, see Ivan Musicant, Battleship at War: the Epic Story of the USS Washington (San Diego: Harcourt Brace Jovanovich, 1986).

temporary fix. What it did, with a four-bladed propeller behind the vertical skeg, you had two blades hitting behind into that wake at the same instant. So you had—bang, bang, bang, bang—every revolution you had four big bangs. With three-bladed propellers, you had one blade goes by, then the bottom blade goes by, then the top blade goes by, so then you have only six, much smaller bangs coming from the arrangement with a three-bladed behind this skeg. And the four-bladed outboard had a pressure pulse that was less on the outboard shafts against the hull than the three-bladed. So we reduced the vibration by a considerable factor by just changing those propellers.

Of course, they weren't designed for that spot, and they didn't have exactly the right pitch, but they were pretty damn good. Then we left the four-bladed propellers outboard, and we put newly designed five-bladed propellers inboard. Well, up to that time nobody had ever designed a good five-bladed propeller, because the feeling was that you can't get the water flow through a five-bladed propeller. The roots are too close together, and the water won't go through. So all we did was unload those roots a little bit. Make them more struts near the bottom of the hub, and then put all the working force out into the five-bladed area, further out. We had to do that by changing the pitch with radius, so they were varied pitch propellers. Well, they were completely successful, the first really successful five-bladed propellers in the world.

Paul Stillwell: Where were those propellers devised?

Admiral Mumma: They were designed in combination between the model basin and the Bureau of Ships. The propeller desk in the bureau was involved in it as deeply as we were. That was before I took the propeller desk. That was when P. D. Gold had the propeller desk.[*] He was a lieutenant commander at that time, and I was still a lieutenant at the Model Basin.

Paul Stillwell: Then the Iowa class, which came along later, had the skegs on the inboard shafts.[†]

---

[*] Lieutenant Commander Pleasant D. Gold III, USN.
[†] USS Iowa (BB-61) was commissioned 22 February 1943.

Admiral Mumma: Yes, and again, we had to change those propellers to five-bladed also. We tried another one in the Iowa class also. I rode every time she went to sea, but I got off before she ran aground in Casco Bay. I switched over to a destroyer and came back to Washington. But Earle Mills went into Casco Bay with her. He was the deputy chief at that time, and he was aboard when she ran over the rocks in Casco Bay. At any rate, then they put her in dry dock. I had to run up and see what the hell damage had been done to her. They cut a nice long ridge right through her bottom with that rock. It was just like a knife.[*]

Paul Stillwell: I talked to Admiral McCrea, who had the conn, and 40 years later he still wished he'd gotten his rudder over sooner.

Admiral Mumma: Well, my classmate took the rap on that one.

Paul Stillwell: Who was that?

Admiral Mumma: Bill Whiteside.[†] He was the navigator.

So we had identified several problems with propellers that we were having, not only this vibration problem, but we also had a singing propeller problem, which was relatively unknown at that time. Nobody knew quite what a singing propeller was, if they had ever heard of it. But we found out by actually pinging on propellers in air that they would sing, they would vibrate. Then the frequency would change due to the mass of the entrained water, along with the mass of the blades. So we experimentally were able to produce a singing propeller. We soon found out that we had singing propellers on some of our submarines. They were making noise. Everybody used to say it was squealing

---

[*] On 16 July 1943, while completing a transit from New York City, the Iowa cut a long gash in her bottom while entering Casco Bay, Maine, shortly after low water. The commanding officer at the time was Captain John L. McCrea, USN. McCrea, who retired as a vice admiral, discussed the incident in his Naval Institute oral history.
[†] Lieutenant Commander William J. Whiteside, USN.

shafts, but we found out it really wasn't squealing shafts at all. It was singing propellers, and the blades were vibrating.

This was caused by very, shall we say, slightly sloppy work on the finish of the propellers, not according to the design where the edges were made a little too blunt, and it would throw a vortex. This vortex would be the exciting force for the tips to start vibrating against the center of the blade. And that would cause a major singing effect at a specific frequency that was identifiable as such. It didn't change with RPM. A singing propeller would sing, starting out at, maybe, five knots, and going up through the whole range at the same frequency, only getting louder and louder and louder.

So our phenomenon, after identification, was easily fixed. All we had to do was to be extremely careful about the very accurate, precision-like work on the blades so that they didn't throw these vortices. We also attempted to design the blades themselves so that they wouldn't be so susceptible to this singing. One of the things we did with submarines, particularly, we skewed the blades, tilted them back, made them scimitar-like in shape. That scimitar-like shape gave a much more gradual entry of the tips into the water that it was to push against. Therefore, it didn't cause as much of an exciting force on the center of the blades, and the blades weren't as much drum-like as they had been. A drum-like blade will have a tendency to vibrate against the edges much more than one that is scimitar-shaped.

Paul Stillwell: By drum-like, you mean more rounded?

Admiral Mumma: Yes, right.

Paul Stillwell: Could you repeat that story about Carney and his cruiser, please?

Admiral Mumma: Yes. Well, another example of that singing was when Captain Carney had command of one of the cruisers.[*] I was called up to Philadelphia Navy Yard because they had a problem. They said they had shaft squeal and that this would take anywhere

---

[*] Captain Robert B. Carney, USN, was the first commanding officer of the light cruiser Denver (CL-58) when she was commissioned on 15 October 1942. As an admiral Carney was Chief of Naval Operations from 1953 to 1955.

four to six weeks to repair—take the shafts out, realign the shafting, and so forth, the bearings, and reinstall. Well, I suspected that we didn't really have shaft squeal. So I had taken some instruments up with me to measure frequency. I said to Captain Carney, "Captain, if you'll take the ship down Delaware Bay a little ways, and maybe we may have to go out into the ocean, depending upon what speeds we have to make. But I would like to control the speed from the engine room if you don't mind, up to a degree. If you have to go beyond, or change that speed, just go ahead and do it. But I would like to cover the range of speeds of the shafts through, up to not full power, but medium power."

He said, "Okay." We got about halfway down Delaware Bay when I learned that she had singing propellers. The singing propellers were characterized by a single frequency just getting louder and louder with increased shaft rotation, which eliminated the shaft as the cause of the problem, because it wasn't at shaft frequency. It was another finite frequency which must be singing. So I went up and told the captain, "Captain, we don't have to go any higher. We can turn around and go back to the yard. What we'll do is take your propellers off. We'll work on them overnight. We may get your propellers installed by tomorrow some time, and we will have you ready to go the following day, I suspect."

He said, "My God, Mumma. You mean to tell me you're not going to take four to six weeks?"

I said, "No, sir, you've got singing propellers, and they're pretty easily fixed. We fixed submarines. We fixed a lot of ships with them." So, sure enough, that's what happened. I stayed with the job, oversaw the work, and made sure the propellers were satisfactory when they went back on the ship. Went to sea with him the following day—quiet as a church. Well, he was overjoyed, of course, and he went to sea happy to fight the wars. It may not have been by accident that he was Chief of Naval Operations when I was made Chief of the Bureau of Ships. I don't know.

Paul Stillwell: Certainly didn't hurt you.

Admiral Mumma: But the worst case I think we had during the war of singing propellers was all the Kaiser-class carriers.[*] Every one of them went to sea with a singing propeller as they were launched. They were launched with propellers on them, and they didn't know anything about singing propellers. They didn't pay any attention to what the Navy wanted to do to those ships, because FDR had said, "Those ships are to be done quickly and no interference from the Navy."[†]

Well, the Casablanca, the first one of these ships, you could hear her for five to ten miles.[‡] So I went out to Puget Sound and flew aboard this little postage stamp of a ship. She only could make 19 knots. She was in Puget Sound, operating within the sound, and she was making enough sound all right. You could hear her for miles. And so I did the same thing on that ship as on Carney's cruiser. Got the skipper to give me control of the speed in the engine room, and I took my instruments and measured the frequency, and so forth, and the amplitude of the noise. Did the same thing: came back in; took the propellers off; fined the edges; put the ship to sea again. She was as quiet as a church. The only difficulty was that Kaiser had dumped several dozen ships already into the water with propellers on them, and we had to redock every one of those ships to put the propellers in shape. And that delayed those ships. In other words, if he had allowed us to do something about the first ship design—he had one naval architect on that job—and if Kaiser had been checked early by the Navy, we wouldn't have that problem with the Casablanca class of aircraft carriers, the jeep carriers.

Paul Stillwell: Did you have to pull the propellers off and take them into a shop somewhere and mill them?

Admiral Mumma: Well, we do, almost all yards had some sort of a propeller shop that we can do that. Bremerton, though, was not a propeller-building yard like Philadelphia was. Philadelphia actually had a propeller profiling machine there that we built before

---

[*] Henry J. Kaiser (1882-1967) was an American industrialist famous for his feats of ship production in World War II. His shipyards built about one-third of the merchant ships constructed during the war and 50 escort carriers for the Navy—a total of 1,460 ships.
[†] FDR—Franklin D. Roosevelt, President of the United States from 1933 to 1945.
[‡] The escort carrier Casablanca (CVE-55) was commissioned 8 July 1943.

the war and put into Philadelphia, and so that machine would take propellers up to about 25-30 feet in diameter.

Paul Stillwell: Well, if the problem was known beforehand, why did they go ahead and build the propellers that way?

Admiral Mumma: Speed of construction and the lack of inspection. You know, there wasn't any Navy inspection on those Kaiser-built ships. All the propellers of that class, because they were all designed and built wrong. They were perfectly designed for singing. You could hear the damn things for, oh, 10 or 15 miles on a hydrophone. It would have been murder to send those ships to sea.

Paul Stillwell: They had enough other problems as it was.

Admiral Mumma: So we managed to get the singing propellers squared away, and then we got everybody indoctrinated about singing propellers. Then pretty much, the problem evaporated, disappeared, because everybody began paying attention to the fine points of how to design and prevent singing.

Paul Stillwell: You mentioned the skegs, and the idea there was to get greater efficiency through taking advantage of that wake. Did that work out?

Admiral Mumma: Now, the only time that that wake going into the propellers increased efficiency without increasing problems of vibration is in a later story—my baby, the Skipjack-class submarines. That's an entirely different story, which I'll get into a little later.

Paul Stillwell: So it didn't achieve the desired result in the battleships; is that what you're saying?

Admiral Mumma: No, it did not improve the efficiency. As a matter of fact, it increased the cavitation at high speeds a little bit. But it didn't hurt too much except vibration-wise.

Paul Stillwell: Well, I talked to one skipper who said he felt that the skegs might have helped him in ship handling in port. He said the propeller wash on the skegs gave him a little greater turning momentum.[*]

Admiral Mumma: That's not technically so. Those ships without skegs would have turned faster. Because trying to turn the skeg against the water made it hard, even though we had twin rudders on there. The reason we put twin rudders on originally was that you had to have twin rudders to counteract the skegs, which tend to prevent turning. Because skegs have a tendency to smooth the water out and keep that ship going straight ahead, just like fins on the rear end of an airplane. So skegs are not effective from a point of view of hydrodynamics basically. They're fine for docking ships. You know when you put them in dry dock, you don't have to block them up so much.

Paul Stillwell: You put the keel blocks right under the skegs.

Admiral Mumma: Yes, so you put the blocks right under the skegs. But other than that, after I got into the act in the bureau, design, we had no more ships with skegs. None whatsoever. We kept them off all ships, all the aircraft carriers, everything. The minimum amount of strut was what we wanted just to hold a shaft, keep it in place. Get the propellers as far away from the ship, out of the wake, as possible, because all the blades going through the wake does is give you momentary cavitation—a noise maker, and vibration causer.

Paul Stillwell: Sounds like the skegs were really counterproductive.

---

[*] This was Captain Edward M. Thompson, USN, who commanded the New Jersey (BB-62) shortly after World War II.

Admiral Mumma: They certainly were. It was a step in the wrong direction. But theoretically good. Practically bad. You learn those things, you know, after you get a little more experience in hydrodynamics.

Paul Stillwell: You mentioned you went on the trials for these ships. I'm interested in the New Jersey because I served in her. Do you remember anything from her specifically?

Admiral Mumma: Yes, I rode her in her trials. I was there at the launching, and I was there on her trials. She was like all the Iowa class in many respects. We'd done some improvements on that class by the time the New Jersey hit the water. We had the five-bladed propellers, I think, on that ship originally, if I remember correctly. So that we thought she went to sea as a pretty damn good ship, considering that she also had skegs.

Paul Stillwell: I've heard that Captain Carl Holden was a demanding skipper.[*] Do you have any recollections of him?

Admiral Mumma: Not, not directly because I was only aboard for trials most of the time.

Philadelphia had done a very good job on the New Jersey, and I rode that ship on her trials, as I did all those ships of those days. I was able to evaluate not only their performance from an economic point of view—for example, their efficiency, their fuel consumption. We had torsion meters on them, and being a model basin guy originally, I knew all those folks and was able to help monitor the accuracy of our prognostications. Because when I was later riding various ships, I had the responsibility in the bureau of the propellers and shafting for all the ships in the Navy from the landing craft on up. I was just as interested in the performance of those ships according to contract, as well as the economy aspects of the Navy and the efficiency of their ability to perform according to design with the radius of action that they were expected to have. So that, basically, I was at sea an awful lot during that period in the early part of the war, either with the

---

[*] Captain Carl F. Holden, USN, was the first commanding officer when the New Jersey was commissioned on 23 May 1943.

model basin gang originally, or later when I had the propeller desk in the bureau to ensure the performance of, no matter what ship or what class, every ship of the class if I could ride it. That's how come I happened to get involved with so many of these skippers, and so forth.

Paul Stillwell: Do you remember working with a guy named Al Dunning at the Philadelphia yard?*

Admiral Mumma: Oh, yes, I knew Al very well, class of '27, good friend of mine, high pockets.

Paul Stillwell: Very tall, yes.

Admiral Mumma: Taller than you.

Paul Stillwell: Yes, he is.

Admiral Mumma: Al eventually went on up to Electric Boat and did a good job up there.
Any time those ships went to sea, I was with them on trials. As a matter of fact, we were at sea in the Washington when the Bismarck was being trailed. She sank the Hood, and she was finally sunk herself. But we didn't have a single round of ammunition on board, and we couldn't have gotten into the fray if we'd wanted to. But some of the guys were going around, "We got to get into this."†

Paul Stillwell: When you were in those trials, could you really go up to speed in shallow water? Wouldn't that present a problem?

---

* Lieutenant Commander Allan L. Dunning, USN, was machinery superintendent for the Philadelphia yard during the construction of the New Jersey.
† In May 1941, the German battleship Bismarck, accompanied by the cruiser Prinz Eugen, entered the Atlantic to operate as a surface raider. In a gun duel on 24 May against the British, she sank HMS Hood and damaged HMS Prince of Wales. The Bismarck herself was damaged on the 26th by British torpedo planes and sunk on the 27th by gunfire from the British battleships Rodney and King George V.

Admiral Mumma: Well, we tried at first—I guess it was the Washington we took up to run on the Rockland measured mile.* I think it was the Washington. Anyhow, we learned that she was too big for the measured mile at Rockland. The water was only 600 feet deep there. No one would believe, before that, that 600 feet of water was not plenty of depth of water for a ship of that size. But we got bottom effect at 600 feet on a ship that was over 700 feet long. These bow waves and these underwater body pressure waves go very deep. And that's the thing that you've got to avoid when you're trying to make accurate measurements. The Wasp was the last big ship that we ran there, and she wasn't very big. I'm talking about the little Wasp.†

Paul Stillwell: Right, CV-7.

Admiral Mumma: Yes, she wasn't very big compared to other ships that we ran at Rockland. But we ran destroyers and cruisers and other ships up at Rockland without a problem. I used to enjoy going up to Rockland and running ships on trials up there. But thereafter we had to go to Guantanamo to get the deep water to run them.

Paul Stillwell: One of the engineers from the New Jersey told me he could tell by the vibrations when the ship crossed the 100-fathom curve.

Admiral Mumma: That's right.

During these trials, we had strain gauges on the shaft to measure torsion; we had strain gauges on the shaft to measure longitudinal extension and contraction; and we proved that those battleships actually had longitudinal vibration of the propeller against the thrust block. When we first took those ships to sea with the four-bladed propellers behind the skegs, we actually got thrust reversal. In other words, the thrust collars came right off the thrust bearings. Then when they went back, it was double the amount of the thrust that hit that. In other words, it was hitting that thrust block with a 200,000-pound sledgehammer. That was what was causing the vibration in that ship, in addition to what

---

* The Navy used a course off Rockland, Maine, for speed trials because the relatively cold water in the region produced higher speeds in a steam turbine plant than did warmer water.
† USS Wasp (CV-7) was commissioned 25 April 1940.

happened outside on the hull. We had to do something about it very quickly. That's why we changed the propellers immediately, and that's why we designed other propellers for it.

The result of that was the first good, really properly designed five-bladed propellers in the world. Now we've got six and so forth. There's no problem nowadays. But this forced us to these things, because we had this terrible phenomenon that we didn't know how to handle until we got these tools to examine it with.

Paul Stillwell: Did you work on submarines in that period?

Admiral Mumma: When I reported to the David Taylor Model Basin in '39, the Bureau of Engineering was about to put a big 24-inch water tunnel over here at the engineering experiment station at Annapolis. And we had a 12-inch water tunnel down at the old Washington Navy Yard that we were going to move out to the new basin at Carderock as soon as it was completed and in operation.

I was going to be in charge of the propeller tunnel at Carderock, so I went to my boss, and I said, "You know, I think that's an absurd thing to do down there. We ought to get that tunnel up here and install it at Carderock, so that the propeller design and development is located at one place with the best qualifications of the people as well as the equipment. In addition to that, the scale effect between those two tunnels will be very, very good in characterizing propeller scale between model and full scale." These are some of the things I had learned in France from my good friend Barrillon.

They decided, okay, that was a good idea. So instead of installing it at Annapolis we installed it at Carderock. So then I had charge of both tunnels. This was the propeller excited vibration research group. So when we got to DTMB, we got Dr. Wesley Curtis with this 24-inch tunnel.[*] When we got this vibration research group going, he was an electronics expert of considerable expertise, and we were not only interested in reducing cavitation from the point of view of power loss, but also from the point of view of noise production. I ended up working with Wes on this phenomenon. He said, "You know, we can characterize any of these ships. All we have to do is bore a hole in the side of the

---

[*] DTMB—David Taylor Model Basin is the official name of the facility at Carderock.

ship, and we can stick a microphone out there, and we can find out what's going on out in the water. We'll bring that stuff in and we'll analyze it, frequency analysis, put it on tape and so forth, and we'll have all the information we need."

We said, "Okay, let's do it." So we did that first on submarines. We started on submarines because we thought submarine quieting was the most important goal. Internally in submarines, they also had a very vigorous quieting program, and we had acoustic people from Western Electric and others that were Naval Reserve people that came in during the war, stayed in, and helped us with that scientific approach to quieting. As you know, Western Electric at this time had already installed sound movies. They were one of the pioneers in sound.

So having this ability to stick microphones out and characterize every aspect of noise, as well as driving by fixed microphones on piles, bollards, anywhere, we could drive right by them at various speeds, and get the noise spectrum. And then from one submarine to another, get how much noise we were getting so we get the attenuation as well as the real exciting force of these noises—not only their frequency characteristic, but also at the speed characteristic of the submarine.

We found that at periscope depth and at high speeds, almost all the submarines were just noisy as hell, not only from the machinery and everything else, but also from the propeller noise. So we immediately had a multi-pronged approach to noise. We not only had to quiet the inside of the submarines, but we also had to quiet the propellers themselves, and the appendages that were sticking out of the submarines that would cause wakes and eddies. So we examined the fleet boats rather completely. I rode any number of submarines during the early part of the war and before the war, actually—'39, '40, '41—in which we were quieting these submarine propellers and the rest of the submarine itself. I wasn't in charge of the rest of the submarine. I was really in charge of the propeller-excited vibration and the noise of the propellers.

Wes Curtis was a tremendous help in this area, and we were able to characterize the noise by the frequencies. Then we began in the water tunnels doing what we felt was absolutely necessary to try and reduce this noise. We found, of course, that one of the primary causes of the noise was cavitation of the propellers. We all suspected that, but the question was, "What do you do about it?"

Any heavily loaded, highly stressed propeller has a tendency to cavitate near full power. So these cavity bubbles ordinarily form either around irregularities in the propeller itself, like any bumps or imperfections in the manufacture, or primarily around the tips, where the actual pressure on the face of the blades spills over into the unloaded side of the back of the blade and forms a swirling eddy. This swirling eddy becomes a cavity if it swirls fast enough. It overcomes the static pressure of the water, and it actually forms cavity bubbles. Later, when these bubbles slow down, they collapse, and ping when they collapse. They make a noise. So that is what causes the noise of cavitation—not only the formation of these cavities, but also the collapse of the cavities. That's cavitation.

Now we were tackling a major problem, and the reason for that was that the war was so imminent. Everybody knew it was coming—in the Navy at least. I don't know whether the general public had figured it out yet, because we were supposed to be staying out of the war.

Have you ever heard of the brutality patrol?

Paul Stillwell: I've heard it called the Neutrality Patrol.[*]

Admiral Mumma: We called it the "brutality patrol." The reason being, of course, that this was supposed to be a neutral operation, but it was not neutral at all, as you probably know. The American ships out there on patrol would spot a submarine, and they'd immediately, by blinker signal, or otherwise, tell the British about it. Then the British would come in, and they'd attack the German submarine. Well, the Germans got wind that this was going on. They couldn't exactly prevent knowing about it after a while, and

---

[*] In the period from 1939 to 1941—when the United States was not yet an active combatant in World War II—the American republics maintained what was called a Neutrality Patrol of a zone in the western Atlantic. Ostensibly neutral, it in fact aided Britain in its war against Germany.

that's why we called it the brutality patrol. I'd been in destroyers a lot, and it was not exactly fun. Well, I suppose you know about the Reuben James.*

Paul Stillwell: She was sunk in October 1941.

Admiral Mumma: She was sunk, and my classmate Tex Edwards was in command, and he was lost, as were a lot of that crew by the German submarine sinking it.

Well, when you get right down to it, this was an act of war on our part. You know, we were not neutral, and it could have caused the start of the war. It did not because it was sort of, shall we say, sort of downplayed. I don't think the public knew about the Reuben James for quite a number of months, if not years.

Paul Stillwell: I think they knew, but I gathered that Hitler was not ready to take on the United States at that point.†

Admiral Mumma: Well, that's perfectly true. There's no question about it, but we weren't ready either.

At any rate, to jump back to the problem, we felt that there are two ways really of attacking cavitation of the tips. One is to unload the tips of the blades by reducing the outer pitch so they don't have as high a pressure to cause the swirls at the tip. The other was to make the entrance into the water of the tip at high velocity much more gradual. In other words, scimitar the shape of the blade. No propellers had ever been made that way before except weedless propellers, you know, for that was the only scimitar-shaped blades we knew of, were the weedless propellers that were on various outboard motors.

We tried weedless propellers in the water tunnels, and we found that they did prevent the early formation of cavities. So we designed the scimitar shape of the propeller blades of our submarines. We took them to sea at various speeds, various

---

* On 31 October 1941, the U-552 torpedoed and sank the four-stack destroyer Reuben James (DD-245) with the loss of 115 lives. She was escorting a convoy from Halifax, Nova Scotia, to the British Isles and was lost about 600 miles west of Ireland. She was the first U.S. warship lost to enemy action in World War II. Lieutenant Commander Heywood L. Edwards, USN, was the final commanding officer of the ship.
† Adolf Hitler was Chancellor of Germany from 1933 until his death by suicide on 30 April 1945.

depths, and with hydrodynamic noise examination, not only from within the boat but also passing other areas, as well as passing other boats. We ended up coming to the conclusion that we had a pretty good propeller design by the time we got into the war, which neither of the other two navies had. Neither the Germans nor the Japs, fortunately, had done the same. So they were not able, even during the length of the war, to make a major change in the quietness of their boats, which, I think, resulted in a lot of our success relative to their success in various attacks. So that's the story of the submarine propeller quieting program that, I think, was one of our more important programs. I just can't feel anything but happy about the fact that that was a successful program.

Another program was the torpedo boats. Higgins built PT boats.[*] Electric Boat built PT boats during the war, and Huckins built PT boats in Jacksonville. The best PT boats were built by Electric Boat; the second best by Huckins in Jacksonville. Both of them were good builders. The Huckins boat was not quite as fast; it was a little fancier from a finish point of view, but it wasn't quite as good a boat. The Higgins boats were terrible. This was a very strange one because when I was in the Navy Department, I kept getting dispatches from my brother, who had command of the PTs in the Southwest Pacific: "Do something about those Higgins boats. We can't get them up on the step out here in hot water."[†]

So I decided we had better have another PT derby, which we had had originally, and we had it down in Jacksonville in hot water. This we set up out of Mayport. We went to sea and ran off the measured mile with each of these boats, light load and full load. I had Jim Farrin along who was in contract design and so forth at that time.[‡] This was during the time I was in the propeller desk during the war. We found out that the Electric Boat's boats did very well. They not only made their speed in light, but also in full military load. Then the Huckins boats did very well. Not quite as well as the Electric Boat boats, but they did their speed with full military load and light. The Higgins boats failed miserably to make the speed. They couldn't even make the full military load speed

---

[*] Andrew J. Higgins manufactured both motor torpedo boats (PTs) and landing craft, vehicle and personnel (LCVP).
[†] Commander Morton C. Mumma, Jr., USN, served from February 1943 to February 1944 as Commander Motor Torpedo Boat Squadrons Seventh Fleet.
[‡] Commander James M. Farrin, Jr., USN.

light. So it was obvious that there was something wrong, and it wasn't just propeller design. It was boat design.

We checked and we found out that Higgins had been actually testing those boats in Lake Ponchartrain, which was fresh water, instead of in seawater. He also had his measured mile. We measured it and we found out his measured mile, which was supposed to be 6,080 feet, was a land mile, 5,280. He was certifying miles per hour, land miles, as knots. The Navy Department recommended that the Higgins contracts be cancelled and that all the remaining contracts for PT boats be spread between the other two contractors. Higgins was a major supporter financially of FDR's campaign. The head of the Senate investigation committee that investigated the matter was Senator Harry Truman. The investigation was dropped.

Paul Stillwell: So did Higgins keep his business?

Admiral Mumma: I make no accusations. I wasn't there at the hearings. I don't know what happened. But it was not processed. We did not cancel the orders with Higgins. However, Higgins faded very, very rapidly after that as a contractor for us.

Now let me talk about the Alsos Mission and the people on that. One was Professor Yappie Den Hartog, who is now the emeritus professor, mechanical of MIT.[*] He was with us during this time. And I've already mentioned three of the names of the Alsos Mission's Navy members. I've mentioned Packy Schade, who went to the University of Berlin in structures; I've mentioned Wendell Roop, who did this explosion research; I've mentioned Yappie Den Hartog; and the fourth one was Al Mumma.

Paul Stillwell: When did that take place?

Admiral Mumma: Now that's the Alsos Mission as far as the Navy is concerned. There were only four of us.

---

[*] Dr. Jacob P. Den Hartog. He was a captain in the Naval Reserve; he served on active duty with the Navy from 1941 to 1945.

This jumps past the performance during the war—the building of all the ships in the Navy; the building of the aircraft carriers and all that sort of thing, into a slightly later period, shortly before the invasion. At that time we were doing some work up at G.E. one time, and Earle Mills, again—he enters the picture all the time—Earle was deputy chief at that time, and I was a commander and head of the propeller desk in BuShips.[*]

Around '42, I guess, we were up in G.E. research lab, and we were talking to Dr. Guy Suits, who was at that time the head of G.E.'s research lab. We were talking about various kinds of propulsion and so on, and efficiencies of this and that. Later, when Earle and I were alone in the elevator going down, after our meeting, I said, "Earle, when are we going to get going with U-235, and build some nuclear power plants? The damn Germans are doing something on that, you know."

He said, "Shut up." I was really surprised.

Paul Stillwell: Where had you heard about the German work?

Admiral Mumma: Well, I knew that Niels Bohr was doing work on it.[†] I'd read about that in scientific stuff. I used to read a lot of scientific stuff. And I knew that they'd had a chain reaction. So Earle called me into the office the next morning after we got back to Washington. He said, "Al, I told you to shut up for a very good reason. We are working on the atomic bomb. It is a very important project, and it is classified at the highest secrecy. What you said up there, U-235, is a secret word."

I said, "Well, okay."

He said, "Okay, now, here's what we're doing." And he told me about it. He briefed me. He told me about the thermal diffusion process that the Navy was doing at the Boiler and Turbine Laboratory in Philadelphia. That was our contribution to the thermal diffusion process, separating uranium-235 from uranium-238. He told me about the electromagnetic process down at Oak Ridge, for separating uranium-235 from U-238

---

[*] G.E.—General Electric.
[†] Niels Bohr (1885-1962) was a Danish physicist who was awarded the Nobel Prize. He developed a theory about the structure of the atom, published in 1913. He also expanded on a theory by German physicist Max Planck on the emission of radiation by atoms. In World War II, after escaping the Nazis, Bohr was an adviser to U.S. scientists in their work to develop the atomic bomb.

by the difference in their electromagnetic properties.* He told me about the Hanford plant out there in Washington that was building plutonium out of uranium-238 in a graphite pile.

So I said, "My God, Earle, when are we going to get going on nuclear power for ships, because it'd really do something for submarines."

He said, "Never—as long as we're working on this bomb project. We are forbidden from touching anything to do with nuclear power until after the bomb project is successful."

Well, in early '44, the British naval attaché for engineering called Earle Mills and asked if he and I could come to lunch over at the Hay-Adams.† Earle called me up, and I said, "Yes, sir, I'll be there." So I went up and joined him at the office, and we went over to lunch. And the admiral—Smiley Burke was his name—was the engineer admiral for the Royal Navy. He said, "Admiral, we know that Mumma's been doing some work in connection with vibration research here in United States. We've got a new aircraft carrier that we're just completing over in Europe of the Implacable class, and we have had considerable vibration in the Victorious-class aircraft carriers. Do you suppose you could loan him to us for a while?"

Earle Mills said, "Sure, if I can carry his bags." So he and Packy Schade and I got a ride in a British aircraft carrier. Packy at that time had the aircraft carrier desk in the bureau, and we three went to Europe to ride the Implacable.

We got to London, and we went on up to the Clyde. As we got in there, we found that the Implacable was about ready to go to sea. It was really imminent. So we reported to the skipper. At this time, Earle was a rear admiral, Packy Schade was a captain, and I was a commander. I had some instruments with me, being a dirty old engineer. So we reported to the captain, who was Captain Victor McIntosh—the McIntosh of the McIntosh clan. He'd had the monster up there in his lake at Inverness.

So we went to sea. We went out the Clyde in the ship. It was built at Fairfields on the Clyde. We went through the Irish Sea, up to the north of Scotland, around the north of Scotland, and we came in below Edinburgh to the Firth of Forth, to the royal

---
* Oak Ridge National Laboratory, Oak Ridge, Tennessee, has long been involved in research and development in the field of nuclear energy.
† Hay-Adams is a hotel in Washington, D.C.

dockyard in Rosyth, during which time we run trials on the ship. I was there with my equipment. They had the same kind of vibration we had—not quite as bad as we had in the battleships because they didn't have skegs.

So I talked to the skipper about it: "Say, I think the solution is going to be a change in propellers." They had three-bladed propellers all around on four shafts. They were getting too much longitudinal vibration from the three-bladed propellers, because they were getting a very large exciting force from those three blades. They had them up close to the hulls where they'd get the wake. So then, when we got back to London, we went to the Admiralty; we went to the British model basin; we went to Stones, who built the propellers; and we went to the Royal Corps of Naval Constructors.

In Britain, the Royal Corps of Naval Constructors had responsibility for the design of the propellers at that time, and the engineering department had responsibility for the strength of the propellers. If you can imagine the design and the strength being separated from each other—I can't. I thought, "What a hell of a strange operational situation." They had never put on a combatant ship anything other than a three-bladed propeller because the three-bladed propeller was the most theoretically efficient propeller you could get because the water could get through the roots very nicely. We said, "Look, we've got good five-bladed propellers. We've got good four-bladed propellers. You can even build a good six-bladed propeller. You've got to put some decent blades on that ship, and you'll get rid of your whole problem. You'll swallow that exciting force way down into the operating range."

They did it finally, reluctantly, but they did it. Then the three of us were there in London, boom, when the buzz bombs started.* They came over one Saturday night, and the barrage balloons were still up there catching them and bringing them down, when some of them might have gone over. The technical division that we were part of was located at Number 8 Grosvenor Square. The bomb disposal squad was a part of that technical division. We contacted the British Admiralty and asked, "What are they going to do about those barrage balloons?"

---

* The V-1 was a pulse-jet flying bomb, also known as a "doodlebug" and "buzz bomb." It was 25 feet long and had a 16-foot wingspan. It carried a one-ton warhead some 150 miles (later increased to 250) at a speed of about 400 miles per hour. It was first successfully flown in December 1943. The Germans fired more than 13,000 V-1s during the course of World War II.

They said, "We agree. They've got to be moved. They've got to come down. Move them down on the coast, and we can do something about them down there. Maybe catch a few of those buzz bombs coming over."

The end of that was that we were going to go over to Guards' chapel on Sunday. We came back from the Implacable on Saturday night. Then we got so busy with this thing that we said, "I guess we can't go." Then the next thing we heard the Guards' chapel had taken a bomb and 175 people killed in there. We might have been there.

Then we went back immediately to the United States after having helped the British solve this problem. We hadn't any more than gotten back when we were called upon by Leslie Groves to set up what was called the Alsos Mission.* Alsos means "groves" in Greek literature translation—orange groves, I guess. At any rate, Earle Mills selected four of us to be members of Alsos. Now, Packy Schade speaks German, having gone to the University of Berlin. Wendell Roop speaks a little German and a little French, and he's a good structures man. He's the one that was doing that research on explosions. Yappie Den Hartog was a Dutchman. Came over to the United States, and he became the top engineer at MIT. Yappie Den Hartog is one of the best men on vibration and mechanical research in the country, in the world. Then I was a French speaker. So we four were briefed by General Groves about the Alsos Mission. The Alsos Mission was supposed to go to Europe to find out how far the Germans had gotten with their atomic bomb project. We were scared to death that they might be ahead of us because they had a two-year head start on us.

When we got there, in Europe, we were four of the about ten people in all of Europe that knew about this. They hadn't even taken too many of the British in on it at that time. So then we had to decide, "Okay, how do we get information on the Germans? Where's the rest of the team? We're not going to do it all by ourselves, just the Navy." We were briefed with the rest of the team as they gradually began to dribble over.

The rest of the team consisted of a leader by the name of Dr. Sam Goudschmidt. He was a Dutchman who had done nuclear physical research years and years before, and he knew Niels Bohr. He knew all those European scientists. He knew the Curies in

---

* Major General Leslie R. Groves, USA, was head of the Manhattan Project that developed the atomic bomb in World War II.

France.* He knew everybody that had anything to do with splitting atoms, and bomb work. And Sam had been working with Teller on the thing up in Chicago. But Sam, they decided, could be spared to head the Alsos Mission, because he not only had French, German, Dutch—every other language in Europe—but he also was a tremendous scientist, and so he was chosen the head of the group. Then we had a young super boy scout by the name of Boris Pasch, a colonel in the Army, who could do anything. He could climb the Empire State Building if you asked him to. You know, nothing stopped him. He was "Mister Yes I Can Do It." He was the administrative head of Alsos.

Paul Stillwell: Did you get special security clearance to be part of this mission?

Admiral Mumma: Oh, we were ultra, ultra, all of us. And then there were other scientific people: the head of the Bureau of Standards, the head of the chemical engineering at MIT, and others that were on the fringes of this thing, but nobody actually connected with the real bomb business of building one. In other words, kept it that far removed. We were the investigators, and the Manhattan District were going to be the digesters.†

The four of us landed in Paris the day Paris was liberated. We were in a C-47—DC-3, in other words. We had a Jeep in the cargo bay of this aircraft. We climbed in the Jeep after I drove it down out of the airplane, and we put a bunch of rations in the back of the thing. We put a lot of cans of gasoline in jerry cans on the rack there in the back of the Jeep. And I, knowing Paris, I got behind the wheel and away we went into Paris. We went to the Ambassador Hotel, which was the headquarters of the ComZone—the Army headquarters. They had just arrived, and they said, "The rule is you are going to have a 75-man mission, total. You're going to have this and that kind of equipment, Jeeps and so forth, which we have for you. You are going to take a hotel that has been occupied by the Germans. Not any French in the hotel. We are not displacing any French. So you

---

* Pierre Curie and his wife Marie were physicists who discovered radioactivity in uranium and isolated two radioactive elements they named radium and polonium. Along with Antoine Henri Becquerel, who discovered natural radioactivity, they received the 1903 Nobel Prize in physics.
† Manhattan District derived from an Army Corps of Engineers term connected with the U.S. program to create an atomic bomb in World War II. The overall effort is often referred to as the Manhattan Project.

are going to have this hotel which is up at the Etoile near the Arc d'Triomphe." So we got in the Jeep, and away we went to Etoile. When we got there and got out, the first thing we discovered was that this was a German cathouse. Well, we decided this was no good. We climbed in the Jeep again, and we went back to the Ambassador Hotel.

Paul Stillwell: You didn't check to see if there were any German cats left, did you?

Admiral Mumma: Look, this is a serious operation. None of this. So I said, "Look, I know several of the hotels up there, and many, many more are available."

They said, "The Royal Monseau."

I said, "That's it. Okay the Royal Monseau on the Avenue Hoche." So we got in the Jeep, and away we went up to the hotel. When we got up there, it had about 100 rooms. It was a beautiful hotel. The German intelligence people had had it. We walked in the door, and out came Antoine, the maitre 'd of the hotel. Antoine said, "Monsieur, [and further French words]," you know. He practically embraced me, you see. I was the first one to speak to him, and then I introduced the others. I said, "Antoine, we're taking this hotel. It's for a mission called the Alsos Mission."

"Oh, that's fine, but I have no food."

I said, "We brought some C rations and some K rations here for us. And the other people are going to be arriving soon," and so on. So I gave him all the C rations and K rations. That night he made a six-course dinner out of those C rations and K rations that the soldiers used to carry around in their knapsack. We had a prune whip, fluffy pudding dessert made out of that old prune bar that you used to have to eat.

Well, by the time the scientists joined us, which was in a very few days, our headquarters grew to about 75 people. Then we had all this logistic support with us too. We could go anywhere. We kept a continuous watch over at the Majestic Hotel, which was where the war room was, as to where the troops were, and how much progress they were making. And, in the meantime, the scientists and Sam Goudschmidt called on Madame Curie. She was still alive there. She had collaborated with the Germans a little bit on fissionable material matters. Then we finally got to a spot where we were in a stalemate for a period of time because things didn't happen very fast. During that time a couple of us Navy guys went down to Bordeaux, where a German destroyer, the Z-37, had been captured in dock, and so we evaluated that ship. We turned it over to the British, and they evaluated it more completely.

Then, finally, by September of '44, our gang had gotten as far as Strasbourg. In Strasbourg, they ran across a large group of scientific people that had been assembled by the Germans. They had kept very meticulous records of everything they had done. Our language beagles got in there and started working on that stuff. They digested everything that they had done, and they found out that the Germans had been absolutely unable to build a nuclear bomb. The reason being that, one, they didn't have quite the proper philosophy. We had three complete successful methods of making fissionable material going at that time. All they had was a graphite pile that was supposed to produce plutonium, and it hadn't been working very well. Then they had the heavy water project up in Norway, which, again, had been pretty well destroyed by the attack on Narvik. So the Germans hadn't really made very much progress.

Paul Stillwell: Despite all these rumors you'd been hearing.

Admiral Mumma: In spite all the head start they had. And in spite of the scientific, supposed secret weapon that Hitler was supposed to be doing so much about. In other words, the Germans weren't nine feet high. They were just ordinary people.

At that time, we Navy members—I am nearing the end of this story—found out that the rest of the group would go ahead and detail the work that the Germans had done and how far they'd gotten, and all that information. We could detach ourselves from that group. Packy Schade was the senior one. We would form what was known as the Naval Technical Mission Europe. Packy was the senior member of that group; I was next senior; and the other two. So now NavTechMisEu replaced the Alsos Mission as far as the Navy was concerned. That was when we started the evaluation of Hellmuth Walter's work at the Walter Werke in Kiel, the high-speed submarine work, the hydrogen peroxide—all that sort of thing, which is entirely, completely another story. And I think we'd better postpone that one.

But I thought the Alsos Mission ought to be gotten into this talk for the reason that it formed a framework and a base from which we operated pretty much in Europe the rest of the time, as separated from the strategic services group, the OSS, you know--Office of Strategic Services—which did a lot of the Army and the other evaluation work in Europe at that time. We had our own separate operation. We could do as we wished, and we had very good logistic support from the Army. As a matter of fact, most of our work was done in the British sector. We got very good support from the British, because almost everything we covered in the Navy was up in the northern part, and that was all British sector.

Now, I'll tell you that story in considerable detail as to how, where, and why things went on and what we did. Packy Schade himself is still alive, but he is in very poor health now out in California.* So I am now the senior guy left. Yappie Den Hartog is very, very sick up in New Hampshire. He's in a nursing home, and he dictates letters to his daughter-in-law, who writes them down and sends them to me and I write him back. And Wendell Roop is gone. So we'd better get that story down.

Paul Stillwell: Okay.

Admiral Mumma: I think that's enough for today, don't you?

Paul Stillwell: All right.

---

* Commodore Henry A. Schade, USN (Ret.), died 12 August 1992 at the age of 91.

Interview Number 2 with Rear Admiral Albert G. Mumma, U.S. Navy (Retired)

Place: U. S. Naval Institute, Annapolis, Maryland

Date: Monday, 20 April 1987

Interviewer: Paul Stillwell

Paul Stillwell: Admiral, we're ready to resume the narrative chronologically. When we ceased the interview the last time, you were talking about your work with the Naval Technical Mission over in Europe late in World War II.

Admiral Mumma: At this time, most of the activity in which we were interested was located in the northern British sector. We had previously been collaborating with the British in every respect relative to a technical exchange with the Russians and the British and ourselves on everything that we learned in torpedo research, primarily that of Professor Hellmuth Walter in Kiel. Well, at this time when the technical mission was formed, Professor Walter was located in Gdynia, and much of the research work was being done there on the southern shore of the Baltic. As a matter of fact, Wernher von Braun was doing his work at Peenemünde.*

Hellmuth Walter provided Wernher von Braun with the launching platform for his rockets and the Army's V-1s; the launching mechanism of the V-1s was a hydrogen peroxide-propelled launch piston in a cylinder. The rapid decomposition of the peroxide caused the expansion impulse to put the V-1 into the air. But he also had designed and built the fuel proportioning system for the V-2.† The proportioning pumps were driven by hydrogen peroxide. The proportioning system then would take the liquid oxygen and the fuel, and combine them in the throat area in such a fashion that the rocket would lift

---

* Wernher von Braun was a German-born rocket scientist who helped develop rockets for his country in World War II, then emigrated to the United States in 1945 and began working with the Army. He subsequently played a considerable role in the U.S. space program. Peenemünde is a German town on the Baltic Sea's Pomeranian Bay. During World War II it was the site of a German rocket complex where the V-weapons were developed.

† The V-2 rocket bomb was first successfully fired on 3 October 1942 at Peenemünde, Germany. It was a liquid-fuel rocket, 46 feet long and weighing 13 tons. It carried a one-ton warhead. The German V-2 offensive against the Allies began in September 1944 and ended in March 1945; it involved some 5,000 rockets.

off the pad and continue on its course. So that Wernher von Braun and Hellmuth Walter were very close, very good friends, and cooperated completely.

But Hellmuth Walter had his own activity. He was also working for the Air Force on the Messerschmitt 163 propulsion system, which was the German rocket airplane.* It had a hydrogen peroxide launch and propulsion system. There was no other power in that airplane. They were intended to rise at a very rapid rate off the ground, like a rocket—as a matter of fact, they were a rocket because they carried their fuel with them. A rocket carries its own fuel. As a rocket, it had also a very high velocity; it got up to 550 miles an hour.

At that time there were no aircraft that were making more than 400 miles an hour in level flight, other than the Gloucester Meteors. There were five of them that had been built by the British, by Whittle, who built the first gas turbines.† These five were able to make about 500 miles an hour. Not as fast as the German rocket plane, ME 163. The Meteors never got into operation in the European theater except over Britain, whereas, the Germans used the 163s in many attempts to knock out the final bombing attacks on Hamburg, Bremen, and the Ruhr. They were quite successful in bringing down a pretty high number of Allied planes from these bombing attacks. But the Germans suffered tremendous, tremendous mortality in the British mass saturation bombing of Bremen and of Hamburg particularly.

Paul Stillwell: Now, was your naval mission getting into these aviation aspects of it?

Admiral Mumma: Not in detail, but you could hardly avoid them because of the ability to run across this whole broad spectrum of propulsion with hydrogen peroxide. So we did it by osmosis, I suspect. At any rate, I had, of course, had the experience at the Model Basin in connection with the wind tunnels. Also, I had a great interest in aerodynamics as well as hydrodynamics.

---

* The Messerschmitt ME 163, also known as the Komet, was the only interceptor-fighter powered solely by a rocket motor to be used in combat in World War II. The first operational use was in July 1944 against American B-17 bombers.
† Sir Frank Whittle was a British aeronautical engineer who developed the first British jet engine with his company, Power Jets, Ltd. He achieved a successful trial flight in 1941, but technical problems developed, and no planes with Whittle-designed engines were used in operations during World War II.

At any rate, when we knew that the Ruhr had fallen and the Americans had crossed the Rhine, we knew then was the time that we could get up into the British zone and really get something going.* By this time we knew that Hellmuth Walter had abandoned Gdynia and retreated to Kiel at the Walter Werke. The reason was that Wernher von Braun, Hellmuth Walter, and their scientific cohorts had agreed they were not going to be captured by the Russians. If they were going to be captured, it was going to be by the British and Americans. So they retreated to the West.

Being cleared for Ultra, we got the information that this had happened.† So that when the Russians closed the pincers on Gdynia and Peenemünde, they got an empty sack with only the lowest levels of routine workers being caught. Somehow the British intelligence got this information out to us in time so that we made no silly assaults on either Gdynia or Peenemünde. However, we did contemplate at one time—this was before we were landing in Paris—possibly going in and dropping in with parachutes to get into some of these spots, to see whether or not we could get in there in time to get it before either the Russians got it. Because the Russians had double-crossed us on Gdynia, and I don't know whether I've told you that complete story or not.

Paul Stillwell: No.

Admiral Mumma: Well, maybe I'd better go back and start with that.

At Yalta it was agreed that there was going to be a tripartite team of five Russians, five British, and five Americans to go to Gdynia and exploit the special torpedo and propulsion work that Hellmuth Walter was doing there.‡ There was a good bay there in Gdynia where they could do this kind of research, far better than at Kiel. So, as a result, this having been agreed with the Russians, we were in contact with the Russians.

---

* The Allies first crossed the Rhine River on March 7, 1945, when men of the U.S. 9th Armored Division, First Army, seized the Ludendorff railroad bridge at Remagen.
† Ultra—short for ultra secret—was a special security classification given by the British to information gained from breaking the code of the German radio enciphering machine. It has come to be used more broadly to encompass other information obtained from interception and decryption of German and Japanese radio communications.
‡ Yalta, a resort city on the Crimea in the Black Sea, was the site of a meeting of the Allied Big Three—Roosevelt, Churchill, and Stalin—in February 1945. The conference reaffirmed the principle of seeking unconditional surrender by Japan and plans for the postwar division of territory.

We had an admiral by the name of Admiral Olsen, who was our naval attaché in Moscow.[*] And the British had a naval attaché, Admiral Archer. In order to avoid compromising of codes, anything that was sent by Archer would be answered by us to Olsen, and they would privately talk together, so that we were not compromising the information going back and forth.

The first plan that we made was to have two airplanes standing by. This was in December of '44, and these were American planes, C-47s. We were equipped with arctic gear of all sorts—fur-lined boots, jackets, helmets, and everything—so that we could fly into Moscow, pick up the Russians, and go into Gdynia. This was a naval effort. The Army and OSS were doing the same thing in connection with Peenemünde.[†] The first difficulty that we had was that the Russians demanded that we all have visas. Apparently, they were worried that some White Russians might be in our group, coming in from either the British or the American group. We sent them visas. The next thing that happened, they said that we couldn't fly in over Sweden direct to Moscow. We would have to come in through Rumania. Well, of course, all that was obvious to us; it was a delaying action. They didn't want us to get there as soon as the Russians could get there themselves.

Archer and Olsen were talking back and forth, back and forth. Finally, the Russians decided we would have to come in through Italy and fly up from Teheran. Well, that was an impossibility from a point of view of logistics. Not only did it make it indecently long to get there, but we knew the Russians would have evaluated the target long before we got there, and we would not be carrying out the tripartite agreement. So what happened was that my opposite number in the Admiralty, Captain Maitland Dougal called me up. We were speaking to each other on the scramble, and he said, "On the bottom of this dispatch, it says, 'Can the leopard change his spots?'" In other words, they were getting a continuous runaround from the Russians.

---

[*] Rear Admiral Clarence E. Olson, USN, whose Naval Institute oral history is devoted almost completely to his recollections of the Yalta conference.
[†] OSS—Office of Strategic Services, formed in World War II to collect and analyze foreign intelligence and to carry out special operations under the control of the Joint Chiefs of Staff.

So I called the chaplain, Chaplain Lash. I said, "Padre, we got this dispatch from Admiral Archer, and I want to answer it through Admiral Olsen. Where do I find such-and-such a passage in the Bible?"*

He said, "You wouldn't be making sacrilegious use of it, would you?"

I said, "Well, it might be just slightly sacrilegious, but it's in a good cause."

And so he said, "It's Hebrews 13:8."

So I looked up Hebrews 13:8, and it said, "Jesus Christ, the same yesterday, today, and tomorrow." So this dispatch went to Admiral Olsen. At that point I went to Admiral Stark, our boss man—he was chief of the European theater in the Navy—and I said, "Admiral Stark, we've been getting an absolute runaround on this tripartite thing. The British and we agree, cancel it and we'll go in and do it ourselves, because we've just gotten word that all the principals have fled to the West, and they're not going to be captured by the Russians anyhow."†

So I prepared this dispatch that said, "In view of the Russian intransigence in not carrying out the agreement for the tripartite visit to Gdynia, agreed to at Yalta, that we recommend the cancellation of any further technical exchange with the Russians." I didn't think Admiral Stark would sign it, but he did, and he sent it to Eisenhower, who was supreme commander.‡ Eisenhower quoted the dispatch verbatim, and at the bottom of it, he said, "This is my policy," and sent it to Washington. That was the end of technical interchange with the Russians, due to the double-cross at Gdynia.

Okay, end of that story. So we found ourselves in Paris, and looking at the northern part of Germany. We took off in two separate groups. One advance group went up to Bremen. I had just a photographer with me in a Jeep, and I came up through the Ruhr. I have never seen such devastation as the Ruhr had suffered. In Dortmund and Essen, there was not a single window in any building anywhere. Most of the water lines had been broken and cut, and most of the population were in the streets lined up at a single spigot to get water. It was complete devastation. We spent the first night outside

---

* Captain Frank H. Lash, CHC, USN.
† Admiral Harold R. Stark, USN, served as Commander U.S. Naval Forces Europe from 30 April 1942 to 15 August 1945.
‡ General of the Army Dwight D. Eisenhower, USA, was the Supreme Allied Commander in Europe in 1944-45.

of Essen, from Paris, just my photographer and myself. He also could speak some German. Everywhere we went, the Germans had been blowing up bridges all the way to try and prevent our Army's advance. The first question we asked every German we came to at a fork in the road, "Ist der brücke kaput?"

They would say, "Ja, ja," or "Nein, nein," and point the way, but we had quite a few dead ends. We turned around when they didn't answer us properly, and we'd keep on going. I joined the group at Bremen. We had taken over a house there, which had been occupied by a widow of a German general. It was a very nice house, and we used it as a headquarters. She welcomed us as, to some degree, liberators. However, we noticed that on the wall, in an entrance foyer, here was a family tree showing that they were all Aryan—no Jews in that family tree at all.

Bremen was not a major target of ours. We did visit the shipyards in Bremen, but there was very little military interest in Bremen. It was mostly commercial shipping. There were some floating cranes and other things that we were interested in, and we catalogued all that kind of information. When some of our group arrived in Bremen, however, the first night, they found that the British combat troops had gone through that day, and I came up the second night. The first night had been a night of pandemonium, apparently, and it was even worse the second night because the troops, as they went through, had released all the slaves that the Germans had working in all of these camps around—every shipyard, every area, they had slave labor from all over—from France, from the Lowlands. So they ended up free, and by the second night, they were all just drunker than skunks, the whole bunch of slaves celebrating their liberation.

I was asleep up in this house on that second night shortly after I'd arrived. I was called by the next senior officer, and he said, "You'd better come on down. Your photographer is in bad shape." I went down and the photographer had his gun out, and he was as drunk as anybody. He apparently had found a place in town where the Germans had stored all this liquor that they had swiped in France, and they had a whole warehouse of it in Bremen. These slaves had stored the liquor for the Germans. He had found out where the slaves were, and he was with them. Had a big night. He came in about 3:00 or 4:00 o'clock in the morning waving his pistol around, and so it became my responsibility to disarm him and to prevent any further happenstance.

I said, "Let me have your gun." So he handed it to me. I said, "All right, now you go to bed and you stay in there, and no more monkey business." So that's what he did. He was an Army file, and, of course I was wearing—in those days when we were in the field, we had no really Navy uniforms for the field except dungarees, and so we wore Eisenhower uniforms complete. The only difference, we wore a black tie whenever we were wearing a tie, and our Eisenhower jackets always carried rank on one side and naval insignia on the other.* Our overseas caps had rank on one side and naval insignia on the other to ensure that everybody knew we were Navy and not Army. So that was our uniform. We looked alike in almost all respects, but you could tell if you looked carefully.

At any rate, we heard that Hamburg was going to fall, and so we moved out of Bremen up to Hamburg. When we got to Hamburg, the devastation was even worse. The Ruhr had been pinpoint bombed by our troops, primarily our Air Force. The British had saturation bombed Hamburg, particularly, and 85,000 people died in Hamburg in that firestorm. That firestorm consumed almost all of the center of Hamburg. It was rubble almost entirely. There were a few isolated buildings that were standing. There would be great big concrete structures standing, and these were the bomb shelters.

Paul Stillwell: How did you react to all this from an emotional standpoint?

Admiral Mumma: Well, it was the most upsetting thing you can imagine, to see all this devastation and tremendous carnage around the place, because they had no time to clean up after the troops went through.

Paul Stillwell: What kind of condition were the survivors in, the German civilians?

Admiral Mumma: Well, German civilians were doing the best they could to take care of the survivors. They had emergency hospitals set up in anything that had a roof on it. And, of course, this time we're talking about now, April, it was still pretty damn chilly in

---

* The Eisenhower jacket was a brown Army uniform jacket that ended at the waist, rather than extending down the hips as the regular uniform did.

northern Germany. They had very little heat. It was miserable. So when we found a place to stay, we always tried to find one where they might have a little heat. When we first got to Hamburg, we stayed in a hotel there that was not as severely damaged as some of the others. Of course, we displaced people when we moved in.

We were a 75-man task force. The 75 men consisted of British Royal Marines. We had the four British officers under Captain Ball, and four Americans under my command. And we had a major in command of the 30th Assault Unit of the Royal Marines. This young man was a very enterprising young fellow. He was really full of beans, and I enjoyed him tremendously.

We got word that Kiel was really a pretty open city, that we could get into Kiel. However, the surrender had not taken place, and we did not at the time know that we were supposed to stay 100 miles back from the Elbe in accordance with the agreement that the Russians and the Americans were not going to touch and fight each other. We didn't know that. So we decided to go on up to Kiel, and we did, boom—the whole 75-man task force and we in our Jeeps. We carried our own gasoline with us. We had weapons carriers full of jerry cans full of gasoline. So everywhere we went we had adequate protection; we had adequate supplies; we had our own C and K rations, and gasoline. So we were self-sufficient wherever we went. When we got to Kiel, we decided that in view of the fact that we were 100 miles behind the German lines, that the best thing to do would be to take and live in the submarine pen. We went in and cleared out the Germans, and then just took over the place, lived there for the few days that we were there.

By this time Hitler was dead.[*] He had been discovered in the bunker in Berlin, and Dönitz had taken over as head of state.[†] We also knew that he had transferred his headquarters to Flensburg up on the tip of the German part of the Danish peninsula. We also knew that the government had pretty well collapsed. On the way into Kiel, we had located the Walter Werke in Kiel, and we knew that Hellmuth Walter was there. So the next day after we took over the sub pen, the group of us officers, with our interrogators

---

[*] Adolf Hitler was Chancellor of Germany from 1933 until his death by suicide on 30 April 1945.
[†] Admiral Karl Dönitz served successively as commander of the Germany Navy's U-boat force in World War II and then as commander in chief of the entire German Navy. He became head of the German Government following Hitler's death.

and our language speakers, and so forth, moved into Hellmuth Walter's headquarters at the Walter Werke in Kiel. In the meantime, this very enterprising young commander of the 30th Assault Unit decided that there was a very great chance that he might be court-martialed for not knowing that we should be 100 miles back behind those front lines. The Germans, very fortunately, had not fired on us on the way north, so that we really hadn't been engaged in any combat. It was so near the end, they all knew that the end was coming. So we worried about that a little bit too. But he was doing special worrying. He was afraid he'd get a court-martial.

Paul Stillwell: Were you ever concerned about your personal safety during this period?

Admiral Mumma: Well, pretty obviously we had some concern about it. But we wanted to get there as fast as we possibly could, and that was the impelling motive.

At any rate, when we went over to Walter Werke the major decided he'd go over and call on the commander of the German forces in Kiel. He went over and he negotiated the surrender of the 150,000 Germans in the Kiel garrison to our 75-man task force.

Paul Stillwell: That was late April?

Admiral Mumma: That was late April, yes. So, obviously, instead of getting a court-martial, he got a commendation. It's on such thin threads that some of these things hang. In the meantime at Kiel, at the Walter Werke, we found Hellmuth Walter welcoming us to some degree. His first thing he said to me was, "When are you going to let me get back into operation so we can help you lick the Russians?" Obviously, he saw on which side our bread was really buttered.

But I said, "Unfortunately, you cannot get back into operation. We have orders that you're not to continue your operation." So he told us quite a lot. There was word that we shouldn't fraternize with the enemy. But I knew we weren't going to get anywhere by antagonism, so I gave him some tea. We had a lot of tea and we had a lot of coffee, and they were short on both of those things. They had just had a new baby, their fifth child. His wife was a lovely person. She appreciated the tea very, very much, and that helped a great deal in setting up where we could talk.

But he refused to talk about the combustion chambers, which were a major part of his hydrogen peroxide propulsion system. He had been personally responsible for setting up the hydrogen peroxide manufacturing in all of Germany. Because of the tremendous power that's released when high concentration hydrogen peroxide decomposes into its two elements, which is steam and oxygen, it forms a tremendous heat thrust of its own. It gets up to about 500 degrees centigrade, which makes a pretty hefty power unit. The thrust and just the decomposition of that material itself, even without fuel, makes a very excellent thrust mechanism. That's the reason why the rocket airplanes had such a tremendous specific impulse.

So I got the gang together, the senior group of us, and we went up to Flensburg. We drove up in our Jeeps and command cars. When we got up there, we suddenly saw this big German command car going by with the top down, and I recognized Dönitz as he drove by. I took a picture of him, but I didn't get a picture of the front view; I got a picture of the car as it went by. But I didn't want to talk to him, anyhow. The fellow I wanted to talk to was the head of the German Navy. So when we found their headquarters we found that the commander in chief of the German Navy was on his way to Compiègne to participate in the negotiations for the surrender. Of course, the French insisted that it take place at Compiègne, where World War I had been successfully completed with the help of the Americans.

Paul Stillwell: It was also where the French had to surrender to Hitler in 1940.

Admiral Mumma: So we then talked to Admiral Backenkohler, who was the Vice Chief of Naval Operations.* Admiral Backenkohler whistled up the chief of each of the major bureaus that had to do with shipbuilding and torpedoes and ordnance. One of the major things that we wanted to know were what had they given to the Japs, and what surprises could we expect from the Japs. Well, Admiral Backenkohler was a little reluctant at first when we began talking. But after we began talking about the Japs and the problems that

---

* Admiral Otto Backenkohler, German Navy.

we'd had, he decided that it would be wise to cooperate, even though they hadn't signed a surrender. So I said, "Well, Admiral, you know, we're having a little bit of difficulty getting information directly from scientific people like Professor Walter. Could you sign a release for these gentlemen, releasing them from their oath of secrecy, their geheimestat?"

He said, "Oh, yes." So he signed one.

I said, "Would you mind signing 50 of those for all of our people?" So that included not only us, but the Royal Navy and everybody else.

Paul Stillwell: What language were these statements in?

Admiral Mumma: German. So all we had to do was pull this out and show it, and immediately we found that Hellmuth Walter not only was willing to show us the combustion chambers, and told us where they were, but our young major had been very enterprising and through inquiries that he had made, he discovered that there was a whole trainload of combustion chambers up on a siding way up in the peninsula. He took a group of Marines up there; he loaded his vehicles onto this train; and he came chugging into Kiel with Germans engineers running it right on into the Walter Werke in Kiel. He had a great big sign on the front of it, "30th Assault Unit." They had all the combustion chambers, not only for the Messerschmitt 163, but also for the launching mechanism for the V-1s, also for the proportioning system for the V-2s, also for the two types of submarines—the type XXI and XXVI submarines, which were of interest to us—as well as the torpedoes.

Paul Stillwell: Did you get to look at the type XXIs while you were there?

Admiral Mumma: Oh, yes. We examined them carefully, and also the type XXIIIs, and type XXVI also. We had captured all of those, not only in Bremen, but in Hamburg.

Paul Stillwell: Now, they were ahead of the technology of our fleet boats at the time, weren't they?

Admiral Mumma: Only insofar as the high-power hydrogen peroxide, which conveyed only ten hours of full power. If you compare the cost of that ten hours compared to even our ordinary fleet boats, at that time the Germans were paying out of their own economy a dollar and a half per kilowatt hour for that power. In a U.S. fleet boat, that submerged power was costing about six cents a kilowatt hour by the time you put it into the batteries and took it back out of the batteries in the form of electric energy. But we only had a one-hour duration at full power as compared to ten hours at full power for these boats, but not one of those boats ever got into service with the fleet. Not a one of them ever sortied in anger.

At that time, while in Flensburg, I interrogated the head of the German submarine force, and he could not understand how our Bay of Biscay offensive had succeeded so well that, of all of the submarines that went out, only 5% returned. This was caused actually by our combined air-sea operations, where we had radar in aircraft, as well as in ships, and were able to coordinate so that no German submarine could sortie without being detected, with a 95-100% chance of being detected, and even with snorkel. They had rubber waffling on their conning towers and on the snorkels, and things like that, to try and evade the radar. But they had no idea, really, originally, that we had radar in aircraft—that we had radar that small. They knew that radar took a big roomful of equipment. That was true for the British radar, but the American radar was a much smaller and much more compact radar, shall we say a businessman's radar.

Paul Stillwell: Did you find out that they had indeed passed on much technical information to the Japanese?

Admiral Mumma: Well, yes, in many respects there were many German subs that made the trip to Japan. They had taken the lead ballast out of those submarines and had replaced it with gold that they had pilfered from conquests. But many of those submarines got sunk on their way to Japan. They went around the Horn.

Paul Stillwell: What was their purpose in putting the gold in there?

Admiral Mumma: They replaced the lead ballast with gold. That was not only to supply themselves with additional support from Japan but to buy war supplies in short supply in Germany. Albert Speer, for example, in his book is obvious in his evaluation that the end was coming, going to be a happy solution for the German people.*

Paul Stillwell: Well, presumably though, they might have provided things to the Japanese a couple years earlier, before the end was apparent.

Admiral Mumma: That's right. They could have, but I don't think there was very much real cooperation between the two. I think it was mostly communications and things of that kind, logistic information.

Paul Stillwell: And the Japanese did not have as good a submarine force as the Germans, so apparently they didn't benefit that much.

Admiral Mumma: Well, this is not very well known, and this may be a separate subject. But we had the best submarines in the war, by far. They were better than the German submarines; they were better than the Jap submarines. They were quieter. We lost approximately a third of the number of ships per attack as did either of those. We had almost a three-time advantage over them. Whenever we found a German submarine, we were able to stay on it and kill it to a much greater degree than they were on ours, and the same thing with the Japs.

Paul Stillwell: Did you have any contact with Armand Morgan?

Admiral Mumma: Well, I knew Armand Morgan when he was at the Naval Academy. He and I were both on the rifle team together. He stood first in his class at the Naval Academy, class of '24, and I stood pretty well up in my class. I never was able to

---

* Albert Speer was Germany's Minister for Armaments and Munitions. He was in charge of all war production. His book was Inside the Third Reich: Memoirs; translated from the German by Richard and Clara Winston ; introduction by Eugene Davidson (New York : Macmillan, 1970).

determine whether he had anything to do with it or not, but his class decided to put in an award at the Naval Academy for the one who stood first in engineering and aeronautics. By that time, it had been renamed the Department of Engineering and Aeronautics instead of the Department of Marine Engineering and Naval Construction, which is what it used to be called. Used to call it ME and NC and it became E and A.

Well, by this time I had set up a pretty fair record in engineering at the academy, and it was too far along for anybody to catch me. So at the end of graduation I got this class of 1924 gold watch for standing one in engineering and aeronautics. Well, Armand Morgan was very happy about that. Later, after many years, Armand and I found ourselves together again in the Navy Department. I was at the Model Basin and he was in the submarine desk. I knew and communicated with him frequently on such matters, and he was very helpful in setting up tests and doing all that sort of thing. It was an extremely good relationship. I admired Armand, and we were good friends.

Paul Stillwell: What was his forte as an engineer?

Admiral Mumma: He was a naval constructor basically. He wasn't as strong in engineering. He was a good shipbuilder, and he knew submarines. He was the submarine, shall we say, expert of the Navy for many years. The strange part about it was that Armand didn't agree on the benefit of single-screw design.

Incidentally, we got Armand Morgan over to assist on the evaluation at Walter Werke at Kiel. He was very helpful in further evaluation. He made considerable number of reports to the Navy Department on that. But I was convinced, hydrodynamically, that the single-screw submarine was a far better submarine than any multiple-screw submarine, because a multiple-screw submarine had the same disastrous effect of having wake go into the propeller disk unevenly, which would cause vibration, and which would cause noise. In other words, this was my philosophy, that you feed wake, if any, into the propeller as smoothly as you can so that it doesn't see variability of wake. The wake is bound to form around any moving hull, and it gets thicker and thicker the further aft you get. So that the more thick and uniform it can be—and uniformity, that's the main thing—and not affected by the rest of the hull in any way, the better off it's going to be not only for propulsive efficiency, but also for noise and vibration. So Armand and I had disagreed on that point. He didn't see my position as I did. As a matter of fact, most of the Navy didn't see my position. [Laughter] I was a little bit out in left field.

So it wasn't until after we went to Kiel and we saw the Germans had—I think it was a XXIII boat, which was a single-screw, small submarine—that Armand first saw some of the possibilities of this, but still wasn't willing to get very enthusiastic about it.

Paul Stillwell: It's interesting that that single screw has been picked up in the nuclear submarines.

Admiral Mumma: It's not only interesting, it's imperative. I fought Rick hammer and tongs on that one.*

Paul Stillwell: I think, really, that would be getting ahead of our story. If we could pick up back there at the end of the war where you're looking at the German facilities.

Admiral Mumma: Okay. All right.

Paul Stillwell: Anything else to cover about what you discovered there?

Admiral Mumma: Well, the first thing was to what degree were we going to use the hydrogen peroxide process of propelling submarines. I was not in favor of it. It was not an economic way of producing power. It cost a dollar and a half a kilowatt hour as against about six cents for the diesel. I knew at that time, because of my experience with the Manhattan District and the Alsos Mission, that we could probably produce nuclear power at a maximum of maybe two or three times the cost of diesel power, not a factor of over 20 or 25. So that I was a nuclear enthusiast from those days. My recommendation, as well as Armand Morgan's recommendation—at that point we were the two senior people with what you might call submarine experience and know-how—was against our

---

* This is a reference to Admiral Hyman G. Rickover, who ran the U.S. Navy's nuclear-power program for many years, from 1948 until he eventually left active duty in 1982.

major activity with hydrogen peroxide. The British wanted it, so they got Hellmuth Walter and the type XXI submarine setup and moved it to Britain at Vickers Armstrong. For a considerable period of time Vickers Armstrong was the major submarine builder in Britain.

So the next episode was that the British, having taken the hydrogen peroxide project, left the way clear enabling the States for something better. So when I came back, there was a question for a period of time as to where I was going to go for duty. I was almost the last guy out of the European theater; I didn't get back until the day before Christmas 1945.

Paul Stillwell: How did you spend that time from April, which is what you mentioned before, to the end of the year?

Admiral Mumma: I was not only assistant naval attaché for engineering matters, and so forth, but we were handling the disposition of this captured German material. I was the only engineer on Commander Naval Forces Europe staff at that time.

Paul Stillwell: Where were you stationed?

Admiral Mumma: London was my headquarters, Number Eight Grosvenor Square, and the embassy at that time was in Number One. The headquarters of the Navy was in Number 15 and 18 Grosvenor Square. So I was stuck until I could get a relief. I worked on that pretty vigorously, because I wanted to get home from the war. I finally managed to get home just before Christmas.

Paul Stillwell: Living conditions were rather austere at that point, weren't they?

Admiral Mumma: Oh, pretty bad. Britain was tough. I tell you, they were still on rationing. At that time the Navy did not eat Army rations at Grosvenor House. The Army had that hotel, and they fed well. All of us on naval attaché status were on absolute British ration. We could occasionally go over to Grosvenor House and have a lunch or something, or we could go out in town and eat, which we did a lot, because we got a little bit hungry. We only got one shell egg a month.

Paul Stillwell: You mean the shell eggs as opposed to dried eggs?

Admiral Mumma: As opposed to dried eggs. And bacon, meat—all that was very severely rationed. I felt so sorry for the British, because it was really a sad situation. Yet I attended several meetings where the British were encouraging—and the Australians wanted—a large, large migration of British to Australia and New Zealand. They wouldn't go; they wouldn't leave the islands. That was their home, and they were going to stay in spite of how tough it was. So all that flux that could have taken place after the war, not only to Canada, but also to the Australians and New Zealand, did not take place in the large numbers that they'd hoped. They hoped to reduce the imports to U.K and be able to tighten their belts more. But it did not happen.

And, of course, the defeat of Churchill made it even worse because when Clement Attlee took over, things began to fall apart even worse.[*] As a matter of fact, times got so tough that in Britain that at that time there was great dissatisfaction with many, many of the problems but not enough for them to take the lead that the Canadians and the New Zealanders and the Australians offered to them to move out and ameliorate the situation in the island of Britain. This got worse, as a matter of fact, particularly when Clement Attlee began to nationalize things.

There's a story that was current at that time. Winston Churchill, of course, was still on the floor of the House but not as Prime Minister. He went to the men's room in the House of Commons, and as he entered the room, he saw in the very first stall, standing there, Clement Attlee. He went all the way down to the other end, and on his way out he found that Clement Attlee was waiting at the front door for him. Clement said, "Winston, I know we have our differences on the floor of the House, but I didn't know we were so personally obnoxious to each other that you had to walk all the way down to the other end of the men's room."

---

[*] Clement R. Attlee, the leader of Britain's Labour Party, defeated Winston Churchill in a general election in July 1945 and served as Prime Minister from then until February 1950.

Winston said, "Clement, you know the trouble with you fellows is you see anything large and running well, you want to nationalize it." [Laughter]

Paul Stillwell: What was the substance of your duties for that latter part of 1945?

Admiral Mumma: Well, in the first place, it was major cleanup; it was turning over of German equipment to the various Allies, like floating cranes. We got a floating crane, the British got a floating crane; and that was the only thing that we could not prevent happening was the Russians did get some of that loot. The only technical interchange was the actual partition of some of the equipment. That had been decided other than Yalta. That had been decided long beforehand and was inviolable. We could not change that. Otherwise, we would have.

Paul Stillwell: I think that floating crane is still used at that Long Beach Naval Shipyard.

Admiral Mumma: That's right. And the old Bremen and Europa hulls, and the partition of the cruisers.* We got the Prinz Eugen, which was used as a target ship out at Bikini.† So that the partition actions were very, very important relative to cleaning things up in Europe as far as the Navy was concerned and shipping out the stuff we wanted. The British got the Z-37 and so on, and they got the hydrogen peroxide plant, and things of that kind. It was all on an exchange agreed basis.

Paul Stillwell: Did you have a program of interrogating the Germans on what they'd done during the war?

---

* The Bremen and Europa were German passenger liners.
† The Prinz Eugen, a German heavy cruiser commissioned in 1940, was probably best known for being a part of the ill-fated Bismarck's last cruise in 1941. The cruiser was turned over to the United States as part of the postwar reparations and was later used as a target ship in the Bikini atomic bomb tests in the Marshall Islands in the summer of 1946. For an account by one of the German officers who remained after the ship became part of the U.S. Navy, see Helmut Raumann, "Life As 'Employed Enemy Personnel,'" Naval History, Summer 1989, pages 28-34.

Admiral Mumma: Oh, yes, we did that. But we did that generally as we were proceeding, and we made reports. Then I had all of the NavTechMisEu people as they finished their jobs in Europe; I was back in London by this time. We'd moved our headquarters out of Paris back into London. I was the, shall we say, residue of NavTechMisEu in Europe, and I had them, whenever they came through, sit down with a secretary and write a report. So that we had a complete report on everything that went on. Also, if they wanted to go and visit British shipyards and came on through, and saw a lot of stuff, sit down and write a report. Numerous friends of mine now say I was very obnoxious in that respect, making them write a report when the war was all over. But those reports are all in the archives now.

I was scheduled to get back the middle of December, but the airplanes weren't flying. In all of Europe there were many, many airplanes stacked up, down in India and in southern Europe. Northern Europe was just completely covered with fog, and fog and smog. You couldn't see anything, and the airplanes couldn't get in. So I waited for almost ten days to get out of Britain. We finally got in the airplane the night of the 23rd and started.

Paul Stillwell: Was this a clipper?

Admiral Mumma: This was a DC-4. As a matter of fact, the pilot was a friend of mine. He'd served in the Saratoga years before and was a contract pilot for Naval Air Transport Service. When we started that night, there were two senior officers on the plane. I was one from naval attaché's office, and the other one was an assistant Army attaché that was going back. He was a colonel, and I was a captain in the Navy. We were the two senior, and there were a lot of people from the CBI, China-Burma-India Theater. Most of them were nurses and doctors and people that had been out there to the bitter end. They'd been delayed getting started home. They came through, with their baggage on this airplane on their way home.

We managed to get a few people on the plane in the U.K., and we put a pile of naval attaché and Army attaché bags on board. This was a mixed cargo airplane with bucket seats along the side. The whole center of the airplane was stacked up with these naval attachés' pouches which had been stacked up for the previous week. We finally got in the air and got headed for Lajes, Azores; Iceland was closed in. We couldn't go directly over to Newfoundland, so we had to go down to the Azores and then fly up. I was in the copilot's front seat with the pilot. He'd given the copilot a little time to sleep.

We were talking, and he said, "We've got a nine-hour flight plan." I was there, I guess, for about eight hours out, and we were supposed to come in. Nine hours passed, nine and a half, ten hours, ten and a half, and it was coming up on 11 hours out. He said, "If we don't see that damned island pretty soon, we're not going to be doing anything but swimming." Pretty soon we saw the lights of the island and we got down. He said, "Well, we got a couple of teacups left of gas." So he went up to make his report. In the meantime, he came back after his report, and he said, "Due to that adverse weather we had coming down, they've changed our flight plan so that instead of nine hours from here to Newfoundland, they've hiked it to 11 hours and we've got to take more gas. We've got to drop off a dozen passengers and their luggage."

I said, "That's the silliest thing I ever heard of. This is Christmas Eve." So this colonel and I went up to the flight commander's headquarters, saw the commander of the field, and said, "Look, that center aisle is full of naval attaché and Army attaché baggage that we both know about. These people have been out in the CBI theater and been waiting for an airplane for a week, as have we. This stuff, when we arrive tomorrow night in Washington, is not going to have any attention at all over Christmas weekend. That can certainly go on the next airplane, all that cargo stuff and mail."

He said, "No, sir, it can't."

I said, "The hell it can't."

The colonel in the Army said, "The hell it can't."

But the field commander said, "I am in command of this station, and those bags go through. They are priority one."

I said, "That's the goddamnest thing I ever heard." We had to go back to the airplane, and they took a dozen people off, all their stuff. I don't know when they got home. This was one of the instances in which militarism took over from common sense. I have always been a guy that said, "Look, you ought to use your brains first; follow the rules second." Well, that was the worst example I think I've ever run into of militarism taking over. I never let it happen again in my watch, if I could help it.

Paul Stillwell: Did you have a choice of duty then when you got back to the United States?

Admiral Mumma: Yes, for a period of time there were three jobs supposedly open to me: one was an assistant in command out at the engineering experiment station using my engineering background; another was go to a navy yard; and third was head of machinery design in the Navy Department. Well, Admiral Cochrane was chief of bureau.[*] Admiral Mills was deputy chief of bureau.[†] They finally decided that I should become head of machinery design, and they gave me a month's leave after I arrived. I reported in late January, I guess it was, to the design division. Logan McKee, Andy McKee's brother, was head of design, and Mike Honsinger was deputy for hull contract design.[‡] I was deputy for ship machinery design, so Mike and I were opposite numbers—machinery and hull.

Obviously, this became a high-priority item for me to get started on nuclear power. I don't think it's generally known, but the Naval Research Laboratory down in Anacostia had been working on a nuclear power project from the very beginning of the war. They had been stopped for the development of that project, by the concentration on the atomic bomb of the Manhattan District, with the Army in charge of the whole works. General Groves and General Nichols were the two top people.[§] Well, Paul Lee was head of shipbuilding in the bureau at that time.[**] So Earle Mills and Paul Lee and I decided we would have a chat with the Manhattan District as to how to go about it. Let's get going on nuclear power.

---

[*] Rear Admiral/Vice Admiral Edward L. Cochrane, USN, served as Chief of the Bureau of Ships from 1942 to 1946.
[†] Rear Admiral Earle W. Mills, USN, became Assistant Chief of the Bureau of Ships in 1942. He was promoted to the rank of vice admiral on 31 December 1945 and became Chief of the Bureau of Ships on 1 November 1946.
[‡] Captain Logan McKee, USN; Captain Leroy V. Honsinger, USN.
[§] Colonel Kenneth D. Nichols, USA, was deputy director of the Manhattan Project.
[**] Rear Admiral Paul F. Lee, USN.

So we had a meeting with General Nichols and General Groves. I had known General Groves beforehand, because I was on the Alsos Mission, which was a part of the nuclear program of the Manhattan District, and General Groves had briefed us when we went overseas on that particular part of the Alsos Mission. When they said, "There is no way that that can be done. We have, at this time, a commitment that every ounce of fissionable material goes into bombs, or a stockpile of bombs. We have to have it; you cannot have one ounce of fissionable material." That's what they told us.

Earle Mills and Paul Lee and I then said to ourselves, "Aha! They won't let us have any fissionable material. We'll build everything else in the system except that. And we'll try several approaches."

So between then, in early February, on through into June we went to G.E., Westinghouse, Mine Safety Appliance in Pittsburgh, Babcock and Wilcox, Foster Wheeler, and Combustion Engineering, and all those people. We said, "Now look, we cannot have any fissionable material, but we can develop the rest of the plant as though there were a fissionable source there. We're going to get a head start on that nuclear program for submarines particularly."

So we let contracts with each of those. I think we must have let $10 million worth of contracts for study purposes, each one about a million or two million, to Westinghouse, Wolverine was the code name on it. Genie was the code name for GE. And Baby was the code name of Babcock and Wilcox.

Paul Stillwell: Why did you need code names?

Admiral Mumma: We used code names because we didn't want to tilt the project toward nuclear at that time. It was just a research study, so we used code names. We had Mine Safety Appliance studying liquid metals as a possible coolant for nuclear power. And sodium, is a possible liquid metal. Potassium is a possible liquid metal; most people think potassium is something you put in salt, have it instead of sodium chloride. There is a eutectic blend of the two metals, which is the lowest melting point of the combination (so-called NAC). NaC is sodium and potassium blended together and it has a melting point eutectic that is down to almost freezing of water. In other words, those two metals blended together could form a liquid heat transfer material which would give you a far faster and greater transfer of heat than any water, whether pressurized or not. So that was one that we wanted to explore, was the liquid metal possibility. And, of course, pressurized water was another one. G.E. wanted to do the liquid metal. Westinghouse wanted to do the pressurized water. Okay, so we decided on those systems, and we did them with those companies. At this time Rickover was out in the reserve fleet out in San Francisco. So we had this system pretty well along.

In the meantime, we were also attempting to rig carriers so that they could handle atomic bombs. The Air Force wasn't exactly enthusiastic about that, but it was an obvious solution to the problem as well as carrying it in airplanes. We carry it in our ships and then launch it in airplanes closer to the target.

By this time, Logan McKee had been replaced by Armand Morgan, and Logan went to other duty. So Armand Morgan became chief of nuclear matters, and I became deputy chief of nuclear matters for the Bureau of Ships. He and I were anointed to do this research work, I for the power side, and he for the ship bomb side. Armand and I worked together, Armand being head of design and I kept the same job at machinery design. We had a very good operating arrangement.

Anyhow, we went down to Sandia, and we discussed various aspects of handling of atomic bombs.[*] They had to be safely handled and put together at the last minute—all the various logistic problems that would come with handling atomic bombs. We also stopped at Oak Ridge and discussed with them the various methods of making fissionable material. Of course, I had already known of the Navy's part in the thermal diffusion process. I think I mentioned that to you earlier, before I went on the Alsos Mission and when I had inadvertently asked Earle Mills, "When are we going to get into nuclear power with U-235?" So we knew that that fissionable material had to come from one of three sources. Number one was at Oak Ridge that had thermal diffusion process; number two was at Oak Ridge with the electromagnetic process; and number three was plutonium from Hanford out in Washington. Those three were the only possible sources of fissionable material. And, of course, we would have to have the authority of the Manhattan District and later the Atomic Energy Commission to use any of that material.

---

[*] Sandia was the site of a nuclear weapons development facility in New Mexico.

This authority was not forthcoming until the stockpile got full. It wasn't until 1948, two years later, that any fissionable material was forthcoming for any of our purposes at all.

In the meantime, having visited Oak Ridge, Earle Mills and Paul Lee and I attended a special course set up here in Washington to learn about nuclear physics, and we had two outstanding physicists as our instructors. One was Dr. George Gamov, the author of <u>The Birth and Death of the Sun</u>, who was head of astrophysics at Cal Tech, and he was here in Washington on temporary duty with the office of Strategic Services. The other one was Dr. Larry Hafstad, who was the head of nuclear physics at George Washington University.[*] Well, we sat at their feet and listened and learned about nuclear physics in much greater detail than I had ever known before in connection with the Alsos Mission. We knew the basic fundamentals but didn't get into it like this. Both of those people became very good, close friends also. Dr. Larry Hafstad later became head of research at General Motors, their tech center outside of Detroit, and I visited him there on one or two occasions. At any rate, Gamov eventually went back to Cal Tech. I think Hafstad is still alive, but I had no further contact with Gamov, and I'm not sure he is still alive.

Paul Stillwell: How did Captain Rickover get into it?

Admiral Mumma: Well, he wasn't in it yet, you see. At about this time then, we decided to send some outstanding young people to Oak Ridge to study. So I selected from a group of people five outstanding young men, and one of them was Lou Roddis out of the class of '39.[†] Another one was Jim Dunford out of the class of '39.[‡] Another was a Lieutenant Dick; I don't know his specific background at the moment; I'd have to look it up.[§] Then there was a man by the name of Blizard whose father was in Foster Wheeler Company.[**] Miles Libbey was the fifth.[††]

---
[*] Lawrence Hafstad, Director of Reactor Development, Atomic Energy Commission.
[†] Lieutenant Commander Louis H. Roddis, Jr., USN, who stood number one of the 581 graduates in the Naval Academy class of 1939.
[‡] Lieutenant Commander James M. Dunford, USN, third in the class of 1939.
[§] Lieutenant Raymond H. Dick, USNR, first in his class at Ohio State in 1942.
[**] Everitt P. Blizard, a physicist for the Bureau of Ships.
[††] Lieutenant Commander Miles A. Libbey, Jr., USN, Naval Academy class of 1940.

At any rate, they were all to go down to Oak Ridge and I was talking with Earle Mills as to who should be their head man. We ought to send a senior guy down there too. I still had my major job in the Navy Department, and I couldn't go down. We did this quickie course for us so we'd be knowledgeable. We thought that two or three people might be good candidates. But Earle Mills said, "Why, Rick is about to come back from out there in the West, reserve fleet job, and he's available for that."

I'd known Earle since he was a lieutenant, and we'd been associated for many years in destroyers and so on. I said, "Earle, you know Rick as well as I do." I had Rick as an opposite number in the technical section when I had the propeller desk during the war, after I left the model basin. I had the propeller desk before I went overseas, and I had that responsibility for all the ships in the Navy. Rick had the same responsibility for everything electrical in the Navy." I said, "Whenever it came to electric drive, we had to talk about power and power and torque, and everything else, RPM. Rick was a very difficult guy to deal with. He doesn't get things done quickly. He mulls it over until he's sure it's going to be all right, and that is not the way to get things done quickly. You have to move faster than that. Once you're convinced, you should move, and you should get convinced sooner than Rick does."

He said, "Ah, forget it."

I said, "Look, Earle, you're going to regret this if you do that. Some day you'll live to regret it, because he will not do it as fast. And he will not do it in a fashion that will be happy. We've got guys around here that can do that job."

Paul Stillwell: Did you have any other specifically in mind?

Admiral Mumma: Yes, I did, Harry Burris, class of '24.[*] Did you ever hear of him?

Paul Stillwell: No.

Admiral Mumma: Harry Burris is the guy who did the DE program during World War

---

[*] Captain Harry Burris, USN.

II.* He was a fabulous individual. He did that DE program so fast and so well, the British, everybody thought there was no one like Harry Burris. I was a good friend of Harry's; I knew him very well. I knew how he operated, and I knew how good he was, because I had to propel every one of his ships. We had three different kinds of propulsion in those ships, as you probably know. We had Fairbanks Morse diesel engines; we had geared drive turbines; we had geared drive diesel engines. We had everything in those ships, anything that you could use for power because we couldn't make enough reduction gears of that size. So Harry had done a fabulous job, and I said, "Earle, Harry Burris is your man."

He said, "Harry can't be spared at the moment."

I said, "Look, you don't want to put Rick in there just because he can be spared." But I lost, and Rick was put in. So I turned it over to Rick, all the stuff we'd been doing for two years.

Paul Stillwell: Were these five very bright guys picked before Rickover was selected?

Admiral Mumma: Oh, yes. Oh, yes. I picked them. Rick had nothing to do with that.

Paul Stillwell: Did you seek applications or did you go on records?

Admiral Mumma: I used to read their theses at MIT, and I thought, "These guys have got it." They showed a lot of brainpower in their theses. And I followed their records, class of '39; they'd done a nice job through the war, and so I figured, "Look, you've got to do a real selective job of picking jobs."

Paul Stillwell: How tight was the security on the propulsion program?

Admiral Mumma: The security was tops on that program at the time. We didn't talk about it at all. The only use of my terminology of deputy for nuclear matters was on

---

* DE—destroyer escort.

correspondence that absolutely had to have it. Other than that, I was head of machinery design.

So finally they recalled Rick and got him. We sent the young guys to Oak Ridge. Rick went down as the senior guy, and he began whipping them into shape, à la Rickover. You know, "Everything I do is right. Unless I say it, it's wrong." That kind of attitude. Well, that wasn't the attitude they were brought up in basically, but they had to accept it. And though they were very loyal to Rick early on—there was no question about it—they were very good. In my book, those young men made Rickover look good. <u>They were the program.</u> I've told them so, many, many times, but, you know, it got so bad for some of them that Lieutenant Dick committed suicide.* He couldn't take it from Rick, and he committed suicide. I don't suppose that's ever been told.

Paul Stillwell: I didn't know that.

Admiral Mumma: Nobody ever tells these things.

In the end, after my stint in machinery design, just before I left the bureau and I went to another assignment, I had the necessity of getting this nuclear thing off the ground. By this time, the AEC had been formed. So Rick and I together wrote a letter, because we saw eye to eye on the necessity of getting this thing done. We signed a joint letter to Earle Mills to have it sent on over to the AEC and Mr. Strauss was head of the AEC at that time.† When it got over there, it got some, I guess, happy response, because the fissionable material had become more available. The Argonne National Laboratory, which was being operated at that time by Westinghouse, was assigned a research program for a nuclear fissionable power plant for potential submarine size of 15,000 horsepower. I selected two more brilliant young guys—one by the name of Turnbaugh and one by the name Naymark—and sent them out to the laboratory to work with the Westinghouse people.‡ Then Rick, of course, began to assume charge of the Argonne job.

---

* Dick died in January 1953 when he was project officer for the nuclear reactor prototype.
† Lewis L. Strauss was a member of the Atomic Energy Commission, 1946-50, and chairman, 1953-58.
‡ Lieutenant Commander Marshall E. Turnbaugh, USN, stood ninth in the Naval Academy class of 1939; Lieutenant Commander Sherman Naymark, USN, stood fourth in the class of 1941.

I was due to be detached that fall, and we put it off until about January of '49, because Ned Cochrane and Earle Mills felt that I had to have a tour in the shipyard, in a production job.* I'd been in research, I had had a long PG, and they wanted to salt me down a little bit, I guess. I'd had this period in the bureau as machinery design, which is a semi-theoretical kind of thing too.

Paul Stillwell: Well, I hope we can cover some of that in addition to the nuclear propulsion. What other kinds of projects were you working on?

Admiral Mumma: Well, at that time, we had built a tremendous number of destroyers all alike, the 2200-ton destroyers. We had built a lot of aircraft carriers, all alike, Essex class, and so on. And we never had looked upon the jeep-class carriers as something to be considered long term in the Navy. We wanted attack aircraft carriers, and so immediately we needed to modernize our propulsion equipment. So at the same time that we were doing this nuclear business, we started a research program for advanced design of ship machinery.

Paul Stillwell: Higher pressures of steam.

Admiral Mumma: Higher pressures, higher temperatures. So Paul Lee, who was the head of shipbuilding at that time, cooperated with us completely, and Earle Mills, of course, was for this. So what we did was we took a destroyer that was on the ways, the DD-828.

Paul Stillwell: Timmerman.†

---

* Admiral Cochrane had retired in November 1947. Mills served as Chief of the Bureau of Ships from 1946 to 1949.
† USS Timmerman (DD-828) was a Gearing-class destroyer that served as a test platform to evaluate advanced design experimental engineering equipment under operational conditions. Her keel was laid in 1945; she was not launched until 1951 and not commissioned until 26 September 1952. She became part of the Operational Development Force and in 1954 was redesignated AG-152, a miscellaneous auxiliary ship.

Admiral Mumma: <u>Timmerman</u>. She was partially finished a little above the keel and was nearing the point where she might be completed or might not be completed, either one way or the other, at the end of World War II. Earle Mills who was deputy chief of the bureau, and Paul Lee, who was head of shipbuilding, and I all agreed that we should do something to further our capability in ship design and machinery design. Because during World War II, we built series upon series of ships of the same design in order to get an adequate quantity of ships for the war. But they were all the same design. We hadn't been able to change any major designs during that period.

Before World War II, the boiler's pressure and temperature were about 600 pounds—before that they were 400 pounds, and around 650 degrees. Then we got up to 750 degrees in temperature. In the meantime, the power plants ashore had been going up to 1,000 pounds and in some cases, 1,050 degrees. We knew this and we knew these plants were operating and operating very well. So here was a potential tremendous saving in weight and space if we were able to adopt something of that kind.

We decided, okay, in that same hull we're going to put 100,000 horsepower, previously designed for 60,000 horsepower. That was quite an ambitious task, weight- and space-wise. We hoped to improve the efficiency so that we could increase the radius by at least 20 and maybe 30% on the same amount of fuel. And, of course, the increase in horsepower in that particular ship would have increased her speed, not in direct proportion to the increase in horsepower, of course, but appreciably.

So how to do this? This necessitated additional contracts over and above anything about nuclear; they were completely separate from the nuclear. So we went to G.E.; we went to Westinghouse; we went to Allis-Chalmers. Allis-Chalmers had never done any major work for the Navy, but they had been big in industry, and there was no reason why they shouldn't have made a contribution. We then made contracts with the boiler companies also: Foster Wheeler, Combustion Engineering, and Babcock and Wilcox. Then we made contracts with the auxiliary machine builders, the turbines, the small turbine builders like Terry and others. But that was supplementary and secondary to the original purpose. So we built one of each type.

How did we decide on what to build? We had William Francis Gibbs as a consultant. He was not in charge of it; he was a consultant to us. And William Francis himself was a pretty good engineer and a devotee of this philosophy. He also fancied himself quite a ship designer, particularly for destroyers.

Paul Stillwell: He had a very good reputation, didn't he?

Admiral Mumma: Had a very fine reputation, but he was not the easiest man in the world to deal with. He was a curmudgeon when he wanted to be. He had very little respect for anybody who didn't have a lot of brains, and it was quite a while before I convinced him I even had a modicum of them. [Laughter]

So, at any rate, we had a meeting with him in New York once a week. We had meetings in Washington with the contractors. We had sometimes meetings in New York with the contractors. Our basic principle with these contractors: "We want you to design the very best possible design you can make. We do not want you to guarantee the result, except in workmanship and manufacture. In other words, we are taking the risk for the design in the Navy Department. In other words, we're taking the salesman off your back, you designers. You don't have to perform according to a price; you don't have to perform according to a specification; you perform according to a goal. We are taking the responsibility."

That had never been done, as far as I know, in the Navy before. That stemmed from Paul Lee, Earle Mills, and myself. The three of us agreed that that was the way we should go, and so we first did research. How far could we go? We went to all the top power plants in the country. Public Service in New Jersey had a 1,050-degree power plant. It was a 2,000-pound, 1,050 degrees. That's pretty high, and that takes pretty hefty pipes. Maybe the pipes would be too heavy. But we found that the engineering of the Electric Institute had a piping committee, and we went to this piping committee and asked them, how did they size piping, and so on. We got all the information we could from them: pressure versus weight of piping. As the pressure goes up, do you make it that much heavier or not? Can you ease up on this to avoid heat transfer, chipping on the inside and cracking on the outside, that kind of stuff? We had members sitting on that committee with the industry people, so that we could pick their brains.

We then did the same thing with boilers, with the three boiler manufacturers. We did it with the three other manufacturers; we did it with the three electrical manufacturers. We wanted to have the least weight, an outstanding electrical system in the ship. So instead of 60-cycle, we investigated 400-cycle, which had been used in aircraft. Why not use it in ships? This makes pretty high-speed stuff, 400-cycle. So we ended up that everything had to be higher speed, if possible; lighter weight in order to fit into this ship of the same size. So we built one of everything. We figured that between 875 and 2,000 pounds with 1,050 degrees, we would bracket the industry as to what would be available and how good it would be. So we built the ship with one engine room 2,000 pounds, 1,050 degrees. The other engine room we built the 875 pounds, 1,050 degrees. The forward machinery plant was one pressure and temperature; and the after machinery plant was the other, all in the same ship. There was no cross connection.

Paul Stillwell: I've heard that one of the problems with the Timmerman was that there were too many variables, too many new things.

Admiral Mumma: She never was intended to be an operating ship. She was a research ship, and we never wanted her to be an operating ship. OpNav thought they were losing a ship. Actually, we had an additional research ship, and we got the authority to do it and we did it. But by the time it came out and she was running in the fleet, why, they began to use her like a fleet ship. Well, she wasn't an ordinary ship. She was a research ship.

Paul Stillwell: Did she serve the purpose that you had intended?

Admiral Mumma: Oh, she served the purpose admirably as a research ship. So we backed off from the 1,050 degrees, 2000 pounds and 875 pounds, down to 1,200 pounds. And instead of 1,050 degrees, we went to 975.

Paul Stillwell: Why did you pick the number of 1,200?

Admiral Mumma: Twelve hundred because that was a compromise in the weight of the piping. The piping helped decide that. For the 2,000-pound version the piping was pretty heavy. For the 1,200 the piping wasn't that much heavier than the 875, and it would take the thermal stresses better. So, therefore, that was the way to go.

We also backed down to get a more reliable ship from the 100,000 horsepower. We got the 100,000 horsepower in the Timmerman. There's no question about it. We made our goal. And we backed down from there to 80,000 horsepower. So the new destroyers were 80,000 horsepower with 1,200 pounds and 975 degrees. Now, what happened then was that we were building two new aircraft carriers, one down at Newport News that was the Forrestal, and the other one was the Saratoga.[*] The Saratoga was being built up in New York Navy yard.

As a result of that, we tried to see whether or not we could get the Timmerman results into the Forrestal. But it was too late. We couldn't do it. So we had to put the old power plant in the Forrestal, and we put the new power plant in the Saratoga. So from that point of view, they're sister ships aviation-wise, but they're different machinery-wise. And that's not the first time that ever has been done. Back in the old days when they went from reciprocators to turbines, half the ships in a class would be reciprocating, and the other half would be turbine. They wanted to run them to see which was better. It turns out that this was just a transition in progress.

Paul Stillwell: The DLs, the Mitscher class got those 1,200-pound boilers.

Admiral Mumma: Yes. Right. The Mitscher was the first of the class.[†] Now, we had an accident in the Mitscher class. I guess that was a pretty hefty part of my career too.

---

[*] USS Forrestal (CVA-59) was commissioned 1 October 1955 as the first of the U.S. Navy's big-deck carriers. She had a standard displacement of 56,000 tons, was 1,046 feet long, 129 feet in the beam, and had an extreme width of 252 feet. Her top speed was 33 knots. She was originally armed with eight 5-inch guns and could accommodate approximately 70-90 aircraft. USS Saratoga (CVA-60) was commissioned 14 April 1956. Her dimensions were similar to those of the Forrestal but not an exact match.

[†] USS Mitscher (DL-2) was originally commissioned as an all-gun frigate on 15 May 1953. She was the first of a four-ship class, and all were noted for having engineering problems. She was decommissioned for conversion to a guided missile ship in the 1960s, reclassified DDG-35 in 1967, and recommissioned on 29 June 1968. She was stricken from the Naval Vessel Register on 1 June 1978.

When I was in machinery design, we had had been using AN steel in the shafts for many years, which is a copper-nickel, steel, and certain stresses were permissible with that design. We decided that we would go with a little higher alloy steel in the shafts of the new destroyers and the Saratoga. Of course, the shafts were of the old design in the Forrestal.

In the Mitscher class, suddenly we dropped a propeller off one of the ships. We investigated, and we found out that apparently we had not done a sufficient amount of research on this new material. This new material was susceptible to a new kind of cracking, which was called stress corrosion cracking. It happened only in seawater. We hadn't done the oscillating fatigue tests in seawater. We'd done the oscillating tests in air, and nothing happened. It had a perfect fatigue limit in air, but its fatigue limit was low in seawater. So this seawater attacked the boundaries of this particular alloy between grains, and caused this eventual early failure. The Mitscher class were involved.

We had the Saratoga involved, because she had the new design shafting in her. This was written up and brought to the attention of the Navy Department—Chief of Naval Operations—and told what would have to be done and how much it would cost. In the Saratoga, it would cost about half a percent of the original cost of the ship. In the Mitscher it was a little higher percentage, was 1% and 1 1/2% of the original cost of the ship to replace the shafting. We didn't have to replace the inboard shafting, just the outboard shafting—the shafting that saw salt water—which we did.

The Chief of Naval Operations wanted an investigation for responsibility for this error having been made. The letter came to my desk. I said, "There's no problem. The responsibility is mine." When I had the machinery design division in the Bureau in 1946, 1947, and 1948, I made that decision as to which shafting was going to go on those ships. We had not done adequate research on the corrosion resistance and fatigue resistance in corrosion.

Paul Stillwell: Were you Chief of Bureau by the time this letter came in?[*]

---

[*] Admiral Mumma served as Chief of the Bureau of Ships from 1955 to 1959.

Admiral Mumma: Yes, I was Chief of Bureau. So I wrote a letter, and I said to the Chief of Naval Operations, "No investigation is needed. The person who made that decision was Albert G. Mumma, then head of machinery design. I made that decision myself, because I found that it was a very superior steel on all the tests that we had made on the steel. Unfortunately, we had not made fatigue testing immersed in seawater. This was a unique failure that only appeared when immersed in seawater, stress corrosion of the boundary layer of the crystals."

It came back, "No further investigation is required. Thank you very much." I thought I was going to lose my job. I really did. But Arleigh Burke didn't think of it that way.[*] [Laughter] Neither did Mick Carney, who was about to be relieved at that time, one relieving the other.[†] So I kept the job of chief of bureau, and that shows it's worthwhile—if you're guilty, admit it. It paid off.

Paul Stillwell: If you had been evasive, they would have found you out eventually.

Admiral Mumma: Oh, they would have had my neck, I'm sure. If I'd been evasive about it, I would have been out. So, boy, I learned that lesson good with that one.

Now, where are we?

Paul Stillwell: Well, maybe we're at a good point to interrupt for lunch because we're right near the end of this tape.

Admiral Mumma: All right, that's a good time.

Paul Stillwell: Well, we were talking before lunch about this time that you were in the Bureau of Ships after the war and working on the machinery. What was Mills like as a bureau chief then to work for?

---

[*] Admiral Arleigh A. Burke, USN, served as Chief of Naval Operations from 17 August 1955 to 1 August 1961. His oral history is in the Naval Institute collection.
[†] Admiral Robert B. Carney, USN, served as Chief of Naval Operations from 17 August 1953 to 17 August 1955.

Admiral Mumma: Earle was a good engineer. He was a damn good man. I liked Earle, a very good friend, and so on. I don't think he was quite as sharp when it came to judging character of people, or he would have gone for Harry Burris.

Paul Stillwell: How was he as an administrator, a manager?

Admiral Mumma: He was good. He was all right. But, again, evaluation of people, I think, is the strongest thing a manager has to do. I think he succeeded in putting the wrong guy in charge of that nuclear program. My personal opinion is that the nuclear program could have been done twice as fast with Harry Burris, than was done, and with better and better people to succeed Harry Burris than Rick has ever had available to him because he killed them all off, all the good ones. Then when they had to get rid of him just before he died, why, then, there was nobody really, of ability, super ability to take over.[*] Whereas, I, for example, had tried to bring in my successors and have them all there, have them all trained and ready, and saucered and blowed, ready to go. He never did anything like that, and he refused to do anything like that.

Paul Stillwell: Not only that, he did the opposite.

Admiral Mumma: He did the opposite; he killed them all off, chopped their head off one after another. The people that should have had those kudos are people like Roddis, and Dunford, and Turnbaugh, and Naymark, and all those early on people that did the job for Rick and made him look good.

Paul Stillwell: It's interesting that you said that he slowed down the process, since one of the things that he's been given credit for is bringing nuclear power in sooner than it might have been.

---

[*] In March 1982, Admiral Kinnaird R. McKee, USN, succeeded Admiral Rickover as Director of the Naval Nuclear Propulsion Program. Rickover died in 1986.

Admiral Mumma: If we had had the impetus of Harry Burris, he'd have done the nuclear job in half the time, with everyone on a happy constructive team. Incidentally, Harry had phlebitis in the leg, and it had to be amputated.* Shortly thereafter, Harry Burris, unfortunately, died.† I think if he had had that nuclear job, he would have stayed alive.

Paul Stillwell: Why do you say that?

Admiral Mumma: Well, it was a tremendous disappointment to him because I think he knew he was being considered. He was up at G.E. and helped G.E. a great deal with their program, in spite of Rick. This is another point that I think I ought to mention before I leave this submarine business.

General Electric had a civilian viewpoint of nuclear power. They wanted to get into the civilian reactors as soon as possible, wanted to get a head start on everybody else. I had a very tough problem with one Dr. Kingdon at G.E., who was one of their research scientists in nuclear physics.‡ Dr. Kingdon believed that you should go with the civilian job first, and then do the Navy job later. I think I helped convince Dr. Suits, who was the head of G.E.'s research, and Harry Winne, who was the executive vice president, who had been vice president of engineering, and the chairman Ralph Cordiner—that the best possible way to get a civilian reactor would be for us to design and build the naval reactor first, where we could afford it if it was just a few cents more for a kilowatt hour than ordinary power.§

We were comparing with a dollar and a half a kilowatt hour with the German hydrogen peroxide job, and that was, I think, what finally sold them. We were comparing with a dollar and a half a kilowatt hour for a Navy job, not with four cents for a civilian power plant. So we can afford to pay six cents, or eight, or ten, or 15, or whatever it takes for us to do it, a nuclear job in a submarine because it conveys so much to us. It conveys infinite submergence at full power. That is the greatest thing that a

---

* For another view on the impact of Burris's health, see the Naval Institute oral history of Captain Harry Jackson, USN (Ret.), another pioneer in the Navy's nuclear power program.
† Burris died 14 October 1955.
‡ Dr. Kenneth H. Kingdon, technical director of the Knolls Laboratory east of Schenectady, New York.
§ Dr. C. Guy Suits, General Electric vice president in charge of research; Harry A. Winne; Ralph J. Cordiner.

submarine can have, is infinite submergence at full power. Anybody that says the Navy was trying to stop the nuclear power plant is just nuts. We were trying to push it from the very, very beginning. Rickover came along Johnny-come-lately just as we managed to push it. He said the Navy was dragging its feet, which is the biggest lie in the history of the Navy.

Paul Stillwell: It's interesting that he has managed to make that a widely accepted "fact."

Admiral Mumma: Oh, yes, absolutely. I don't know any naval officers who believe Rickover deserves that place in history. I don't know how the public decides; this is what I worry about in history. That so many of these things get established, and then you can't disestablish them. It's caused by the press, the public. They accept it. They think it's true. Anybody is turned down that tells the truth, the real story. This is one reason I've never published anything about this whole story, about Rickover. I've been urged by several people to tell the whole story about Rickover and the truth of the matter. I don't know whether you've read the new Rickover book or not.[*]

Paul Stillwell: Yes, I have.

Admiral Mumma: It's fairly full of me and the author never, never interviewed me. I don't know why.

Paul Stillwell: That is curious.

Admiral Mumma: Never interviewed me because it was my friends and associates apparently that injected me into that book. I never did. My granddaughter read the book. She said, "Grandpa, I never knew that you did all that kind of stuff." There you go.

Paul Stillwell: Well, we're right at the end of this side of the tape.

---

[*] Norman Polmar and Thomas B. Allen, <u>Rickover: Controversy and Genius</u> (New York: Simon and Schuster, 1982).

Albert G. Mumma, Interview #3 (3/3/88) – Page 143

Interview Number 3 with Rear Admiral Albert G. Mumma, U.S. Navy (Retired)

Place: U.S. Naval Institute, Annapolis, Maryland

Date: Thursday, 3 March 1988

Interviewer: Paul Stillwell

Paul Stillwell: Admiral, when we were together the last time we talked about your service in the Bureau of Ships from 1946 to 1949. After that you moved out to the shipyard in San Francisco as production officer. Could you resume the narrative at that point, please?

Admiral Mumma: At that time Captain Ben Manseau was the shipyard commander.[*] He was a naval constructor, and I, of course, as you may have learned earlier, had training in both areas, both naval construction and engineering. We were primarily interested at that time in the more recent destroyers built during World War II and converting them to radar pickets. We had two of those to do at San Francisco. Boston was the lead yard for those, and our regular overhaul load consisted mostly of aircraft carriers, because the big carriers couldn't get up to any other yards except Long Beach or Bremerton. They couldn't get into Mare Island because the water's too shallow up there. That's why Hunters Point, the San Francisco Naval Shipyard, was not a permanent station for the carriers. It was an intermediate spot for them to overhaul, and particularly for any short availabilities that they might need. So we had a large number of ships of that type. Then along came the Korean affair at about that period, and so we had quite a heavy workload of putting ships back in commission, including the Iowa and several other of the major combatant types.[†] This was primarily for the purpose of getting ships into the Korean action in a short time.

---

[*] Rear Admiral Bernard E. Manseau, USN. He later served as Commander Mare Island Naval Shipyard from 19 June 1950 to 18 June 1952.
[†] The Korean War began on 25 June 1950, when six North Korean infantry division and three border constabulary brigades invaded South Korea.

Paul Stillwell: Your classmate, Captain Smedberg, was the CO of the Iowa.* Are there any specifics you remember from that job?

Admiral Mumma: Very, very well. Of course, he was an old, old friend of mine. We'd been in destroyers together years before, and he was a very, very highly esteemed classmate.

Paul Stillwell: That seems to me it would be a big industrial job reversing the effects of inactivation. How did you go about that process?

Admiral Mumma: Well, the main job was to try and ensure that there'd been no deterioration during the inactive period—such as making sure that all the machinery was in adequate operating condition, degreasing, and dehumidifying, and all that sort of thing wherever there had been any leaks in the system. This resulted in rather short turnaround in those ships from inactive to active ships. It was an experience that we all had in the navy yards, wherever we had inactive ships. Philadelphia, in particular, was a very large source of ships going back into active duty. But we on the West Coast got it a little faster because of the fact that we were so close to the Korean affair. At any rate, an item that might be of interest.

The conversion of destroyers to radar picket ships was primarily aimed at ensuring that we had adequate radar coverage for either incoming aircraft or incoming missiles. These radar pickets were equipped with a very highly capable radar—highly capable in elevation as well as distance. The ships were spread over several shipyards in order to ensure their early availability, and Boston was the lead yard for them. We were a follow yard, and so was Mare Island a follow yard. We each had two ships. We were rather proud of the fact that we did the conversion in about 60,000-some man-days. As contrasted, Mare Island was about 70,000, and Boston was up near 90,000 man-days. We even actually beat the lead yard in the completion of our ships, which we were very proud of, as a matter of fact, because of the necessity of getting those ships out early.

---

* Captain William R. Smedberg III, USN, commanded the battleship Iowa (BB-61) from her recommissioning on 25 August 1951 to 29 July 1952. The oral history of Smedberg, who retired as a vice admiral, is in the Naval Institute collection.

Paul Stillwell: Would their total be higher because they had some design work as well?

Admiral Mumma: Oh, yes. But because Boston was a little slow, we had to fill in quite a bit of the design work ourselves. So that, particularly when we finished our two ships ahead of Boston, a lot of the latest work had to be done in-house, so to speak, rather than follow the lead yard. The net result was that we were very proud of our work. San Francisco always had a gung-ho bunch of people, many of them having been trained at Mare Island originally, and Mare Island was a good yard. We had people that were anxious to do a good job and a good day's work, and they made a new reputation for the yard.

Shortly after Korea, there was a big pitch to put Long Beach and San Francisco out of commission. And that we fought pretty vigorously, because we felt here was one of the best yards in the country, talking about deactivation because we were one of the smaller yards. We never did have more than about 6,000 men, so that we didn't compare in size with some of the big yards that had 10,000-12,000 men that had more political clout.

Toward the end of that period our son was graduating from the University of Virginia, and we drove all the way back to his graduation from San Francisco on leave. During that time I stopped in to see the chief of the bureau. He told me that I was going to go to fleet maintenance officer in Hawaii on my next assignment to go on back to San Francisco and relax for at least six months. I went back to San Francisco.

A rather amusing part of the story was we had a pipe fitter master, and his brother another pipe fitter master up in Mare Island were raising cattle on the side. They asked me if I wanted to help them butcher a very nice prime steer that they'd just raised. I said I sure would, and so we split the steer three ways, which is a little hard to do since a steer only has two sides. We ended up in doing it, so I filled our deep freeze with some beautiful, beautiful prime beef. I hadn't any more than finished that job when I suddenly got orders to command the Model Basin. I had hoped someday to be able to command the Experiment Station or the Model Basin, having had duty at the Model Basin before, as a young officer. But I had no idea that I was going to be jumped into it that soon.

When I'd first gone to the Model Basin in '39 I had a nice long tour of duty there. I became very enamored of that work, and so that it was very, very pleasing to me to be ordered to the Model Basin in command.

Paul Stillwell: Before we get to that, I wonder if you could explain in more detail, please, what the production officer does and what the impact the Korean War had on your work. Did you have to beef up the yard force?

Admiral Mumma: The production officer has the responsibility of having the masters of all the trades report to him, the various shops. He also supervises a repair superintendent, who is a senior officer, usually a commander. The production officer is almost always a captain, and a man who'd had considerable experience in shipyards, or in design, or in some other aspect of it.

The planning officer is ordinarily the officer who has charge of the design work itself in the yard. The planning officer and the production officer are supposed to see that the work is done according to a good design, and done properly. So that it's a team operation reporting to the shipyard commander. Then, of course, there's the supply officer, and there are a lot of other auxiliary jobs there that support each project.

Well, an interesting sidelight is that during the time that we were there, the Shah of Iran came to the United States and was very interested in seeing how we ran shipyards, because he was planning to build himself a pretty fair-size navy, as well as bolstering all the military capabilities of Iran.[*] At that time he was a single man, and he came in a naval officer's uniform as having served in the Navy there himself. He promoted himself to considerably higher rank than he had held before, as he had already become the Shah. His wife had not produced any sons, so he divorced her. But he, shortly thereafter, got himself another wife who was able to produce the proper gender of offspring. But, of course, this was long before he got into trouble with Khomeini and the rest of that crowd. But he was a very knowledgeable young man. He spoke very good English, and he was very interested in current technology.

---

[*] Mohammad Reza Pahlavi (1919-1980) became Shah of Iran (or Persia, as it was then known) in 1941 and held office until his regime was ousted in 1979 by the Ayatollah Khomeini.

I personally showed him all through the shipyard, took him on board ships, and observed the work in progress, how we managed the work, and how we ensured that the manpower was available, and that it was completed on schedule. Because it was quite a job, of course, on an aircraft carrier's overhaul to have everything finished so that you can get the carrier out on schedule with a little time left over for shakedown and painting, and so forth, before the ship actually leaves the yard. We'd seen too many cases where ships left the yard with too many painters hanging over the side, and we were ensuring that that didn't happen at San Francisco. As a result, we got very good recognition from the fleet for the kind of work that we were able to do.

Production officer was a very interesting job for a design man, because there you have to really eat your designs and see that it works. In other words, it's a salting-down process. I suspect that was one reason they sent me there, was to salt me down from this fantasy of design and research. It had its desired effect. I became very pragmatic.

Paul Stillwell: Did you have to beef up the work force at the shipyard with all these reactivations for Korea?

Admiral Mumma: Yes, we went up to around 8,500. In addition, we had the responsibility of reactivating the Marine landing tanks and making them all into swimming Marine Corps landing vehicles, which was a real overhaul of these amphibious tanks. We set up a real production line there and had it running on three shifts just exactly like an automobile production line. The engines had to be taken out and overhauled and ready for action when they were reinstalled. Same thing on the tracks and on the propelling mechanism, etc. So that that was, again, primarily for Korea. Those were tanks that had been deactivated down in the desert in Southern California and were then shipped up to us and reactivated, put back into commission. The Marine Corps, incidentally, thought we did a good job on that, as well.

Paul Stillwell: What are your recollections of Captain Manseau as the shipyard commander?

Admiral Mumma: Ben Manseau was an old friend of mine. I had known him for many, many years. He had specialized, to some degree, in salvage work and was highly respected by everybody that knew him. Ben went from command at San Francisco to command at Mare Island at the same time while I was still there. And he was, shall we say, the father confessor at Mare Island for San Francisco Shipyard, because they always considered San Francisco as sort of an offshoot of Mare Island. He was basically responsible as the senior shipyard commander in the area for the total production work. We could ship people back and forth between the two yards as the workload required. But Mare Island was basically a small shipyard and a building yard for submarines. We were a counterpart, being the big ship part of Mare Island as such. Ben was very capable, a very good leader, and I would say, very highly esteemed by all who knew him, particularly me.

Paul Stillwell: When you increased the size of the work force, were that many trained people available, or did you have a training program?

Admiral Mumma: Well, San Francisco had a pretty good-sized work force there for us to draw from. There was the old Bethlehem yard there and, not that we proselyted those people, but because there wasn't always that much work in the various civilian areas. Oakland was nearby and had a good basic manpower pool. So we were able to get pretty capable men on fairly short notice. We gradually built up, which we then had to build down later.

Paul Stillwell: Did you have a unionized work force at all in the shipyard?

Admiral Mumma: Well, parts of the various trades were unionized, but, as you know, the trades are organized according to specialties like machinists and boilermakers. But they are not authorized to strike in government civil service and what they do is bring their union knowhow and technical expertise point of view to bear on how we handle things in the Navy. It was the master mechanic, and the foreman, and the chief quarterman, and the quarterman, and all of them bring things to the surface by getting them to the master mechanic. The master mechanic will bring it to our attention if he thinks it's a valid complaint. There really has very rarely been a standoff between any of these labor unions in shipyards and any of the management by the Navy. So it is, to a considerable degree, constructive rather than, shall we say, destructive as it is in many industrial areas.

Paul Stillwell: Well, it must have been a great pleasure and source of satisfaction to move from there to the Model Basin.

Admiral Mumma: Well, I had told you that I had this beef in my deep freeze. I had been back from Washington about three weeks, just having been assured that my next job was going to be the fleet maintenance officer in Hawaii, when I suddenly got orders to command the Model Basin. We ate beef as fast as we could, had all kinds of parties, all of them were full of beefsteak. Then we drove east and in driving east, we had a car icebox, and instead of putting ice in the icebox, we put frozen beef. As it thawed, we ate it all the way across the continent, in cookouts and all sorts of things with our sons. We had two of the sons with us. The oldest son had already graduated. So that was a very interesting period because we had to get rid of that beef. We lived pretty high on the bull for that period of time.

We had rented our house in Arlington during the time that we were on the West Coast, so we moved back into our house. I took over the Model Basin command and got really back into the saddle there, because I knew almost all the people very, very well. I really enjoyed that period at the basin. It was technically good.

In the meantime, you know, we'd done this research on the submarines during the time when I was in the bureau in machinery design, and we had let contracts for a lot of research jobs with General Electric, Westinghouse, Mine Safety Appliance, and everybody else trying to look toward the nuclear. But the big thing I wanted to do, which wasn't really very well understood by most of the submarine service, was the necessity of getting a true hydrodynamic design for the submarine, because our submarines of World War II had been basically semisubmersibles. They had a reasonable capability on the surface and a much less than desirable capability submerged. So what we were looking for was a very highly qualified submarine, for submergence that would be almost ineffective on the surface. Anybody that sees a picture of a modern submarine under way on the surface can figure that out by themselves. Because it pushes a wave the likes of which nobody ever saw in front of it. But it certainly smoothes out the performance submerged, because it acts just like a dirigible in a much more dense medium than a dirigible in the air.

Paul Stillwell: In the Model Basin, were you doing the tests on the Albacore hull design?*

Admiral Mumma: The Albacore was a research submarine developed by the Model Basin—not completely during my watch, but it came to fruition during my watch. We had started the seed some time before, and so the Albacore was the guinea pig, our research vehicle. I went up to Portsmouth, and I rode the Albacore when I had command of the Model Basin. By this time, I was a captain with adequate authority. I'd had design experience, and so forth, and, I'd been seasoned enough so that, not only in the building of ships, repair of ships, but everything, that I was accepted, even though I had some pretty dirty hands, you know, being an old engineer originally. They began to accept me on hydrodynamics, which was, I thought, my forte.

After the Albacore trials I visited SubLant and all of his squadron and division commanders. I told them what we had done at the Model Basin with a model submarine, single screw, standing on the carriage. I did it myself, maneuvered the submarine with the electric controls of the rudder and speed. I showed them that these single-screw ships, in model form, could outperform any twin-screw ship in maneuvers—evasive maneuvers, anything that you wanted to do. But the single screw did not really affect you very much from a point of view of rotational worry that would put a rolling torsion on the submarine hulls. Most people thought you had to have twin screws in order to get maneuverability. We proved that you could cut the turning diameter in half with properly

---

* The diesel submarine Albacore (AGSS-569) was commissioned in December 1953 as an experimental vessel to test the feasibility of the teardrop-shaped hull. The test was successful, and the hull shape has since become standard in U.S. nuclear-powered submarines. For details on the design of the Albacore see the Naval Institute oral history of Captain Harry Jackson, USN (Ret.).

designed rudders and a single-screw submarine. Because this submarine had much less resistance to turning than did the old semisubmersible submarine.

It also became obvious, when I was able to show them the results of the <u>Albacore</u>, that here was a submarine that verified our model scale. We'd now been able to jump from the model that had this fabulous performance. At model scale, those submarines could turn in three diameters. There was no submarine in the world that could turn in three diameters, even backing full on the inboard screw. Two reasons for that—not only the single screw, but also the hull form was stubby. It was airfoil shaped, and it didn't have the resistance to turning. So the combination of these two effects gave an ideal submarine. That's what a submarine should look like.

Paul Stillwell: That's what God meant for them to be like.

Admiral Mumma: Exactly. All you got to do is take a look at a bonita, you know, beautiful fish. Looks exactly like that. Not all fish look that way, but the bonita was a good example.

Admiral Mumma: So I went to the two squadron commanders, one of whom was my brother-in-law, Brooks Harral.* You know him, I think.

Paul Stillwell: I've heard from him, yes.

Admiral Mumma: And the other four division commanders. I got four votes out of six for the single screw. I went back to the Navy Department, and I talked to the submariners in CNO. I talked to Armand Morgan. I said, "Armand, we've got to do this. There's no way in the world that we can't improve the performance of submarines if we do this and go to single screw. I've got the votes of four out of six of those fellows in submarine operations at New London."

He said, "Oh, Al, I don't think so."

---

* Captain Brooks J. Harral, USN, who was married to Mumma's sister Sarah.

Paul Stillwell: He wasn't all that easy to convince.

Admiral Mumma: Well, it wasn't an easy sell because of the fact that there was so much history of experience with twin screw. Everybody said, "Well, what happens if you lose a screw? How do you come home?" You know, that sort of thing.

I said, "It's the easiest thing in the world to build a shaft and a propeller that you won't lose." Under those circumstances, we finally got those votes in that framework.

Paul Stillwell: What other projects do you remember from that time at the Model Basin? What else were you working on?

Admiral Mumma: Well, among other things, during World War II, we'd had terrible vibration problems with battleships. We'd run into all sorts of difficulties with those ships, and had them put on five-bladed propellers and different thrust block arrangements and all sort of things, to try and correct the vibration. So what we did was immediately start a full-scale program. We still had the same vibratory experts that we'd had when I was there before when I'd had charge of the propeller-excited vibration research. These same people were very, very anxious and ready to go into real design of vibration-free ships, and we were able to do that. We took all the skegs off of newly designed big ships like carriers. We didn't take them literally off of the ships, but we took them off any succeeding ships, aircraft carriers in particular. We never put any skegs on aircraft carriers as a result of having had the bad experience on battleships.

Paul Stillwell: What was it about the skegs that produced the problem?

Admiral Mumma: The original idea of skegs was twofold from a hydrodynamic point of view. One, it would usher a good considerable amount of the wake that was generated in a ship into the propeller, where it would be recovered because the wake fraction improves the efficiency if it is evenly distributed in the propeller. That was one thought. The second thought was, with these big, very heavy ships, like the battleships with their turrets, that if you had these skegs landing on the building blocks and on the docking blocks when you dock the ship, that it was much easier to have a fully supported after end of the ship, just as you did with the forward end, with the forward end of the keel. In other words, you didn't want a single skeg coming down amidships if you had a large number of propellers. So they decided to put the skegs inboard on the Washington and the North Carolina, on the two inboard shafts. On the South Dakota and the Massachusetts and the Indiana class, they put the skegs on the outboard shafts. In other words, they really had a tunnel in the inner section of the ship going to the inner propellers. The thought was that that would put even more wake into the propellers.

What was not visualized by that design and those designers that went for that was that the wake would not be uniform going into the propeller. It would be concentrated in areas directly associated with the skeg itself up to a certain boundary layer thickness, the boundary layer being the wake that's carried along with the ship due to the frictional movement of the ship and as contrasted to the undisturbed water outside. In other words, that water's moving to some degree with the ship. If you can reaccelerate that water uniformly, it does improve performance. But if you increase cavitation in the ship, such as momentary cavitation of each blade as it goes through that wake area, the loss of thrust due to the cavitation, causes torsional vibrations, because it has a tendency to slow the propeller's rotation. In other words, winding up the shaft and when each blade gets past the wake, then the shaft unwinds again, you see, because of the torsion in the shaft. People did not really think of big shafts as pieces of spaghetti that could be wound up, twisted, bent, so forth.

A case in point was when I went out on the Richelieu, the French battleship, which was in New York yard being repaired after the damage at Casablanca.[*] Being a French speaker and also having the propeller desk, I went up and rode the Richelieu, and examined her before we did the repair on her and then rode her afterwards. Well, when I examined her before the repair, she had taken a torpedo on one of the shafts and it had bent the struts very seriously. She had bossing and struts, and these bossings and the struts were all bent over on one side, so they couldn't operate that shaft. I took one look at it, and I said, "Well, there's no way in the world you're going to realign that. So what

---

[*] It was the Richelieu's sister battleship Jean Bart that was damaged by American gunfire at Casablanca, Morocco, in November 1942. The Richelieu was nearly complete when France fell in 1940 and escaped to Africa. After that she joined the Allies and was completed at the New York Navy Yard in 1943.

we're going to do, we're going to admit that a shaft is a piece of spaghetti, and that you're going to have to just take out the bearings, compute the angle in which we're going to have to make the bearings nonconcentric with the bushings outside and have the bearing really support the shaft in the direction in which it wants to be bent, because of the deformation of the struts and the bossings.

So we did that and instead of moving the struts and the bossings and so forth, trying to redo the whole stern of the ship, we just took the bearings out, computed the angles in which they should be rebored, and put in new bearings that were nonconcentric with the housing in which they sat. Well, of course, the French were concerned that we were doing a half-baked job on their ship. So I rode the ship on her trials. She not only was as quiet as a church, everything was fine. She made her speed; there was no problem, whatsoever; and the shaft acted like a piece of spaghetti and followed the curvature around and went into the newly aligned bearings. No problem.

Well, this is a very serious problem. More money has been spent on realigning shafting than ever should have been done because of the fact that in many cases you don't need to realign the shaft. All you have to do is make sure the bearings support the shaft in whatever line the shaft takes. And that's it. Nobody ever thought a 30-inch shaft would be a piece of spaghetti, but it is. It sags between bearings. We can prove it. All you have to do is sit down and compute it. That proves that what you really should do is to design bearings for the sag, and design bearings for any misalignment that you may have. After you do that, you're home free. Well, so that, that was the way in which we were able to ensure that the Richelieu was able to go to sea with all propellers operating.

And that's the way in which we were also able to ensure that the newly designed struts, and so forth, to replace skegs on aircraft carriers and everything else that's built since World War II, does not have any detrimental effect on either noise or alignment, or anything else. You just fit the alignment and the bearings to each other. I hope it's still continuing.

Paul Stillwell: What do you remember about the design of the Dealey class destroyer escorts that came out in the '50s.*

Admiral Mumma: Oh. Well, I don't remember too many details of that class of ship. I personally felt that the ship was under-powered. I personally felt that the characteristics had been somewhat loosely chosen and that the ship itself should have been a more capable ship than that class turned out to be. As a matter of fact, the tendency to under-power and under-equip ships of that type is pretty rampant because of the thought that they're a one-purpose ship. I had enough time in destroyers to know that destroyers and ships smaller than that can't just be one-purpose ships. They've got to be pretty flexible. They have to have adequate speed and adequate capability to do almost anything you ask them to do, under almost any circumstances. And so that, the Ship Characteristics Board and in the old days the General Board used to do some of those things that would, shall we say, try to keep a ship very simple. Single-purpose ships was a goal to be desired but rarely worked out in practice at sea. You almost always found yourselves doing things that you hadn't expected to be doing.

Paul Stillwell: What do you remember about some of the amphibious warfare ships that came along in the 1950s. There were new classes of LSTs and LSDs.†

Admiral Mumma: Well, those ships had proven themselves very, very capable ships during World War II. The Marines had a big, big desire for improvements in those ships that they had had. The British had shown the way on some of those designs during World War II. And we began to feel the pressure of the Marine Corps to do a good job on landing ships of all types, including helicopter ships, helicopter carriers, and so on. So we listened very strongly to the Marine Corps as to what they wanted. And I'm sure the Ship Characteristics Board was very, very influenced by the Marine Corps. They did a

---

* USS Dealey (DE-1006) was the lead ship of the first class of post-World War II destroyer escorts built by the U.S. Navy. She was commissioned 3 June 1954. She had a standard displacement of 1,280 tons, was 314 feet long, and 37 feet in the beam. Her design speed was 25 knots. She was armed with four 3-inch guns and Weapon A.
† LSTs—tank landing ships; LSDs—dock landing ships.

good job, generally, in the characteristics, design and building of those ships. They were pretty versatile ships, and they had a capability of doing things that could not have been done during World War II. And they still do have that capability. They're basically good ships.

Paul Stillwell: Well, for example, they designed a new class of LST during the Korean War that was certainly faster than the World War II variety.

Admiral Mumma: Well, that was one of the problems, of course. We couldn't put enough machinery in those World War II ships to let them keep up with any kind of a fleet. Even almost a cargo fleet could run away from them. So the high speed, so-called, LSTs and other ships had to be more mobile and get there quicker. You know, speed is a very important ingredient in getting to the action where you need it on time.

Paul Stillwell: How closely did you at the Model Basin interact with the design people in BuShips, people like John Niedermair?

Admiral Mumma: Every single model that we ever made, we got the bureau people out, the design people, to come out to the Model Basin, observe the tests, observe the good and the bad that we would see in any test, and attempt to design something that would improve it. Could we get a little bit better performance by doing thus and so, and thus and so, and so on? And this was a continuous operation.

Because I'd been at the Model Basin many, many times; I used to go out to the Model Basin a lot, and that's where we got going, in the late '40s, on the Albacore. Got going on many other things that later ended up in things that we did, like not designing skegs on ships anymore and things of that kind. And in basic improvements in the fundamental design, including the tremendous increase in the size of the bulbous bows.

As you know, those sonar bows became a very big thing in destroyers in later years. It was important because we were accentuating the sonar capability in ships, as well as its other performances. It was soon discovered that, gee whiz, you could afford a lot bigger bow, and some of these big tanker scows that are running around with enormous great big bows on them just show how far you can go without hurting yourself. David W. Taylor had proved that years and years before, and the British were the only ones that didn't believe him. The French believed him and put bulbous bows on their ships. But the British didn't, for some unknown reason.

Paul Stillwell: Do you remember dealings with Niedermair specifically?

Admiral Mumma: Oh, yes, I'd known John since '36, because in 1936 I came back from France after having my postgraduate over there. I underwent at least a month's debriefing at the Bureau of Construction Repair and the Bureau of Engineering as to what I had learned over there in France about ship design. Because the two bureau chiefs that had sent me over there—that was Jerry Land who was chief of Bureau of C and R, and Mike Robinson who was chief of the Bureau of Engineering. They were very good friends and had agreed that this would be a good thing to send a PG student over there to find out what was going on in France, particularly because of the Normandie's good performance.

Well, so when I came back, they asked me questions. John Niedermair and Les Kniskern was in design at that time, he having been over there with me at Genie Maritime for one year. But he became an auditor libre and didn't take the whole course. I took the full two-year course and got the diploma. Unfortunately, he got there when they were spending most of the time on engineering, and he felt that that was a waste of time to some degree.

Well, I being an engineer, as well as a potential naval constructor, wanted to get all I could get out of both years, and so I attended two years and took the whole course. I was very happy I had, because it turned out later that my training in naval architecture was even more important than my career in the engineering aspects of it. Because I thought that what I learned over there from Professor Barrillon in theory of ships was outstandingly important, not only in ship design but for my own knowledge and curiosity. So, at any rate, John Niedermair was head of preliminary design at that time in the Bureau of Construction and Repair. I thumbed through all my notes, one page after another, and when he'd see something that interested him, why, he'd ask me about it. One of the things that he was particularly interested in was, I had a sketch of the inclined armor, inside armor on the Nelson and Rodney.* He said, "What? We've been trying to find out about that for years. The British wouldn't tell us, but the French knew all about it." And here I had a sketch about it. That's when we went to the inclined armor on the new battleships.

Paul Stillwell: The North Carolina class and after that.

Admiral Mumma: Yes. And it was one of the things that we just stumbled upon really. And then, of course, the high-speed performance of the Normandie, as well as French naval vessels, including destroyers. They had had quite a number of destroyers up around 40 knots before World War II, and so this was of interest to us. Well, what the French had no magic except good hydrodynamic design of the hull in those destroyers, because they'd sacrificed firepower and radius to high-speed performance. So they didn't carry quite as much weight, and they could perform faster and do better in speed, because they didn't feel the global responsibilities that we did with two-ocean, three-ocean navies, you know, that kind of thing.

Paul Stillwell: Were there any special problems in having the inclined armor rather than the straight vertical?

Admiral Mumma: I would say that yes, to some degree. In case of a hit near the waterline, it would have reduced the waterline area. But it had a tendency to improve the capability of the armor to resist penetration, to have not only the inclination, but also because of the angle of fall of the shell, but also the fact that it would have to be detonated a little further from the armor by blisters and things of that kind, on the outboard side of the inclined armor. I suspect that that was the best compromise between the two. If you put it way inboard, why, then you lost waterline area radically; if you put it partially inboard, it was about what the British did. It was about the best thing you could do. That's what we ended up with.

---

* These were British battleships that were designed in the early 1920s, following the 1922 international naval disarmament treaty.

Paul Stillwell: Any subsequent relationships with John Niedermair after that time in the '30s

Admiral Mumma: Oh, actually, John was a very good friend almost from the start. And we had a lot of association in the Society of Naval Architects. We had a lot of association when I was at the model basin, because most of our work was done with the preliminary design section.

Paul Stillwell: Do you remember any specific things that you worked with him on when you were at the model basin?

Admiral Mumma: You see, when I was at the Model Basin in '39, '40, '41, '42, those four years, we were doing almost every known kind of design work out there. And, of course, I was tied in with propellers mostly at that time. That was my primary responsibility, propeller design. John was one of the fellows, along with Captain Saunders, (who was head of the Model Basin at that time, that felt that skegs would be good for ships). I'm not pointing fingers at people, but it was just another one of those things, just like my shaft that broke, you know. You do make some mistakes, but this was a rather big one when the skegs got on so many battleships and we had to undo some of that design work later. It was theoretically good. It was practically not so good because the theory didn't go quite far enough. The theory didn't get into the non-steady state areas as greatly, you see. Because this was the thing we used to take averages, generally, in the old days. The average was so-and-so; the average wake was so-and-so. The instantaneous wake was what was the problem.

For example, we found that behind those battleships that the thrust variation got as high as 12 to 15% of the thrust. In other words, if you had 300,000 pounds of thrust, the thrust variation could be as much as 45,000 pounds of thrust. But there was a very peculiar phenomenon that we didn't recognize originally. But we thought we might have a problem. It was the only reason we put the instrumentation on those battleships, was we thought we might have a problem. That was one of my theories that we might have a problem due to the instantaneous change of thrust. Because I had learned a lot more about that in France talking to Barrillon.

Well, what we learned later, that propeller was an exciting force at the end of a long spring. That long spring was the shaft. And you wouldn't believe it, but that long shaft was in compression like this—longitudinally. It's very hard to visualize that big shaft being in compression. But the impulses of that shaft being 15%, say, if you had a magnification factor of eight, that's 120% of the thrust. That means that the thrust collars would come off of the bearings and actually pound against them, and that's what happened the first time we went to sea in the Washington. We encountered thrust reversal.

Fortunately, we had the material on board on the shafts, and the strain gauges, and everything else to measure what we had. Thank God we put it on, and that was what we at the Model Basin did. It was a very important thing to have, be able to correlate the actual difficulty with the measurements we had. Incidentally, we put a quadrangle of strain gauges on these shafts, and we recorded them in oscillographs. The oscillographs were cathode ray oscillographs made by Du Mont, who was one of the original pioneers in the cathode ray tubes, and original pioneer in television, as well. The strain gauges were the work that had been really, originally done for aircraft wing stress.

That was done by Professor De Forest and Ruge at MIT. And we had them as consultants to us at the Model Basin on the strain gauges. You glued them onto the shaft in the direction in which you wanted to measure the stress. For example, to measure thrust or torsion, we had different arrays of strain gauges. For thrust we'd have a longitudinal strain gauge and we would make a four-sided bridge out of it, and then connect the corners to slip rings, and then take the slip ring information out to oscilloscopes and oscillographs. For torsion we had the strain gauges at 45 degrees so they could measure the torsional vibration of the shaft in actual torsion. And we'd take that to another cathode ray oscilloscope. That way we knew what had happened when we observed this tremendous vibration. The whole stern of the ship was practically jumping up and down. It was terrible.

Paul Stillwell: Were you on board the Washington for that?

Admiral Mumma: Oh, yes, I rode all those ships on all their trials. As we approached full power, we finally came to the conclusion that we couldn't stay there. We had to get down out of that range. The first thing we did, because the four-bladed propellers were behind skegs, four times a revolution, the same blade would go by, see? I mean a blade would go by there four bumps per revolution of the four blades. But because of the fact that you had a skeg above and a skeg below, it amounted to the fact that it was twice as great an impulse. In other words, if every time the shaft made a revolution, a full revolution, each blade would go by the skeg twice. It was twice as bad as it would been otherwise.

So we immediately reasoned, "Ah, we've got three-bladed screws on the outboard. If we put them on there, instead of having four times the revolution of the major impulses, we can cut it down to six times a revolution and swallow it down in the range where we can go through it without getting thrust reversal." Which we did, and we were able by just switching the propellers, putting three blades on the inboards and four blades on the outboards, we improved both shafts. But that's why we later put five blades on, on the inboards, in order to make sure that we would keep it further down in the operating range. We went through the critical but did not get into the second harmonic.

Paul Stillwell: You talked about working with Du Mont, and so forth. Did you work with private companies during that time in the '50s when you were commanding the Model Basin? Did they do tests in the basin?

Admiral Mumma: Yes, but it was not as great as the Navy work. We had some of the best brains in the country helping us. We had Du Mont, J. P. Den Hartog, Professor Den Hartog, who had been professor of mechanical engineering at Harvard, and was later professor emeritus at MIT of mechanical engineering, he is a very, very good friend of mine. And he was a vibratory expert. And we had Dr. Jesse Ormendroyd, who was also a reserve officer, who was head of mechanical engineering at Michigan. We had both of those. We had Ruge and De Forest at MIT as consultants, and we had Du Mont as a consultant. Then we had Professor Harold Edgerton at MIT, and he helped us with cavitation research in the model basin. We used him in connection with some of this other research on photographing underwater explosions and photographic work on vibrations. He's a very, very outstanding person, and his personal business firm is E.G.G. It's on the big board, the New York Stock Exchange.

Paul Stillwell: You described the process of measuring strains, and so forth, on board the actual ship. How did you take data at the Model Basin in the early '50s?

Admiral Mumma: We weren't able to produce it in the identical fashion at the Model Basin. That's why we had to work on the full-scale ships. Because we could not simulate the cavitation completely in the Model Basin itself. We could simulate cavitation in the water tunnels, but we could not simulate the combination of the two in the basin and in the tunnels, and come up with a single measurement that we could measure.

We did our analysis at the basin, and the fellow that was really an outstanding help to me was Dr. Wesley Curtis. He was originally hired by the Navy to help with the water tunnel down at the engineering experiment station. I think I told you that at the time of the consolidation of the two bureaus, that it was decided that instead of having a water tunnel down at the experiment station and a water tunnel out at the Model Basin, we'd combine the two and have them both out at the Model Basin. So I had the job of moving that water tunnel from down here at Annapolis out to the Model Basin, and we put the two water tunnels adjacent, head-to-head to each other so to speak. So that we could, compare the scale ratio effects. One was a 24-inch water tunnel and the other was a 12-inch water tunnel, 12-inch being a very old one and the 24 was newer design. But correlating those two, we were then able to get better data. But the biggest thing we ever got out of that big water tunnel was Dr. Wesley Curtis. He was the fellow that invented the Hammond organ, the electronic organ (Hammond bought Curtis's patents). And so you can see what kind of brain power we had there. He was the fellow that helped us to, not only do this hookup with Du Mont, and so on, but also Ruge and De Forest.

Prior to that the only way of measuring strain was on string oscillographs, and they had inertia and they didn't respond to this fast phenomenon accurately. And so we had to have the immediate response of a cathode ray tube. That's why we got a hold of Du Mont.

Paul Stillwell: Well, I'd think you'd still want to make tests and measurements in the Model Basin. You can't do everything, but that's the purpose of having the basin, isn't it?

Admiral Mumma: Oh, well, the Model Basin gives you average performance, basic average performance of everything, including ship resistance. That's all fine because that is not dependent upon minuscule laboratory problems. Once you make certain corrective factors for scale ratio, then the Model Basin is valid within a very few percent. But it's not valid for very, very fast phenomena, because you cannot reproduce the very fast phenomena in model scale. It just doesn't happen. For example, you're working in water which is of nearly the same basic density as the sea water. You can't scale the water to the model scale. For instance, where you have a 30-ratio scale model. And you are scaling that 30-ratio scale from model to full scale by, in some cases, not only the linear factor but also the square sometimes the cube of 30. You see, you get up around 9,000—27,000 actually—as the scale differential with the cube of the scale ratio. Well, what that amounts to really is that many of these very, very rapid things are not measurable in model scale.

Paul Stillwell: Well, how do you go about comparing two different hull forms, let's say? How do you run the tests on those?

Admiral Mumma: Well, you have very sensitive dynamometers that measure the resistance of towing at various speeds. Then you change the attitude of the model; you change its characteristics in some fashion or other; you add appendages to it; or you put bilge keels on it, or you put a bulbous bow on it. Then you test it again.

The tracks on that model basin towing carriage are set for the curvature of the earth within, about now, I suspect it's within two or three thousandths of an inch. Now, in the length of that basin the curvature of the earth amounts to about an inch and a half. So that the water takes the curvature of the earth when it is still, and, therefore, the tracks have to take the curvature of the earth in order to avoid any uphill or downhill effects. In other words, we're attempting, within a measurement of a few thousandths of an inch, to measure things that we can multiply by sometimes a cube or certainly the square, of a scale ratio and get reasonable accuracy. That's the reason why that Model Basin is on bedrock out there. And you have to reset those tracks every few years. It was done the second time while I was there. I suppose it may have been done a third and a fourth time by now.

Paul Stillwell: How is the resetting done?

Admiral Mumma: You close the basin off entirely so there's no chance of wind circulation, no change of air, no nothing. Everything is as still as you can get it, and the water actually looks like you can walk on it. It looks like glass. Then it takes the curvature of the earth completely. Then you have a very, very sensitive electronic device that you put on the top of the rail, and you can measure the instant that it touches the water within a thousandth of an inch. Then you know whether it's up or down, from the rail. You do that throughout the whole length. When you get through with it, you then know where your humps and hollows are, due to either the movement of the concrete, in aging, or movement of the rock foundation underneath, or whatever the reason is, and then you know how much you have to correct it by. You do that by putting shims under the rail and then clamping the rail down onto the shims so that the rail is following exactly the curvature of the earth within a thousandth or two.

Paul Stillwell: How long is that basin?

Admiral Mumma: Well, the original basin was 500 feet long. It's now, I think, about 1,500 feet long, so that you can imagine that in 1,500 feet you've got a lot of curvature to worry about.

Paul Stillwell: Did you have computer programs to deal with these data that you gathered, say, from your dynamometers and so forth?

Admiral Mumma: Yes, yes. As a matter of fact, originally it was done by analog computers. Well, before that, it was hand computing way back in the old days in the old model basin in the navy yard. But then, later, it's done now with electronic computers that are very, very accurate and very quick.

Paul Stillwell: How sophisticated were the computers when you were there in the early '50s?

Admiral Mumma: Well, as you may know, we put in the very first Navy computer, the big computer out there, the Univac number four. The Bureau of Census got number one; the Air Force got number two; the Army got number three; and we got number four.

After we had this computer installed, that thing had thousands of vacuum tubes in it. Wes Curtis was my expert, and I was in command of the model basin at the time we put that in in 1950 for a maintenance contract. After completion Univac came around. By this time General Leslie Groves was with Univac.[*] He was a good friend of mine because I'd been in his business during the war, during the time we were doing the nuclear business. So Les was very interested in what we were doing at the Model Basin, as well as with the computers going in. I was approached by Les to get a contract for maintenance of the computer from Univac. And I checked with Wes Curtis, who was my expert in computers.

I said, "Wes, should we take a contract?"

He said, "I think we can maintain that computer."

I said, "Wes, I'll give you one year, and if at the end of the year, we don't have as good a maintenance uptime record as the rest of those other three computers, we're going to have to have a contract with them." At the end of the year we had over 96% uptime in that doggone computer. None of the others had even made 90%, and we were doing our own maintenance. That's when Les Groves came back and said, "How do you do it?"

Paul Stillwell: Understandably.

---

[*] Leslie R. Groves, head of the Manhattan Project that developed the atomic bomb in World War II, retired from the Army as a lieutenant general in 1948. Subsequently he served as vice president of the Remington division of the Sperry Rand Corporation.

Admiral Mumma: Gee, that was something, Wes Curtis's ability with electronics.

Paul Stillwell: Was Grace Hopper involved in that operation?*

Admiral Mumma: Not directly, no. We were doing this primarily for the nuclear, and mostly the Bettis Field nuclear people were involved in utilizing that computer for that purpose.†

We also did one other thing on that computer which was a little bit unique, first time it was ever done. The armed services—Army, Navy, Air Force—were all interested in a survivors' benefit program for dependents. So a task force was set up using the actuaries from all of the five big insurance companies—Prudential, Metropolitan, Travelers, and others—and these five people got together and came up with an actuarial program as to what should be fed into the computer to be able to come up with the cost each individual would have, the life expectancy of the individuals, including dependents. Not only your wife, but also your children if they were dependent upon you.

This was an actuarial job that had never been done by hand and would have taken a long, long time to do it by hand, so they wanted to do it on the computer. It was the first job, and they programmed the computer. None of the insurance companies had a computer like this then. This was the first actuarial job ever done on a big computer, and it took us about a month to grind that out. That was the beginning of the retired servicemen's protection program, and then later the survivors' benefit program, both of which were done on that computer. Since then, of course, they've got much more powerful computers.

Paul Stillwell: With these outsiders coming in using your computer, how much use did you get of it?

---

* Dr. Grace M. Hopper was one of the Navy's computer pioneers. She was commissioned as a Naval Reserve officer during World War II; she finally retired from the Navy as a rear admiral in 1986 at the ate of 80. For details she Rosario M. Rausa, "Grace Murray Hopper," Naval History, Fall 1992, pages 58-60.
† Bettis is the name of a nuclear laboratory in West Mifflin, Pennsylvania, not far from Pittsburgh.

Admiral Mumma: Oh, we used it for everything that was of that stature and required that volume, because it had a capacity to do things. For example, in the old days to do the computation for a floodability capability of a ship with its compartmentation, you had to take each compartment; you had to calculate its volume; you had to flood it; and when you flooded it, it would flood more or less depending on how much it sank. So it was an indeterminate figure. By ordinary means, you had to do it by approximation, successive approximation. By hand that would take, oh, six months or so, to do a floodability curve for a ship. We built what was called a "BuSAC," a Bureau of Ships analog computer out there, and that was built by Wes Curtis. That analog computer we could use to cut that period down to something like two weeks. Then on the big computer you could run that through that machine in a few days. So that you could shorten the time required to do jobs, and you could do things that you couldn't do otherwise, like compute a nuclear reactor.

Paul Stillwell: How much were the computers used for the hull forms in the nuclear submarine program?

Admiral Mumma: Every, every program. Everyone, every reactor went through that computer, or a successor.

Paul Stillwell: What's the capability of that Model Basin to simulate rough water?

Admiral Mumma: We always wanted what we called a maneuvering basin. The Model Basin always used to have wave-makers at one end to be able to send waves down the length of the basin. Then you could see the performance of the ship in rough water as it hit certain size waves, depending upon how fast and the amplitude. Not only the amount of motion, but the speed of the motion, you would generate the response of the model to waves going right down the basin, and at various ship speeds. Then in the maneuvering basin, you have the ability to do this in 360 degrees, not just longitudinally. That maneuvering basin out there was one of our dreams that we didn't have when I had command, but now is in existence.

You can predict the performance of ships in waves very, very accurately. The only one that you have difficulty producing is the very strange, phenomenal wave that sometimes occurs in the ocean, where you get almost a vertical wall of 40 or 50 feet. That happens occasionally, due to a very peculiar combination of circumstances in the atmosphere, the wave formation, the winds, and everything else. That can happen, and it has happened. Some ships have encountered waves of that type. When you hit one like that, it can bash in the whole side of the ship, or the whole superstructure of the ship. It's a phenomenon you don't want to go through more than once—if ever.

Paul Stillwell: What were some of the specific issues you remember dealing with as the commanding officer? What kind of problems came to your level?

Admiral Mumma: Well, the main problems had to do with performance of the Model Basin in predicting accurately. We always sent teams out on trials to check exactly what the ships did do, and then we compared always on the basis of full scale versus model scale, to correct our model scale predictions, and predict more accurately for the future. That was a continuing effort. But you also were doing theoretical work all the time as to what it should be and how could you do it better. You put some of that on the computer and try it and see if you can predict accurately by a computer or not. So that in the long run, it was just a long, long search. That's where the word research comes from, because if you don't get it the first time; you search again, research it every time. It's a continuous program.

We also encouraged a tremendous amount of self-improvement by our staff, by additional courses at the University of Maryland, George Washington, and anywhere else that they could get expertise to improve. Many of them got doctorates. We were able to be sure that we had the best brains in these areas. We kept importing people. We actually imported a couple of Germans right after the war, and they stayed for quite a while. The one that we had went back to Germany and became head of their model basin.

We always had associations with all the major model basins in the world. It was called a towing tank conference, and the Davidson Laboratory up there in the Stevens

Institute of Technology was one. Ken Davidson was an old friend of ours. He used to come down to the Model Basin and compare his stuff with our stuff. He's the fellow that did almost all the work on the yacht hulls that was so phenomenal in our winning the America's Cup races for years, and years, and years. He's gone, and so is Olin Stephens, who was the designer of those boats that won all the time.* And now we've lost the cup.

Paul Stillwell: Well, we have it back again.†

Admiral Mumma: Yes, but, I tell you, it's getting tougher. We don't have the monopoly we always had.

Paul Stillwell: What incentives could you offer these very intelligent people to get them to come and work there?

Admiral Mumma: Recognition, I think, more than anything else, and making a real contribution to national defense. We had really top-quality people, and they were respected worldwide. See, it wasn't just the Navy; it was the United States, because we did work for everybody, civilians and everybody. So the word was always, "Go to the Model Basin and see what they say about it." There has been no towing tank like it in the world—I believe I may be a little biased here—that has quite a reputation as the David Taylor model basin has, because David W. Taylor started it that way. When he began the Model Basin over here, of course, he tore a page out of the British book. He'd seen a model basin in Britain. He came and he sold it to Congress in 1898 when he was a lieutenant. He got the Model Basin built down at the old navy yard.

Well, he surrounded himself with the most excellent people he could get his hands on always. For example, the head of aeronautics at MIT, Dr. Jerry Hunsaker, was a lieutenant there at the model basin; Mr. Curtiss, of the later Curtiss-Wright fame was down there. He was a co-designer with the Navy on the NC flying boats that crossed the

---

* Olin J. Stephens II was a noted naval architect and yacht designer.
† In 1983 the Australian yacht Australia II won the series of races, breaking the U.S. monopoly on the America's Cup that had existed since its inception in 1851. In 1987 Dennis Conner's boat Stars and Stripes, recaptured the cup for the United States.

Atlantic with Albert Read, you know in 1919. And Dr. W.F. Durand, who was the founder of the NACA, used to spend quite a lot of time down there at the old model basin. In other words, it was surrounded with the brainiest people in the world at that time. They also built the first real research wind tunnel down there. It was a 10-foot section, 10-foot-square section, up to 100 miles an hour. That was the only research wind tunnel in the world when it was built in 1913. So you can see that it's been on a basis of excellence that it has survived and continued to be world-renowned and world-recognized. Most of that credit goes to David W. Taylor. That's why when a few years ago, they changed the name of it by edict in the Navy Department to the Navy Research and Development Center, I wrote Secretary Middendorf and said, "It's a travesty that you have removed the name of David W. Taylor from that establishment."[*] It is once again the David W. Taylor Research and Development Center. Thank God, he changed his mind and put the David W. Taylor back on it.

Paul Stillwell: Was one of your responsibilities to ensure funding for this operation as the commander?

Admiral Mumma: Oh, yes, you had a budgeting problem always. But another thing we instituted in the fairly early days out there—we improved it when I was there by a considerable margin—was unprogrammed funding for research of the scientific community out there on the things they hoped might work. In other words, we had a reasonably sized fund—I think it started out at $500,000—on which we could afford to do some of the things that nobody saw anything immediate need for, but was a research program that really should be done so that we'd move forward the scientific capability of the basin. That has been very, very effective in not only retaining good people, but attracting them, that they have some of this uninhibited research that they can do.

Paul Stillwell: Was the funding adequate in your judgment?

---

[*] J. William Middendorft served as Secretary of the Navy from 20 June 1974 to 20 January 1977.

Admiral Mumma: Well, I would put that into the program and then get it funded. And we were successful with that. I don't know what's going on there now, unfortunately. I hope it's still being done and with an adequate uninhibited research fund. It never was an enormous fund, because it costs quite a bit of money to fund that Model Basin. It never was a tremendous percentage of the total cost, but it was an enticement.

Paul Stillwell: You talked about the ability to predict actual results from the use of the models. Do you have any overall reliability figure, say, on towing tank results?

Admiral Mumma: Well, in one or two instances we came a cropper; for some reason, we had difficulty. I think one of those was an auxiliary ship, a tender, where we missed it by something like 20%, and we always accused the torsion meters of being wrong. We were never able to prove it, because we never got a chance to do the trials over again. The ship went to sea. Ordinarily you can predict within 1% or 2%, and at least within 3% or 4%. Then we run trials and we continuously check back, and continuously modify, make sure that if we've got correction factors in, we know how much they are and why they are either increasing or decreasing. Because you must admit that water is water wherever you are, even though salt water is a little different from fresh water, that you can't scale the water; you can scale the model.

In air you have the same problem. You can't scale the air; you can scale the model. So that aeronautical research has the same basic problem. But we frequently do corresponding research between air and water. We do a model in air, and then we do a model in water, and then we check that kind of a scale differential. You frequently can find that you've got a scale factor that is quite similar between the air model and the true airplane, and the ship model and the true ship because of the scale factor being so enormous. But if you run them both, you run a ship in air and you run a ship in water—you can't run the major ship in air, the big ship in air, but you can check between water and air and get a scale factor due to the density of the medium in which you are running.

You can do it with dirigibles; you can do it with aircraft; you can, you know, tow aircraft submerged in water. And you can tow aircraft in air, and so forth. So you can really get a feel for scale factor. You see, the difference in the density between air and water is about a thousand. That's a big scale factor, and you can zero in on some of those variations by testing in air and testing in water. That's one of the things we did with the submarine hull form. We checked against dirigibles, we checked against air and water and dirigibles, and we checked submarines against air and water. We were able to get a reasonable factor for that form in both air and water and the way in which they differed.

Paul Stillwell: Were you involved in the test to the Albacore itself, that is, the real submarine?

Admiral Mumma: At that time I was in the bureau when we were actually doing the specific model tests on the Albacore. The Albacore was in existence when I got back from my tour in San Francisco. She had been built in the meantime. But I went to sea on her and rode her on trials up there in Portsmouth several times, and then came back and began working over the people trying to get approval of that design while still at the basin. But, of course, I didn't get anywhere until I became chief of the bureau.

Paul Stillwell: Helps to have that kind of clout.

Admiral Mumma: It helps.

Paul Stillwell: I don't have any more specific questions about the Model Basin. Are there any other things that you want to mention?

Admiral Mumma: Well, except that those two tours of duty were a very, very important part of my life, because it was so strange that my PG in France led to that. It was also strange, as a matter of fact, that the personnel people in the Navy Department thought that that was a good idea, not only for me to go there, but also a good idea for me to go to the Model Basin.

What you wonder about is how in the world such things happen to you that are such a major part of your life. I was so profoundly affected by those three events, really, the postgraduate, and the two tours at the Model Basin, and then, of course, being salted down and practicalized in the shipyards. And then being chief of the bureau, where I had the basic responsibility for the whole damn works, and maintenance of the fleet. The blending of the research, the design, the maintenance, and the responsibility of that was kind of overwhelming, that anybody had the brilliance to try to train a guy along those lines, because I couldn't have done it on my own. Somebody had to do it, and I lay it at people like Jerry Land and my good, good friend Mike Robinson, and Ned Cochrane, and Earle Mills, and Paul Lee.

Those men had such a tremendous influence on what eventually happened to me that you wonder how in the world anybody could be such a good mentor for an individual, that they would see that I would get to the ultimate in my profession in the Navy. Of course, I had daydreams of someday being that kind of a guy, but you never know. My happiness in contributing over the years has been entirely one of attempting to give credit to the people who, somehow, had sufficient faith to put me in the jobs that I was able to do something about.

I tried to do the same thing when I was in the Navy Department. When I was in design, for example, in the late '40s I used to read all the theses of the postgraduate students. I was trying to see where I thought they would be good and where they could make a contribution, maybe that they didn't even recognize themselves.

Paul Stillwell: Did you spot some potential comers by this process?

Admiral Mumma: Well, actually, among those were Lou Roddis, Jim Dunford in the nuclear area. Both of them were brilliant young officers, stood one and two in their class, and were the real people that made Rickover look good. They did the work that eventually should have been recognized by either one of them being the head of the nuclear power program. But Rickover got rid of them both. Now Roddis is the consultant on whom the government is leaning in connection with the Hanford Pile, which is the only one which could possibly have an accident like Chernobyl.* They're

---

* Hanford, Washington, has long been the site of a U.S. nuclear facility. On 24 April 1986 the power station at Chernobyl, near Kiev in the Soviet Union, suffered an explosion and fire in the graphite core of one of its four nuclear reactors. The accident released radioactivity that spread over the Soviet Union, Europe, and Scandinavia.

leaning on Roddis to do that.* But you can see that he could easily have replaced Rickover to great advantage, very early. But Rickover hoodwinked the Congress and the public into believing he was indispensable.

Paul Stillwell: Well, do you want to move on then and discuss your tour in command at Mare Island, please?

Admiral Mumma: My Model Basin experience was excellent, and I had no idea what I might have as a next tour of duty. While still in command of the Model Basin in the late summer of '54 I made flag rank. I was fairly sure I would be transferred, and so I was happy to be assigned to be the shipyard commander at Mare Island.

We had had plans for some time to put Mare Island in the business of building nuclear submarines. All that had either been done at Electric Boat or some of the work done at Portsmouth, and there were no other major contractors at that time. So we felt that it was vital that we have another nuclear shipyard for submarines. Fortunately, the bureau at the time agreed that it was a very, very good thing to do.

The chief of the bureau at that time, Admiral Durward Leggett, decided to put Mare Island into nuclear program, and so when I went out there we had a double job to do.† One was to put Mare Island in the program, and number two, to celebrate the 100th anniversary of Mare Island, in 1954; that was 100 years since Mare Island was founded in 1854. Then you realize that the miners came in '49, and that was only five years later.‡ Farragut was the one who founded the Mare Island Navy Yard.§ He was at that time a captain. It was started as a shipyard there opposite Vallejo on the island and, of course, has been a shallow-water shipyard ever since. It wasn't an ideal spot for a big shipyard, but it was an ideal spot for a small-ship shipyard.

---

* Roddis died 15 September 1991, subsequent to this interview.
† Rear Admiral Wilson D. Leggett, Jr., USN, served as Chief of the Bureau of Ships from 1953 to 1955.
‡ On 24 January 1848 James W. Marshall discovered gold at Sutter's Mill in the Sacramento River Valley. News spread quickly, and people began rushing to California from all over the world. Because of the large influx of prospectors in 1849, those who took part in the gold rush came to be known as "forty-niners."
§ Commander David G. Farragut, USN, served as the first commandant of the Mare Island Navy Yard; his tenure was from 16 September 1854 to 16 July 1858. He gained fame in the Civil War and in July 1862 became the U.S. Navy's first admiral.

Paul Stillwell: What made it ideal for that?

Admiral Mumma: Well, at first, the island itself had a lot of waterfront. It had a rather unique contour there of the island, and it was well protected, back in from the ocean, and from the sea, and any other effects that could affect the quality of the work. And good reasonable climate the year round, even nicer than San Francisco, because San Francisco had those afternoon fogs and Mare Island did not. So I particularly enjoyed that.

Now, we had the Secretary of the Navy come out there for, not only the centennial, but also, putting the shipyard into the nuclear program.* We had the Chief of Naval Operations come out—that was Mick Carney at that time—and Charlie Thomas was the Secretary of the Navy.† We had a very distinguished group of people from Washington came out for this celebration. We had Ed Sullivan as the master of ceremonies at this event.‡ It was a big event. We took over one of the warehouses and converted it into a dining room. They had boxcars full of food that had been prepared in the navy yard kitchen. People moved in the boxcars directly down alongside of the warehouse and then served directly to this enormous crowd. It made quite a splash and was very interesting.

For this nuclear role we immediately set about the job of training people, sending them away for additional training to various locations, at the laboratories at Bettis and other places for nuclear training. Some went for long-term training, some for two years, some for one year, some for six months. Depending upon the degree of involvement of that particular job with the nuclear portion of it, it would be longer or shorter depending upon how theoretical they had to get in connection with it. Usually the one- to two-year program was for the top theoretical people that had to be responsible for the design.

Well, that was quite successful, and it got going very, very well. By the time I was detached, which was in late February, we had that going quite well. In the meantime, a lot of my old associates at the San Francisco yard—some of them had

---

* The celebration began on 16 September 1954 and ran for four days. A book was produced to describe the shipyard's long history: Arnold S. Lott, <u>A Long Line of Ships : Mare Island's Century of Naval Activity in California</u> (Annapolis: United States Naval Institute, 1954).
† Admiral Robert B. Carney, USN, served as Chief of Naval Operations from 17 August 1953 to 17 August 1955. Charles S. Thomas served as Secretary of the Navy from 3 May 1954 to 1 April 1957.
‡ Ed Sullivan was then the host of a popular variety show televised each Sunday evening by CBS.

moved up to Mare Island and a lot of the old friends at Mare Island—I'd been at Mare Island several times on ships, cruisers as well as destroyers. So I knew the operation quite well. We had a good operation. It was an excellent yard. They went into the nuclear program readily and easily and did a good job. I think the Scamp was probably the first real high-speed nuclear boat they ever built.[*] It was a Skipjack class, of which I was very proud, and I was proud of Mare Island for producing it. At any rate, of course, the time was awfully short.

Paul Stillwell: How closely did Admiral Rickover monitor your developments on that line?

Admiral Mumma: Very little. Very little. He had learned that it wasn't too profitable to interfere very much when I was in various other jobs that he and I had been associated with. Like when I had the propeller desk when we did the work on the North Carolina and the Washington, he had the electrical section. He would come snooping around and try to see what we were doing, and I'd explain it to him. He got the idea that we kind of knew what we were doing, and so he never challenged me as such. He always bored around behind the scenes and did things.

Well, take for example, the fellow that sponsored him more than anybody else was Senator Scoop Jackson.[†] But Scoop Jackson was a good friend of mine. I had him out to the house for hamburger cookouts and things like that. But Scoop would talk freely to me about Rick. He said, "As a matter of fact, Rickover recommended you for the chief of the bureau job. So that we didn't have any quarrel up here on the Hill about it either." Because Rickover had said that I was the best qualified to get the job.

Paul Stillwell: How did you come to know Jackson?

---

[*] USS Scamp (SSN-588), a Skipjack-class nuclear submarine, was commissioned 5 June 1961. She was 252 feet long, 32 feet in the beam, and displaced 3,075 tons surfaced and 3,500 submerged. . She had a top speed on the surface around 20 knots and a speed in excess of 30 knots submerged. She was armed with six 21-inch torpedo tubes.
[†] Henry M. Jackson, a Democrat from the state of Washington, served in the House of Representatives from 1941 to 1953 and then in the Senate from 1953 until his death in 1983. He was chairman of the Senate Armed Services Committee and a strong proponent of nuclear-powered warships. The ballistic missile submarine Henry M. Jackson (SSBN-730) is named in his honor.

Admiral Mumma: Primarily through the nuclear contacts. I knew he had later sponsored Rickover, and then he got in the job at the Senate of the Atomic Power Subcommittee. I didn't have any direct connection with him when I was in connection with the Manhattan District because we were remote from the Hill in connection with that. But it made sort of a camaraderie out of it when we did meet and get together. He was much more understanding for someone that knew something about the program before we got into the power program. There were only four of us that had been involved in that Alsos program. None of them were still around, unfortunately, at the time that we finally got into the power program ourselves. They'd gone back to civilian life, and so forth, like Den Hartog, and Roop had retired, and Packy Schade had gone to the University of California.

Paul Stillwell: What were the steps that you had to go through to get to the Mare Island yard ready to begin building nuclear submarines?

Admiral Mumma: Primarily training of personnel. That's the real crux of getting anything done is to get the personnel trained so that they know what they're doing. You have to send them to other places to not only observe what's going on, but you also have to send them to get the educational background and the theoretical moxie to go with it. We had to coerce Electric Boat into loosening up some of their know-how, because they were not happy about getting more competition.

Frank Pace was at Electric Boat at that time, had been former Secretary of the Army.[*] I had a little tussle with Frank Pace on more than one occasion about putting additional yards in submarine work, because he liked his monopoly in the civilian part of the business. He kind of objected to Portsmouth, and he objected to Mare Island, but we had him where the hair was short. Because, after all, he couldn't refuse to do our work for us, and he also needed the competition to keep his prices within limitations. We knew what the prices should be because of our navy yard costs of work. Even though the navy

---

[*] Frank Pace, Jr., served as Secretary of the Army from 12 April 1950 to 20 January 1953. He was with General Dynamics from 1953 to 1953, serving successively as executive vice president and chief executive officer.

yards weren't supposed to be as efficient as private yards, on some occasions, like at San Francisco, we had beaten private yards with similar work. So you don't always lose by doing a government job. Like overhauls, we had had many competitive overhauls between private yards and navy yards, and we were usually able to prove that the navy yards could do it more economically, because they had deeper background.

Paul Stillwell: What means did you use for coercing him?

Admiral Mumma: Well, Frank Pace actually went to the Secretary of the Navy and complained about me. Then, of course, I would just muster my own forces and be able to show them it was absolutely essential that we expand the base to build submarines. We could not have just one or two yards building submarines. Because anybody could see that the Russians, with a 300-submarine fleet, were going to have to build submarines at a rate of something like six to a dozen a year. And they did, and have. So that was obvious. I mean, it didn't take too much to convince the Secretary and the Secretary of Defense that we had to put additional yards in. That's the reason I put Pascagoula and originally New York Ship into submarine work, so that they could potentially possibly grow into the nuclear, but Wolfson in New York Ship was a disaster, and that didn't turn out well.[*]

Paul Stillwell: Were you involved in any surface ship programs out there at Mare Island during your tenure?

Admiral Mumma: None that were of a vital importance at that time. We were pretty well tied up. We had overhauls and things like that, but we didn't have a serious building program for surface ships. We had no major problems. I enjoyed the duty out there. I had nice quarters, but it didn't last long. You know, in my whole naval career, I only had

---

[*] Ingalls Shipbuilding at Pascagoula, Mississippi, was a private yard. It has since been taken over by Litton Industries. The New York Shipbuilding Corporation, Camden, New Jersey, was founded in 1899. It was liquidated in the autumn of 1967 by its parent firm, Merritt-Chapman & Scott, which was headed by Louis Wolfson. For a summary of the events surrounding the closing of the yard, see The New York Times, 3 September 1967, Section 5, page 13.

quarters at two places—two and a half years at the San Francisco Naval Shipyard, and the six months at Mare Island. No other places did I have quarters.

Paul Stillwell: That was the time when the Essex-class carriers were getting the hurricane bows enclosed, but that wouldn't affect you since you were a small-ship yard.

Admiral Mumma: No, no.

Paul Stillwell: Had you done the model work on those bows at the Model Basin?

Admiral Mumma: Actually, I don't think we were able to scale the hurricane effects as such. I know that some work was done in the wind tunnels with ship models, but I don't know the degree to which you could scale the structural effects. For example, the Saratoga and the Lexington had closed bows and then some of the other ships, particularly the jeep carriers, had these decks on top of tankers, and so on, and they had problems. And then some of the other later ships had problems. But generally speaking, I think that kind of a problem is empirical. I don't know that you can model it.

Paul Stillwell: How much, as a shipyard commander, did you get involved with the local community around Vallejo?

Admiral Mumma: Well, I'd known a pretty fair percentage of that community in earlier years, and so they were very nice, and very congenial group. And the Vallejo people, including the state senators, the congressional people, and the others, were all very vitally interested in the shipyard. They kept California in line, to be kind to the shipyard, because they certainly didn't want to lose it. The town of Vallejo was pretty heavily dependent upon that shipyard.

Paul Stillwell: Anything else about that particular job that stands out in your mind?

Admiral Mumma: Well, among other things, one of the aircraft carriers that went out of there was commanded by Red Raborn.* So I got to know Red quite well during that time. Of course, as you know, he was an aviator and knew hardly anything about submarines. But I had quite a respect for Red's general attitude relative to the job of getting that aircraft carrier in shape. He was a good man. I liked Red, and I knew he was capable and would be a good skipper, as, of course, I also had the same feeling about my classmate Bill Smedberg. We got along, in other words. We had no confrontation of any nature, and we had good amicable relations with everybody. We were considered a good, can-do navy yard, which I was proud of.

Paul Stillwell: What else do you want to say about that tour of duty?

Admiral Mumma: No, except that I was very surprised to be yanked out of there as young as I was and, shall we say, junior as I was. I'd been there only five or six months—nice and beautifully ensconced in the second set of quarters in my whole life in the Navy with mess boys, etc. I had just gotten myself well settled in at Mare Island as shipyard commander and was actively engaged in getting that shipyard into the nuclear submarine building program with educational programs for all sorts of levels of management

Then I got a telephone call from Jimmy Holloway, who was the chief of the Bureau of Naval Personnel.† He said, "Al, you have been chosen to be chief of the Bureau of Ships. You've got to come back to Washington right away. You're going to have hearings right away for confirmation." He went on to explain that there was a bit of a youth movement going on, that they wanted to get younger people into some of the more important jobs in the Navy Department. They had already selected a classmate of mine to be Chief of the Bureau of Aeronautics, and they were talking about Mick Carney

---

* Captain William F. Raborn, Jr., USN, commanded the USS Bennington (CVA-20) in 1954-55. Later he was director of the Special Projects Office, which developed the Polaris submarine-launched ballistic missile system. He held the post from 1955 to 1962, being promoted to vice admiral in 1960. His Polaris oral history is in the Naval Institute collection.
† Vice Admiral James L. Holloway, Jr., USN, served as Chief of the Bureau of Naval Personnel from 2 February 1953 to 31 January 1958. His oral history is in the Columbia University collection.

eventually being relieved by a younger CNO, and it turned out to be Arleigh Burke later on.*

Well, the shock was pretty severe, because at that time I was number 16 on a list of 17 flag officers in the ED group. I wasn't sure that all my seniors were exactly happy about that. I knew them all very well. Strangely enough, one of the happiest of all was Armand Morgan. He was the most loyal and supportive guy I have ever known in the way in which he rallied around.

I was told that I had to get back to Washington post haste; I didn't have time to drive. I had driven overland to get out there, and I was planning to do any travel by automobile, because I had a very fine rocket engine Oldsmobile at that time, which was a brand-new car. I was told that I would have to fly, so we flew back to Washington.

Paul Stillwell: What was the reason for the urgency—to get back for congressional hearings?

Admiral Mumma: Apparently. As a matter of fact, my predecessor was going to retire on the 31st of March, and so I had to get back as soon as possible so that I could be confirmed by that time, and let him retire. That was Durward Leggett, who was chief of bureau at that time, had a commitment. He had made all his plans to retire, but then a group of senators delayed my confirmation while they examined all aspects of my background, including my extreme youth—at the age of 48. Today, I don't know that that's extremely youthful.

Paul Stillwell: Were you the youngest officer to hold that job up to that point?

Admiral Mumma: Well, that was one of the things they thought, but I was able to do enough research to catch them off base and find that before World War I, there'd been a

---

* Admiral Robert B. Carney, USN, Naval Academy class of 1916, was CNO from 1953 to 1955; he was relieved by Admiral Arleigh A. Burke, USN, class of 1923, who served as CNO from 1955 to 1961. Rear Admiral James S. Russell, USN, a classmate of Mumma, served as Chief of the Bureau of Aeronautics from 4 March 1955 to 15 July 1957. The oral history Russell, who retired as a four-star admiral, is in the Naval Institute collection.

chief of the Bureau of Engineering, Admiral H. I. Cone, who was made an admiral and took that important job at the age of 38.[*] That stopped them very quickly on the age program. They hadn't done that research themselves. So it ended up that they dropped the age program immediately.

Durward Leggett did retire before I was confirmed, so they made Ben Manseau, who was deputy chief, acting chief in the interim. Ben Manseau was the class of 1922, a very fine officer. I had served with him when he was shipyard commander at San Francisco and I was production officer. We had a very fine relationship. He was an excellent person, and we were very fond of each other. He was a regular naval constructor. He had no specific research expertise, but a damn good man. So when I reported to Washington as prospective chief of bureau, I had to be confirmed by the Senate. I found Ben Manseau enthusiastic about my coming as chief of bureau. I said, "Ben, if I get confirmed all right, would you stay on as deputy?"

He said, "I certainly would."

I said, "That's one of the greatest things I've ever heard, because, as you know, I have a great admiration for you."

He said, "It's mutual, Al." So that started that way.

So then I had to go down on the Hill for confirmation hearings. Styles Bridges was the senior head of the Armed Services Committee on the Republican side, because at that time we had a Democratic Senate, as well as a Democratic House.[†] Styles Bridges called me up on an advance hearing. The advance hearing was because I had had duty in San Francisco, not only as shipyard commander at Mare Island but also at San Francisco as production officer. All the East Coast shipbuilders figured I was a West Coaster, afraid I'd put an awful lot of shipbuilding on the West Coast.

So they had a meeting up in a little dinky room up above the old Supreme Court chambers on the Senate side of the Capitol. In this little room there were about six senators and me. Styles Bridges ran the show, and Margaret Chase Smith was there and, oh, gosh, everybody from the Northeast.[‡] I can't remember half of them now. They

---

[*] Rear Admiral Hutch I. Cone, USN, served as chief of the Bureau of Steam Engineering from 21 May 1909 to 18 May 1913. He was born 26 April 1871.
[†] Senator Styles Bridges (Republican-New Hampshire).
[‡] Senator Margaret Chase Smith (Republican-Maine).

interrogated me about what was my feeling about East Coast, West Coast. I said, "Well, the West Coast has some facilities, but they don't have the experience or the expertise at the moment. They have facilities that could build ships of certain sizes, but so far nothing of large size has been built on the West Coast. The biggest thing is jeep carriers during the war. The naval shipyards should not be used for that kind of big ship building. San Francisco, itself, would probably be the best for building an aircraft carrier, but I would not recommend it."

Well, this was music to their ears. They had delayed for a month getting me called before the Senate Armed Services committee. In other words, they let me cook. Finally about the first of April, I was called for a hearing down in the Senate. Lyndon Johnson was then the senior member of the whole armed services group, and he presided.[*]

Of course, there was a whole gang of senators. On the starboard side were the Republicans; on the port side over here were the Democrats. Stu Symington was over there on the left, and here was Styles Bridges and Margaret Chase Smith on the right.[†] Margaret Chase Smith, in particular, asked me where was I born. I told her I was an Army junior. I happened to be born in Ohio. And was I a West Coaster or an East Coaster. I said, "Well, I've had duty on both coasts. It doesn't really make that much difference to me."

She said, "Well, what about shipbuilding capacity?"

I said, "Well, the East Coast has far more shipbuilding capacity. There's no question about that." Well, that seemed to satisfy them.

The Secretary, Charles Thomas, was supposed to take me down and hold my hand during this hearing, but he couldn't go. He got called to the House for a hearing, so he had Albie Pratt, a brand-new assistant secretary in personnel go with me.[‡] It was his first hearing on the Hill of any kind. So he was not exactly much help at holding my hand. I'd been down there for hearings when I was in command of the Model Basin.

---

[*] Senator Lyndon B. Johnson (Democrat-Texas), later Vice President, 1961-63, and President, 1963-69.
[†] W. Stuart Symington was first Secretary of the Air Force, holding office from 18 September 1947 to 24 April 1950. Later he served as a U.S. Senator from Missouri.
[‡] Albert Pratt served as Assistant Secretary of the Navy (Personnel and Reserve Forces) from 1954 to 1957.

So they started asking me questions about this and that and the other, most of which I could answer pretty well. Scoop Jackson was there, and Scoop, having been the proponent for Rickover for all the years, knew me and he knew all my past history, and so forth. And Scoop was quite enthusiastic. But Stu Symington I also knew from hearings previously about aircraft, because at the Model Basin I had the wind tunnels as well as the ship tank, you see. So I worked for BuAer as well as BuShips.* Stu Symington had experienced a little bit of this interplay between air and sea, and he started asking a question: "Admiral, what would be your view of aircraft carriers versus aircraft?" In other words, Navy versus Air Force.

Paul Stillwell: And he was a former Secretary of the Air Force.

Admiral Mumma: Oh, yes. It was a loaded question, no question about it. I started to answer, and this young, brand-new assistant secretary jumped in.† Pratt got a little confused in his answer and he said, "Well, Admiral Symington . . ."

Then Lyndon Johnson, who was in the chair, interrupted and said, "Mr. Secretary, it doesn't appear that we have too many objections to the confirmation of Admiral Mumma as Chief of Bureau of Ships. But we object very strongly to your promoting Senator Symington to admiral." So that stopped that question cold. Everybody went into roars of laughter. That was the end of the hearing. That was the most amused I ever saw Lyndon Johnson.

Anyhow, at the end of this whole thing, I then was appointed on the first of May, and Ben Manseau became the deputy again. He was the most loyal deputy you could ever have. He did everything exactly in accordance with our agreed wishes. He never once pulled seniority on me or indicated in any way that it was obnoxious to him to serve in that capacity. Unfortunately, he wasn't there too long before he had a heart attack. I was called from the lunchroom to go down and see him in the dispensary in the Navy Department, in the old Navy temporary building on Constitution Avenue.

---

* BuAer—Bureau of Aeronautics; BuShips—Bureau of Ships.
† Pratt was 42 years old at the time.

They said that his heart had actually fibrillated for a long period of time, and that his ability to survive was questionable. Well, he was moved out to Bethesda, and I went out and saw the senior doctors there.[*] The senior doctors violated a little bit of protocol by taking me to see his X-rays, and pointed out the whole one half of his heart, the heart muscle had just evaporated into a thin membrane. They said, "Now, don't you ever talk to him about coming back to active duty. It would kill him instantly, the stress of active duty. So you are going to be kind and considerate to him, but don't give him any thought about coming back to active duty, because we've told him it's impossible."

He lived on for about six to eight months and passed on.[†] His wife and his children are still very close friends of ours. So that's when I had to go after another deputy, and I got Mike Honsinger to come in as my deputy.[‡]

Paul Stillwell: Well, we're getting pretty close to the end of the tape. Maybe we ought to save the chief of bureau for the next session.

Admiral Mumma: Okay.

Paul Stillwell: Thank you.

---

[*] The National Naval Medical Center at Bethesda, Maryland.
[†] Manseau retired on 1 August 1957 with a retirement promotion to vice admiral on the basis of his combat awards; he died on 4 November 1957.
[‡] Rear Admiral Leroy V. Honsinger, USN, became Deputy Chief of the Bureau of Ships in April 1957. He served in that billet until 1959.

Interview Number 4 with Rear Admiral Albert G. Mumma, U.S. Navy (Retired)

Place: Naval Historical Center, Washington, D.C.

Date: Friday, 4 March 1988

Interviewer: Paul Stillwell

Paul Stillwell: Admiral, when you were considering whether to remain as a line officer or switch to engineering duty, you hoped to rise to the top of your profession. Everybody has ideas about what he would do if he became boss. Did you have an agenda when you came in as chief of the Bureau of Ships?

Admiral Mumma: Well, of course, immediately the first one that came to my mind was the real high-speed nuclear submarine, because I was very unhappy from my experience at the Model Basin with the tests of the Nautilus and the Skate class.* I knew that they were completely inefficient from a propulsion point of view, and that there was great improvement possible if we could adopt the Albacore-type hull. That was my number-one priority. My second priority was the fact that we were in the process of modernizing the Navy. We had to have a real up-to-date cruiser-destroyer force with missile capability. We were embarked on that program, but we, also, had to further the nuclear power program, not only for submarines, but also for surface ships. So these were things that needed doing very, very urgently.

The first thing I did after I was sworn in was to go see Mick Carney, the Secretary of the Navy, who was then Charlie Thomas, and I also talked to Tom Gates.† I said, "Now look, we've got six Skate-class submarines scheduled. The Skate class is really not

---

* USS Nautilus (SSN-571), the Navy's first nuclear-powered submarine, was commissioned 30 September 1954. She was 324 feet long, 28 feet in the beam, and displaced 3,533 tons. She had a top speed on the surface of 22 knots and undisclosed higher speed submerged. She was armed with six 21-inch torpedo tubes. Because she did not have to come to the surface frequently to recharge batteries, the Nautilus revolutionized submarine warfare. USS Skate (SSN-578), commissioned 23 December 1957, was the first ship of her class. She was 268 feet long, 25 feet in the beam, and displaced 2,570 tons surfaced and 2,861 submerged. She had a top speed on the surface of 15.5 knots and a speed in excess of 20 knots submerged. She was armed with eight 21-inch torpedo tubes. The hull forms of both were along essentially traditional lines, compared with the Albacore-type hull that Admiral Mumma discussed in interview number three.
† Thomas S. Gates, Jr., served as Under Secretary of the Navy from 7 October 1953 to 1 April 1957.

a very great submarine. It's a twin-screw, small power, really not a very effective submarine. I've done a lot of research over the years on single-screw submarines. The single-screw submarine has tremendous advantages hydrodynamically and speed-wise over a twin-screw submarine." To give you an order of magnitude, the Nautilus and the Skate-class submarines had a maximum propulsive efficiency of about 68%. The design of a good single-screw submarine with adequate control of wake, and so forth, and entrance into the propeller, and so on, to smooth out the flow, can be as high as 94 to 96% propulsive efficiency.

Paul Stillwell: What do you mean by efficiency in that sense?

Admiral Mumma: Propulsive efficiency means the effective thrust forward of the submarine relative to the horsepower developed by the machinery. In other words, if a 15,000-horsepower submarine has propulsive efficiency of, say, 95, it's got about 14,000 horsepower actually pushing it through the water at a much greater speed than if it had 60-some. All right. The Nautilus was twin screw; the Seawolf was twin screw, and the six Skates were supposed to be twin screw. In other words, we were embarked on the twin-screw Navy in submarines. I felt it was absolutely wrong. In other words, I had not been able, in my absence from the model basin and from the bureau, to convince anyone to do it without my being present.

If you had that efficiency, coupled with the maneuverability improvement, you had a real submarine. It didn't make any difference about the performance on the surface. You could stay submerged forever in a nuclear submarine. What difference did it make what its surface capabilities and characteristics were? You had a true submarine, which is the thing that Professor Abelson visualized originally when he tried to sell the nuclear submarine during World War II.[*]

When I went to Mick Carney and the Secretary, and so on, I said, "Now, what I want to do is to go down to the Congress and tell them that we're taking the last ship of the Skate class that is authorized already by the Congress and redesign it to a new

---

[*] Dr. Philip Abelson was a physicist with the Carnegie Institute. For details on the development of nuclear submarines, see Richard G. Hewlett and Francis Duncan, Nuclear Navy, 1946-1962 (Chicago: University of Chicago Press, 1974).

single-screw class of submarines completely different from the Skates, and which will be a submarine that you can all be real proud of." I told them the stories that I told you before about the submarine people being ready and willing to accept something of this kind, and what it would do from a point of view of maneuverability, what it would do from a point of view of speed for the same horsepower, and so on, without specifying any actual speeds. The submerged speed practically doubled. Part of that was due to the hull form, and the other part was due to propulsive efficiency itself of the single screw.

Those gentlemen agreed with this. Then I went down and got authority from the Congress to redesign that last submarine into what became the Skipjack, the 585.* We went up on the Hill later with a full explanation of the changes, and the Skipjack was actually built in a relatively short time. We started that submarine design from scratch in the middle of '55, and that ship went to sea in '58, in three years, a completely new, completely different submarine, completely different machinery. The only thing that was the same was the reactor, like the Nautilus, a 15,000-horsepower reactor. We didn't allow him to change anything; we kept him out of the design, so it could be done fast, and efficiently.

Paul Stillwell: By him, you mean Rickover?

Admiral Mumma: Yes, Rickover. He had nothing to do with the design; he had nothing to do with the machinery except the reactor. We designed and built that submarine in the Bureau of Ships.

I went to sea in the Skipjack, and she performed exactly as I expected her to perform. She was the most maneuverable submarine we have ever had. She also dove more abruptly; she surfaced more quickly and effectively; and in every respect was a true underwater boat. Of course, she made waves on the surface, but what the heck. She wasn't built to run on the surface; she was built to run submerged.

---

* USS Skipjack (SSN-585), commissioned 15 April 1959, was the first ship of her class. She was 252 feet long, 32 feet in the beam, and displaced 3,075 tons surfaced and 3,500 submerged. She had a top speed on the surface around 20 knots and a speed in excess of 30 knots submerged. She was armed with six 21-inch torpedo tubes.

Well, Wilfred J. McNeil was the assistant secretary of defense for financial management.* I knew Bill McNeil and had dealings with him and so forth, supporting the BuShips budget. I took him with us on about the second trip of the ship to sea. I said, "Bill, I want you to see something. I want you to see something that's different." And so we went to sea in the Skipjack. Of course, I got Armand Morgan and all the rest of the submariners in this act, too, at various times, to make sure that they really knew what we had, and what it would do, and how it could handle, and so forth.

As a matter of fact while on board, I had Bill McNeil fly the ship submerged. And you really fly that sub, just like an airplane. It's the most beautiful and nice handling thing you've ever seen in your life. It responds just like a flash. Well, he was very enthusiastic about it on the trip. He came back. He called me the next day. He said, "Al, you know, we've been examining the budget this year. I think we've got room for one more of those submarines." We already had in for several of them, and he said, "We can slide in one more."

Paul Stillwell: That was a good time for test then.

Admiral Mumma: Yes. In addition to the submarines, a very high priority was given to the nuclear aircraft carrier, the Enterprise.† In attempting to justify such a ship on the basis of operational capability before the Ship Characteristics Board in the Navy Department, and before the powers-that-be in the Navy Department, we had to prove that such a ship would be an operationally superior ship to a conventionally powered ship. That wasn't too difficult to do when you got right down to doing it. So we made several studies of what a nuclear-powered ship could do compared to a conventionally powered ship. The big, big difference, of course, was in the fuel in the ship itself. Because if you could count on a nuclear-powered ship not having to be fueled for any purpose except for

---

* Wilfred J. McNeil served as Assistant Secretary of Defense and DoD Comptroller from 1949 to 1959.
† USS Enterprise (CVAN-65) was commissioned 25 November 1961 as the world's first nuclear-powered aircraft carrier. She is the only ship of her class. She has since been modernized and refueled a number of times and remains in the active fleet. She has a standard displacement of 61,000 tons, full-load displacement of 81,500 tons, is 1,052 feet long, 130 feet in the beam, and has an extreme width of 250 feet. Her top speed is 33 knots. She can accommodate approximately 90 aircraft.

the aircraft, you could immediately see a tremendous saving in time and in weight and space on the ship.

Now, some of that weight was lost in the shielding of the nuclear reactors. But it was regained completely in the additional fuel capacity that the aircraft could have on board for their sorties. When you put all those factors together, you could prove that a nuclear-powered ship, on a wide assortment of expected sorties, would be able to almost double the performance of, shall we say, aircraft over the target of a conventionally powered ship with her escorts, because the conventionally powered ship would have to fuel her escorts as well as herself, during extended operations, so that immediately slowed down the capability of any ship to do extended operations.

Paul Stillwell: Well, that would work only if you had nuclear-powered escorts as well.

Admiral Mumma: That gave us the incentive for going nuclear powered escorts, which we did with the Bainbridge.* We started that program and the first nuclear-powered ship was done for the same reason as the aircraft carrier, the Enterprise, and then the nuclear-powered cruiser as well.† So that we had those three programs going simultaneously, practically, but with the highest priority on the Enterprise.

Paul Stillwell: Was Admiral Rickover a staunch ally in this?

Admiral Mumma: To some degree. I think he considered himself being stretched, but I had confidence in those young fellows that he had, Roddis and Dunford, and so forth. I knew that these fellows could do the job, and if we used very similar reactors in those ships, only different in size, we would be able to get the design going and proceed with a

---

* USS Bainbridge (DLGN-25), a nuclear-powered frigate, was the only ship of her class. She was commissioned 6 October 1962. She had a standard displacement of 7,600 tons, was 565 feet long, 58 feet in the beam, and had a maximum draft of 29 feet. Her top speed was 30-plus knots. She was armed with two twin launchers for Terrier missiles, two 3-inch guns, ASROC, and six torpedo tubes. She was redesignated a cruiser, CGN-25, on 1 July 1975 and eventually decommissioned 13 September 1996.

† USS Long Beach (CGN-9), the Navy's first nuclear-powered cruiser, was the only ship of her class. She was commissioned 9 September 1961. She had a standard displacement of 15,540 tons, was 721 feet long, 73 feet in the beam, and had a maximum draft of 31 feet. Her top speed was 30-plus knots. She was armed with two twin launchers for Terrier missiles, one Talos missile launcher, and ASROC. She was eventually decommissioned 3 May 1995.

very logical program. The big sell was how to sell the second one after we had sold the first nuclear. Well, I don't think we succeeded in selling the second one immediately until after the first one got into operation. When the Enterprise got in operation, why, it was duck soup for many other reasons. For instance, instead of having big stacks with all the necessity for smoke exit, and so forth, to get away from the airplanes, all we had was a nice big island with a big antenna on it for radar coverage.

Paul Stillwell: Well, in fact, it was another ten years before the next nuclear carrier was sold.*

Admiral Mumma: Yes. It was unfortunate that people couldn't be more far-seeing. Now, Arleigh Burke was willing to go on that, but he wasn't willing to go for the second until later. As a matter of fact, at that time, also, Tom Gates had moved up to Secretary of Defense.† The new Secretary of the Navy was Bill Franke.‡ He was very much less enthusiastic, because he was not a technical man; he was an accountant. Like all bean counters, he wasn't far-seeing in the technical areas as to what the tremendous importance was. So he didn't push for it.

As a matter of fact, that was one of the terrible, terrible problems I had with Franke when he was Under Secretary.§ He had the idea that because one or two chiefs of bureau had not been postgraduate and had not been EDs, engineering duty officers, over the history of aeronautics as well as ships, that, therefore, there was no necessity for the engineering duty designation. He constituted a board called the Franke Board to study the necessity for the ED designation. That was the biggest fight I had, because I knew if our engineering postgraduate program and naval construction program, which had been started back in the 1870s, was ever terminated by the lack of necessity for technical excellence in the technical fields, that our Navy would go kaput.

---

* The next two aircraft carriers, America (CVA-66) and John F. Kennedy (CVA-67), were conventionally powered. It wasn't until the approval in the late 1960s of the Nimitz (CVN-68) class that the Navy went exclusively to nuclear-powered carriers from then on.
† Thomas S. Gates, Jr., served as Secretary of the Navy from 1 April 1957 to 7 June 1959.
‡ William B. Franke served as Secretary of the Navy from 8 June 1959 to 20 January 1961.
§ Franke served as Under Secretary of the Navy from 17 April 1957 to 7 June 1959.

So I fought like a tiger, and I got all EDs together, talked to them, gave them a fight talk, that they should contact every person they knew as to the importance of the technical know-how that they had to their job and how necessary it was for the excellence of the Navy. The naval constructors had fought like tigers to prevent being made EDs instead of naval constructors. That stems from the olden days in the U.K. where the Royal Corps of Naval Constructors was a royal corps, and they were untouchable. They were not even civil servants as such. They put on uniforms when they went to sea, and they were civil employees when they were ashore. But that's another story which I'll tell later. That has to do with my friend Mountbatten when he was the head of the Royal Navy.

Paul Stillwell: How much contact did you have in your job with Admiral Carney when you first took over?

Admiral Mumma: He was extremely supportive and a very intelligent fellow. I told you earlier that I had had experience with Mick Carney when he was in command of a cruiser in Philadelphia about to go to war. Well, I think my reputation with Mick Carney was made from that day.

Paul Stillwell: Well, since you had this good relationship with Admiral Carney, what issues do you remember working with him on when you were chief of the bureau?

Admiral Mumma: Well, he was very receptive to almost all the ideas we had, particularly on the first one, had to do with the change of the last Skate-class ship to our fancy new submarine. He went along with that after I managed to convince some of the submarine people, and, shall we say, played down the importance of twin-screw over single-screw from a safety at sea point of view, because we over-designed those shafts to make sure they didn't drop off. And we had the Mitscher problem very strongly in mind at that time.[*]

---

[*] Admiral Mumma discussed the problem of propellers on the Mitscher (DL-2) class in interview number two.

Paul Stillwell: Did you have contact also with Secretary Thomas?

Admiral Mumma: Yes, Charlie Thomas was not a technical man. He had been a haberdasher, more or less, like our President Truman. But he was an intelligent man, and you could talk to him about programs, and you could get his backing. But he never, shall we say, had very much original thought to bring to bear, particularly to design or operational matters. He was a good administrator, as such. He had Tom Gates as an Under Secretary who was very good. I had a very good relationship with Tom Gates.

Paul Stillwell: Gates was one to get in and study the technical aspects.

Admiral Mumma: Yes, he, he could understand it when you told him what was going on. And he was a very open-minded individual. He had quite a bit of influence on Charlie Thomas.

This didn't have anything to do with the Bureau of Ships, but it was a very interesting little anecdote, anyhow, about Charlie Thomas. We had Engine Charlie at one time; that was Charlie Wilson, who was Secretary of Defense.[*] Electric Charlie was Charlie Wilson of General Electric. But later we had another Charlie; that was Charlie Thomas. But he got a special name through a very special system. I think it was the General Accounting Office in Congress found some large amount of mobilization reserve materials. They were searching to find overruns and any excesses of any kind, and they found 175,000 tins of canned hamburgers. This was in the Marine Corps mobilization reserve. Of course, they made a big flap about the waste of government money, and so forth, and how this was going on.

So they called Charlie Thomas down, and he was accompanied by General Randy Pate, who was Commandant of the Marine Corps.[†] At this hearing, of course, the Congress brought up this terrible waste of material in the mobilization reserve,

---

[*] Charles E. Wilson served as Secretary of Defense from 28 January 1953 to 8 October 1957. He was nicknamed "Engine Charlie" because he had previously been chairman of the board of General Motors.
[†] General Randolph M. Pate, USMC, served as Commandant of the Marine Corps from 1 January 1956 to 31 December 1959.

tremendous expense—175,000 large cans of hamburgers. When Charlie Thomas was asked about this, he was kind of nervous and didn't have a very good position, because they brought this up sort of out of the blue, you know, without any preparation during other hearings. They were always looking for an opportunity to do that, to catch you off guard. But General Pate was there, as were a lot of the rest of us, in connection with the hearing on readiness, and so on. When this was brought up and Charlie Thomas wasn't able to supply a good answer immediately, General Pate said, "Gentlemen, there are 175,000 men in the Marine Corps. Those Marines can eat up those 175,000 cans of hamburgers in one day." That immediately ceased all further discussion of that matter by anybody in the Congress. Thereafter, behind his back, we all called Charlie Thomas, "Hamburger Charlie."

Paul Stillwell: How frequently did you yourself testify on the Hill on Navy programs?

Admiral Mumma: During the budget process, it could be as much as once a week and go on for long periods of time, sometimes into the evenings.

I remember one time in the House, I was the last bureau chief to come up, and it was rather late in the afternoon, but we went on and on and on. Finally the chairman got to the point where he said, "And now we hear from Admiral Mumma, who is the mayor of Olongapo."[*]

I said, "Mr. Chairman, I appreciate you bestowing that title upon me, but I have very little to do with the city of Olongapo in the Philippines, except to say that it is adjacent to our naval base there, and it is rather important that we improve the conditions in that city." And so we had an appropriation there to improve sewage and drainage of that area because there used to be in the native portion of that town, there were pigs underneath the buildings, and the buildings were on stilts. I'd lived in the Philippines years before, so I knew about this, with my dad who was regular Army in the Philippines. So this condition had to be improved because on a heavy rainstorm all that sewage from Olongapo was running right on down into our base. So we had to do something about

---

[*] Olongapo, the town right outside the U.S. naval base at Subic Bay in the Philippines, was noted for its raunchiness

seeing that it got properly taken care of. The Navy furnished some money to provide that sewage disposal plant for really the base, as well as part of Olongapo.

Paul Stillwell: Why were you given that title by the congressman?

Admiral Mumma: Well, because I was justifying this item for the city of Olongapo.

Paul Stillwell: That sounds to me more like Civil Engineer Corps than Bureau of Ships.

Admiral Mumma: Well, it was under our program, and, of course, the civil engineers would actually have to do it. But the Navy base was under me, just like any other navy yard, as was also the bases in Japan at Sasebo and Yokosuka. So I had those three bases in addition to my 11 naval shipyards.

Paul Stillwell: Did you have a murder board set up with your staff to get you ready for this testimony, asking you the hard questions, potential ones?

Admiral Mumma: We had a quarter of 8:00 meeting every morning on every item that we thought might come up during the day. It was only for 45 minutes. All the assistant chiefs were to attend, the deputy chief would attend. It functioned to bring up important items that were going to come up during the day or had happened overnight at sea—some ship had had a casualty of some sort. So we were on top of everything immediately, every day. These fellows also knew that I could be called at any time in the night if we had a real emergency of any major importance. But the budget process was one in which you prepared quite assiduously for potential questions, and make sure that you were not only economically correct, but technically correct in your answers. Because if you made a mistake in replying to one of these fellows and he happened to have some accurate knowledge to the contrary, you were in deep trouble. So occasionally you'd have to answer and say, "I haven't looked into that. I'll have to report back to you." I frequently had to use that.

Albert G. Mumma, Interview #4 (3/4/88) – Page 196

The minute you try to gun-deck an answer, you get trapped.* It's very dangerous, so we always tried to adhere to honesty is the best policy.

Paul Stillwell: How well did you do in selling your budgets year after year when you were in that job?

Admiral Mumma: Actually, we didn't have much of a problem because we had some outstanding people like Stennis in the Senate.† Senator Hayden in the Senate was the Appropriations chairman.‡ In the House, Carl Vinson was head of the Armed Services Committee, a most understanding gentleman.§ Even though all those guys were Democrats, they were really interested in doing a job for the government. They were non-partisan when it came to Navy programs in particular, particularly Carl Vinson.

Paul Stillwell: What are your recollections of him specifically?

Admiral Mumma: Well, he was always throwing quips into the hearings of various kinds. And the various navy yards were always vying with each other via their congressional constituents, like Norfolk against Charleston, and so on. We had Margaret Chase Smith against New Hampshire because she said that the navy yard was not the Portsmouth Naval Shipyard; it was the Kittery Naval Shipyard.** Therefore, it was in Maine and there was no necessity of calling it the Portsmouth Navy Yard. So that there were always these little rivalries going on between the various congressmen and senators on their constituencies, trying to get real plus points with their constituents. But in the long run, they all seemed to be basically interested in an improvement in the Navy at that time. It was a very fortunate period. We had just had Korea, and it brought upon us in a

---

* "Gun-deck" is Navy slang for faking or falsifying something, such as a report or a record.
† Senator John C. Stennis (Democrat-Mississippi). The aircraft carrier John C. Stennis (CVN-74) is named in his honor.
‡ Senator Carl T. Hayden (Democrat-Arizona).
§ Carl Vinson of Georgia entered the House of Representatives in 1913 and was appointed to the Naval Affairs Committee in 1917. He became the ranking Democrat in 1923 and chairman in 1931. When the Armed Services committee was formed in 1947 Vinson became chairman and held that position, except for two short periods when Republicans held the House, until his retirement from Congress in 1965.
** Though officially known at the time as Portsmouth (New Hampshire) Naval Shipyard, it is actually on an island at the mouth of the Piscataqua River and officially part of Kittery, Maine.

big way our global responsibilities. So that we had very little, shall we say, partisan heckling as such.

Paul Stillwell: Well, Vinson had been around so long, he was sort of above that anyway.

Admiral Mumma: Well, not only was he above it, but there was one between Portsmouth, Virginia, and Charleston. Vinson was there, and during my discussion about those two yards, and what ships were going to those yards, there was a question as to whether or not the Norfolk Naval Shipyard in Portsmouth wasn't getting a little too much work; probably some of it should go to Charleston. The question was asked by a congressman from Charleston, "Why shouldn't we lean a little bit more toward Charleston, put some of this work in Charleston?"

Paul Stillwell: Was this Mendel Rivers?

Admiral Mumma: Yes, Mendel Rivers.[*] I knew Mendel pretty well. He was almost immediately silenced by Carl Vinson. He said, "Mr. Rivers, that is an improper question for the off-year." Off-year meaning not an election year.
  So there were some of these things that made it a lot of fun.

Paul Stillwell: How did you go about deciding where to assign the work?

Admiral Mumma: Well, that was a tough job. One of the first principles was that we had to distribute the work so not only could the ships be done on time economically, and not too many ships in one yard, so that when we had a technical improvement of some magnitude, we could put it into the next design and spread it over the same group of yards with the same distribution, so to speak, and get the follow-on ships improved.
  This was one of the biggest mistakes that Mr. McNamara ever made.[†] McNamara

---

[*] L. Mendel Rivers (Democrat, South Carolina) served in the U.S. House of Representatives from 1940 until his death in 1970. He was chairman of the House Armed Services Committee from 1965 until his death and was credited with getting a great deal of military money funneled into his district in Charleston.
[†] Robert S. McNamara served as Secretary of Defense from 21 January 1961 to 29 February 1968.

had the brilliant idea, being a bean counter, that the more ships you put into any single yard, the more efficient it would be—just like building automobiles on an assembly line—which was the most erroneous thought I think he ever had. Second, he was not cognizant of the fact, and apparently could not be convinced of the fact, because this happened after my time—if I had been there, boy, I would have sat on his doorstep until he understood this problem. Because if you have 30 ships in a shipyard like he had at Pascagoula, all the same design, by the time you finish three or four ships, you want to make some changes, improvements because the state of the art continues, and your research is progressing and providing new stuff all the time.[*] The minute you invade those contracts to make corrections of that magnitude, you immediately open Pandora's box for tremendous overruns.

Paul Stillwell: And you destroy the very cost savings you were trying to achieve.

Admiral Mumma: He destroyed, he completely inundated it. There were no cost savings on those ships. There were tremendous overruns. And the same thing happened in airplanes. I'm not an aviation expert, but due to the background of the model basin and aviation, and wind tunnels, and so forth, I can assure you that he made another horrendous mistake and that was the TFX.[†] Here he had the brilliant idea that the Navy had fighters, and our Air Force had fighters. They should be the same fighter. Why? Why not? Why have Grumman build the Navy fighters and have somebody else build the Air Force's? So I think he got Chance Vought to build the TFX.[‡] Billions of dollars in the program. When you imagine an Air Force jet fighter taking off from an 8,500-foot runway and flying a long distance to its target, escorting bombers or whatever, and then has to return to its base a long distance, you see that fuel is of basic importance, more important almost than any military load.

---

[*] This was known as total package procurement, which refers to buying an entire class of ships from one defense contractor. The most notable case involved the <u>Spruance</u> (DD-963)-class destroyers, 30 of which were built by the Litton/Ingalls yard in Pascagoula, Mississippi. The first was commissioned in 1975.

[†] The F-111—originally designated TFX—was a controversial fighter plane that Secretary of Defense Robert McNamara tried to develop in the 1960s for use by both the Air Force and the Navy. The Navy was eventually able to thwart its role as a carrier plane and developed the F-14 instead.

[‡] General Dynamics won the contract to build the F-111.

But in a Navy fighter, to take off and land on aircraft carriers, where they are jerked into the air by a catapult in a short space of a couple hundred feet, and they land on a deck, angled deck to make it longer on an aircraft carrier and yanked out of the air at 200 knots and slammed on to the deck four or five G's, you can see that not only the landing gear, the oleo gear, but the fuselage itself is a completely different piece of machinery. You are not required to have the tremendous fuel capacity because your aircraft carrier's taking you a lot closer to your target than the jet fighter of the Air Force is. So you don't have to have the fuel capacity, but you have to have structure in that fuselage so that tailhook won't pull the plane in half and so the jet can be yanked into the air by a catapult.

Now, you can see that that airplane was completely worthless to the Navy. It was only of some partial use to the Air Force. It wasn't even a good airplane for them because of the compromises in it. So there was billions of dollars down the drain. That is what has made our whole program seem so completely uncontrolled by the military when actually, during the Eisenhower Administration, we not only controlled it but we controlled it very accurately.

If I had a 2% or 3% overrun in a program, I was embarrassed going to the Congress for it. When I was called down to the Department of Defense some years after I retired and was asked about Navy overruns by the Department of Defense, I found that the questions they were asking primarily accounted for overruns by Rickover. He had a much freer hand after my departure, because he could boondoggle some of those other fellows that had very little nuclear experience. But he couldn't boondoggle me, and so I kept him under control. I had ahold of that moneybag at the top, and so we were able to really see that everything stayed in proper relationship. That nuclear-powered aircraft carrier did not cost double an ordinary aircraft carrier. It was only about a 20% increase over a normal aircraft carrier, and it was more than double the effectiveness.* So that that was an easy sell, not only in the Congress, but elsewhere in the Navy Department. Whereas, many of those overruns that came from Rickover, he would get a low price to

---

* <u>Enterprise</u> (CVAN-65), commissioned in 1961, cost $444 million. The next carrier, the conventionally powered <u>America</u> (CVA-66) was commissioned in 1965 and cost approximately $300 million.

start, and then he would force them to take changes. He would look good at the beginning, and then the overruns would show up later.

Paul Stillwell: How did you correct that when he was still working for you? Did you force him to have realistic initial estimates?

Admiral Mumma: We had people sufficiently expert in that field that we could second-guess him. Rickover had no free hand in the Bureau of Ships when I was around, because he knew I knew what he was doing. He also knew that he couldn't get by with it if he was pulling any fast ones. If he had turned that job over to Roddis or Dunford, boy, the Navy would have been so much better off. But he chased every one of them out of the program.

Paul Stillwell: You talked about this political pressure from congressmen trying to get projects assigned to the various naval shipyards. What about the competition between private versus naval shipyards for business?

Admiral Mumma: Well, we had the Vinson-Trammell Act to fall back on there.[*] The Vinson-Trammell Act said that a certain portion of the work should be in naval shipyards, and I had the authority of the President backing me up on that. I had to go see Ike at least three or four times a year in connection with the shipbuilding program as required by the Vinson-Trammell Act.[†] We usually went with the Secretary of the Navy and the Secretary of Defense going along to ensure that we had the highest level of backing for that kind of a program, any program changes.

For example, I think one of the biggest ones was when 11 western states attempted to get an aircraft carrier built on the West Coast. Their senators and congressmen all ganged up together to try and force the Navy Department to build an

---

[*] Representative Carl Vinson (Democrat-Georgia) and Senator Park Trammel (Democrat-Florida) were chairmen of the respective naval affairs committees. The Vinson-Trammel Act, 27 March 1934, called for the construction of 102 new ships in the Depression era and specified that a certain amount of the shipbuilding work be done in navy yards.
[†] Dwight D. "Ike" Eisenhower served as President of the United States from 20 January 1953 to 20 January 1961.

aircraft carrier on the West Coast. Well, Bremerton had always been a Navy yard for aircraft carriers; Long Beach had a big dock and they'd done repair work, but Hunters Point was a possible building yard for it without interfering with repair work on the fleet. So they sort of seized on Hunters Point as being a proper spot to do this. I personally did not think that was a wise move.

First place, because in a small yard of that size, the tremendous hiring hump that you would have to do for building a big job like an aircraft carrier, and then the falloff of those same jobs as each hump went through each of the shops would be very catastrophic for a small yard because of its inability to absorb these men on other jobs in the meantime, because that 6,000-man-day job would require every man you have to build an aircraft carrier; whereas, the bigger yards would always be able to put men on repair work in the interim. So that was finally defeated. If you'd like an anecdote along that line, I might tell you right now.

Paul Stillwell: Sure.

Admiral Mumma: Well, the President had to approve any changes in shipyard assignments as well as the original program each year. So this 11-state gang was trying to force the President to do this. So we were called over. I went and I prepared a study as to how it would affect the yard—these workload snakes going, humping through each of the shops—and had it on a chart. Took it and showed it to Secretary Thomas. He and I went up and showed it to the Secretary of Defense Charlie Wilson, and then we made an appointment to try to go over to the President, who was Mr. Eisenhower. The President had a very strange way of going to the youngest guy in the room and asking him what the story was. And I was, obviously, the youngest in the room. So he asked me what this was all about, and I gave him the briefing on the subject. When I got through, the President pounded his desk, and he said, "I'll be goddamned if I'll be pushed into anything like that. So the answer is no, they will not get a ship assigned to San Francisco Naval Shipyard, to build an aircraft carrier."

Paul Stillwell: What was his objection?

Admiral Mumma: Well, actually, Charlie Thomas then said, "Well, Mr. President, we have a chart here that shows this, how it does, what the problems are."

Charlie Wilson grabbed his sleeve and pulled him out of the oval office, and we got outside. When he got outside, he turned to Charlie Thomas and he said, "Charlie, after you've made the sale, you know you get the hell out."

So that was the end of that job, because there was no possibility of really doing an efficient job by building that aircraft carrier in San Francisco. I was able to verify that pretty strongly, having been production officer there. So that's just one way in which your experience as a production officer brings to bear on later decisions.

Paul Stillwell: What do you remember about the contracting business, the negotiations, and so forth, with the various private shipyards?

Admiral Mumma: Well, the private yards always knew that we had a benchmark from naval shipyards to compare with. And they always knew that we were not going to hold still for any major overruns. As a matter of fact, some of the contracts had been already made when I got to the bureau, with Bath Iron Works—and Bath Iron Works was, among others, was always being renegotiated for excess profits in case there were any.

To avoid renegotiation if there were any excess profits, Pete Newell of Bath Iron Works would come down and he would say, "Admiral, I've got about $10 million on that last batch of destroyers that I know if I get before the renegotiation board, I'll probably lose. I would much rather, instead of it going back into the treasury, have it go back into the shipbuilding program. I'd like you to take it back if you would."* So I would get bonanzas of that type from the various contractors, because they knew the renegotiating board would take it away from them if we didn't.

But we didn't have big changes. With short ship programs, we had very, very few changes during the life of the contract. We put the changes into the new contract for the next run of ships. We would have four or five shipyards building the same type of ship.

---

* John R. Newell joined the staff of Bath Iron Works, Bath, Maine, in 1938 and became president of the company in 1950.

That would get competition as well, and then ensuring that no one got the lion's share. The lion's share would always go to the low bidder. The one or two extra ships made a lot of difference to their ability to bid low.

Paul Stillwell: Well, for example, the Forrest Sherman program was going through then.* Do you have any specific recollections of that one?

Admiral Mumma: Not in detail, I don't think, at this stage of the game. It's so long ago. We had not only a good financial group in the bureau, but we also had a good civilian bunch of lawyers and a bunch of negotiators that had had good experience during World War II, and they knew what the facts of life were. I had to take the Bureau of Ships down in size during my regime. We had around 125,000 employees in the Bureau of Ships, including the 11 naval shipyards and eight laboratories, at the time I took over. President Eisenhower put in shrinking budgets for the maintenance of the bureau, the bureaucracy in the Navy Department, and we reduced that during my four years to about 105,000. In other words, we dropped about 20%. I think we got lean and mean. I don't think that we hit muscle. I think we were doing as good a job at the end of that as we were in the beginning.

One of the places that I had a problem was with New York Naval Shipyard. They had 20-some congressmen, and anything I wanted to do that was contrary to their wishes, they'd go to the Secretary of the Navy. Then I'd have to come over and tell the Secretary what the story was. Because instead of coming to me, they'd go to the Secretary first to try and embarrass me. But that didn't make me any happier with those fellows, because they usually didn't have the facts, and it was pretty easily refuted.

Paul Stillwell: What sorts of things would they come up with?

---

* The Forrest Sherman (DD-931) class was the Navy's first new destroyer design after World War II. The class eventually comprised 18 ships; commissioning dates ran from November 1955 to August 1959. For details see Daniel G. Felger, "Retrospective: the Forrest Shermans," U.S. Naval Institute Proceedings, May 1987, pages 162-175.

Admiral Mumma: Well, I was cutting down on the New York yard. It had been about 12,000. I got them down to about 8,000 men, and they were just raising a big stink about that. They wanted to get another aircraft carrier, and I didn't want to put another carrier in the New York yard. They were already the highest priced yard we had for aircraft carrier construction. Newport News was beating the devil off of them. Even New York Ship was doing better.

Paul Stillwell: Why were the prices so high in New York?

Admiral Mumma: Well, the labor unions were extremely militant in that area, and they had the backing of what I guess you might call the rabble-rousing congressmen.

Paul Stillwell: And they undoubtedly brought up these charges again about you being a West Coast guy when you were cutting down the New York yard.

Admiral Mumma: Yes, but I didn't put much of it on the West Coast away from them. Most of it stayed on the East Coast. So they didn't have a real excuse.

Paul Stillwell: Was there pressure to close any of the yards completely?

Admiral Mumma: I tried to close New York yard during my regime, and I could not get adequate support in the secretariat to do it. I think they were a little bit intimidated by the size of that New York delegation.

Paul Stillwell: Why was that the target? Because of the high costs?

Admiral Mumma: Yes. High costs, and it eventually was closed.[*] It was the proper thing to have done.

---

[*] The New York Navy Yard, popularly known as the Brooklyn Navy Yard, was established in 1801. In late 1945 it was officially renamed the New York Naval Shipyard. In 1966 the yard was decommissioned as a result of cost-effectiveness initiatives on the part of Secretary of Defense Robert McNamara.

Paul Stillwell: We've talked about the nuclear carrier program. What do you remember about construction of the conventional carriers?

Admiral Mumma: Well, New York Ship in the old days had done a good job on the Saratoga, way back.* In those days it was called the American Brown-Boveri Corporation. It was part of the Swiss company of Brown-Boveri. I had been a young officer in putting that ship in commission as a part of the commissioning detail. The net result of that was that they had a background of capability in that yard, and Wolfson very much wanted to get into the shipbuilding business for big carriers. And so he wanted to put in a dry dock for big carriers. He collapsed, unfortunately. We had our qualms about him, and they were justified because after he'd been in business, the Kitty Hawk was built there, and there were some other jobs that he did.†

I even put one conventional submarine in there to see if they could do a job on a conventional submarine. At the same time I put one down at Pascagoula. I did those on specific assignment without bidding, which I was authorized to do under Vinson-Trammell, to ensure the proper broad base of shipbuilding capability. I was afraid to put Newport News in because we already had so much business in Newport News, and it wasn't until we got in real trouble, and New York Ship went out of business and pretty much Pascagoula eventually went out of business when McNamara put all those destroyers down there, that we had to have Newport News in the business of building submarines. That was done after my day. But I was resistant to putting Newport News in because we had so much aircraft carrier work in Newport News, that I didn't want to divert them at that time, or show partiality to Newport News in putting submarine work in there. I was getting enough flak out of Electric Boat as it was.

Paul Stillwell: It would be interesting to run through the various yards, both civilian and commercial, and see what specific recollections you have of them. You've mentioned

---

* This is a reference to the Saratoga (CV-3), commissioned in 1927.
† The contract for the aircraft carrier Kitty Hawk (CVA-63) was awarded 1 October 1955 to the New York Shipbuilding Corporation, Camden, New Jersey. Her keel was laid 27 December 1956. She was launched 21 May 1960 and commissioned 29 April 1961.

Pete Newell up at Bath. Anything else about that yard that springs to mind; certainly they had a fine reputation.

Admiral Mumma: Bath always did a good job. They had a good group of men. They worked well. The Newells, Pete and his son John, did a very fine job for the Navy, and they were very patriotic and did a good job.

Portsmouth always did a good job. Portsmouth yard, Kittery, whichever you want to call it. The Boston shipyard was marginal in some respects, because they were pretty well unionized and some of them were kind of rabble-rousing unions.

Did I ever tell you my story about Jack Kennedy?

Paul Stillwell: I don't believe so.

Admiral Mumma: Jack Kennedy and Leverett Saltonstall were the senators at the time.[*] What happened was there was a group of so-called veterans decided to form what was known as a veterans' union up in Boston. Well, veterans is not a trade union. We had trade unions in shipyards. We might as well have had a Republican union up there, a Democratic union up there as veterans. So it didn't make any sense. Admiral Bill Howard was the shipyard commander up there when I was chief of bureau.[†] He sent me down a letter telling me what the situation was against this rabble-rousing bunch of so-called veterans. I went down with this information and copies of the letter, and I gave them to Leverett Saltonstall and discussed the matter with him and discussed it with Senator Jack Kennedy. Both of them assured me, "Admiral, don't worry about it. That's no problem. I understand your position. It's perfectly okay. You won't hear any more from me." Both of them told me that.

It was a couple of months later that I was up in Boston on another matter and I was told by Bill Howard, the shipyard commander, that this matter had erupted again in a big way, and that Senator Jack Kennedy was in the yard and had been making talks to

---

[*] Senator John F. Kennedy (Democrat-Massachusetts); Senator Leverett Saltonstall (Republican-Massachusetts).
[†] Rear Admiral William E. Howard, Jr., USN.

these groups, these so-called veterans' groups, to try and up the demand for recognition. Completely against the law.

Paul Stillwell: And against his assurances.

Admiral Mumma: Yes, against his assurances. That day I went back and climbed into the shuttle plane to get back to Washington, and I was sitting in the airplane by myself when Senator Kennedy came in. He said, "Admiral, do you mind if I sit with you?"

I said, "No, sir, sit down, Senator."

So we sat down and I turned to him and I said, "Senator, I've been informed that you have been making speeches to groups in the yard concerning a matter that I discussed with you some weeks ago on the recognition of this so-called veterans' group."

He said, "Well, ah, yeah, well, I changed my mind."

I said, "In spite of your assurances to me that I'd hear nothing further from them?"

He said, "Yes, well, you know, you got to pay attention to these people."

So the next thing that happened was this group, encouraged by Senator Jack Kennedy, started a suit against the shipyard commander for a million dollars, and a billion dollars against the Navy Department.

Paul Stillwell: What was their basis for their claim?

Admiral Mumma: That it was illegal for us to deny them recognition. They won in the Massachusetts court. They won in the Massachusetts court of appeals, where we appealed it. It went to the Supreme Court of the United States. They based it also on the fact that we had violated the separation of powers between the Congress and the executive branch by providing copies of this letter that the shipyard commander had written to me. I thought that was an absurd thing for them to try to prove. Of course, the Supreme Court immediately threw it out and said it had no merit whatsoever. So we won the case. My shipyard commander didn't have to pay a million dollars, and the Navy Department didn't have to pay them a billion dollars, and the union was completely discredited. But you can imagine my enthusiasm for then Senator Jack Kennedy.

Paul Stillwell: Lack of enthusiasm. That yard was later closed, as was the New York yard.* Were there some vulnerabilities there that you saw?

Admiral Mumma: Yes. For example, we beat the Boston yard on the radar picket program by a large number of man-days. It was not as efficient a yard. But they had been able to live on the Vinson-Trammell clause which provides a certain percentage of stuff be put in navy yards. My predecessors and others had stuck a little more closely to Vinson-Trammell than I did. I would get the President's authority to deviate from Vinson-Trammell. That's what was needed; if you deviated from Vinson-Trammell, you had to get the authority.

I'll give you another little anecdote along this line. There was a congressman by the name of Tom Pelly out at Bremerton, Washington, and the Bremerton yard was in his area.† I knew him pretty well because every time anything came up, why, he would always be bugging me to try and find out what Bremerton was going to get so that he could jump the gun and tell everybody out there before it was announced.

Paul Stillwell: As if he were personally responsible.

Admiral Mumma: Exactly. That's the idea. So Tom called me up one day, and he said, "Al, when are you going to announce the shipbuilding program?"

Admiral Mumma: I said, "Well, it's going to be coming out tomorrow. I've got an appointment with the President tomorrow, and I've got an announcement that'll be ready at the end of that meeting with the President. Then we will be able to get it distributed through the Congress. We will have yeomen up there with these releases, running like antelopes through the Congress so that everybody gets it as near simultaneously as we possibly can. So that everybody gets it."

---

* The Boston Naval Shipyard closed in 1974.
† Representative Thomas M. Pelly (Republican-Washington).

He said, "Ah, come on, Al. You know there was a fellow that died and left in his will that he be buried exactly between his two previously deceased wives. And he said he wanted to be exactly between them because he loved them both very much. But at the bottom of the will he put in, tilt me a little toward Tillie. Al, can't you tilt a little toward Pelly?"

I said, "No, sir." So you can see it wasn't all unfriendly. And there were a lot of funny anecdotes in connection with it which I enjoyed.

Paul Stillwell: What do you remember about the Quincy yard?

Admiral Mumma: I had had two experiences with Quincy. I had taken a ship out of Quincy, the USS Clark, as a young officer when I was chief engineer of this 361, the so-called destroyer leader group. And she was a good ship. I appreciated the yard's work, and I had ridden several of the ships out of the yard. I rode the Massachusetts, and I rode the last of the treaty aircraft carriers out of that yard years before.[*] The workmanship was good, but for some unknown reason, they were unable to be completely economic. They seemed to lose money, and I think part of that was that Boston area's labor rates and labor militancy. They weren't able to control their labor force as well as they should, and even though it went through several hands attempting to put it into shape. It was a sad thing to see Quincy yard go under. They built the Lexington at the same time that I was a young officer putting the Saratoga in commission down in Camden. The Lexington never was quite as well built as the Saratoga. We beat her in the engineering competition, and we beat her in almost everything, even though Ernie King was the skipper.

Paul Stillwell: There's no parochialism showing, is there?

Admiral Mumma: Well, I lay an awful lot of it to the skippers. I think I told you earlier who they were, didn't I?

---

[*] The battleship Massachusetts (BB-59) was built by the Bethlehem Steel Company yard at Quincy, Massachusetts. The hull was launched on 23 September 1941.

Paul Stillwell: Yes.

Admiral Mumma: They were all very fine men and great leaders starting with Harry Yarnell, who set the pace.

Paul Stillwell: We've talked about the New York yard. What about Philadelphia?

Admiral Mumma: Philadelphia always did a reasonable job. They weren't our lowest cost yard. Newport News could almost always beat them and usually did. Part of that was the labor force, and the other part of it was they had a very good management group at Newport News. I was there during the time of Bill Blewett, who was a very, very fine shipyard operator.* He was not only an excellent man but a good friend and could be trusted to come up with reasonable costs.

As a matter of fact, in the Forrestal and the Saratoga, in the basic design of the ship, we had Newport News people come into the bureau to assist us in the contract design stage so that it would be an easier transition from contract design into final design by the design team at Newport News. That was a smooth operation. We did that occasionally with difficult ships, particularly like the tremendous changes that were made in the Forrestal class from any previous aircraft carriers. Now, the bigger design change on the machinery, we did an awful lot of that ourselves in the bureau and then worked it out with New York yard when she built the Saratoga. In all other respects than the main machinery, she followed the Forrestal. So basically, Newport News was good; Philadelphia was good.

Paul Stillwell: We haven't talked too much about the Electric Boat yard. What are your recollections of that from your period as chief of the bureau?

---

* William E. Blewett, Jr., was president of Newport News Shipbuilding and Dry Dock Company from 1954 to 1961, when he became chairman.

Admiral Mumma: Well, at that time Frank Pace was there as head of the Electric Boat, and he had done a good job in connection with it. They had some old-time people from the submarine building of old that, really, were very, very capable people. They had good design capability. They were what you might call, open-minded and could accept new ideas, which we shoved onto them quite frequently, like the first Polaris boat, which was really a <u>Skipjack</u> opened up and put a missile in the center.* That was a design innovation to save time. We were able to cut almost two years off the procurement of those first three Polaris submarines by doing that in the design stage and in the budgeting stage. So we eliminated all that and were able to proceed with the missile compartment and the development of the missile, which were the major projects of that Polaris program.

To give you an order of magnitude of speed of accomplishment, the <u>Skipjack</u> was the first of her class. The Polaris came along shortly thereafter, starting in '57. The fleet ballistic missile submarine was supposed to be a submarine that carried a missile, and in the first case it was a Redstone missile. A Redstone missile was a liquid oxygen, liquid hydrogen missile. One of the worst things in the world to carry on a submarine, those two ingredients—a potential bomb, if anything went wrong. The nuclear, on the other hand, was not a potential bomb. The nuclear, we had actually done a melt-down years ago out at Arco, Idaho. We had actually done a melt-down to see what would happen. And it was a hell of a melted mess; there's no question. But there was no explosion; there was no spreading of contamination all over the place. That melt-down, all you had to do was dig it up and bury it someplace, which they did.

Paul Stillwell: When was that, would you guess?

---

* Polaris was the name for the U.S. Navy's first submarine-launched ballistic missile, which became operational in the early 1960s. Its more-capable follow-on was the Poseidon missile, which entered the fleet in 1970. For more on the design of the first Polaris submarines, see the Naval Institute oral history of Captain Harry A. Jackson, USN (Ret.). There is also an entire volume of oral history devoted to the development of the Polaris program.

Admiral Mumma: Oh, that was early on in the program. I think our melt-down job was done in maybe '51 or '52.

Paul Stillwell: Was it deliberate?

Admiral Mumma: Yes, deliberate. Oh, yes, absolutely. We had done all the tests on it. That was the <u>Nautilus</u> reactor. We had a prototype out there, and we melted it down intentionally to see what would happen. Of course, Rick was in the nuclear saddle by that time. I was in command of the Model Basin at that time. As a matter of fact, shortly thereafter, I was out at San Francisco Shipyard. And shortly thereafter, I was out at Mare Island in command before I came back to the bureau.

So then, the next stage in this came was the building of the Polaris. We had to get rid of that confounded liquid oxygen, liquid hydrogen rocket. It was impossible to visualize that in a submarine. But that was the only thing we had to try and do to get a seagoing rocket at that time, because they were all liquid fuel rockets. But out at Cal Tech they'd been doing some work at the Applied Physics Laboratory, work on solid fuel for rockets, and they were developing pretty rapid "specific impulse" progress. And when the "specific impulse" got to a specific figure, we could go with a solid fuel rocket. Sputnik went up in October of '57.[*] That put a little goose behind the impetus of this project. And obviously we were lagging in some of these areas, and it was time to get moving. So we ended up talking to Arleigh Burke and, by this time, Tom Gates, about a possible get-going on this fleet ballistic missile program, FBM so-called. Red Raborn was chosen.[†] I knew Red Raborn. Even though he was an aviator, I knew him to be a good leader. So I supported Red Raborn. I knew him when he put an aircraft carrier in commission during the Korean War when I was in San Francisco Naval Shipyard and I knew Red pretty well. So I enthused about Red as a choice for this job. We had to do it well and do it fast.

---

[*] On 4 October 1957, the Soviet Union launched Sputnik I, the first artificial earth satellite. It caused great uproar in the United States, which had expected to be first in space.
[†] Rear Admiral William F. Raborn, Jr., USN, was director of the Special Projects Office, which developed the Polaris submarine-launched ballistic missile system. He held the post from 1955 to 1962, being promoted to vice admiral in 1960. His Polaris oral history is in the Naval Institute collection.

One of the problems, of course, was how were we going to give him adequate authority to do this job? My suggestion to Arleigh Burke and to Tom Gates was, "We have to give him authority within our bureau as though he's a member of our bureau. In other words, make him a deputy chief of the Bureau of Ships, and make him a deputy chief of the Bureau of Ordnance." At that time the chief of the Bureau of Ordnance was Fred Withington.* Fred was a good friend of mine, and he was a classmate of Arleigh Burke's, class of '23. Fred kind of balked at that idea. He said, "Oh, I don't know about that."

I said, "Look, Fred, there's only one way to really do it. You can have control over him to some degree if he's a deputy of yours. But he's going to have authority to go in to your bureau and get your support on a top priority program. It has to be top priority. The only way you can do that, give him one of your best people that will keep him in line." I said, "For example, I'm going to give him Jimmy Farrin. Jimmy Farrin is my top design man in the Bureau of Ships. He's been on the design of everything since the war, and Jimmy Farrin is the man I'm going to put on that job."†

He said, "My God, that's not a bad idea." We agreed on that. We went to Arleigh Burke and told him, "Okay, we're with you. Okay, we'll go ahead with a special projects officer to run that show. He'll be a deputy to our two bureaus. Bang! Let's go." This was in late November of '57. We got Tom Gates to set up a special meeting on the Sequoia, the Secretary of the Navy's yacht, for the purpose of briefing and getting support from all the heads of the major industry that would be involved.

So we individually called up our support people that we wanted down there. I got Mark Cresap, the chairman of Westinghouse; I got the GE chairman, Ralph Cordiner. And we got the head of the propulsion laboratory out at California. We got Stark Draper who was the head of the guidance research area up there in MIT.‡ We got all those fellows down, and we had a lunch on the Sequoia out in the Potomac. Obviously,

---

*Rear Admiral Frederic S. Withington, USN, served as Chief of the Bureau of Ordnance from November 1954 to March 1958. His oral history is in the Naval Institute collection.
† Captain James M. Farrin, USN.
‡ Dr. Stark Draper of the Massachusetts Institute of Technology had an important role in the development of the inertial navigation systems used in Polaris missiles and later in the space missions sent to the moon.

nobody could spy on us out there. We had a presentation on the way this would be done by Red Raborn and our specialist people in the ship and in the rocket area.

This was the non-Redstone missile by this time. It would have to be a solid-fuel rocket. It was expected that the solid fuel rocket's specific impulse would be adequate by the time this ship would be finished. At this meeting we all agreed that we could do it in two years' time—the Polaris submarine program from scratch. The way in which we could do it, in the Bureau of Ships, would be not to change the whole bow of the Skipjack class, not to change the whole stern of the Skipjack class. Move the two apart and put in the missile section. That would give us untold additional time in design, to design only the missile section, and the sail, and stuff in the mid-section. Well, that's what we did from the ship's point of view. Red Raborn said, "You're not going to get that damn ship ready."

I said, "We're going to have the ship ready. I'm worried about you, Red, and your ability to get that damn missile." And he did have problems with the missile. The problems were, he not only had a couple misfires, but also the impulse wasn't up at first that had to be improved, and the burning mechanism inside the missile had to be improved, so that it would burn more smoothly and efficiently. But I said, "Now look, that ship is going to go to sea in December of 1959, and I hope your missile is ready, Red."

He said, "The missile will be ready." He said, "We should be operational by June of 1960—two and a half years total time."

I said, "Okay, that's a deal." Sure enough, after one or two flubs in the original testing, the missile testing did go very well. And it finally—the size of the missile, the housing, the length, everything, fit into the submarine perfectly. Stark Draper came up with an inertial system, the guidance of that missile and the whole thing got married together. The submarine went to sea in December of '59. The missile was fitted in and the first ship, the George Washington, fired its first test missile in operational test in June of '60.[*]

---

[*] The keel for the ballistic missile submarine George Washington (SSBN-598) was laid on 1 November 1957. She was launched on 9 June 1959 and commissioned on 30 December 1959. Her first deterrent patrol began in November 1960. She served until being decommissioned on 24 January 1985.

Paul Stillwell: Well, just an indication of the caliber of the guy Stark Draper was, he was the one involved in putting the man on the moon in '69.

Admiral Mumma: Oh, hell, yes. He was a terrific guy, Draper was. Well, the Draper Laboratory is not by accident named after him up there at MIT.

In other words, Red Raborn deserved a tremendous amount of credit. Jimmy Farrin deserved a tremendous amount of credit. The Bureau of Ordnance deserved a lot of credit in doing this job faster than anything had ever been done except the atomic bomb, which had number one national priority. This is the reason I say that Rickover took too long.

Paul Stillwell: Andy McKee was up there at Electric Boat, a very capable guy.[*]

Admiral Mumma: Yes, and Andy was a terrific help. As a sup-ships, he was without peer. He, Andy was a real old-time ship design submariner. His brother Logan, who was a good friend of ours also, was in design. But Logan never quite had the feel for design that Andy had. Both of them were terrific people.

Paul Stillwell: Well, Andy McKee, you could probably call an artist in that particular profession.

Admiral Mumma: Oh, no question about it, yes.

Paul Stillwell: So that was the right place for him to be at that time.

Admiral Mumma: Yes, it certainly was. And he indoctrinated all the rest of that group up there that did a good job. I spent a lot of time up there over the years. I enjoyed their ability to understand what you were getting at, and do it quickly and accomplish it. For

---

[*] Rear Admiral Andrew I. McKee, USN (Ret.), was a noted naval constructor and submarine designer while on active duty. Following his retirement he went to work in private industry for Electric Boat. For details on his remarkable career, see John D. Alden, "Andrew Irwin McKee, Naval Constructor," U.S. Naval Institute Proceedings, June 1979, pages 49-57.

example, they accepted the Skipjack design very, very quickly, which was a major departure. I just couldn't believe that these people would be quite that receptive.

Paul Stillwell: What are your recollections of the Nautilus going into service?

Admiral Mumma: Well, she went to sea in January of '55, shortly before my watch started.* I was on the West Coast at the time, so I didn't get to ride her on her trials. But I thought she went into service quite well, because the Bettis Field group and the Argonne National Laboratory had been very closely coordinated during the design stage of that nuclear power plant. As you probably know, we had a test reactor out at Arco, Idaho, where we actually tested the reactor before installing it in any ship. And so that I was familiar with all those aspects of the ship's design.

But, again, hydrodynamically, she was not a very good ship, even though she was a good success as a nuclear ship, as contrasted to the Seawolf.† The Seawolf was a design which encompassed the General Electric project of a liquid metal cooling reactor. In other words, a sodium potassium, eutectic. As you know, those are both liquid metals, sodium and potassium, and they have rather low melting points and become liquid at fairly low temperatures within the atmospheric range. The blending of the two to form a minimum temperature metal, liquid metal, is called the eutectic, and that's where the two metals blended in a certain percentage would be the lowest possible freezing point. That was done in the Seawolf at the insistence of General Electric.

This was caused by Dr. Kingdon of General Electric, who was quite a theoretician in the matter of heat transfer. He knew that a liquid metal would have a much higher heat transfer than the pressurized steam, or pressurized water, and so that under those circumstances, you'd have much higher efficiency. He was looking, really, down the

---

* For details see the Naval Institute oral history of Vice Admiral Eugene P. Wilkinson, USN (Ret.). As a commander Wilkinson was the first commanding officer of the Nautilus.
† USS Seawolf (SSN-575), commissioned 30 March 1957, was the Navy's second nuclear-powered submarine. The first, USS Nautilus (SSN-571) had a pressurized water reactor. The Seawolf served as a test bed for a reactor cooled by liquid sodium. The latter was not deemed a success, so the Seawolf was later equipped with the pressurized water type. For the first skipper's view, see Richard B. Laning, "The Seawolf's Sodium-Cooled Power Plant, Naval History, Spring 1992, pages 45-48.

road toward commercial utilization of nuclear power. There were some liquid metal reactors built, and there are some of them still in operation. But the trouble with liquid metals, is that both sodium and potassium are somewhat corrosive, and it takes a very fine stainless steel type of material to build the housings for this liquid metal so that it won't corrode. Well, unfortunately, we were not able to prevent that happening in the Seawolf, and so the liquid metal did corrode the heat exchangers. We had to re-engine that ship with a nuclear reactor that was pressurized water.

This is another peculiarity of Rickover. I was at the bureau the time this developed. He came to me and he said, "Admiral, would you announce that we have to re-engine the Seawolf because of the leakages caused by this work?"

I said, "Rick, you announce everything else in connection with the nuclear program. Why don't you announce it?"

Paul Stillwell: He wanted to put out only good news.

Admiral Mumma: Exactly. [Laughter] But we announced it.

Paul Stillwell: Do you have anything else to say about the New York Shipbuilding yard at Camden?

Admiral Mumma: Well, it was fairly obvious in the long run that Wolfson was not going to be an ideal shipyard capability, and that proved out. It eventually went bust.

Paul Stillwell: What was the quality of the workmanship?

Admiral Mumma: Well, it was not only that, but poor management. Wolfson was an entrepreneur—an in-and-outer, so to speak. He had, I think, shown his colors a little bit earlier that we probably didn't take adequately into account. We probably should not have put that much confidence in his yard.

Paul Stillwell: Well, that was a trend that was coming along—getting more of the financiers and the conglomerates, as opposed to the old-line shipbuilders.

Admiral Mumma: Well, unfortunately, that trend went overboard, and later I was in an industry that eventually got conglomeratized as well after I retired from the Navy and went into civilian industry. So that trend was unfortunate.

Paul Stillwell: What about any of the yards around Baltimore. Did you work with them in that time.

Admiral Mumma: Yes, though we didn't build many combatant ships in the Baltimore Bethlehem yard. We had a lot of pressure to do so of one kind or another, and they did a pretty darn good job for commercial ships. We had a close liaison with them, and they did repair work and other work for us. But they never were an enormous factor in the military area.

Paul Stillwell: On the business of repair work in general, did you parcel that out with some of the same considerations?

Admiral Mumma: On the bidding process, generally speaking, plus trying to keep it near the home ports of the ships to ensure that we didn't upset the families too much, because, after all, a yard overhaul is supposed to be a time when the men and the officers can be with their families. Life in the Navy was tough enough without having to have everybody move all over creation every time you went to a naval shipyard.

Paul Stillwell: Moving down the East Coast, you've talked about Newport News. What about the Norfolk Naval Shipyard?

Admiral Mumma: Norfolk was a very good repair yard basically. They had also done considerable work on landing craft and things of that kind because of the landing craft proximity during World War II. We had a design section there that was primarily expert in small boats as well as landing craft. They were the ones that originally dieselized our ships' boats with, originally "Buddha" diesels. Then the Navy took over the building of those diesels themselves, and they built those diesel engines right there. The purpose, of course, was to get rid of the gasoline fire hazard in ships' boats.

Paul Stillwell: Moving further on down the East Coast, what do you recall about the Charleston yard?

Admiral Mumma: Charleston was a good yard, particularly in those days for minesweeps and all the auxiliary-type ships. We had good relations with the Charleston yard, and then, of course, eventually it got into the submarine business, which it was well fitted to handle. We didn't need that many submarine yards originally, but as we got more and more nuclear submarines, why, it was absolutely imperative we have more yards. And they were a good yard. We had no problem with them.

Paul Stillwell: What do you recall about the Ingalls yard at Pascagoula?

Admiral Mumma: Well, originally that was part of the Ingalls Steel Company yard operation, and Monroe Lanier was the president of that organization originally when I first knew it. He was a very fine, very fine shipbuilder and he ran a good yard. That was one of the reasons why we began more business into the yard because of its location and year-round ability to carry on work, plus the fact that Monroe was a good shipyard operator. Because of that, I eventually chose it as one of the potential submarine yards, and put first a conventional submarine in there, and let them bid later for other submarine work. That was, in other words, to get them oriented in submarine work. Now, we had to give them logistic support from Electric Boat. We had the legal authority to do this, but Electric Boat didn't like it.

Paul Stillwell: You mentioned that yesterday on the Mare Island situation.

Admiral Mumma: Same thing. Same damn thing. So under the circumstances we went ahead with it, anyhow, and that was the way it was.

Paul Stillwell: What do you remember about the Long Beach Naval Shipyard?

Admiral Mumma: Long Beach was a very fine repair yard basically. They had capability for aircraft carriers on down. Did very well with them. It was a can-do yard. A little along the lines, about the same size and about the same capability as San Francisco, though they did not have the building capacity to build ships that San Francisco had.

Bremerton was an excellent yard. It eventually got more and more into some of the shipbuilding, although they were a basic big ship repair yard.

Paul Stillwell: Had been for years and years.

Admiral Mumma: Yes, they did a good job. I had plenty of experience at Bremerton in ships, not only in the aircraft carriers, but also later, cruisers and so forth, though I went to Mare Island for destroyers.

Paul Stillwell: You've talked about both Hunters Point and Mare Island. Anything to add about those two from your times as chief of bureau?

Admiral Mumma: No, no, I don't think so. You see, when I was in the bureau, we had over a 1,000-ship Navy. So when they talk about a 600-ship Navy, that doesn't impress me too much.[*] However, they are talking about replacing some of these aircraft carriers to keep up the 15 aircraft carriers, which is an almost absolute minimum because of the fact that we've expanded our three-ocean Navy to about a five-ocean Navy now. Trying to police all the gulfs and all the oceans, and it's a pretty tough job.

---

[*] When John Lehman became Secretary of the Navy in 1981, he established a 600-ship Navy as a goal. When he left office in 1987, the Navy had not achieved that goal and has declined rapidly since then. In the year 2001 the U.S. Navy has approximately 315 active ships.

Particularly, we don't get adequate support from some of our allies that we helped build ships for in the offshore procurement program right after the war. I was responsible for it in shipbuilding for those recipient nations that had suffered so during the war, like France and Belgium and Holland and Italy, even Italy and even Yugoslavia—to assist them to get back into the business of building ships, to our account for the first few ships under the Marshall Plan.* Then after that, not only did they build additional ships to their own account, after having finished design, and so forth, but also they were then stuck with manning and maintaining those ships, which is a big part of the expense, which we're now beginning to get into in a 600-ship Navy.

Paul Stillwell: Are there any specifics you remember from that offshore procurement program? Any programs that you were especially interested in?

Admiral Mumma: Well, I remember that almost all of them were doing a pretty darn good job. Belgium and Holland, particularly. And Italy was doing pretty darn well. As a matter of fact, during one of my visits in connection with this offshore procurement is an interesting story. I was going to fly originally on this trip all across the Atlantic and all over Europe coming back. I suddenly got a call from William Francis Gibbs in New York. He said, "Admiral, I know you're going on this trip. I've discovered that you're heading for Europe. I would like to ask a favor of you if you don't mind."

I said, "What's that?"

He said, "Well, I know if we ever get the job to build another United States—the United States Lines is planning to bring it up this year to the Congress—you're going to be asked to testify."† He said, "You rode the original United States. You know all about her. You know her machinery, you know everything about her. I would like you to go on the United States to Europe, if you would, and look her over very carefully and as critically as you can from the point of view of any improvements that we ought to be able

---

* At the Harvard University commencement in 1947, Secretary of State George C. Marshall made an address in which he outlined a plan for the economic rebuilding of war-ravaged Europe. Congress passed the European Recovery Act, and the program of American support came to be known as the Marshall Plan.
† SS United States was a 990-foot-long passenger liner that went into service 1952. At 53,329 gross tons, she was the third largest liner in the world. Her top speed of more than 38 knots was considered a potential military asset. She was removed from service by the United States Lines in late 1969.

to make in a second ship. After you've had that experience, I would like you to give me a summary of what your recommendations would be."

I said, "Well, that's going to cost me an additional four days, but I guess I can do it in the interest of national defense because the ship actually would be naval auxiliary as well." So as chief of bureau, I went ahead and assigned myself to go that way. As a slight emolument, he put me in the owner's suite.

Paul Stillwell: What year was that?

Admiral Mumma: I think it was early '56.

At any rate, he was in the habit of calling the skipper and the chief engineer every single day the ship was at sea. Talked to them on the transatlantic radiophone. He added me to the list and so I talked to him every day, from New York he would call. He had a way of asking questions, what was I doing, and how much had I seen, and all that. Were the captain and the chief engineer cooperative, and all that sort of business? And they were. Of course, we couldn't have had better treatment obviously. But the morning we arrived in Southampton, there was an urgent telephone call from William Francis Gibbs. He said, "Brace yourself. The Andrea Doria has just sunk outside New York Harbor. That is going to really shake the shipbuilding world and particularly the Italians."[*] He said, "I know you're going to Italy and you're going to be talking to Dr. Liacono who is the head of the Italian shipbuilding operation. See what you can find out about the Andrea Doria design and how she might have been improved to prevent the sinking."

I said, "Okay, I'll see what I can do."

He said, "I've got another request if you don't mind. After you do that, and you find out all you can about the Andrea Doria, I would appreciate it if you would come back on the United States and see if any of the things you have learned would happen on the United States, and whether or not we could make the United States more invulnerable to any such collision."

---

[*] SS Andrea Doria was a 700-foot-long, 29,082-gross ton Italian passenger liner launched in June 1952. She sank off Nantucket on July 26, 1956 after colliding in dense fog with the Swedish liner Stockholm, which survived. As a result of the collision 51 lives were lost.

I said, "Well, I don't think there's a hell of a lot we can do to the United States to improve her in that regard because she's already pretty well designed. As you know, we insisted on quite a few things when you first came to us for additional military features, and additional cost of the ship to support those military features." We were pretty resistant to ensure that she was a good ship in the beginning, because I was in design at the time that the first United States was being designed. I forced him to change the shaft lines and a few other thing on that ship. But I said, "Okay, I'll do it." So I did. I came back on the United States.

But in Italy I learned from Dr. Liacono something that apparently has never been published. I have checked that with Bob Young, who is the former chairman of the American Bureau of Shipping, and he thinks that it's correct— that the Andrea Doria had a longitudinal bulkhead down the middle of the ship, fore and aft. That is something we eliminated a long, long time ago in naval ships because unless you're very, very fast on your feet and adept at counter-flooding on the other side of the ship, your ship floods on only one side, and you begin to lose stability. Well, I was able to determine that that was the case.

Now, in the United States we didn't have any longitudinal bulkhead down the middle of the ship. We haven't had a longitudinal bulkhead down the middle of a naval ship for years. Many merchant ships were built that way, because that's the cheapest way to build a ship to get girder stability in the vertical, in flexing and bending. So rather than making the outboard side of the ship and the ship protection areas so important—well, that's apparently what happened to the Doria. When one compartment was ruptured, it apparently ruptured—as the bow on the Stockholm went further in, it apparently ruptured the top of a second bulkhead. It went from the skin of the ship to the central longitudinal bulkhead, and as the ship heeled over, that second compartment flooded and caused her to heel over further. As she heeled over further and the main deck went under, I mean the—it was the main deck; it was not the promenade deck but the main deck on which the bulkhead stopped, flooded and it spread through the air-conditioning ducts all the way fore and aft. She flooded completely on the starboard side, and, of course, she turned over.

Paul Stillwell: Get one side full of water, she would.

Admiral Mumma: So all naval ships have been designed for many, many years to flood—we make the bulkheads very short between bulkheads athwartships, so that if the compartment floods, it floods all the way starboard and port and it doesn't flood fore and aft. If you rupture another bulkhead, why, it floods all the way starboard and port, and doesn't flood fore and aft. On that basis the United States was a four-compartment ship. She could flood four major compartments. The Stockholm's bow only ruptured one compartment and a half, and they lost the ship. So this is again a basic point of ship design which we've adhered to for so many years which has prevented the loss of a large number of American ships. This is incorporated very firmly in the minds of the maritime safety and life at sea people.

Paul Stillwell: What conclusions and observations did you make on the basis of your two voyages on board the United States?

Admiral Mumma: Well, I didn't learn too much extra actually. She had a few lower deck openings that I would have recommended way down below, between firerooms, and so forth, that should have been up and over and closed up to the bulkhead deck. But she was not particularly vulnerable. This was pretty much all within the basic longitudinal restriction that you have only real athwartships bulkheads with only interrupted longitudinal bulkheads.

Paul Stillwell: What factors prevented the construction of the follow-on ship that Gibbs envisioned?

Admiral Mumma: Well, the general increase in aircraft travel, and the general decrease in ship travel. It finally ended up that they began worrying about the subsidy, and the Congress got leery of putting more money into another ship. So the merchant marine suffered accordingly; whereas now, these so-called cruise ships being built all over the world, some of them are even bigger than the second United States would have been.

The ability to use the first United States has been extremely limited. Nobody's really been able to put her into a real amount of service. She's too fast. Most of these ships are really puddle jumpers of 19, 20, 21 or 22 knots.

Paul Stillwell: She's probably too big too.

Admiral Mumma: Oh, they're enormous. They just go from port to port.

Paul Stillwell: What are your recollections of Gibbs as an individual, a person?

Admiral Mumma: He was a tough cookie. He had a brother, and his brother was almost completely invisible. But he consulted his brother a lot in connection with design and financial matters. His brother was a very good financial man, but most people didn't even know he existed. Gibbs himself was a very tough taskmaster. He was a hard man to work for, but he was an intelligent guy. He was a peculiar combination of an engineer and a lawyer. He was both and had degrees to prove it, so he was what you might call a sea lawyer. He was always working the angles. We had worked very, very closely, almost every week on the Timmerman design. So I knew him very, very well. He knew me pretty well, too, and he knew that we were just as tough as he was.

Paul Stillwell: In what ways was he tough?

Admiral Mumma: He was always trying to pull a little fast one on you, that you didn't know about it. He wouldn't tell you right away, and then he'd pull something that would shock you and attempt to get you to say yes quickly in order to avoid embarrassment or something. But basically, he didn't know as much about big ships as he thought he did. He was a good designer of destroyers and did a good job on destroyer designs, which he did most of. He did not do the Phelps class that were done at Fore River. But he did the Farragut class of destroyers, and they were good ships.[*] So gradually he worked more

---

[*] The first of the "gold-platers," the modern destroyers designed in the 1930s, was the USS Farragut (DD-348), commissioned 18 June 1934. They replaced the old four-pipers as the front-line destroyers in the U.S. Fleet.

and more. He did design work for Newport News in some of their stuff. That was on smaller aspect of things. He did design work very, very heavily for Bath Iron Works and did almost all their basic fundamental design.

He had done the rehabilitation of the Leviathan after she became a U.S. ship in World War I.* He got most of his experience in big ships, redoing ships for a while. Then he always was after the Secretary of the Navy to give him an aircraft carrier to design. But we didn't look upon that with favor because of his experience in big ships, particularly when I had to force him to put more bulbous bow on the United States and to move the shaft lines to remove part of the vibration on the United States because of the experience we had had during World War II and before. In other words, he didn't understand the big ship vibration problem which was a very, very, tough thing. For that reason, I had to prevent him from getting in the big ship design.

Paul Stillwell: It's curious that you see that as a shortcoming when his reputation, I guess, rests primarily on the big ships like United States and Leviathan.

Admiral Mumma: I know, but the United States would have been a disaster if it'd been built the way he designed it originally. She would have had terrible vibration, very severe vibration. And if she had had the original bow he had on that ship, didn't have the larger bow that we insisted on, she wouldn't have made the speed she did. So there you are. We insisted on those as military features.

Paul Stillwell: Do you have any recollections of these fast ones that he tried to pull, any specifics?

Admiral Mumma: Oh, he was always asking for more speed in ships. He was a great speed enthusiast. Well, we always had to balance speed against endurance, against

---

* The Hamburg American Line put the 950-foot-long, 54,282-gross-ton passenger liner Vaterland into service in May 1914; she was then the world's largest ship. When World War I broke out a few months later, the liner was interned in New York. Renamed Leviathan, she became a U.S. Navy transport when the United States entered the war in 1917. After the war she was rebuilt by naval architect William Francis Gibbs and became a passenger liner owned by the U.S. Government and operated by United States Lines. She continued operation into the 1930s and was scrapped in 1938.

firepower, and all these other features that were mostly military features that he didn't worry about to such an extent we did. So we always had to knock him down on those things. He was always trying to pull an end run. He'd go over and call on the Secretary and tell him things like that. But, fortunately, I had a pretty good liaison with the aides over there, and they knew who was talking to the Secretary.

Paul Stillwell: Was he an irascible, difficult person to deal with, disagreeable?

Admiral Mumma: He would be difficult. For example, on the 445-class destroyers, which was the beginning of the war before we got into the 692s, he had a design that was made by the chief engineer of a propeller for that class of destroyers.* And we had a bureau design made by the Bureau of Ships. We were testing these out at the Model Basin in the water tunnels, which I had charge of. William Francis Gibbs came down to observe the tests, and he brought his chief engineer along. We ran the two model propellers in the water tunnels and showed them that his design cavitated before you got to full power, whereas the bureau design did not cavitate. He got so mad he walked out of that observing room and refused to look anymore. But his chief engineer stuck around, and he picked our brains until we told him what to do to the design of the propeller to fix it, which he did. So the propeller was satisfactory when it was finally done, but William Francis showed his true colors when he stalked out of the room and wouldn't look anymore.

Paul Stillwell: Was there generally a lot of sharing of information between the Navy and private industry?

Admiral Mumma: We had to. We had to keep these fellows up to snuff because we had top scientific talent at the model basin, and we gave them more or less a free hand do things that were new and different. And we had to keep industry up to snuff, and so we

---

* USS Fletcher (DD-445) and her sisters comprised the largest class of destroyers ever built for the U.S. Navy. All told, there were 175 ships of the class, commissioned 1942-44. Characteristics as originally built: standard displacement of 2,050 tons, 376 feet long, and 40 feet in the beam; top speed of 37 knots. Each ship was armed with five 5-inch guns, ten 40-millimeter guns, and ten 21-inch torpedo tubes.

encouraged them to come down and observe tests of equipment that they had anything to do with even somewhat remotely. So we had a very large group of design people that spent quite a bit of time at the model basin. I enjoyed these associations, because I got to know all the people very well, all the design people in all parts of the country. I guess that helped me a lot later on, when I got into the bureau.

Paul Stillwell: I'm surprised that Gibbs would have so much clout, as you describe the daily calls and so forth, after the United States was built. I mean, he didn't work for the shipping line.

Admiral Mumma: No. He wanted to know first if anything went wrong. That's what he was after. He didn't want any criticism of that ship ever to come out that he didn't know about first, and could offer a possible solution to the problem.

Paul Stillwell: The U.S. Lines must have been very accommodating to let him do all this.

Admiral Mumma: Oh, sure, sure they were. They had a close liaison with William Francis. They did. They talked very frequently, and I think it was relatively good. William Francis gave me a little plaque he wanted me to put in my office which says, "I do not wish to have anything to do with a ship that does not sail fast because I intend to go in harm's way. Signed John Paul Jones." And he said, "Now that's something that you ought to remember."

I said, "I have it pretty well in mind, William Francis." But I still have it. I've got it in my office up in New Hampshire.

Paul Stillwell: But you knew there were other things in a ship than just speed.

Admiral Mumma: That's right. The ship does other things besides go fast.

Paul Stillwell: Well, there was a trend that developed in the '50s and has accelerated since then toward habitability. How much was that a concern when you were the chief?

Admiral Mumma: Oh, that first became important during World War II. We didn't operate in the South Pacific or the tropics a great, great deal in the old days. The worst climate that we operated in was Southern California pretty much. Occasionally Panama transits and so forth. But long-term habitability in the tropics was a serious problem. Many of our ships did not have adequate capability to operate in the tropics because they didn't have very much air-conditioning, if any, in World War II. Even our clothes were not designed originally for tropical duty. The British had their short sleeves, polo shirts, and their shorts that they used in their tropical assignments. They knew all about India and Singapore and that area. We hadn't that much experience, so that we learned a pretty rough lesson during World War II as to what we should do, not only for the men's comfort in the tropics but also for their long-term survivability in a climate of that kind, and to be able to function. So every ship postwar had a primary requirement of habitability from aircraft carriers right down to destroyers and minesweepers, and everything else. It was vital. It was one of our fetishes.

Paul Stillwell: You step aboard some of today's ships, you may think it's gone overboard.

Admiral Mumma: I don't know. I haven't been aboard some of the more recent designs enough to be able to say. You know, in the old days the Farragut class and the Phelps class, the Porter in the Phelps class of destroyers--we were destroyer leaders in that Phelps—they were considered gold-platers, you know. They weren't all that gold when you look back on it.

Paul Stillwell: In retrospect, no. How would you evaluate the Fletcher class?

Admiral Mumma: Good ships basically. As a matter of fact, I thought our destroyers did a very good job. The only mistakes that were made were mistakes in operational judgment, like when we lost the three destroyers during fueling.[*] That should never have

---

[*] While operating off the Philippines, ships of the Third Fleet ran into a ferocious typhoon on 18 December 1944. In all, three destroyers—Hull (DD-350), Spence (DD-512), and Monaghan (DD-354)—sank, and a number of other ships were damaged. For details, see C. Raymond Calhoun, Typhoon: The Other Enemy: The Third Fleet and the Pacific Storm of December 1944 (Annapolis: Naval Institute Press, 1981).

happened because with a typhoon coming, we should never have gotten those ships down to the point where they didn't have any ballast in them at all.

Paul Stillwell: Well, the Sims class had had problems being top-heavy even before that.

Admiral Mumma: Yes, but they weren't really that bad.

Paul Stillwell: We've talked about these various shipyards. There were the Todd yards also. Any recollections of them?

Admiral Mumma: Well, I had known the Todd yards for many years, and I knew Jack Gilbride very well who was the head of the Todd yards during my regime. Jack was a very good technical manager, and he did very well with Todd over the years. He got a little bit overextended toward the end. They put in quite a lot of innovations, and so on, in their yards. He was trying to get ready to take some of the business that was going elsewhere, and he got himself a little overextended with it. He's retired now, but his heirs have had a problem.

We put an adequate amount of business with Todd. They did a good job on their ships.

Paul Stillwell: Then there was that little yard that Lockheed later took over in Seattle, the Puget Sound Bridge and Dredge.

Admiral Mumma: Yes. Lockheed did well with that yard too. They were all right. We didn't have any real quarrel with them. By and large, we attempted to help all the yards in their qualifications to bid for Navy work, and we did not like any fixed quota for the private yards, or fixed quota for the navy yards. We tried to put it where it would be best done. I had no real ruckuses with private yards during my regime. They thought I was being fair, which I felt was about as far as you could go. I don't think you could've made any of them completely happy or, nor the naval shipyards completely happy because there wasn't that much business to go around so that everybody would be completely happy. But we did the best we could. And I was able to stand my ground. I had the backing, particularly, of the Under Secretary, Tom Gates.

Paul Stillwell: We haven't talked about Admiral Burke.* How much of a relationship did you have with him?

Admiral Mumma: Well, I knew Arleigh very well, and we talked very frequently on things. During one of the times, you know, when I went overseas in '56, I was asked to stop and call on the First Sea Lord, who was at that time Lord Louis Mountbatten.† So I went to see him, and he apparently had done his homework. During World War II, I had talked to Sir Harold Yarrows, who was head of the Yarrows Yard up on the Clyde, and was the father of the Yarrows boilers and so on. Sir Harold was on the Tizard Committee. The Tizard Committee was a committee that was set up by Winston Churchill to examine the organization of the Admiralty and see if there could be any improvement made, particularly in shipbuilding. And so Sir Harold and Sir Stephen Pigott, who was the head of John Brown's Yard, were on that committee, and I was asked how did we build ships in the U.S.? So I explained our general philosophy on shipbuilding and how we engineers and naval constructors got together, and particularly during the war we had a common bureau called the Bureau of Ships.

These fellows were quite concerned over the fact that the Royal Corps of Naval Constructors was all-powerful because of their royal status, and that the engineering aspects of a ship design were not very well handled. Also, that there were 15 departments in the Admiralty concerned with the building of a ship. Well, to coordinate 15 departments was quite a job. They had a Department of Torpedoes, and they had a Department of Ordnance. They had a Department of Engineering, and they had all these other auxiliary departments. Even a Department of Navigation—one built magnetic compasses and another one built gyro compasses. So you could see that that led to some problems. I told him what we did and how we did it.

---

* Admiral Arleigh A. Burke, USN, served as Chief of Naval Operations from 17 August 1955 to 1 August 1961. His oral history is in the Naval Institute collection.
† Admiral of the Fleet The Earl Mountbatten of Burma served as Great Britain's First Sea Lord and Chief of Naval Staff from 1955 to 1959.

The report, as usual, went on the shelf. But, apparently, Lord Louis Mountbatten dug out the report and read it. He apparently found my name in there, though I had not appeared as an official witness by any permission of the Navy Department. I just answered some questions for these fellows, and so he said he wanted to see me when I next came to Europe. I came to Europe on this offshore procurement thing, so I went and called on Lord Louis Mountbatten. He and his wife had us over to lunch, and we had a very nice relationship. Then he said, "I'd like you to appear before my committee that I have set up to do this, and they stand ready for a short session with you."

I was, again, completely unofficially, without any government sponsorship of the United States, I told them how we were organized. He thanked me profusely and so forth. He said, "I want to come over and see you. It probably won't be until next year, but I want to come over and see you."

I think it was '57 he came over, and he told Arleigh Burke, "You know, I'm not really interested so much in spending time with the Chief of Naval Operations. I want to go over, spend about a week with the Bureau of Ships and see how they do business because, you know, your ships had more firepower than our ships of the same tonnage; they had more speed than our ships of the same tonnage; and they had more range than our ships of the same tonnage, not only in destroyers but all the way up the line." He said, "Your aircraft carriers of 33,000 tons had 88 aircraft. Ours only had 44. You know, those things are important, and we've got to do something about it."

So he came over, and I had a reception for him at our house and had most of the senior people come and meet him and so on, and his staff that he had brought with him. Then we let him and his staff shop around the Bureau of Ships for a week as much as they wanted. When he left, he thanked us profusely, and he went back to the U.K., and he reorganized the Admiralty. He consolidated all of the departments into five really sections and with basic responsibilities. To give you a horrible example, the Royal Corps of Naval Architects had the responsibility for the design of the propellers. But the chief engineer had the responsibility for the strength of the propellers. Now, how you could separate the design and the strength of the propellers, I don't know. But that was how bad the situation was.

So when he consolidated these departments, he did it quite logically. These departments were all consolidated in five main sections. Then he had what was called a Director of Ships. And the Director of Ships was a former commander in the submarine section who, during World War II that I knew. He was knighted and made Sir Alfred. The Director of Ships had the basic responsibilities the same as we had in the Bureau of Ships now, or shall we say the Sea Systems Command now.*

Paul Stillwell: What are your recollections of Mountbatten personally?

Admiral Mumma: Oh, he was a charming individual. He really, he really had a charisma the like of which you never saw. You always wondered whether he was putting it on or whether it was natural. I thought it was pretty natural.

Paul Stillwell: How did it manifest itself? I mean, what examples might you give of this charisma?

Admiral Mumma: Well, in meeting people, in talking with the people, he could get the most out of them. They'd open up; they'd talk with him. He was most cordial to us when we were there.

Now, another instance. After I retired from the Navy, I was the president of the Society of Naval Architects and Marine Engineers. And the Royal Corps of Naval Constructors had their 75th anniversary in 1960. In other words, they were formed in '85. I was appointed the delegate to the society meeting. I was then employed by Worthington Corporation, and so I went to the meeting as the delegate of the United States. We were welcomed by Prince Philip.† Lord Louis, by this time, was Minister of Defence.‡ Lord Louis had a big reception for us, and, of course, I met him again

---

* In 1966 the material bureaus were abolished. Under the new setup the Bureau of Ships became the Naval Ship Systems Command (NavShips). In 1974 the Naval Ordnance Systems Command (NavOrd) was merged with the Naval Ship Systems Command to form the Naval Sea Systems Command (NavSea), which exists to the present.
† Prince Philip, the Duke of Edinburgh, is the husband of Britain's Queen Elizabeth II.
‡ Mountbatten was Britain's Chief of Defence Staff from 1959 to 1965. The Minister of Defence was a civilian cabinet secretary.

personally and had a very nice chat with him, and so on. I was very, very fond of that fellow. I thought that any people that denigrated either his intelligence or his intentions were very mistaken. Because I thought he was a great patriot for the United Kingdom.

Paul Stillwell: You mentioned the Society of Naval Architects and Marine Engineers and there's also the ASNE.* How much association did you have with those two groups as chief of bureau?

Admiral Mumma: Well, I joined both of them rather early in my career as a young officer in the '40s and so forth, because in my business at the Model Basin, I had a lot of association with many people that were members of these things. I thought that a good professional naval architect or professional engineer had to be a member of both of those societies. I joined willingly and enjoyed working in the society on spare time and additional, and I got a lot out of many of the assignments I had on the papers committee, on the ship research committee, and so on. Eventually, I was assigned the job of the finance and auditing committee of the society—this was before I became president. So I had had a lot of experience on the committees before and written some papers and contributed to the thing. I thought that this professionalism of our naval officers was absolutely important to the future of the design capability of the United States Navy. I still feel that way.

Paul Stillwell: In what ways do these organizations serve the profession?

Admiral Mumma: Well, in the first place, they are scientific societies basically, not just engineering design societies. They sponsor scientific research with the dues that are paid in universities and other places, and so that it is an auxiliary to government support of research. And these people serve on these research teams. They're appointed due to their capability by the president of the society, and recommendations of others that were made to the president as people that would be well on this society, that society, a committee. Instead of governing really by committees, it's a learning process on

---

* ASNE—American Society of Naval Engineers. Mumma served as ASNE's president in 1957.

committees. All we expected of the government was to get the people to the meetings. That's all. We didn't want them to put any money in—none of that. Just get them to the meetings, and we'll help train them. And that's what we did.

Then along comes this so-called ethics problem. Some people seem to think that because you accept a dinner from somebody, or lunch from somebody, that you're beholden forever and you're going to give him a big contract, which is the furthest thing from the truth because very frequently most of these committees meetings were with a lunch, associated with it. Sometimes we never knew who picked up the tab for the lunch. Sometimes the society did; sometimes some individual would do it who was particularly interested in that particular work. I never accepted anything. I never accepted a hotel bill. I never accepted anything from anybody. The maximum was up to a dinner. I never accepted from any one group a lot of dinners. So under the circumstances I felt that I was completely free to give them as much hell as I wanted any time. And they felt that way, too, so that when they started this so-called ethics thing, that it was illegal for anybody in the government to go to a meeting and accept a dinner because you would compromise your integrity. I thought it was the silliest thing I'd ever heard of. As a matter of fact, due to that thinking which permeated, oh, a period of maybe 15 years, it has resulted in lack of professionalism in a lot of these naval officers. That's why they have trouble finding guys to be really hot-shots in the design business of ships.

Paul Stillwell: How much do those journals contribute? How useful are they that the two organizations publish?

Admiral Mumma: Well, in my mind, they're going a little too far in some cases by putting stuff in there that should be classified. But I have no control over that now. I used to when I was president of both societies. I wasn't ever president at the same time of both societies. I was naval engineers first, then naval architects last. But then I continued to serve on the executive committee for years, and I still am on the naval architects' executive committee, and I'm invited to the so-called presidents' courses, and so forth, meetings here for the naval engineers. I'm participating in the May meeting of the naval engineers when we have our centennial, 1888 to 1988. The naval architects' organization is five years younger, 1893, so that centennial doesn't come for a while.

Paul Stillwell: What is the difference between the two organizations?

Admiral Mumma: Well, naval engineers is engineering only. It hasn't really to do with ship design, whereas, naval architects is both. It originally was almost all naval architects, not quite as much engineering. Now it is pretty well both. In view of the fact that I was what you might call the first "congineer," which is a constructor and engineer because I had both kinds of training, we are now attempting to train almost all the naval officers at MIT as congineers so that they're both and are not so narrow minded as to be just engineers, and so on. In other words, we're trying to make the hull and the engines part of the same ship.

Paul Stillwell: How much interaction did you have with the other bureaus? Obviously, a ship, an aircraft carrier involves the airplanes, any ship's got guns on it. How much did you deal with the other bureaus?

Admiral Mumma: Well, Jim Russell was the chief of BuAer and he was a classmate of mine. I knew him very well. Jim Russell, I think, was the original cause of Bill Franke thinking that you could do away with the engineering group as such. Because Jim Russell stood very high in my class and he was a smart guy, he could be a good Chief of Bureau of Aeronautics as well as a good line officer, and you didn't have to separate him, so to speak, to be a good one.

But when I came up, I was a lieutenant commander, and I'd been at sea a long time. I'd been in aircraft carriers, cruisers, destroyers of both types, and I was headed for command. I had the problem of deciding what the heck I should do when it came to being a specialist or being a straight line officer. A lot of the fellows that came to that point chose the command route. I talked about it with Earle Mills, as I told you, and became an ED. I've never regretted it. I some days might have delusions of grandeur and think I might have had four stars if I'd stayed in the line. Maybe. I don't know. But I can tell you this, that I got to the top of my profession and I'm proud of it. I think that I did more for the Navy than if I had been a four-star, I really do. Otherwise, I wouldn't be living very well with myself. I wouldn't be very happy. And neither would my wife. She's a happy girl, and she is very, very satisfied with the way we made our career, because she's been a very vivid part of it. We've been married 60 years now.

Paul Stillwell: Well, maybe you can talk more about that point. In what ways has she contributed?

Admiral Mumma: Well, in the first place, she's been the most supportive person I have ever known of, wife or otherwise. Because, not only did we have sons, but we had our third son was a handicapped son. He has cerebral palsy, and that frequently happens with the third child when you have a positive/negative arrangement in the blood count. That's what happened to us. But that in itself made both of us so cognizant of the frailty of the human race that we decided to make the best of whatever it was and really work at it. That's why we're going up and see our son this weekend in Philadelphia. He's at a sheltered workshop up there. He's now 53 years old, 54 years old this year, and he's happy, we're happy.

When you have, shall we say, a major, major problem of that type in a family and you overcome it because Carmen gave him physical therapy herself under Dr. Phelps, over in Baltimore, for years till she finally got him on his feet at the age of about seven or eight. Then, you know, it's tragic that we sometimes get saddled with something of that kind, but it is not only character-building; you can take almost any adversity in stride and you don't get picky at each other. As a family, you're a unified entity, unlike what's happening to so many families. They're falling apart. And so talk about supportiveness, she actually has helped me not only morally and mentally and physically in every way, but she has actually, in some cases, pitched in, and she did some drawings for me one time when I was in PG school and had to get something out real quick. She's an artist in her own right, and so I just told her what to do and she helped me with some drawings.

Paul Stillwell: Ship drawings?

Admiral Mumma: She can do mechanical drawing too. So she actually helped me, but I only called on her on that one occasion when I was really strapped. So under the circumstances that life and—you can do a better job when you're happy. There's no question about that. I'm convinced that if you have a positive way of thinking and you are not subject to negativism, you end up with doing a better job and you feel so much happier with the whole result. I sound like a Pollyanna, I suspect, but quite truthfully, it's been the story of our life. In spite of the handicap problems that we've run into, and the other problems, everything's fine. We had our 60th anniversary reunion last October 1, and we had every one of our descendants there from all over the United States. All of them are blood.

Paul Stillwell: Well, we're right near your time deadline, Admiral, so maybe that's a good note to end on for the day.

Admiral Mumma: Okay.

Paul Stillwell: We'll resume at some other time.

Interview Number 5 with Rear Admiral Albert G. Mumma, U.S. Navy (Retired)

Place: Admiral Mumma's home in Melvin Village, New Hampshire

Date: Saturday, 3 September 1988

Interviewer: Paul Stillwell

Paul Stillwell: Admiral, I put together a list of topics that we did not finish up with during our last interview in Washington. One of the things I was interested in from the time that you were Chief of the Bureau of Ships was what leadership the chief of the bureau provides for the EDO community at large.

Admiral Mumma: Well, the chief of bureau not only had to do with the approval of the assignments of all the ED officers by our ED personnel office. He also had to monitor the educational programs that were required in connection with becoming an ED, not only the ones at MIT but also at the postgraduate school in Monterey. We always felt that those postgraduate periods in an ED's career were of vital importance in the development of expertise and professionalism. Once that was developed, it then should be salted down by practical experience to apply it. So that we almost always had a great deal to do with officers' careers—where they went and what they did.

To some extent you were playing God, I presume, in trying to shape a man's career, sometimes more so than he would do for himself. I suspect that that fine Italian hand had an awful lot to do with the shaping of my career by very senior officers. We have a way of calling them mentors. As a matter of fact, the amount of recognition that those men should get from us who have succeeded in business and in our business in the Navy is so important that we recognize it wasn't just ourselves that did it. It was people putting us on the right path that made us do it. I am forever grateful to so many of those people that provided that kind of leadership in my own career, so I hoped to provide that same kind of leadership for the young officers coming along during my term.

I particularly felt, for example, that postgraduate education was vitally important. I used to read the theses of these graduates to attempt to make up my mind as to where I thought they would do the best job—to see what their thinking was and where they could make a contribution to the Navy, in what specialty. Because I always felt that a man should have a specialty of his own to be able to make a contribution. Then, after he had made his contribution in his specialty, to broaden him out to become a generalist so that he could be in charge of major programs and not just his specialty.

This was one of the disadvantages that Rickover had actually, when you analyze his training. After he got into the nuclear program, he was a specialist in the nuclear program and only that. He did not have, actually, the management skills that are required to get the maximum out of people and to motivate people other than by fear. So that he was not really a good manager. He was a specialist who went to the top. Most specialists that go to the top, they hit the top of their ceiling and stay there.

Here was a specialist that was not a manager, not a broad-scale man in many, many areas, whom you couldn't assign, shall we say, to a flag officer's job anywhere. So that's why he originally was passed over. He was not a broad-scale individual. So when the time came for his selection and he was passed over, that's when the Congress jumped in—and assuming that he was a practicing Jew—apparently rode that program right to the hilt to get him promoted. So the Secretary of the Navy finally gave in and promoted him. That's how they pushed him right on up to four stars, the same way, but he never was a broad-gauge four-star admiral.*

Paul Stillwell: He was certainly an exception.

Admiral Mumma: Yes.

So now, going back to the other basics of leadership and how to develop people, I always had a feeling that after you had given to these people experience in education and practicalized them in, say, a shipyard, why, then after the shipyard, you send them to a laboratory and theorize them again in connection with some research programs. Then after they finish that and go to sea for a period of time, again to practicalize their experience in not only education but in shipyards, and in laboratory, and at sea, you have

---

* For details on his selection for flag rank, see Norman Polmar and Thomas B. Allen, <u>Rickover: Controversy and Genius</u> (New York: Simon and Schuster, 1982).

all the possible applications of that theoretical knowledge. That is when we were supposed to put that man in the bureau as the most expert guy in that particular specialty.

Now, no industry goes to the trouble of training men to that degree to make them really, truly professionals. They do not run the risk of moving them around from one job to another to that degree to broaden their educational capability. So that's the reason why we felt that we had in each of the bureau's technical sections, the best qualified man in the whole United States because he'd had that background of technical experience. Well, then, of course, after that period of contribution, which might be 10 or 15 years long as a technical specialist of great note, you then broadened him out to become a generalist. I think that's vitally important in trying to make an overall manager out of a technical specialist. You shouldn't be too narrow that you can't broaden.

This was the type of leadership that we hoped to engender in our professional group.

Paul Stillwell: How did you go about recruiting particular officers to come into the ED community?

Admiral Mumma: We always tried to get people, not only that had the educational capability, to broaden and become expert in the field—this usually had to do with standing reasonably high in the class indicating that they were able to study and understand—but also that we would be able to build on that base. We used to examine very carefully the applications for engineering duty because of that, shall we say, selective program. It was very helpful.

Paul Stillwell: Did you have some means of communicating your ideas, your philosophy, to set a tone for the community while you were the chief?

Admiral Mumma: I not only wrote a monthly newsletter to the ED groups that gave them general philosophical views on various things, but also we had occasional seminars in the bureau itself on the various subjects for the various purposes, particularly if we were going into a new program of some sort. These were, shall we say, semi-seminars; they were not really commercial-type seminars, which are followed by a big dinner. We used them as daytime work jobs in which we would get together and study various approaches to programs.

This was started in a big way immediately after World War II got started by Cochrane and Mills when they became chief of bureau. Immediately after World War II, after the production had been established and we were, shall we say, going into a new era of management of a new type of Navy—all new ships, all new technologies—we then had this technique pretty well developed to train ourselves, as well as other people, how to do these advanced things. We picked everybody's brains that we could in industry or everywhere else in an attempt to mobilize it for our own purpose.

Paul Stillwell: What were some of the topics that you covered in the newsletters?

Admiral Mumma: Well, everything from ordinary news to general changes in philosophy that we ran into. One of the things that I particularly remember was when we ran into the program—I have mentioned to you earlier, I think, about the Franke Board.[*] See, Under Secretary Franke was an accountant basically. He felt that everything should be done mathematically and on a cost basis. He had no appreciation whatsoever for our educational program that I've just described and didn't understand it. He did not feel that engineering officers had to have that kind of training, that anybody could do the job as long as they understood how to run the mathematics of accounting.

The result of that was that he set up what was called the Franke Board, and he had several Navy members on it. Tom Moorer was one of them, and the Vice Chief of Naval Operations was also on that.[†] So that Tom was not yet in that high level position; he was a rear admiral. We felt that that board was constituted in such a manner that it was a little bit loaded to do away with the ED program. I personally felt that it was a tremendous danger. So what I did, I got all the ex-chiefs of bureau down and had them testify before

---

[*] The Franke Board issued its report in 1959. One of the consequences was the merger of the Bureau of Ordnance and the Bureau of Aeronautics to form the Bureau of Naval Weapons. For details, see Paolo E. Coletta, editor, American Secretaries of the Navy, Volume II, 1913-1972 (Annapolis: Naval Institute Press, 1980), pages 884, 897-898.

[†] Rear Admiral Thomas H. Moorer, USN, who subsequently served as Chief of Naval Operations and Chairman of the Joint Chiefs of Staff.

the Franke Board, including Ned Cochrane, Earle Mills, Jerry Land. Every single one of those old bureau chiefs that I could get ahold of, I had them come in and testify before the Franke Board about the necessity of that educational program.

So that when the Franke Board came up with their recommendation that possibly the EDs could be done away with, I had also had a meeting with all of the EDs in Washington and anywhere near Washington. They came in, and I discussed the matter with all of them in a central meeting, and got them aroused to the danger of their extinction. The net result of that was that Tom Gates, who at that time was Secretary of the Navy, was thoroughly convinced that this was not the thing to do. So the report on the Franke Board, even though it had been made a little bit wishy-washy by the testimony of all these ex-bureau chiefs, came to the conclusion that it could not be done to the benefit of the Navy, and that it was very important to the Navy to continue its training of professionals to be professional designers and builders of ships and of aircraft.

Paul Stillwell: What do you mean by saying it was made wishy-washy by the testimony of the ex-chiefs?

Admiral Mumma: No, it was, shall we say, made less effective a recommendation, because they would have made a very much stronger recommendation had they not had that testimony from the ex-bureau chiefs.

Paul Stillwell: A strong recommendation in the other direction.

Admiral Mumma: To do away with the EDs. They would have been, I think, successful if I hadn't brought those bureau chiefs in.

Paul Stillwell: You've mentioned these men that you looked up to, your mentors. Did you serve as a mentor for other junior officers coming along?

Admiral Mumma: There are a few of them, maybe.

Paul Stillwell: Any you remember in particular?

Admiral Mumma: Well, particularly Dunford and Roddis and all those young fellows that went into the nuclear program: Turnbaugh, Naymark, and so on. Another one was John McMullen. He was coming along very well, and I thought, "Well, we really ought to know more about air flow and fluid flow of all sorts, as well as air and water flow to combine—" At that time Dr. Accura in Switzerland was the foremost scientific brain in that area in the world, so I sent young John McMullen over there as a young student, as I had been originally sent by both Land and Robinson to study in France.

John McMullen, therefore, spent two years at the Techniche Hoch Schule in Zurich. He graduated from that as a doctor in fluid flow mechanics as his specialty. When he came back, he went into preliminary design in the bureau and so on, and I suppose he also felt that he was pretty highly educated and a pretty smart young man, because he'd learned some habits in France and Switzerland that didn't seem to jibe completely with our method of operation in the Navy Department, like being on time at 8:00 in the morning, etc. He was called on it by then-Captain Snyder, who felt that he should have been more assiduous in getting to the bureau on time. Well, it came to a bit of a loggerhead. Why I'll never know because I wasn't involved in the bureau at that instance. I was not in the bureau. I was on duty elsewhere or I would have probably been able to intervene and do something about it.

But before I knew it, McMullen got his ire up and resigned.[*] He later built his own company called J.J. McMullen Associates. Then he was actually made the maritime administrator. He now, of course, has built that firm of his up into a worldwide business, putting in shipyards for all the Far East countries and so on. So he now owns the Houston Astros and runs a lot of activities on the side, including the New Jersey Devils.[†] So he's become quite a guy. He's parlayed that money he inherited from his father and put into his own business into quite a fortune. John is a very good friend of mine, and I

---

[*] McMullen resigned in December 1954 when he held the rank of commander. He founded John J. McMullen Associates in 1957.
[†] McMullen owned the Houston Astros baseball team from 1979 to 1992; He has owned the New Jersey Devils hockey team since 1981.

think he says some of the kind of things about me that I've said about those other two gentlemen.

Paul Stillwell: It's unfortunate that that kind of talent was lost to the Navy.

Admiral Mumma: I felt it was a very serious loss to the Navy as such. He still is doing work for the Navy but from the outside. He could very well have been such a leader inside the Navy too.

Paul Stillwell: What qualities have made him so successful, do you think?

Admiral Mumma: Well, he's got good judgment; he's a very intelligent and understanding scientific man; and he makes friends easily. He has always done extremely well in business with his business associates, and he's got a lot of clout. So he's successful. That's all there is to it. He would have been a success in the business of the Navy as well as in the industry. Very, very successful.

Paul Stillwell: Was it those same qualities that led you to try to develop him as he was coming along in the Navy?

Admiral Mumma: I thought I could see those qualities to some degree when I sent him in particular. Of course, he was a fairly isolated case, because we weren't able to send very many overseas for educational purposes. It was a fairly expensive proposition, and there weren't very many places left after the war that you could send people overseas. For example, the Génie Maritime that I had attended had almost evaporated during World War II. The Royal Naval College in Greenwich was not of the same stature that it had been many, many years ago. And the University of Berlin was kaput for all practical purposes. The University of Glasgow didn't have the stature it had had. So that some of these foreign sources for educational institutions had dried up, and we had our own educational institutions, which were pretty well developed by this time.

Paul Stillwell: Exactly.

Admiral Mumma: So we weren't as, shall we say, dependent upon foreign education. But we should never lose sight of the fact that sometimes these foreign outfits do blossom with a tremendous rose that needs plucking. We should be alert to that, and that's what I tried to do with John McMullen with Accura in Switzerland.*

Paul Stillwell: When you were the chief of the Bureau of Ships, how much did you do personally in seeing about the assignments of the top EDs?

Admiral Mumma: All the top jobs were cleared with the chief of the bureau, even to including captains going to production officers or going to planning officers in shipyards, or going to a laboratory or anything of that kind. Those were all the top-quality jobs that were a part of this blossoming and, shall we say, toward the end, broadening program.

Paul Stillwell: Did you pretty well know the service reputations of the captains and above?

Admiral Mumma: Yes. Yes, we had access to their records for purposes of assignment to see what kind of jobs they'd had, how well they'd done in them, and what their requests had been, what kind of duty they wanted. So that we would automatically be able to, shall we say, use judgment in connection with those assignments. It was an important job. Why, I think I'm amazed when I look back and see how well it was done before my day when I was one of the young guys coming up. I was amazed that they had done as well as they did.

Paul Stillwell: It was probably easier then because the community was smaller.

---

* McMullen received a doctorate in mechanical engineering from the Swiss Federal Technical Institute and a master's in naval architecture and marine engineering from Massachusetts Institute of Technology.

Admiral Mumma: Oh, yes, of course, before World War II we only had 8,000 graduates of the Naval Academy. Almost all the officers in the Navy at that time you knew either by reputation or personally.

For example, at the academy the time I was there you knew about 4,000 people total that had been ahead of you and behind you at the academy, and that was quite a few people. I happened to know every single member of my class that graduated, because I made a point of it to get to know them, and it was helpful.

Paul Stillwell: What qualities were required for an officer going to be a supships at a private yard as compared with somebody in one of the naval shipyards?[*]

Admiral Mumma: Ordinarily we wouldn't send them as a supships in a private yard until they'd had experience in a navy yard, because it was important that they know in general how such a job was handled. The supervisor of shipbuilding took the same general responsibility actually as another arm of the bureau. Therefore, he had a lot of delegated responsibility and authority. So ordinarily he was a man of judgment who had proved himself in various activities in naval shipyards and was a broad-gauged man that you could trust to make good Navy decisions relative to the contractor's activities and the installation of other contractors' equipment in ships. They were excellent people, generally speaking. I think of one in particular. There was a man by the name of Leonard Kaplan in the class of 1922.[†] Have you ever heard of him?

Paul Stillwell: Certainly have. He was on a detachable page in the Lucky Bag.

Admiral Mumma: That's right. He was a Jew and a very fine man. I knew him personally, and I liked him very, very much. He was the one that had a cause célèbre

---

[*] Supships—supervisor of shipbuilding; this is a naval officer who is the Navy's on-scene representative to monitor the progress of construction and repair of Navy ships.
[†] Midshipman Jerauld L. Olmsted, USN, had the top standing at the graduation of the Naval Academy's class of 1922. Midshipman Leonard Kaplan, USN, finished second in the class and was the victim of prejudice and mistreatment because he was Jewish. His entry in the 1922 Naval Academy yearbook, the Lucky Bag, was printed on a perforated page so it could be removed from the book by those who so desired. For more on the Olmsted-Kaplan rivalry, see Polmar and Allen, Rickover, pages 53-58.

against the Navy, who never exercised it as Rickover did. He was the one that was so smart and so intelligent, he would have stood one in the class of 1922 had it not been for prejudice, I'm sure. Jerry Olmsted stood one, and he was the editor of the Lucky Bag that perforated the page.

But Jerry Olmsted I knew, and I knew the Olmsted family. They were originally from Iowa. Jerry was the class of '22, and he had a brother at West Point as well.[*] They were twin brothers, the Olmsted twins. Then there was another Olmsted in the class of '27, Fred Olmsted.[†] So that the Olmsteds never quite got over that. It was a very bad smear on the Olmsted name to have had that problem with Leonard Kaplan.

But what I started to say about Leonard Kaplan, he was one of the very, very good and great naval architects. He also was a very fine supervisor of shipbuilding in New York. So that there is a man that got nowhere near the credit he should have had, who was an excellent, excellent brain and a very practical engineer and naval constructor.

Paul Stillwell: What made him so good? What qualities?

Admiral Mumma: Well, he was smart. He was so intelligent. He grasped things instantly. Rickover was a dolt, in comparison; he was just incapable of being the same kind of a man as Leonard Kaplan.[‡] Well, that's my personal opinion.

Paul Stillwell: I remember talking with Admiral Elliott Strauss who was in the class of '23 and who was the first CO of the USS Fresno, which was built at Kearny.[§] He remembers Kaplan very favorably from that period for his work.

Admiral Mumma: He did a very nice job.

---

[*] Cadet George H. Olmsted stood second in the class of 1922 at the U.S. Military Academy.
[†] Midshipman Frederick L. Olmsted, USN, resigned from the naval service prior to graduation from the Naval Academy.
[‡] Kaplan and Rickover were Naval Academy classmates. Kaplan retired in 1949 as a captain.
[§] See the Naval Institute oral history of Rear Admiral Elliott B. Strauss, USN (Ret.).

Paul Stillwell: What are the responsibilities that fall to a supervisor of shipbuilding?

Admiral Mumma: Well, he is the on-site representative of the bureau, or the Navy Department, to ensure that the specifications are complied with; to ensure that the timeliness of the work is accomplished; and to ensure that any communications back and forth between the Navy and the contractor are properly handled. Not only from a monetary point of view but also from the efficiency of the program. It's a broad-gauge job and it requires a lot of good judgment. This was where Kaplan was superior.

Paul Stillwell: Do you remember any examples of his superior judgment?

Admiral Mumma: Not in detail because I had very little to do, actually, with monitoring of a supervisor of shipbuilding except in instances later in my time when Leonard had already retired.

Paul Stillwell: Do you think that this stigma, or whatever, that had plagued him at the Naval Academy went with him throughout his later career?

Admiral Mumma: Well, a lot of people knew about it, but I don't think it plagued him. I think it indicated that the Navy had changed and would no longer tolerate that kind of bias. That's the reason why I was so surprised and shocked that they were able to accuse the Navy of so much bias in connection with Rickover. There wasn't that bias against Rickover. That wasn't the problem. Rickover was a vertical specialist, and he hadn't broadened.

Paul Stillwell: I think part of it was his personality too.

Admiral Mumma: Oh, well, of course, I can talk about that for quite a long time.

Paul Stillwell: Well, it sounds as if Kaplan was a big man, that he didn't let that get him down too.

Admiral Mumma: That's right, he was. He was a man of stature and real, real judgment.

Paul Stillwell: We haven't talked about the business of change orders, but I think that would be a thing that would fall to the supervisor of shipbuilding also, to negotiate with the yards on.

Admiral Mumma: Yes, yes, and minimize any unnecessary changes—trying to get the job done effectively and quickly and, shall we say, with maximum performance.

Paul Stillwell: And there again it calls for judgment. What change is so much better that it's worth causing the inconvenience and the extra price and so forth?

Admiral Mumma: This is one reason why we used to do ships two or three at a crack in one shipyard, so that we had time to make changes in the next group of ships and not upset the contract that was in progress at the time, which is a complete philosophy change with McNamara. I don't know if we'll be able ever get back to a good and decent method of doing it, which is to spread the program, to put the competition in the various yards, and to ensure that you don't open up contracts for changes that should come in later models of that same class of ship.

Paul Stillwell: Well, I think it's gotten back somewhat to the idea that you like, with more competition and spreading them out some more—the Aegis cruiser program, for example.[*]

Admiral Mumma: Not enough. Not enough. Take the destroyer program—the Arleigh Burke ships—they're not spread enough.[†]

---

[*] The Aegis air defense system, which involves the use of computers and phased-array radars, is installed in the cruisers of the Ticonderoga (CG-47) class and destroyers of the Arleigh Burke (DDG-51) class.
[†] USS Arleigh Burke (DDG-51) was commissioned 4 July 1991. She has a standard displacement of 6,624 tons, is 504 feet long, and 67 feet in the beam, and maximum draft of 31 feet. Her design speed is 31 knots. She is equipped with the Aegis system; a 90-cell vertical launching system for missiles; two quadruple Harpoon canisters; one 5-inch gun, ASROC, and two triple torpedo launchers.

Paul Stillwell: Well, of course, the shipbuilding base is shrinking too.

Admiral Mumma: Todd Shipyards hasn't been given any of them, you see, and they're going out of business. That kind of thing is wrong, because Todd Shipyards, even though they might be having a little higher price of manpower per hour on the West Coast, could have done, I would think, a very economical job in the long run. The more they got into it, the better they would have done. So that I don't say that just because the West Coast has a higher manpower per hour rate, that you should avoid putting stuff on the West Coast. You've got to broaden the base so that we have a broad shipbuilding base in the United States. Even with that little slight additional variation that there might be, it's far more valuable to have that base than have that few extra dollars that would have been saved.

Paul Stillwell: Well, you told me that was part of your philosophy when deciding where contracts would go.

Admiral Mumma: Exactly. Exactly.

Paul Stillwell: How much did you get around to the various shipyards when you were chief of the bureau to see how things were progressing?

Admiral Mumma: I did a lot of it. I rode ships as the chief of bureau—which didn't used to happen very much; most of the chiefs were too busy to ride ships—but I used to like to ride ships. After all, I'd had a lot of sea duty, and I liked sea duty. So I'd go and see how they were doing. I liked the new aircraft carriers. One time three of us landed on the Ranger—three flag officers in one airplane.[*] It was one of the first times that anything like that had happened in recent years. That was the beginning of the jet operation in those days on ships, and we were curious as to how everything was going at sea. You had to stay with it and find out firsthand how things were. They would give you

---

[*] USS Ranger (CVA-61) was commissioned 10 August 1957.

information that they wouldn't write and send you in a letter or a dispatch. So I always used to like to get the information by word of mouth from people that were experiencing it. It's a hands-on approach, and I always liked that. As a matter of fact, I had a hands-on approach enough that I was a really, really dirty-handed old engineer.

Paul Stillwell: But you have a capable deputy to leave things with if you're going to go out riding these ships.

Admiral Mumma: That's exactly right. I wasn't there long enough that they took over the job.

Paul Stillwell: I was interested in your work with the design section of the bureau when you were the chief. How much input did you have into that?

Admiral Mumma: Having been a design man in various parts of the program, starting with research and going right on up through into actual riding ships, I always had a terrible curiosity, as well as an interest, in what we were doing. I used to go up and hang over the drawing boards and see what people were doing in design. I got to know most of the people pretty well, and they would pretty well level with me as just one engineer to another, one naval architect to another. You could get quite a bit of information that way as to how things were going and should go. I got in the habit of reading drawings upside-down, you know, leaning over the backside of the drawing board, watching. You could pretty well learn a lot more than they thought you were learning. That is a trick that instructors in colleges learn and others learn, and I had learned early on—how to read drawings upside-down. So that always stood you in good stead. Not only knowing the people, chatting with the people about their work, giving them a little boost, a little goose occasionally, something of that kind.

But take, for example, I had been at sea in the 115, the Waters, a destroyer, and it was a flush-deck destroyer. Before that there had been forecastle deck destroyers in the old time with waist guns shooting past the forecastle. That was the old time—the Barry was like that. Then we had flush-deck destroyers in the mid-'30s, except along comes the Phelps class, and she was a forecastle destroyer. I served in both types, and the forecastle destroyer was a so much better sea boat than a flush-deck destroyer, because those flush-deck destroyers in heavy waves would stick that nose under and, boy, it'd take forever for them to rise out of it.

Paul Stillwell: Not as much freeboard.

Admiral Mumma: Well, they didn't have enough freeboard forward. As a matter of fact, we probably would have lost the Clark if she had been a flush-deck destroyer at that time when we had that trough.

As a long-term view, I insisted when we had a new destroyer program that we go to a forecastle because they were so much better sea boats. And then, also, that we attempt to make stacks in such a fashion that they would not interfere with the operational equipment—either higher stacks or whatever to ensure that we did not have anything that was being smoked out aft of the stacks. Or if we had a following wind, smoked out forward of the stacks. For instance, at sea in the Clark I actually put hoods on the stacks to smooth the flow of the gases out of there so we wouldn't get as much gas eddying onto the bridge area. Well, that was completely illegal to put a hood on the forward end of the stack. But then later everybody finally got hoods on their stacks so that they didn't eddy anymore like that.

Well, those are the kinds of things that you have to do occasionally to feel, know how it goes and what the problems are. I remember one instance when I was at the bureau in the propeller desk, and we were running the battleships. I think it was the Iowa class that we were worrying about the bridge area and from the forward guns and the after superstructure area from the after guns when they were trained at full train.

I volunteered to be a guinea pig, and, knowing all the model basin people, why, they thought that would be great. So I would stand at a position where the gun crews would be, and where they would see maximum train of the big guns while they were on a gun crew station for smaller caliber guns. When those guns went off—the big ones, the whole salvo of six of them at one time—Wham! I had on a brand-new commander's hat, and it flew off my head and over the side. I thought I'd been smacked in the chest with a

Albert G. Mumma, Interview #5 (9/3/88) – Page 254

ten-ton tank, and I just felt almost as though I'd been knocked out by this thing, the concussion was so great.

Paul Stillwell: Was that the Iowa herself?

Admiral Mumma: Yes, it was the Iowa.* So we immediately came to the conclusion that they'd have to limit the angle of train, otherwise you'd just knock those gun crews galley west. The blast pressures were measured in the area. Apparently, I'd taken an over-pressure at least 30 to 40 pounds per square inch over atmospheric pressure on my chest and my hat, and everything else. I never got the hat replaced. The government never replaced my hat. I bought another one.

Paul Stillwell: What do you remember about the repair of the damage to the Iowa after she scraped her bottom?†

Admiral Mumma: Well, I was worried about propellers at that time. I went up and visited her in Bayonne where she was dry-docked. I examined the propellers and couldn't find any damage to the propellers. But I did examine, and saw that tremendous rip down through the whole bottom of the hull just inside of the rolling keels. It was a very sad, sad experience. I came back and reported how bad it was, and, of course, they had official reports from the yard and from the dockyard people as well. That took her out of operation for quite a while while they did that repair work, because it had, I think, affected maybe half a dozen, or maybe a dozen lower deck compartments in the ship's bottom that had flooded. The loss of buoyancy was adequate to be a problem in case that had happened in wartime or in action. But the repair of it took, I think, several weeks and

---

* USS Iowa (BB-61), the lead ship of her class, was commissioned 22 February 1943. She had a standard displacement of 45,000 tons and full-load displacement of 57,600 tons. She was 887 feet long and 108 feet in the beam. Her top speed was 33 knots. Initially she was armed with nine 16-inch guns, 20 5-inch guns, and 80 40-mm guns in quad mounts, and 49 20-mm guns in single mounts.
† On 16 July 1943, while completing a transit from New York City, the Iowa cut a long gash in her bottom while entering Casco Bay, Maine, shortly after low water. The commanding officer at the time was Captain John L. McCrea, USN. McCrea, who retired as a vice admiral, discussed the incident in his Naval Institute oral history.

delayed her going to sea. Other than that, she was a pretty fine ship, I thought. It was one of those accidents, and I guess McCrea always felt pretty bad about that.

Paul Stillwell: He did. He told me that. He said that he was saved by having been the President's naval aide, so no ill consequences came to him.*

Admiral Mumma: I think that's true. I think there's no question that he'd gotten a little tougher action if he hadn't had that President's assignment.

Paul Stillwell: We talked when you were discussing that assignment about the singing propellers and about the skegs and about the five-bladed and the four-bladed. What other aspects about that particular job do you remember?

Admiral Mumma: Well, the long-term effect of that was that people had to do an awful lot of thinking before they installed propeller combinations, certain numbers of blades, certain lengths of shafts, certain sizes of bossings, sizes of bulbous bows. All those things were accentuated in more recent years because of the necessity to avoid vibration and to improve performance. For example, I don't think anyone would ever have visualized the tremendous bulbous bows that have been put on these enormous tankers.

Everybody took the position that bulbous bows were very, very dangerous to have on ships because of slamming. That if the ship rolls above the wave and slams down, you'd have this big flat surface forward and you'd do a lot of damage to the underwater portion of the ship forward. That's why the British never adopted bulbous bows, because they were afraid of slamming. But we adopted a much bigger bulb on the United States than anybody would ever put on, because I sort of forced them to put a bigger bulb on there, but I still didn't get as big a one as I wanted. As a result of that, why, she never had any slamming problem. As a matter of fact, those big bulbs have a tendency to stabilize the ship, acting as sort of a horizontal fin forward to assist in stabilizing the ship rather than forcing the tremendous slamming that sometimes would happen.

---

* Captain McCrea had been naval aide to President Franklin D. Roosevelt in 1942-43, until shortly before taking command of the battleship.

The ship is a very, very movable item in a very, very heavy sea. There's no way in the world you can predict how bad a sea is going to be because you get such phenomenal waves sometimes. So occasionally you can get a slamming problem even with a minimum bow. So you can't generalize too much by saying, "Oh, well, that'll cause slamming." So that bulbous bow was always a very, very fine thing to put on ships. We had to put them on destroyers when we began putting all that sonar equipment forward. And it didn't hurt them at all. It helped stabilize them.

Paul Stillwell: Do you remember any other specifics from that time on the propeller desk, any other projects, any other types of ships or classes of ships you worked with?

Admiral Mumma: Well, I've told you all the things I think that are of considerable importance. Certainly the quieting, the cavitation, and I think in general it's in much better hands now, much better shape than it used to be. We had more unsolved problems in those days that had not ever been worked on sufficiently. But we solved quite a few of them during World War II having to do with the design and elimination of vibration, improvement of performance and so on. We had a pretty good record in solving the problems as they appeared and became more important. The higher the speed we went to, the more important they became. For years before then, we didn't have any battleships that made over 20 knots. Nobody ever thought of 30-knot battleships, 30 or above. So we moved up into an entirely new field.

Paul Stillwell: One of the ironies of it was that so many ships were built during the war itself that the knowledge you acquired from operations you couldn't apply to many new ships in the postwar era because there were already a lot on hand.

Admiral Mumma: That's right, we learned a lot during the war, but we didn't learn it on what the new designs were going to be. So we had to do quite a bit of, shall we say, research-type programs like we did at the model basin and so on, as well as we could do it in the model scale and apply it in full scale. But you had to do it in full scale to check it out, because model scale is all right, but you cannot extrapolate from a 30-scale ratio with great accuracy. Particularly in a phenomenon that has to do with mass and time, you can't do the mass/scale ratios. You can't do the density/scale ratios. It's just impossible to do.

Paul Stillwell: Well, one solution to this thing was that in the 1950s a number of these war-built ships were converted in the FRAM program.* What do you recall about that one?

Admiral Mumma: Well, of course, this was just to modernize and upscale these ships into what would be the current requirements, and I thought it was a pretty efficient program because of the fact that we got much more effective ships. They had better equipment for detection, radar. They had better capability in firepower than they had had. We didn't get a brand-new ship out of it, but we got an awful lot more than we had had. I suspect that it was money well spent. I think it turned out that way in the long run. We converted some radar pickets. We did some other kinds of things which were similar but slightly different from the FRAMs, but we were able to extend our capability in those ships.

Paul Stillwell: What kind of a requirement does it put on the bureau to plan and manage a program like that?

Admiral Mumma: It's tough from some points of view, because we had other regular shipbuilding programs going on at the same time, and some of the same talent that you would have used on the one was used on the other. So it spread us a little bit thin in spots, but overall, I think we were all pretty gung ho about the changes that were going on, and we wanted to see them accomplished. An example that I think you put on the list was the guided missile cruisers.

Paul Stillwell: Right.

---

* FRAM is an acronym for the fleet rehabilitation and modernization program. Under this program many U.S. destroyer-type ships of the 1950s and 1960s were substantially modernized by extensive rebuilding that incorporated later technology than that available at the time of original construction.

Admiral Mumma: We felt that those cruisers needed a better antiaircraft capability. There was no way in the world that we could put enough gun power on those ships to bring down aircraft in adequate numbers. If there were kamikaze attacks in any quantity against a bunch of ships, those cruisers couldn't be very effective in bringing down aircraft. We'd had that experience with the kamikazes. So under the circumstances, you had to have a better way to bring down aircraft attacks with antiaircraft equipment. Well, the best antiaircraft equipment, of course, were guided missiles.[*]

You may have heard this story before, but it's becoming something of a classic in that when we first started, we had two-barrel approaches, firing two missiles at a time, one a little ahead of the other out of a single launcher. The plan was that you'd fire two missiles and that the first missile missed, the second missile would hit, just being slightly different in time of firing or something else. Your chance of hitting would be increased considerably. Well, you may know and may have heard that the very first firing that was done down off of Guantanamo, one of the missile cruisers against a drone aircraft, that the first missile fired hit the drone and it broke in half. The forward end of the drone was falling rather rapidly because it had the heavier equipment in it, and the tail section of the drone was falling slower. The second missile went and hit the tail section of the aircraft, and I think those missiles were quite expensive at that time—I think several thousand dollars each. So one of the sayings was that that was the most expensive piece of tail the Navy ever had. [Laughter] So, thereafter, they changed the technique to firing only single missiles rather than double firings, instant double firings at every aircraft, because the missiles did a much more effective job than originally expected. And that has proved out over the years.

Paul Stillwell: No, I hadn't heard that story before.

---

[*] USS Boston (CAG-1), which had previously been a conventional heavy cruiser, was recommissioned on 1 November 1955 as the world's first guided missile cruiser. She retained six of her original nine 8-inch gun and was fitted with two twin launchers for Terrier surface-to-air missiles. She was soon joined in the fleet by her new sister ship, Canberra (CAG-2), which was recommissioned 15 June 1956.

Well, a conversion like that involves several bureaus. Obviously you've got the electronics; you've got the missile itself, so you've got aviation and ordnance. How did you coordinate all that?

Admiral Mumma: Well, the bureaus weren't islands like they had been at one time. You know, it was just a couple of personalities that caused the interaction between those bureaus just before the war. We had a good cooperative group of people in the bureaus. There was very little jealousy, or, shall we say, dogmatic attitudes. The Bureau of Ordnance, for example, with this guided missile thing, our preliminary design people and their preliminary design people would work just at the same desk and come up with a complete solution to any problem. We loaned people back and forth, experts in various areas, so that as we were sitting down putting something in a ship, we had the best brains capable to tell us what to do with it and how to do it. So that the Bureau of Ordnance and the Bureau of Ships got along extremely well, not only because when I was chief of bureau, I knew the chief of the Bureau of Ordnance very, very well. We tried to ensure that that filtered all the way down through the organization. But the same thing with the Bureau of Aeronautics. We had a very close relationship with each other, and there was no dogmatic attitude.

Paul Stillwell: What do you remember about the specific bureau chiefs that you worked with? For instance, Admiral Withington was the Chief of the Bureau of Ordnance there for a while.

Admiral Mumma: He was Chief of the Bureau of Ordnance, class of '23, very good friend of mine. We had minor differences of opinion. He didn't understand the engineering aspects quite as well, of course, and I didn't understand the ordnance aspects quite as well, though I'd had a lot of sea duty and I had worked with ordnance. We got along all right—there was no problem.

At first Jim Russell was the chief of the Bureau of Aeronautics when I was there, and he and I were very close friends. Got along extremely well. Then he was relieved by

Bill Schoech—S-C-H-O-E-C-H is the way it's spelled but it's pronounced "Shea."[*] And then Fred Withington was relieved by my classmate P. D. Stroop.[†]

Paul Stillwell: What qualities do you remember from Admiral Russell? He later became VCNO.[‡]

Admiral Mumma: Jim was a very intelligent guy. We got along very well. He stood high in the class. So we had a good mutual respect for each other. But Jim stayed in the line and did not become a specialist. So he did well in the line—got four stars out of it, which I didn't begrudge him because he was a good man, earned it.

Paul Stillwell: Certainly a broad-gauged individual.

Admiral Mumma: Yes. I had told you, I think, earlier about when he was in command of the patrol squadrons up in the Aleutians during the war.

Paul Stillwell: I don't remember specifically.

Admiral Mumma: It was a rather short story. The Aleut Indians out on these islands had lived on these islands for centuries. He was invited to dinner with one of these Aleut groups; he was a commander at that time. He went to this dinner, and when it came time to cook the meal, why, they went to this great big pot of oil that was right in the middle of the cave. It was a very deep cavern, apparently, full of oil. Whenever they made a kill—a seal or walrus, or anything of that kind—they'd throw the meat in there, bones and all. After trimming it out, they'd throw it in there. Then when it came time to get something out for dinner, somebody would dive in the pool and come up with a haunch of

---

[*] Russell was relieved by Rear Admiral Robert E. Dixon, USN, who served as Chief of the Bureau of Aeronautics from 15 July 1957 to 1 December 1959.
[†] Rear Admiral Paul D. Stroop, USN, served as Chief of the Bureau of Ordnance from March 1958 to September 1959. The oral history of Stroop, who retired as a vice admiral, is in the Naval Institute collection.
[‡] Admiral James S. Russell, USN, served as Vice Chief of Naval Operations from 1 August 1958 to 1 November 1961.

something. You wouldn't know whether it was a dinosaur or what it was. [Laughter] But that's what you'd have for dinner.

Paul Stillwell: That's aged meat.

What do you think has been lost by the abolition of the old bureaus?*

Admiral Mumma: Well, the first thing that's been lost is access to high levels in the Navy Department and access to the high levels in the Department of Defense.

When I was chief of bureau, I reported directly to the Secretary of the Navy for shipbuilding and to the Chief of Naval Operations for maintenance of the fleet. Next up the line, of course, was the Secretary of Defense, and the next up the line from that was the President. So I was only, really, three removed from the President. Whereas, now the Sea Systems Command is about five or six or seven down the line from the Chief of Naval Operations, and has no access whatsoever to the Secretary in person officially. He may do it unofficially but not officially. The Secretary of the Navy doesn't have the authority he used to have. It's all centralized pretty much in the Department of Defense. So, therefore, it's a double whammy in losing clout.

Then the individual secretaries don't have the ability to act as independently as they used to from the Department of Defense because of that centralization. The Joint Chiefs of Staff are supposed to be completely operational and the secretaries of the Navy have very little to do with operations. The secretaries of Air Force and Army same thing. So the Joint Chiefs and the Secretary of Defense, you notice, are the all-powerful areas today, which removes them even further from what used to be the Bureau of Ships.

The Chief of Naval Operations, for example, does not have the authority for operations that he used to. His title is to some degree a misnomer at the moment.

Paul Stillwell: That's right.

---

* In 1966 the material bureaus were abolished. Under the new setup the Bureau of Ships became the Naval Ship Systems Command (NavShips). In 1974 the Naval Ordnance Systems Command (NavOrd) was merged with the Naval Ship Systems Command to form the Naval Sea Systems Command (NavSea), which exists to the present.

Admiral Mumma: So, under the circumstances, his authority comes really as a member of the Joint Chiefs rather than as Chief of Naval Operations. So it's a much more radical change than most people realize. It's had a very serious effect on the ability of the Navy, or the Air Force, or the Army to bring their expertise to bear on individual areas.

I used to be able to make decisions myself having to do with things that were pretty far-reaching as far as the Navy was concerned. Well, let me say that I hope that I was doing it well because of my training. When I saw my associates in industry that were making similar decisions, I knew that I was better trained in my business than they were in theirs. In other words, I had a broader background of experience in my business than they had in theirs, and, therefore, I didn't hesitate to back them down if I thought they were wrong, which is something you can't do anymore.

Paul Stillwell: Do you have examples of that—where you would back down the industry counterparts?

Admiral Mumma: Well, William Francis Gibbs—I told you about that. I forced him to put more bulb on the United States because she had military features. And I forced him to change the position of the propellers on the United States to increase the ability to prevent vibration and change the bossings as much as we could. If I'd had complete authority, I would have had him take the bossings off entirely and put struts on, but I managed to at least make him move the propellers. And so as a big ship, she was nowhere near as bad a vibrator as any of the previous big ships. She was a much better ship.

Paul Stillwell: Do you recall other examples of that?

Admiral Mumma: Well, I had the same arguments with the number of blades on propellers; I had the same arguments with other vibratory problems with various people. They wouldn't believe that it was important—the same arguments in connection with singing propellers. In other words, there's a tremendous amount of ignorance in the world about ships. People don't realize that a ship is the most complicated system of systems ever devised by man, because a ship has every system that a city has; and it has everything that an army has; everything that a navy has in the way of weapons for protection and for projection of your authority. In other words, you've got all the defense; you've got all the offensive weapons; you've got everything a ship has.

Well now, that's a pretty complicated system of systems. Most people don't understand that a ship is that complicated. You know, it has to go out there and be independent for an indefinite period of time—submarines particularly. My gosh, with submarines you've got to provide your own atmosphere. That's a tough assignment. That was one of the toughest things we ever had to do, was to ensure that that atmosphere inside of that submarine would stay livable.

Paul Stillwell: Admiral Rickover, of course, was legendary for his confrontations with the commercial shipbuilders. Did you ever get involved in adjudicating some of those?

Admiral Mumma: Oh, yes, you always ran into that, because he would make them so damn mad and they couldn't talk to him. He was dogmatic about everything. It was too bad that—well, quite frequently Roddis or Dunford or some of those other fellows would be able to be intermediaries and be more reasonable with the contractors. And the contractors would very frequently try to get them to handle it, if possible.

Paul Stillwell: That's certainly understandable.

Admiral Mumma: But when Rickover would call them up at 3:00 o'clock in the morning and raise hell with them, it was a little difficult to get the young fellows in the act.

Paul Stillwell: As you've been talking here this morning in your office, you pointed occasionally to the signed portrait of Admiral Burke. What were your relationships like with him when you were chief and he was CNO?

Admiral Mumma: I knew Arleigh Burke early on. He was a first classman when I was a plebe at the Naval Academy, but I didn't know him directly. We weren't in the same battalion. But over the years in destroyers and other places, I knew him from time to time. But I didn't get to know him really well until he became Chief of Naval Operations and I was Chief of the Bureau of Ships before he got there because I had reported originally when Mick Carney was there. But Arleigh, apparently, was a part of the youth movement that was planned at that time. I think part of that must have stemmed from Eisenhower.[*] I don't think it was primarily the Secretary of the Navy, who was Charlie Thomas. But there was a feeling that we had quite a few fairly older men in the major jobs, and so they wanted to move down and get some younger people in. I've already told you that they jumped way down to grab me, and I was really shocked when they did that.

But I was very happy to see that they grabbed Arleigh because of his record during the war in destroyers and so on. He was a very good choice. There had been so many aviators in recent years and been in that job just before Arleigh, in spite of Mick Carney not being an aviator, that I liked seeing a destroyer man in there.[†] I'd spent a considerable amount of time in destroyers, and I thought he'd bring a good small-ship point of view to some of the problems. I think he did that.

He, also, made a broad-gauge approach to the Navy problems. He was quite a bit younger than any of the previous chiefs of naval operations.[‡] So, automatically, it was a younger point of view. He was emphatic, very definite mind of—had his own ideas about things. But he also was a very hard worker. He spent an awful lot of time in the office, so much time I thought that that almost was wearing him out. He would be in the office until 11:00 o'clock at night, having started maybe at 7:00.

I remember one time in particular I got home in Chesterbrook Woods, and Carmen told me that Arleigh Burke had called. I got home about 7:00 o'clock from the bureau, and he had just called a few minutes before. So I called him at his number in the Navy Department where he had left his proper number. He said, "What the hell are you

---

[*] Dwight D. Eisenhower served as President of the United States from 20 January 1953 to 20 January 1961. During World War II he had been Supreme Commander of the Allied Expeditionary Force for the invasion of Europe. In the early 1950s, as a five-star general, he served as Supreme Allied Commander in Europe when the military portion of the North Atlantic Treaty Organization (NATO) was established.
[†] The first naval aviator to serve as Chief of Naval Operations was Admiral George W. Anderson, Jr., USN, who relieved Burke in August 1961.
[‡] Burke was born in 1901; his predecessor, Admiral Carney, was born in 1895.

doing, taking a half holiday—getting home about 7:00?" So that was his attitude. He was going to be there three or four more hours, and I had been in the Navy Department for about 12 hours at that time, so I thought that was almost enough.

As a matter of fact, we did work pretty heavy hours in those days. I was always in the office around 7:30. We had a quarter of eight meeting of all the assistant bureau chiefs, and we'd go over anything that came up during the night, or anything that we would want to plan to do during that coming day. Everybody get on base together and knew what was going on and where we were headed that day. You could always say, "Well, I'm going down to the Hill at such and such a time, and So-and-So, you take over this, that, and the other thing," and delegate your authorities as necessary.

At any rate, we got to know each other mostly at either meetings over in the Pentagon with the Secretary, with Arleigh, and so on, of the bureau chiefs or some other special program. Or occasionally we would have special opportunities when we had visitors of some sort, like when we had Mountbatten or somebody like that come over, why, we'd get together and talk about the various programs and problems.

He also was a very good observer of what was going on, and he had definite ideas of how to handle things. I never hesitated to voice my opinions to him directly on any item that came up, and he was receptive in hearing this kind of thing. I don't know whether I told you that when I had my potential successors in Washington, I trotted them all out, took them all over at one time or another—individually and so forth—to be interviewed by Arleigh and the Secretary.

We had a five-man committee when I was about to be detached, to choose the successor as Chief of the Bureau of Ships. This five-man committee consisted of the Chief of Naval Operations, the Vice Chief of Naval Operations, and the Secretary of the Navy, and the Under Secretary of the Navy, and myself. That made the five of us. Everybody had a chance to view and talk with all the potential candidates, which were three of them. One was Mike Honsinger, my deputy; another one was Jimmy Farrin who had been in design for many, many years, and had done the Polaris program for BuShips with Red Raborn; and the third one was Jimmy James up there above the Vancouver picture, who was primarily a naval constructor with considerable sea experience—but as a maintenance man, and so forth, rather than design experience.

So I had these fellows each appear in one fashion or another on the Hill defending programs or telling about various items, or at the Navy Department to talk about a various subject matter. So they all got exposure to the five members. Of course, I knew them all very well. They didn't need exposure with me, but they did for these others. Finally I said, "Look, Arleigh, we've got to make up our mind pretty soon which one of these fellows is going to relieve me, because my four years is up at the end of April of 1959." I suppose I told you that Tom Gates offered me a four-year appointment to succeed myself.

Paul Stillwell: I don't remember that.

Admiral Mumma: I said no, I didn't want to do that. I said, "Four years is enough for any one man to have that job, because there's a lot of young fellows down the line looking up to that job." I remember looking up myself. I said, "I don't want to clog the promotional opportunity nor the job opportunity—four more years. That would really set back the whole ED operation very, very seriously. Besides, I think I can get a job in industry if I get out at a reasonable age." I was young enough. I said, "If you can't give them ten years in industry, they don't want you. I can give them more than ten years if I get out and get a job."

Because at that time my total value was the equity in my house. I'd sold every bit of stock years before because of all the contracts I'd been making for years, ever since I was in design. I didn't own any stock at all, and it was all in that real estate. So I knew that I'd better get out and start making some money if I was going to have enough money to live on. I knew my naval pay wasn't going to keep me at a very high status of luxury. So I told Arleigh, "We've got to make this decision pretty quick."

He said, "Al, you know what the trouble is? There isn't a single one of these guys that's as big a son-of-a-bitch as you are."

I said, "Oh, that's what you're looking for?"

He said, "Well, not necessarily."

So it turned out that Jimmy James was the one that the five-man committee selected.* He did a very good job, though he did not have nuclear experience, nor did he have an adequate amount of design experience. So that's why we put a nuclear-experienced deputy in with him. That was Admiral Bob Moore, who relieved Mike Honsinger.† Mike Honsinger went to be shipyard commander out at Mare Island.

Paul Stillwell: What qualities in Admiral James led to his selection?

Admiral Mumma: He had had a lot of fleet experience during World War II. He'd been out in the South Pacific and had a lot to do with battle damage repair, and was a very good ship repair man. He'd had a lot of shipyard experience, and he also had a very good record at Long Beach Naval Shipyard, where he was shipyard commander. So Jimmy was a good fleet man; he didn't have an extensive postgraduate other than at MIT. In other words, he had had almost no experience at laboratories or anything of that kind. But he had had such an extensive fleet experience that he was a good man to come in at that stage of the game. I think it was a good choice. In other words, you don't want to have exactly the same kind of fellow every single tour in the bureau. You want to have a little move this way, and a little move that way, and a little variation in expertise so that you cover all the areas. Jimmy did a good job in that area.

Paul Stillwell: It's interesting that Admiral Burke would talk about you as a son-of-a-bitch since you told me a story before the tape started of the reaction on board the Clark that was just the opposite. Maybe you could put that one on the record, please.

Admiral Mumma: In what respect?

Paul Stillwell: This is about the clock you got.

---

* Rear Admiral Ralph K. James, USN, served as Chief of the Bureau of Ships from 1959 to 1963. His oral history is in the Naval Institute collection.
† Rear Admiral Robert L. Moore, Jr., USN.

Admiral Mumma: Oh. Well, actually, what he meant was that I think he was referring to my talking up when I thought there was a change needed. For example, I remember very vividly going over and having concocted the base on which we were going to build a nuclear aircraft carrier and the ways in which it would be an operational much finer ship than any aircraft carrier we had or could build with ordinary power—that it would have additional endurance; that it would have additional ability to put airplanes over the target and keep them there. So that, that we worked up in the bureau and took it over to the Chief of Naval Operations. That demand did not come from the Ship Characteristics Board; it had originated in the bureau, that we should have a nuclear aircraft carrier. So we sold that very heavily to him.

Paul Stillwell: To Burke?

Admiral Mumma: To the Secretary of the Navy, and to all the rest of that operational group in the Naval Operations because we were able to show them that it could be almost twice as efficient in keeping aircraft over the target as a conventionally powered carrier, due to its ability to carry more fuel for the aircraft and due to its ability to stay on the target for a longer period of time. In other words, its effectiveness was nearly double. And the increase of cost was a very small percentage—20 or 30%, something in that order of magnitude.

Well, we sold that and it was approved by Arleigh Burke and the whole CNO group, as well as the Secretary, and as well as the rest of the line right on up, including the President, because we had to get the President's approval on anything of that kind due to the Vinson-Trammel Act. So I made the contract for the <u>Enterprise</u> with the Bill Blewett of Newport News, knowing that they would be the best to do the job. We invited their design crew—that were going to do the contract design work—into our bureau to work with us in developing the contract plans for giving to Newport News. So they were in on the early stages, as well as the transition period when we go from contract design to the contract. Blewett, of course, was very enthusiastic about that. That's the reason I've got the box over there where I laid the keel for the Enterprise, as well as the Constellation.* I've got two hammers over there that I laid keels with.

Even Rickover came down for that keel laying. He was very generous in that respect. But it wasn't Rickover that sold that program. It was the operational aspects of that nuclear power plant and its effect on operations that sold that power plant and that ship to operational people. In other words, Rickover didn't have anything to do with that. So we went ahead and were able to produce that ship, and it did what we wanted it to do. The Enterprise is still a hell of a good ship. He had to come up with new and better and larger reactors for that ship.

That was his part of the program, just to build the reactors. We designed and built the ship. Then, of course, some, I guess, resistance began to build up against having a second ship nuclear powered. But then pretty soon that was broken down again and they built some more nuclear-powered aircraft carriers, which was absolutely essential. They were so much better than conventionally powered ships that I have never understood why they built any more conventionally powered carriers.

Paul Stillwell: I think that was Mr. McNamara's belief that you could save on up-front costs that way.

Admiral Mumma: Exactly. And the up-front cost was more than halved by the time you got those carriers operational.

Paul Stillwell: Do you remember other examples of why Admiral Burke would refer to you as an SOB?

Admiral Mumma: No, he was kidding, of course. But I was a positive character in pushing our views. I was not about to be pushed around in, shall we say, advocating some of these advancements that I thought were absolutely essential to our Navy.

---

* The keel for the Enterprise (CVAN-65) was laid at Newport News on 4 February 1958. The aircraft carrier Constellation (CVA-64) was built by the New York Naval Shipyard. Her keel was laid 14 September 1957. She was launched 8 October 1960 and commissioned 27 October 1961.

Paul Stillwell: What other advancements might you point to?

Admiral Mumma: Well, from the very beginning we had a necessity for, not only a nuclear carrier but also a nuclear destroyer and a nuclear cruiser. The <u>Bainbridge</u> and the <u>Long Beach</u> were the result of that study. In other words, we were strongly dedicated to nuclear in the bureau at that time—not just because Rickover was interested in nuclear, but because all the rest of us were interested in nuclear. It's not by accident that we have now, by this time, almost 40 years of experience of operating nuclear power plants without a single accident involving damage or fatality to an individual in the Navy, and they live right adjacent to the reactor all the time. They live in the same ship; they live sometimes in the next compartment. How in the world there has grown up this resistance to nuclear power in the United States, I cannot understand. It is a complete fabrication of fear.

Paul Stillwell: Well, but, private industry has not done as well as the Navy in running these things.

Admiral Mumma: Yet, surprisingly, private industry has not done all that badly when you get down to analyzing it. The Three Mile Island thing was very heavily overblown.[*] It was not a major catastrophe at all. The amount of radiation that escaped there was infinitesimal. No one was killed; no one was hurt; no one has been injured even in civilian power plants by nuclear power. When you compare that with ordinary power plants—if you take an ordinary fuel power plant, you'll have, probably, a higher accident rate if you catalog them, than in nuclear plants. But nobody's ever done that.

Paul Stillwell: Well, back to the <u>Clark</u>, you told me this enjoyable story before we started the tape about how the engineers treated you when you left the ship. Could you repeat that one, please?

---

[*] On 28 March 1979, at the Three Mile Island commercial nuclear power plant near Middletown, Pennsylvania, a partial meltdown occurred and released radioactive material.

Admiral Mumma: Well, we had had a very interesting time on that gold-plated destroyer leader, the Clark. We'd done a fair amount of pioneering in connection with the squadron leader job, and we had a very good engineering department. We trained a lot of people to do the kind of things that they ordinarily weren't used to doing in ships like repairing a pump, tearing it all the way down, and miking all the clearances, and putting it back together with new bearings and everything else—a real overhaul of a piece of machinery. That challenged them and increased their knowledge tremendously. Well, the minute you do that, you get these fellows all interested in their job, and they want to excel in it. Everybody is an enthusiast for getting good marks in their performance of duty. And the first thing you know, it feeds on itself. These people get so gung-ho about what they're doing. I think I told you about that overhaul.

Paul Stillwell: You did, yes.

Admiral Mumma: About where we did it for $25,000. That in itself was an outstanding performance to do anything that economically. But we did it all ship's force. So the ships—this was right after that overhaul—that the ship's force, having gone to sea, made a beautiful job of post-repair, full-power run and everything else. The ship looked like a million dollars. It was all spit-and-polish, finished painting. We didn't go to sea with painters hanging over the side. So when we ended up that overhaul, here we were, about to leave Mare Island, and I was about to be detached before leaving Mare Island; I left from there. By golly, these fellows were so gung-ho about everything that I think that had a lot to do with their presenting me with this presento, which I didn't expect. I had no idea they were going to do anything like that. The chief electrician's mate came up to the wardroom as I was preparing to leave the ship, and he said, "Lieutenant, would you mind coming back to the fantail for a few minutes?"

I didn't know what was going on, but I went back to the fantail with him. It was the whole engineers' force packed on the fantail in a solid mass of about 55 guys all ranks all the way from chief petty officer on down, and their spokesman was this chief electrician's mate. He made a very flowery speech, how happy he was that I'd been their chief engineer, and how much they regretted that I was leaving, and that sort of thing. So

I made a little speech to them telling what a fine bunch of people they were, and they'd made the ship a very fine ship, and the morale of the ship and themselves had improved so because of their wonderful performance of duty, and so on, and so on. Well, then they handed me this clock, which is an eight-day ship's clock inscribed with a presentation plaque on it. So I thanked them and I said I was going to be leaving the ship in just a few minutes, and I certainly appreciated this indication of their affection on my, for my part. I went back to the wardroom with this under my arm, and the captain, Rafe Bates, said, "What you got there, chief?"

I said, "Why, it's a ship's clock, Captain."

He said, "Let me see it."

I handed it to him. He looked at it, and he looked at the inscription on the base of the plaque. Then he said, "You know, when enlisted men give you a present like this, do you know what it means?"

I said, "No, sir."

He said, "It means you're soft."

I said, "Is that so?" And I didn't say any more.

He didn't say anything more for a while, and finally he said, "Well, I don't know. In this case, maybe not. You can keep it."

I said, "Well, thank you very much, Captain." I put it back under my arm, took my bags, and away we went over the gangway, having been detached from the ship, and on my way back to the model basin in Washington, D. C.

Paul Stillwell: You added an afterthought before and said there was no way he was going to get that away from you.

Admiral Mumma: Well, that's perfectly true. I don't think he would have had much luck in getting it away from me.

Paul Stillwell: Well, back to Admiral Burke. How much contact did you have with him during the course of your respective jobs?

Admiral Mumma: Well, when I was chief of the bureau I saw Arleigh about several times a month as a minimum, and usually in connection with any problem that came up—any operational problem at sea, anything of that kind. As a matter of fact, I was always visiting shipyards which were part of my bailiwick; I was always visiting the laboratories; I knew what was going on in those places; and I would tell him what I thought about my visits to those places when I'd get back to Washington. Like the Mine Defense Laboratory, where we were doing a lot of training down in Florida in connection with minesweeping—with helicopter minesweeping and everything else. And like the Boiler and Turbine Laboratory up in Philadelphia when we'd make a change or an improvement of some kind that we knew about up there, I let him in on it. I let him know what we were doing because it was important that we were putting these things to work in the fleet as fast as we could, any improvements that we learned in the laboratories.

Second, also, my visits to shipyards. I kept him informed when I visited a shipyard what the result was and how I felt about such and such a yard and its performance, and any deficiencies that we found. I was quite candid with him about deficiencies in case we found some. Then in connection with that sort of thing, I had, also, responsibility for not only offshore repair facilities like at Guam and, of course, the Pearl Harbor Naval Shipyard, but also at the Philippines, at Cavite, and in addition to that at Yokosuka and Sasebo in Japan. Therefore, it was imperative that occasionally we'd take a look at those.

I remember the last time I made around that Pacific area, we left Washington with a group of nine of us. On that trip we had people covering all aspects of the ship problems from design on down to maintenance. Anything that came up in connection with that trip was to be reported back to the Chief of Naval Operations when we got back, as well as to the commanders of each of the facilities as we went around.

Well, we got to Hawaii, and we were given a plane by Commander in Chief Pacific Fleet, who at that time was Admiral Hopwood.[*] Hoppie gave me a special airplane which had, incidentally, been Nimitz's airplane during the war. It was a DC-4

---

[*] Admiral Herbert G. Hopwood, USN, served as Commander in Chief Pacific Fleet, 1 February 1958 to 30 August 1960.

with large facilities for rooms in the airplane, and it was a command airplane but hadn't been used that much because it was an old non-pressurized, four-engine plane.

So he gave me that, and we went first to Japan and Sasebo, Yokosuka, then on to the Philippines, then on back through Guam. On our way back we ran into some problems, one in particular at Cavite, where one of the destroyers had had a problem during overhaul, and we managed to help solve that problem for them while we were there in connection with a turbine. It would have been very severely damaged had we not evolved a method of getting a bolt out of a lower portion of the turbine. Things of that kind. There were always problems coming up everywhere.

At that time, for the Japanese in Sasebo and Yokosuka, the difference in the pay rate between United States and their shipyard workers was about a factor of nine. In order to ensure that we had, say, some motivation to work for us, we paid them about one fifth, which was almost twice their normal wage, to work for in Yokosuka and Sasebo. Well, that was the beginning, I think. By this time Admiral Withington was Commander Naval Forces Japan.[*] I stayed with him and his family while in the Japan area for a while until we went to Sasebo, and we flew down there and then flew on from there to the Philippines. So I learned quite a bit about how things were going from Freddy Withington during his tour out there.

Went on and spent a little extra time in the Philippines because of this problem with the destroyer there and these turbines. Then we went on to Guam. On the way back from Guam we stopped at Wake Island, and there we lost an engine on this plane as we were taking off for Hawaii. We had to go back and, in view of the fact that they couldn't get an engine there in any reasonable period of time, why, we left the plane. We unpacked all our stuff, moved it all over to a Japanese Airlines plane that was coming in, and came back from there to Hawaii commercially while waiting for them to send an engine out to repair that plane at Wake. When we got to Hawaii, why, Hoppie decided that, heck, he'd send us back in his plane. So we were sent back to Washington in his DC-6, a nice pressurized job. That worked out very nicely for the rest of our trip.

Well, I reported to Hoppie, as well as to Arleigh, when we got back as to what we'd found, what our problems were as far as I could see. In general, things were

---

[*] Admiral Withington held the billet from April 1958 to April 1961.

working quite well in connection with this additional repair facility we had in Japan. Eventually I'm not sure but what our policy in Japan at that time isn't what has made an even better Japan out of defeated Japan than it would have been if they had won the war. Because MacArthur was obviously the best president Japan ever had, and they prospered.* They did a magnificent job of recovery, much better than Britain. They were better off than Britain almost immediately. Of course, the European theater was rather slow in recovery. The Japs recovered very, very quickly. So by the time I got there in the last trip in '59, they were really on their feet and going very well. They were building a lot of ships—oh, golly, commercial ships just coming out of their ears.

Paul Stillwell: Did you have any overall findings on the Japanese and the others you visited in the Pacific during that trip?

Admiral Mumma: Well, actually, they were all doing their job well. I have no complaint with the quality of the work that they did, or the fact that they were doing it out there. Because, even though people could take a position that we were farming out work that should be done in the United States, to some degree these ships that were assigned out there, their families were living out there, and the ships should stay out there as much as they could and operate in the area in which they were assigned. I couldn't find a reason to bring them all back to the United States for repair. It wasn't that important to put that little bit of extra work in the United States.

Paul Stillwell: What were the kinds of things that Admiral Burke was interested in talking to you about?

Admiral Mumma: He was particularly interested in maintenance of the fleet, of course. That was my responsibility to him, the maintenance of the fleet. And he was interested in new designs. He was forward looking in that respect. In 1956 and '57 we were beginning new experimental designs of ships that were quite a bit new like the DLGs, and

---

* General of the Army Douglas MacArthur, USA, commanded Allied occupation forces in Japan from 1945 to 1951.

so forth, which were a very, very radical departure from any ship we'd built up to that time. The Dewey was one of the first of those, and I laid her keel up there on the day that Mrs. Mumma launched the Hull, the 945.* That was, again, a little bit of a fetish with Bath Iron Works. They liked to lay a keel the same day that they launched the ship, which had a way of reassuring the workmen that they had a continuous flow of work ahead of them. It's a good ploy for a shipyard to be able to do that, and Bath made a little bit of a fetish of that.

Paul Stillwell: As a destroyer man, did Burke make any inputs on the DLG?

Admiral Mumma: Oh, I'm sure in the Ship Characteristics Board, that many, many of the aspects that got into that ship were directly from Arleigh. He didn't actually transmit that so much directly to us as to the Ships Characteristics Board.

Paul Stillwell: Do you remember in 1956 the collision between the Eaton and the Wisconsin, and having to fix the Wisconsin by putting a new bow on her?†

Admiral Mumma: I don't remember the details of that collision and how serious it really was. I'm trying to remember exactly what yard that work was done in, I can't remember.

Paul Stillwell: I think it was Norfolk. That was her home port.

Admiral Mumma: I think it probably was.

---

* The hull of the destroyer Hull (DD-945) was launched at Bath Iron Works on 10 August 1957 with Mrs. Mumma, as sponsor, christening the ship. The frigate Dewey (DLG-14) was the first U.S. Navy ship designed from the beginning to carry guided missiles. Previous guided missile-armed ships had been converted from earlier configurations.

† On 6 May 1956, while operating with a group of ships off the Virginia Capes, the battleship Wisconsin (BB-64) plowed into the destroyer Eaton (DD-510) in a heavy fog. The collision tore a gaping hole in the battleship's bow, which soon replaced by the bow from the incomplete battleship Kentucky (BB-66).

Paul Stillwell: Maybe we could talk some more about the Ship Characteristics Board. What was your relationship with that organization?

Admiral Mumma: Well, in some of the cases, like the nuclear aircraft carrier, we, shall we say, purloined some of their business and did it ourselves. We didn't undertake all aspects of their business, like the operational aspects of a ship. We figured that if we synthesized an existing conventional ship in our advanced ship, that that would suffice for the time being until they got their teeth into it and changed it what way they wanted to do it.

So when we put forth a ship design of some sort that was different, why, then they would come back with recommendations for characteristic changes. We would then work those in if they were workable. If they weren't workable, we'd tell them why and what the differences were and the difficulties. Then they would come back and say okay. We don't need this and we don't need that, but we do need this—some other aspect of the problem. So we would work that into the design to make sure that almost every aspect of the Ship Characteristics Board requirements were in every design that finally got approved.

The General Board used to do that in the old days, and I used to appear before the General Board occasionally in connection in those days.[*] But the General Board was a bunch of old men who were looking at the olden days, and how to do it in the olden days fashion. They were not as forward-looking a group as the Ship Characteristics Board. The Ship Characteristics Board was not only a more modern-thinking group but they also, in this case after, ten years after the war, had a considerable amount of experience in World War II and what they were after in new ships. But they sometimes even did not have in World War II ships.

So it wasn't a difficult situation; it was a give-and-take situation that went very smoothly. We got along very well with the Ship Characteristics Board. They must have relied quite heavily on us because they didn't have any quarrel with us, generally; it was entirely a matter of, "Well, can you do this or can you do that? What can you do to

---

[*] During the first half of the 20th century, the Navy's General Board was comprised of senior naval officers who helped shape strategy, policy, and ship characteristics.

improve this or that?" And we'd make studies and report. It was a good arrangement. The Ship Characteristics Board was what the operating fleet wanted. I saw to it that that's what he wanted. Arleigh saw to it that we tried to give them what they wanted.

Paul Stillwell: Do you remember any specific discussions that went on with that board?

Admiral Mumma: Not in detail because there were so many discussions and so many aspects of it, and there was an awful lot of give and take on size of ships, on characteristics in ships, whether to put guns in ships or not because there was getting to be a feeling more and more, "Well, you don't need guns any more." You know, "Why put guns?"

We used to say, "Well, what are you going to throw at them? Potatoes?" So we used to ask that question occasionally: "Look we can't just invade the spud locker and throw potatoes at them. You've got to have something in the way of low-level gunfire capability." Not just knocking down airplanes. That's not the only purpose of these ships.

Paul Stillwell: Do you remember any pet projects that Admiral Burke had as far as the Bureau of Ships was concerned?

Admiral Mumma: I hesitate to say that there were pet projects. He generally was a pretty broad-gauge thinker. In other words, he wasn't pushing destroyers at the expense of cruisers or at the expense of carriers. He was a task force man. He knew that you needed them all. As a matter of fact, we not only started several things that are now coming to fruition, but we started them in our watch, believe it or not, way back then, including the no-hands landing on carriers. We were researching that and pushing how we were going to get no-hands landing because with jets and so forth coming in, the possibility of errors was increasing. And ships couldn't get that much bigger. So, therefore, we had to do something about being able to handle landings without as much error, individual errors, as had tended to creep in with hand landings. As an indication, which I didn't previously mention, the "Lex" had 25,000 landings and seven fatalities.

We had 25,000 on the Saratoga and no fatalities, which indicates that the personnel angle gets into it.

Well, okay. The second thing, I think, was that these ships had to have a complete offensive and defensive capability, and to balance those, as well as survivability was always a problem. How far do you go? How much offensive capability do you put on; how much defensive capability? And what about the single-purpose ship? Well, after my day they began to go overboard on single-purpose ships, more so than I think would have been wise. In my day I would have argued more and more against single-purpose ships.

Arleigh Burke stayed on for two more years after I left. We had discussed that privately, just the two of us. I said, "Arleigh, I'm going out. I'm not going to stay anymore." I gave him the reasons, and I said, "I don't think you should either."

He said, "I don't know whether I will or not." You know, that sort of thing.

But in the end Tom Gates said, "I'm going to leave also. I'm not going to stay." But he did stay and went on to the Department of Defense for a while. Arleigh did stay for two more years. I think Arleigh really had in the back of his mind that he might make Chairman of the Joint Chiefs. I think he would have made a very good candidate for it, but I think the rotation of the services, and things of that kind, entered in those decisions to a much greater degree. I don't think they wanted any one guy that had quite that length of time in, as a member of the Joint Chiefs. So that it didn't react in his favor as he might have expected it to. I don't know that he expected that. He never told me, but I suspected that. So I felt that Arleigh had made his contribution. I thought it was a good time for him to bow out at the end of four years.

Paul Stillwell: I take it you found him a good CNO to work with from your purposes.

Admiral Mumma: Oh, sure, and Mick Carney was a terrific guy to work with too. I was lucky as I could be to have those two, because both of them were excellent. Mick Carney was brilliantly sharp. He still is, as you know, in spite of his age, and he has a tremendous sense of humor. Arleigh is a little less immediate in his sharpness, but he's a very good thinker and he thinks things out. But he's a little more of a plodder than Mick Carney, who's almost volatile in his thinking. Do you agree with me?

Paul Stillwell: Well, I haven't had enough exposure to either one of them to be able to make a judgment, but I've heard that from others.

Admiral Mumma: Well, Mick and Arleigh are still very good friends of mine. I have letters from both of them very occasionally. I just admire them both very, very much. The only thing I miss is the fact that I don't have a good picture of Mick Carney.

Paul Stillwell: Well, you've got good ones of nearly everybody else.

Admiral Mumma: I sure have. I'm going to get a good one, too, before he dies.[*] I'm going to see him, probably, this fall.

Paul Stillwell: You mentioned that you, as chief of the bureau, reported directly to the Secretary of the Navy. What do you recall of your relationship with Mr. Gates?

Admiral Mumma: Tom Gates was a very intelligent former naval officer.[†] Acting Secretary was right up his alley, because he brought to it an understanding of the Navy that very few secretaries have had. Because many of them had very little experience in the Navy, if any—like Charlie Thomas, for example. His experience was minimal. He brought to it a view of a businessman. Tom Gates was a pretty good businessman in his own right, I think, but he also had the viewpoint of a naval officer. That was very important to us because we could understand him and talk to him, and get response from him in a way that you wouldn't—say, Bill Franke wouldn't know what you were talking about if you talked to him about a design matter. You'd have to explain it to Tom Gates because he wasn't a design man, but he would understand it after you'd explained it. So ordinarily we got along beautifully with Tom Gates. As you can see, we really ended up

---
[*] Admiral Carney died on 25 June 1990.
[†] For an essay on Gates as Secretary, see John R. Wadleigh's chapter in Paolo E. Coletta, editor, American Secretaries of the Navy, Volume II, 1913-1972 (Annapolis: Naval Institute Press, 1980), pages 876-893.

quite good friends. I was awfully sorry when he passed on.* His wife is still a good friend of ours.

Paul Stillwell: Well, I've gathered that he was one who did his homework more than most civilian secretaries would.

Admiral Mumma: To some degree I guess that might have been it, but he also had a better understanding of what the Navy was all about. That's a gift, and it doesn't happen that often. I knew Tom later when I was at Worthington Corporation and Tom at that time was chairman of Morgan Guaranty in New York. He was just as interested, just as interesting—we had meetings in New York occasionally and—at that time I was an executive VP, I believe. The chairman and the president and I would go on over and have a meeting with them in connection with some financing of something or other at Worthington. Tom was good. He welcomed me like an old brother whenever I'd walk in the room. That didn't hurt any.

Paul Stillwell: No. Do you have any examples you could give to show his understanding of the technical type things?

Admiral Mumma: Well, I think the primary things were that I could get his support on something like the nuclear aircraft carrier, like the nuclear cruiser, the nuclear something or other without, shall we say, dragging Rick into the act. See, Rick would sometimes spoil it. He was not diplomatic in the way he would present things. But Tom Gates would ask questions and he'd get these very serious answers from us. Rick occasionally would give facetious answers: "What do you know about that type of thing?"

Whereas, Tom didn't mind if he didn't know. "I don't know anything about that. What's the dope?" And he would listen. So I liked Tom Gates. I thought he was a great, great Secretary of the Navy. I was very happy when he took over and stayed as long as he did. Because very rarely did you get somebody—the only thing was I wish he'd stayed longer in the Department of Defense. Then we wouldn't have had McNamara.

---

* Thomas Gates died 25 March 1983.

Paul Stillwell: We talked earlier some about the Polaris program. Do you have any additional thoughts on that subject?

Admiral Mumma: Well, you've got to realize that that program is one of two programs in the world—well, the Skipjack program was almost as fast and almost as good as that. We did the Skipjack program in about three years from scratch to operational, all during my watch, which took a bit of doing. I was so proud of the Polaris program because we were able to do that in a very short period of time because of its extremely high priority. We were able to cut the corners that needed cutting without affecting either the responsibility or the capability of the equipment to do what it was intended to do, or the responsibility of the Congress. We told the Congress what we were doing. The Congress approved what we were doing, and we did it. We eliminated the whole budgeting process in that case, which would have taken a year and a half. In other words, you can do those things if you have the confidence of the people. Eisenhower had the confidence, not only of those people but in those people. When anything approved by Ike went up there, the first thing you know, why, Vinson and Stennis would approve it. And the armed services committee—they were for it.

We could go down to the Congress—and we did frequently—and talk informally to those gentlemen in the armed services committees of both houses, as well as the appropriations committee in both houses. We opened up and told them what we were doing and why. In spite of the fact that they were Democratic congresses, they were patriotic individuals. They felt that it was important to do these things, which we did. We didn't have the confrontation that has developed in the Democratic side of the House.

For example, Sam Rayburn was a real Speaker of the House, who spoke not only for the House but the whole United States Congress.* He was a masterful individual. He was a leader. Now, you can't compare any of the current crop of people like that, even though O'Neill—as highly as some people think of him—was just not a speaker of that

---

* Representative Samuel T. Rayburn (Democrat-Texas). He served in the U.S. House of Representatives from 1913 to until his death. He served as Speaker of House from 1940 until 1961, except for interruptions in 1947-48 and 1953-54 when Republicans were in the majority. The ballistic missile submarine Sam Rayburn (SSBN-635) was named in his honor.

caliber.* And so that the whole tone of the Congress has changed to one of antagonism, particularly when they got a Democratic Congress as against a Republican President. We didn't have that to the same degree with Eisenhower. He was more a people's President as far as, as was Reagan, basically.† But the development of antagonism in the Congress is more adamant than it ever has been. I don't understand why we can't get back on a non-partisan basis for most of these things.

Paul Stillwell: Well, they seem to like to have all sorts of issues to beat each other over the head with, and defense has become one of them.

Admiral Mumma: Right. And there Dukakis has gone now and got his hatchet man back.‡ Did you read that?

Paul Stillwell: No.

Admiral Mumma: Yes, his hatchet man that brought up the Biden situation is—he fired him.§ Said he wouldn't have him anymore. He's got him back now so that he'll dig up more hatchets to throw.

Paul Stillwell: I notice one of the photos you have on your wall is Homer Wallin. What do you remember of him?

Admiral Mumma: Oh, he was a very fine naval constructor, and very highly regarded, very intelligent man—not so strong in design as he was in shipyards. Homer was the one who was chief of bureau when Rickover first came up for selection.** That selection

---

* Representative Thomas P. O'Neill, Jr. (Democrat-Massachusetts) served as Speaker of the House from 1977 to 1987.
† Ronald W. Reagan served as President of the United States from 20 January 1981 to 20 January 1989.
‡ Michael Dukakis, governor of Massachusetts, was running for President at the time of this interview. His opponent, George Bush, was elected.
§ Senator Joseph Biden (Democrat-Delaware).
** Rear Admiral Homer N. Wallin, USN, served as Chief of the Bureau of Ships from 1951 to 1953.

board failed to select Rickover, and Homer Wallin took the beating for it, supposedly from the Congress.*

Paul Stillwell: Why was it considered Wallin's fault?

Admiral Mumma: Well, that he probably could have insisted that they select Rickover if he wanted, I suppose. But he was perfectly happy not having Rickover selected because Rickover wasn't a broad-gauged guy at that time. He was a specialist in a certain area— not a very popular one in that area either.

Paul Stillwell: Wasn't it unusual for someone to go from Chief of the Bureau of Ships then to command one of the shipyards as he did?

Admiral Mumma: Well, I always felt it was a step down, and I always felt, also, that it spoiled job opportunity and promotional opportunity for others in the area. There were others that did it besides Wallin. But I never liked it. I felt after you'd had the top job, out you go.

Paul Stillwell: Why was it done in his case, do you know?

Admiral Mumma: Well, I suppose he wanted to retire in the Puget Sound area, and that was a good way to do it, which he did.† I remember when I went out there to visit one time in connection with Bremerton, why, he showed up with others, and we went to a Rotary meeting or something of that kind, and he enjoyed association again with the bureau. He was a nice guy.

Paul Stillwell: Anything else? You've exhausted my list of questions concerning the Bureau of Ships. Is there anything else you have to add that I haven't asked about?

---
* For details on the Rickover selection, see Polmar and Allen, Rickover.
† Wallin commanded the Puget Sound Naval Shipyard at Bremerton, Washington, following his tenure as Chief of the Bureau of Ships.

Admiral Mumma: Well, there's one thing I think I ought to mention, and that has connection with Arleigh Burke as among others. Arleigh and Bobbie Burke were a very nice couple. They never had any children, but they were a delightful couple—very fond of each other, very devoted. Arleigh always felt that the naval officers' wives didn't really get enough recognition for the kind of life they had to put up with. So he and Bobbie, I think, must have been the prime movers in this, although it's been a little behind the scenes, hard to find exactly who did, but they started the Naval Officers Wives' Club.

The purpose was to get a little more esprit de corps among the wives of the naval officers to ensure, not only that they stuck together—hung together or whatever. So that was one of the things that I thought was very, very well done, and a good thing. Because those wives are left alone for such a hell of a long part of their lives. They carry on, and they raise kids, and they do everything that they're supposed to do. And we're supposedly off at sea having fun. Well, we don't have so damn much fun, come to think of it. But I do believe that the separations are a very tough part of the Navy, always have been. I had over ten years of sea duty, so I know a lot about separations, in addition to the war, and had a couple of years during the war. And it's a tough thing for wives.

Now, the more the wives can stick together and, shall we say, comfort each other during such times, the better off it is. The Naval Officers Wives' Club was started in Washington. It happened that my bride, Carmen Mumma, was the very first elected president of the Naval Officers Wives' Club. It was a very, very fine thing for her to be recognized as such—and, as a matter of fact, an ED's wife to be recognized as such. She was a terrific help to those girls. For instance, through our previous connections with my uncle, Uncle Harlan who was the class of '16 at West Point—and Ike was the class of '15.[*] They knew each other very well. They were married on the same day—that kind of thing.

So Carmen was able to call up Mamie Eisenhower and ask her to be a guest at the Naval Officers Wives' Club, which she was. They sat next to each other and talked about old times, and so forth, knowing my Uncle Harlan and Patty Mumma, and so on, and so on. It went on very, very well. So that that in itself put a stamp of great approval on the

---

[*] Cadet Dwight D. Eisenhower graduated in the Military Academy's class of 1915. Cadet Harlan L. Mumma was in the class of 1916. Mumma retired in 1948 as a brigadier general in the Army.

Naval Officers' Wives' Club when, in the middle of a snowstorm, that Mamie Eisenhower comes and goes to the luncheon meeting—2,500 gals there. Boy, that was a big boost in morale, not only for the girls, but for us.

Paul Stillwell: What did the organization set out to do, and what did it accomplish?

Admiral Mumma: It set out to do good, not only for themselves but, also, for the enlisted wives. And it was not by accident that my wife was, also, one of the two members of the board of the Navy Relief Society. The Navy Relief Society is a big, big item in the helping of enlisted wives, particularly if they run into financial trouble or something that has to do with a handicapped child or anything of that kind. They were very, very helpful. We still support the Navy Relief Society in a moderate way.

So these things are morale builders, and Arleigh Burke is a good one. The people that served with Arleigh are very loyal to Arleigh, because he does that kind of morale building, and so does his lovely wife Bobbie.

You see the picture out here of the four of us together.

Paul Stillwell: I remember seeing that on the way in.

Admiral Mumma: Well, this was a Valentine party, I think. Here's Arleigh and Carmen and Bobbie and myself. Arleigh said to Carmen, "Carmen, I understand you're a SOGPIP."

Carmen said, "What? What is a SOGPIP?"

He said, "Silly old grandmother, pictures in purse."

We had just had our first grandchild. So you can see he has a sense of humor, and he gets a lot of mileage out of it.

Paul Stillwell: What specific things do you recall that the wives' club accomplished?

Admiral Mumma: Well, in the first place, they helped the Navy Relief Society. Their luncheons would make a little money, and they could make contributions to the Navy

Relief Society; they could make contributions to any really nice purpose that would be furthering the interests of naval officers' wives, or Navy wives in general—either one of them. Very gung-ho group of gals, and they loved it. They did a good job. Specifically it's pretty hard to say exactly what they do do, you know, but I can get Mrs. Mumma to testify if you'd like.

Paul Stillwell: Well, this is your history. I was hoping that we could get it through your eyes.

Admiral Mumma: Well, all I can say is, "Thank God, I married that girl." Most wonderful thing that ever happened to me.

Paul Stillwell: You had your 60th anniversary last year.

Admiral Mumma: Sixtieth anniversary last year; 61 coming up this year the first of October. I've told you before how supportive she's been—not only me, but my career in every way. And I've tried to reciprocate. We've had a marvelous life.

Paul Stillwell: Well, just before when you were talking about Admiral Burke, you got to the verge of your career with Worthington. How did that come about?

Admiral Mumma: Well, when I had decided that I would not take a reappointment, I then had about a month to do before I was going to retire. My relief would be appointed as of the first of May, so it became known that I was retiring. There were a lot of people that didn't believe I was retiring, because shortly before Christmas of the year before—in other words, the Christmas of '58—we had taken a double garage that was on the end of our house, closed it up, and made a family room out of it. Then we built another double garage just off that area at the end of the driveway. Everybody said, "Well, obviously he's not leaving Washington. He's going to retire right here in Washington. Nobody would do that if he's going to leave Washington."

I said, "No way would I take a job in Washington." I said I did not have Potomac fever, and I was not going to take a job in Washington. So they didn't believe me. As a matter of fact, the representative of General Electric Company in Washington was convinced that I was going to take his job and become a representative in Washington for General Electric Company. I knew everybody in General Electric—Ralph Cordiner on up and down—there's no doubt about that. But that would have been so close to conflict of interest; it would have been an impossible job for me to take. I just wouldn't do it. Did I tell you about Ed Hebert?

Paul Stillwell: No, you didn't.

Admiral Mumma: Well, I'll tell you that story in a minute.

But I was so confident that I had to get out of Washington and take a job elsewhere and have nothing to do with the Navy, if possible, because I knew immediately everybody would raise conflict of interest. So I had about five or six jobs that immediately began to appear. Sure, the General Electric people did come in and talk to me about a job. I wouldn't talk to them. Not about the Washington job, not about a job in GE. I wouldn't take it. I had about five or six people that wanted me to interview with them. About a month before, I had a call from some of these people, and I would say, "No, I'm not talking to anybody until after I'm out of the Navy, after I've retired. Because I'm letting contracts every day, and I cannot in any way be influenced on contracts, because if I let a contract now for somebody and then I go with that company later," I said, "that's the kiss of death."

Admiral Radford, my good friend over there, knew I was retiring.* He was former Chairman of the Joint Chiefs, and he had gone on the Worthington Corporation Board, among others. He told the chairman of Worthington that I was retiring. They were about to fill a new job as vice president of engineering. Their vice president of engineering was going to be moved up to vice president of administration. They had a new job for a VP of engineering, nobody to fill it right away. Though Helmuth Walter

---

* Admiral Arthur W. Radford, USN, served as Chairman of the Joint Chiefs of Staff from 15 August 1953 to 14 August 1957.

was there, they didn't think he had the administrative capability to run that sort of a job in the United States. So then the chairman of Worthington called me up, Hobe Ramsey.[*] He said, "Admiral, I understand you're retiring. When can I come and see you and talk to you? Admiral Radford has recommended that you be considered for a job. And we are looking for a vice president of engineering."

I said, "Well, Mr. Ramsey, I can't talk to anybody until after I'm retired."

He said, "When will that be?"

I said, "The first of May."

He said, "Can you have lunch with me on the first of May?"

I said, "Where?"

He said, "I'll come down to the Carlton Hotel."

So I said, "Yes, sir, I can have lunch with you on the first of May." So I did, and he offered me the job of vice president of engineering. But I went and I talked to the other five people. One of them was American Standard, you know, the plumbing people. They were in air-conditioning and quite a few other things.

Then there were others. Even Bill Blewett wanted me to come work for him.[†] I said, "Unh-unh."

Monroe Lanier down at Ingalls wanted me to come and be president. I said, "Unh-unh. No. I'm not going to go near any shipyard. I'm not going to go near anything that has anything to do with the Navy."

So, finally, I investigated to find out how much Navy work Worthington had. I found out they had only about one and a half percent of their total business was Navy. I said, "Well, that's all right then. That's no problem." So I called up Hobe Ramsey, and I accepted his offer. I went to work for him on the first of July. In the meantime, I took two months off, and decided I needed two months' rest after four years in the bureau. And what happens? My good friend Bud Thebaud called up and he said, "Al, I know you're retiring. I've heard it's the first of May. Is that right?"[‡]

I said, "Yes, sir."

---

[*] Hobart C. Ramsey served as chairman and chief executive officer of the Worthington Corporation from 1955 to 1961.
[†] William E. Blewett, Jr., president of Newport News Shipbuilding.
[‡] Vice Admiral Leo Hewlett Thebaud, USN (Ret.).

He said, "Babs and I are going to Europe, and we're going to be away most of the month, the end of May, last part of May, and about the first part of June for about a total of a month. How about you coming up and babysitting our house up in Murray Bay, Canada?

I said, "Bud, that sounds like heaven." I said, "I'd be delighted." And we did. During that time was when Carmey and I debated all of those possible jobs—hiding away up there in Canada. He had a place on a promontory of the St. Lawrence looking 75 miles down one way and 75 miles down the other way. He said, "You know, that climate up there is very nice in June, early May—late May, June. You'd love it. So we did. And when we decided on Worthington, I then called up two weeks before the first of July and said I'd come.

He had up there a French couple and their daughter. The daughter was the maid, the wife was the cook, and the man was the gardener. And here we were with all that luxury sitting there, enjoying life while we made up our mind. It was marvelous, that kind of friends, you know. It was absolutely wonderful—my old skipper.* And so then, that friend, Radford, I saw a while during the Worthington years—not only later when I became chairman, but also, all during the intervening time when I was—and he died shortly after I became chairman. Wonderful man. I had a great admiration for him. Radford was the class of '16; Thebaud was the class of '13. Hobe Ramsey was the class of '15, but never got his commissioned. I think he frenched out first class year, and so he didn't get a commission.†

Paul Stillwell: What, in general, were your duties with Worthington?

Admiral Mumma: I started as a vice president of engineering in connection with the engineering division. We had an advanced products division, new stuff that we were trying to develop and build. And this advanced products division came under Helmuth Walter. He was the director of research for Worthington, reporting to the vice president of engineering.

---

* In the 1930s Thebaud was commanding officer of the destroyer Clark when Mumma was in the crew.
† "French out" is midshipman slang for leaving the Naval Academy without authorization.

Paul Stillwell: Was his presence one of the things that stimulated you to go with that company?

Admiral Mumma: Not particularly, no. I knew he was there, and it didn't hurt, but I wasn't even sure that he would report to me, but it turned out he did. And he was happy in doing that. We became, again, quite good friends. He was really not a Nazi in his attitude. He was having to do what a patriotic German had to do for his country, which was do what he could.

Well, at any rate, in Worthington, the vice president of engineering had the responsibility for monitoring the engineering departments of all the divisions all over the world. We had two divisions in France—separate companies; we had two in Italy; we had one in England; we had one in Germany; we had one in Austria; we had a company in Australia; we had a company in Japan; we had a company in Colombia, South America; we had another one in Brazil; we had another one in Argentina. So that those European and Far Eastern companies were part of the international operations.

Well, I had general charge of all of the engineering aspects of all of those far-reaching companies. But I did not have operational charge over them at all as regards what business they took, or anything like that. This was sort of design monitoring their programs engineering-wise. Then later, when I became executive vice president, I had all the operational aspects of the domestic operations but not the international. Then after that, when I became president, I became president of everything, including the international—and then later chairman. But the purpose of that really was to consolidate the products used—American products along with Japanese products—to make a package that could be sold together. That sort of thing. And the same thing in Europe. Maybe the Italian company and the French company, or the German company, would get together and put together a package for sale to Australia—or something of that kind—when it was beyond the capacity of the Australian company. So that kind of thing was always going on internationally. The designs were fundamentally the same, though not necessarily so. If the French needed a specific kind of a thing, why, the French company could probably build it for them, and they would.

Paul Stillwell: What products were you making?

Admiral Mumma: Well, Worthington was a very wide-ranging company. They made not only turbines, pumps, compressors, engines, generators, as well as valves and fittings of all sorts. So you can see it's a very wide-ranging capability. The Navy's interest in Worthington only was some pumps, and it wasn't a very high percentage of their business at all. Everybody in the Navy knew of Worthington pumps, because it was a very old company. It was started in 1840, and it went overseas in 1852. The Eiffel tower elevators were run with Worthington hydraulic pumps in 1888. How about that!

Paul Stillwell: That's noteworthy.

Admiral Mumma: Still working as far as I know.

Paul Stillwell: You said you were going to tell me about Hebert. You mentioned him in passing and said you'd come back to him.

Admiral Mumma: Okay. When I retired from the Navy, they called up four—I think it was four of us. One of them was Dutch Will, class of '23; I was the other Navy; one Army—I forget his name at the moment; an Air Force general who had been vice chief of the Air Material Command—a four-star general. He went with General Mills; I went with Worthington; and Dutch Will went with American Export. I can't remember exactly where the Army fellow went. But the four of us were called down there by Ed Hebert of Louisiana, who was chairman of the Government Operations Subcommittee of the House.* I went to see Ed—I knew him from the old days, hearings with Carl Vinson and so on. I said, "Ed, what's this all about?"

He said, "Well, we want to talk to you fellows about your civilian employment."

So I said, "Well, anything . . ."

---

* F. Edward Hebert (1901-1979), a Democrat from Louisiana, was elected to the House of Representatives in 1932. He retired from office in 1976 after being stripped of his chairmanship of the House Armed Services Committee.

He said, "Oh, it won't amount to anything."

So they asked me first. "Admiral, what company are you employed with now?"

I said, "Worthington Corporation."

"How much money do you make?"

I knew they'd ask that question so I cleared it. It's supposed to be confidential information. Not any more is it confidential in companies, but it was then.

He said, "How much money do you make?"

I said, "Well, [such-and-such an amount]."

He turned to all the other congressmen in the room. He said, "A lot more money than we make, isn't it?" And great laughter from all of them, you know. Here I was rolling in wealth, according to them. It wasn't very high actually. It wasn't the highest job I was offered by a long shot to a point of view of money. But I thought they needed me more. That's the reason I went there.

Anyway, then he asked, "Well, how much time do you expect to spend in Washington in connection with your new duties at Worthington Corporation?"

I said, "I don't ever expect to see my former associates ever unless they send for me."

He said, "Oh?"

I said, "No, sir, my job won't have anything to do with that. As a matter of fact, Mr. Chairman, Worthington only makes one and a half percent of their total business for the Navy. And the total Defense Department is between three and four percent of their total product. Therefore, they are a civilian company. As close to a civilian company as I could have gone with—completely civilian. Therefore, I don't ever expect to have anything to do with any conflict of interest item in Washington, D. C."

He said, "Well, okay." Then he went to the others.

But, you know what they did? The law as applied to the Army, the Air Force, and the Navy was different in those days. The Navy law originally was that you could not do business with your own service for two years; you could do business with other services after two years, but not your own service for the rest of your life. And I knew that. And so what they did—the others they didn't have any restrictions like that. So they made the restrictions the same for everybody. Everybody is prohibited for life ever doing anything for their own service. But look at the consultants and the beltway bandits.*

Paul Stillwell: They're notorious.

Admiral Mumma: They don't do it directly, but they do it through the beltway bandits. It's criminal what they do. They're evading the law. And some of those fellows that got retired didn't have, shall we say, quite the capability to stay in and be promoted. They are the ones that are now the beltway bandits that are going as consultants and providing all this information to the Pentagon, and half of it's wrong. See, second guessing people that really know with people that don't really know. They're supposed to be smart consultants, but they don't really know. That's the problem that we've run into in this country today with the Pentagon depending on consultants to do things that—they've got more brains right in the military services to decide those things. They ought to talk to the people in the services that know.

Paul Stillwell: How long did you stay with Worthington?

Admiral Mumma: I was there for 12 years, and so I retired at age 65, as normal. I fortunately was able to invest my stock in various kinds of things that have paid rather handsomely in appreciation, as well as income, and so I'm able to live in a reasonable fashion today as compared to what I would have been if I'd stayed in the Navy for, say, four more years. In other words, I made the right decision at that time. It was the proper thing to do, because I helped Worthington, and I also helped ourselves. Besides, I had that tremendous drain of our handicapped son every month.

Paul Stillwell: What sort of activities have you been involved in in the years since you have retired?

---

* "Beltway bandits" is a nickname for consulting firms that work for the Department of Defense. The name comes from their office locations near the Capital Beltway that surrounds Washington, D.C.

Admiral Mumma: Well, I retired in '71 at age 65, which was normal retirement. In civilian life I had taken on quite a number of boards of directors' jobs. I was with the Prudential Insurance Company; I was with the New Jersey Manufacturers Insurance Company until Prudential got into casualty business, and then I had to get off of the New Jersey Manufacturers because of conflict. I was on the bank board in Newark, the First State Bank. I was on the New Jersey Chamber of Commerce board; and I was on the Newark Chamber of Commerce board; and I was on the United Hospitals of Newark board; and I was on the Coyful and Esser board; and I was on the C.R. Bard board.

So these board jobs, I didn't want the income then. I wanted to put it away if I could, get it later after I retired completely. So I finally got some of these companies to defer my fees and my retainer so that I could get it when I was retired. I started that program in Worthington—that was the first time anybody had ever heard of doing that—and Prudential was the first one I did it with, and they hadn't done it before. Now it is common practice to not take this when you're in a high bracket. Take it later when you're in a lower bracket. So they defer it, and they get to use the money in the meantime. Sometimes they pay you some interest on it; maybe they don't. You know, you never know.

But, at any rate, it's better to take it later on. So I deferred almost all of those board incomes until later, which means that now, as I take that employment-deferred income, I'm self-employed. That is self employment; that is not company employment. That is self employment. So I'm a self-employed consultant. I call myself a management consultant-investments, which I've been doing quite a number of people, particularly the boards that I've been on. And I'm still a consultant to those companies.

Now, another thing that came along in addition to being president of both of these societies, naval architects and naval engineers, which took a fair amount of time—I also was appointed by the naval architects to be their member on the National Research Council in Washington, which is a part of the National Academy of Sciences. After that, the first thing I know I'm suddenly elected into the National Academy of Engineering, which is a corresponding group to the National Academy of Sciences. They have meetings several times a year. And I'm going to the annual meeting on the 28th and 29th of September down in Washington, which is another interesting kind of a thing, because this year they're going to be covering all aspects of environmental effects having to do with, not only pollution, but also energy. It's going to be a very interesting meeting.

By these methods, these societies and the National Academy of Engineering I keep up to date with what's going on in the scientific world. I still am fairly interested in scientific stuff. I take a couple scientific journals here. I keep up with that sort of thing, so that I try to be able to make a contribution at these meetings, and to advise people if I have any knowledge that is applicable. I enjoy staying active to that degree. In other words, I don't like to just sit around and play nothing but golf.

Paul Stillwell: You do some of that too.

Admiral Mumma: Oh, I do some of that because that's good for you. It's a very good relaxing exercise, and it's not too demanding except in time; it takes four hours. And other than that, it keeps you in good health. Now, Mrs. Mumma and I just took a complete comprehensive physical at a clinic, where they give you a real working over, including a treadmill and everything else. We both came through with flying colors, which is good. We eat right; we sleep right; we do the right kind of things from most health points of view. Maybe my belt's slipped a bit, but, in general, we're in good health and we enjoy life very much. And the partnership as in Newark, very, very well.

Paul Stillwell: Well, I have one question that's been raised about that partnership and your time back in Washington that gives me some curiosity. Why did you build the new rec room and garage when you weren't planning to stay in Washington?

Admiral Mumma: That was a good question, because most people didn't believe us. We said that that improved the value of that house by thousands upon thousands of dollars, three or four times as much as it cost us to build it. We had the benefit of it our last Christmas in Washington. And it was just terrific. Then when we sold the house, we got it all back in, several times over. So that was just an investment, you see. Again, like this deferring of all this income. That's an investment.

Paul Stillwell: Well, we have just a bit of tape left. Any final thoughts, Admiral?

Admiral Mumma: No, except that I certainly appreciate your kindness and consideration in taking all this time and helping put this down on paper. I really have enjoyed it very, very much. I want you to know that, Paul.

Paul Stillwell: Well, let me thank you, Admiral, because this is a valuable contribution to naval history. And in a sense it's a legacy to the future because this will be available for generations to come. Thank you very much.

Index to the Oral History of Rear Admiral Albert G. Mumma, U.S. Navy (Retired)

Accidents
In the late 1920s Lieutenant Richard Whitehead crashed an O2U on the deck of the aircraft carrier Saratoga (CV-3) when his tailhook caught the barrier wire, 28-29

Aircraft Carriers
The effort in the 1950s and 1960s to justify nuclear-powered aircraft carriers, 190-191, 268-269; rejection in the late 1950s of a congressional effort to build an aircraft carrier in a West Coast shipyard, 200-202

Air Warfare
The German Air Force used the ME 163 rocket-powered airplane against the Allies in World War II, 107, 116

Albacore, USS (AGSS-569)
Experimental test vehicle used in the early 1950s to demonstrate the feasibility of the teardrop-shaped hull as the best hydrodynamic form for a true submarine, 150-151, 172

Alcohol
In 1945, in Bremen, Germany, Mumma had to disarm an Army photographer who had gotten drunk and was brandishing a pistol, 111-112

Alsos Mission
At the end of World War II, U.S. officers visited France and Germany to ascertain German technical developments during the war, 97, 101-105

See also: Naval Technical Mission Europe

American Society of Naval Engineers (ASNE)
Professional society that contributes to the advancement of knowledge in the field, 234-236

Andrea Doria (Passenger Liner)
Italian ship that sank in July 1956 off Nantucket after colliding with the Swedish liner Stockholm, 222-224; a longitudinal bulkhead was probably a factor in the sinking, 223-224

Antisubmarine Warfare
German U-boats were surprised during World War II by the effectiveness of American airborne radar, 117

Arkansas, USS (BB-33)
Battleship that in the summer of 1923 made a midshipman training cruise to Europe, 7-9

Army, U.S.
In the early years of the 20th century, Morton C. Mumma was one of the top rifle shots in the Army, 1-2; in the early years of the 20th century some Naval Academy graduates went into the Army, 3-4; in 1945, in Bremen, Germany, Mumma had to disarm an Army photographer who had gotten drunk and was brandishing a pistol, 111-112

Atomic Energy Commission
In the first years after the end of World War II controlled all U.S. fissionable material, 127-129, 132

Attlee, Clement R.
Amusing anecdote from 1945 when Attlee replaced Winston Churchill as British Prime Minister, 122-123

Backenkohler, Admiral Otto, German Navy
In 1945 Admiral Otto Backenkohler gave permission for German scientists to talk to Americans about their research work, 115-116

Baker, Newton D.
As Secretary of War during World War I assigned Morton C. Mumma to teach soldiers how to shoot well, 2

Barrillon, Engineer General Emile-Georges, French Navy
In the 1930s did pioneering hydrodynamic work in developing the hull form of the French passenger liner Normandie, 48-49, 92, 157, 159-160

Bates, Commander Richard W., USN (USNA, 1915)
Tough, overbearing individual who served in the late 1930s as commanding officer of the destroyer Clark (DD-361), 68-70, 272; provided shipboard input to a study on destroyer operations, 70-71

Bath Iron Works, Bath, Maine
In the mid-1950s the shipyard's president, John R. Newell, gave back excess profits to the shipbuilding program rather than having them seized by the government, 202; did a fine job for the Navy, 206; launching of the destroyer Hull (DD-945) and keel-laying of the guided missile frigate Dewey (DLG-14) in August 1957, 275-276

Battleships
Work of the David Taylor Model Basin in the early 1940s to correct vibration problems with the propellers in various ships, 79, 81-82, 88-89, 91-92, 152-153, 159-160

Bethlehem Steel Company Shipyard, Quincy, Massachusetts
Construction of such warships as the destroyer Clark (DD-361), aircraft carrier Lexington (CV-2), and battleship Massachusetts (BB-59), 209

Blewett, William E., Jr.
In the 1950s did a fine job of running the Newport News Shipbuilding and Dry Dock Company, 210, 268-269; in 1959 tried to get Mumma to work for his shipyard, 289

Bluestone, Dr. Henry
Naval Academy professor who, in the mid-1930s, provided French language instruction to Mumma to prepare him for postgraduate study in France, 45-46

Boatner, Captain Mark J., Jr., USA (USMA, 1918)
Was stationed in France in the mid-1930s and had a son who later served in the Air Force, 54

Boston Naval Shipyard
In the early 1950s was the lead yard for the conversion of destroyers to radar picket ships, 143-145; in the late 1950s some of the employees tried unsuccessfully to form a veterans' union, 206-208; was not an efficient shipyard, 208

Boston (CAG-1)-class Cruisers
In the 1950s these cruisers were modernized to fire guided missiles, 258-259

Bridges, Styles
U.S. Senator from New Hampshire who was involved in the confirmation process in the mid-1950s when Mumma became Chief of the Bureau of Ships, 182

Budgetary Considerations
In 1939, with modest funding support from the type commander, the crew of the destroyer Clark (DD-361) did a ship's force overhaul at Mare Island Navy Yard, 71-72; in the late 1950s, after steering the nuclear submarine Skipjack (SSN-585), Assistant Secretary of the Navy Wilfred J. McNeil agreed to fund another ship of the class, 189

Bureau of Aeronautics
Rear Admiral James Russell served as chief of the bureau from 1955 to 1957, even though he was an unrestricted line officer, 236, 259-260

Bureau of Construction and Repair
In the late 1930s was squabbling with the Navy's Bureau of Engineering, 76

Bureau of Engineering
In the late 1930s was squabbling with the Navy's Bureau of Construction and Repair, 76

Bureau of Navigation
In the mid-1930s would not ease promotion rules concerning U.S. naval officers serving in Europe, 50-51, 56

Bureau of Ordnance
Rear Admiral William Raborn was given authority within the bureau in the late 1950s as part of the Polaris ballistic missile submarine development program, 213; involved in the conversion in the mid-1950s of the Boston (CAG-1)-class guided missile cruisers, 258-259

Bureau of Ships
In the early 1940s dealt with a number of problems involving shipboard propellers, 79-92; in 1944 sent representatives to Britain to aid the Royal Navy with propeller problems on the aircraft carrier Implacable, 99-101; nuclear power developmental work shortly after World War II, 126-132, 140-141; in the early 1950s did experiments on a high-pressure, high-temperature steam plant tested in the experimental destroyer Timmerman (DD-828), 133-137; in the early 1950s the propellers in the new Mitscher (DL-2)-class destroyers were susceptible to cracking in seawater, 138-139; assessment of Vice Admiral Earle Mills as bureau chief in the late 1940s, 139-140; design in the early 1950s of the Dealey (DE-1006)-class destroyer escorts, 155; design of amphibious warfare ships, 155-156; in 1955 Congress went through the process of confirming Mumma to serve as chief of the bureau, 181-184; the last ship planned for the Skate (SSN-578) class was redesigned with a teardrop hull and became the Skipjack (SSN-585), which performed well on trials, 187-189; in the late 1950s, Under Secretary of the Navy William Franke constituted a board to study the necessity for engineering duty officers, 191-192; Mumma's testimony before Congress and preparations to appear, 193-196; allocation of work among various shipyards, 197-198, 202-203, 230-231; because of Admiral Hyman Rickover's methods, shipbuilding cost overruns increased once Mumma retired in 1959 as bureau chief, 199-200; the effect of the Vinson-Trammell Act, passed by Congress in 1934, was still felt in the 1950s because it allocated a certain proportion of Navy shipbuilding to naval shipyards, 200-201; rejection in the late 1950s of a congressional effort to build an aircraft carrier in a West Coast shipyard, 200-202; bureau employment decreased during Mumma's tenure as chief, 203; involvement in the Polaris ballistic missile submarine program, 211-215; Rear Admiral William Raborn was given authority within the bureau in the late 1950s as part of the Polaris ballistic missile submarine development program, 213; role of the bureau chief as a leader and shaper of the Navy's engineering duty community, 239-242; role on the bureau in the late 1950s in the assignments of engineering duty officers, 246-247; in the 1950s a number of ships built during World War II were converted or substantially upgraded, 257-259; loss of access and authority that resulted from the abolition of the various bureaus in the mid-1960s, 261-262; daily routine in the bureau in the late 1950s, 265; in 1959 a committee chose Mumma's successor as bureau chief, 265-266; in the late 1950s Secretary of the Navy Thomas Gates offered to extend Mumma's tenure as chief of the bureau by four years, 266;

as bureau chief Mumma visited the naval shipyards and other BuShips facilities, 273-274; relationship in the late 1950s with the Ship Characteristics Board, 277-278

Burke, Admiral Arleigh A., USN (USNA, 1923)
As Chief of Naval Operations in the latter part of the 1950s provided a strong push for the Polaris ballistic missile submarine program, 212-213; hosted Admiral of the Fleet Lord Louis Mountbatten during his visit to the United States in the late 1950s, 232; assessment of Burke as a fine naval officer, 263-264, 278-280; worked long hours as CNO, 264-265; involved in 1959 in the process to replace Mumma as Chief of the Bureau of Ships, 265-267; interest in the maintenance of the fleet, 275-276; long tenure as CNO, 279; involvement in the 1950s with the Navy Wives' Club, 285-286; sense of humor, 286

Burris, Captain Harry, USN (USNA, 1924)
Shortly after World War II was a candidate to lead the U.S. Navy's program to develop nuclear power, but the job went to Captain Hyman Rickover instead, 130-131, 140; health problems and death, 141

Carney, Admiral Robert B., USN (USNA, 1916)
In the early 1940s was the commanding officer of the light cruiser Denver (CL-58) when she had a problem with "singing" propellers that was solved at the Philadelphia Navy Yard, 84-85; in 1955 was Chief of Naval Operations when Mumma became Chief of the Bureau of Ships, 85; in 1954 attended the centennial of the founding of the Mare Island Naval Shipyard, 175; listened to Mumma's pitch in the mid-1950s for an improved hydrodynamic shape for submarine hulls, 186-187, 192; replaced as CNO in 1955 in order to get a more youthful individual into the office, 264; was a bright and articulate individual, 279-280

Casablanca, USS (CVE-55)
During sea trials in 1943 demonstrated a phenomenon known as "singing" propellers, 86-87

Casablanca (CVE-55)-class Aircraft Carriers
From the time they went into service in 1943, the ships of this class had problems with "singing" propellers, 86-87

Chicago, USS (CA-29)
Heavy cruiser that in the late 1930s served as flagship for Commander Cruisers Scouting Force, 57-58

Churchill, Winston
Amusing anecdote from 1945 when Clement Attlee replaced Churchill as British Prime Minister, 122-123

Clark, USS (DD-361)
Destroyer that was commissioned on the East Coast in the late 1930s and then operated in the Pacific, 58-60, 66-70; in the late 1930s the ship's black messmen were replaced by Filipinos to save on food costs, 59-60; black sailors had limited job opportunities on board the ship, 62-63; quality of the propulsion plant, 64-65; requirement in 1937 that water and oil not be mixed in fuel tanks, 64-65; the ship rolled heavily as a result of not being well ballasted, 65; in 1939 made a long cruise to the East Coast, 67-68; in 1939, with modest funding support from the type commander, the crew did a ship's force overhaul at Mare Island Navy Yard, 71-72; hoods attached to smokestacks to smooth the flow of gases, 253; when Mumma left the ship, the engineers presented a clock to him, 271-272

Coal
In the summers of the mid-1920s Naval Academy midshipmen made training cruises in several coal-burning battleships, 6-9

Collisions
In the early 1930s a collision involving the destroyers Waters (DD-115) and Rathburne (DD-113) resulted in damage to the former, 40-41; the Italian passenger ship Andrea Doria sank in July 1956 off Nantucket after colliding with the Swedish liner Stockholm, 222-224

Combs, Lieutenant Thomas S., USN (USNA, 1920)
In the late 1920s served as landing signal officer on board the aircraft carrier Saratoga (CV-3), 28, 30-31

Commercial Ships
In 1956 ship designer William Francis Gibbs asked Mumma to ride the liner United States to Europe to provide a technical assessment in the event a follow-on liner were to be built, 221-225, 228; in July 1956 the Italian liner Andrea Doria and Swedish liner Stockholm collided off Nantucket, 222-224

Computers
Use of in the 1950s by the David Taylor Model Basin, 164-167; used to calculate actuarial information for survivor benefits, 166

Congress
In 1959 Congress passed a law that retired pay would no longer be based on active duty pay, 51-52; as an engineering specialist, Hyman G. Rickover needed support from Congress to become a four-star admiral, 75, 240; in the late 19th century David W. Taylor sold the idea of a model basin to Congress, 169; in the 1950s Senator Henry M. Jackson was quite interested in nuclear power issues, 176-177; in 1955 went through the process of confirming Mumma to serve as Chief of the Bureau of Ships, 181-184; in the late 1950s questioned the Marine Corps about a large supply on hand of canned hamburgers, 193-194; congressional concerns in the late 1950s about the effect of sewer drainage problems in the city of Olongapo on the adjacent

U.S. naval base at Subic Bay in the Philippines, 194-195; heard testimony on behalf of BuShips programs, 196-197; the effect of the Vinson-Trammell Act, passed by Congress in 1934, was still felt in the 1950s because it allocated a certain proportion of Navy shipbuilding to naval shipyards, 200-201; rejection in the late 1950s of a congressional effort to build an aircraft carrier in a West Coast shipyard, 200-202; in the late 1950s congressmen objected whenever Mumma tried to impose cuts on the New York Naval Shipyard, 203-204; senators from Massachusetts were involved in the late 1950s when a group of employees at the Boston Naval Shipyard tried unsuccessfully to form a veterans' union, 206-208; Representative Thomas Pelly from Washington tried to get advance word when the Puget Sound Naval Shipyard would be getting jobs, 208-209; in the late 1950s supported the Polaris ballistic missile submarine program, 282; Sam Rayburn was an excellent Speaker of the House, 282-283; in the late 1950s Representative F. Edward Hebert raised conflict-of-interest questions with Mumma and other retired flag officers about their civilian employment, 292-294

Curie, Marie
Scientist who was interviewed by the Alsos Mission in Paris in 1944 concerning her work on fissionable material, 101-103

Curtis, Dr. Wesley
As a consultant, did important research work on propellers in the early 1940s at the David Taylor Model Basin, 79, 92-93, 162

David Taylor Model Basin, Carderock, Maryland
Propeller research in the early 1940s, 73, 79-82, 92-94, 161-162; construction of in the late 1930s, 75; installation in 1939 of a water tunnel at Carderock rather than in the experimental station in Annapolis, 92, 162; testing in the early 1950s of a true hydrodynamic design for submarines, 149-151; interaction in the 1950s with the design people in the Bureau of Ships, 156, testing of hull forms, 163-169, 171-172; recalibration of the towing tank, 164; use of computers in the 1950s, 164-167; the work of the Model Basin involved top-notch personnel, 168-169; allocation of funding in the 1950s to support the work of the command, 170-171; testing in the early 1940s of propellers for the Fletcher (DD-445)-class destroyers, 227

Dealey (DE-1006)-class Destroyer Escorts
When designed in the early 1950s were not equipped with sufficient power, 155

Den Hartog, Captain Jacob P., USNR
MIT professor who took part at the end of World War II in the Alsos Mission to assess German technical developments, 97, 101, 105

Denver, USS (CL-58)
Light cruiser that in World War II had a problem with "singing" propellers that was solved at the Philadelphia Navy Yard, 84-85

Destroyer Flotilla Two
Study conducted in the late 1930s on condenser problems in the engineering plants of the ships of Destroyer Flotilla Two on the West Coast, 60-62; in 1939, with modest funding support from the type commander, the crew of the destroyer Clark (DD-361) did a ship's force overhaul at Mare Island Navy Yard, 71-72

Destroyers
Study conducted in the late 1930s on condenser problems in the engineering plants of the ships of Destroyer Flotilla Two on the West Coast, 60-62; at San Diego in the late 1930s ready destroyers maintained steam pressure so they could intercept and board suspicious-looking ships, 66-67; in the early 1950s several naval shipyards converted destroyers to serve as radar pickets, 143-145; impact in the 1950s of large sonar domes on the bows, 156-157; in the 1930s the French designed destroyers that sacrificed firepower and range in order to achieve high speed, 158; sea-keeping characteristics of various classes, 252-253; in the 1950s a number of World War II destroyers were modernized, 257

Dewey, USS (DLG-14)
Guided missile frigate whose keel was laid in 1957 at Bath Iron Works, 275-276

Dick, Lieutenant Raymond H., USNR
Was selected shortly after World War II to be one of the initial participants in the Navy's nuclear power program, 129

Disciplinary Problems
In 1945, in Bremen, Germany, Mumma had to disarm an Army photographer who had gotten drunk and was brandishing a pistol, 111-112

Draper, Dr. Stark
Massachusetts Institute of Technology professor who had a key role in the late 1950s in the development of the guidance system for the Polaris submarine-launched ballistic missile, 213-215

Du Mont, Allen
Consultant who worked with the David Taylor Model Basin in the early 1940s, 79, 160-162

Dunford, Lieutenant Commander James M., USN (USNA, 1939)
Was selected shortly after World War II to be one of the initial participants in the Navy's nuclear power program, 129, 140, 173, 200

Durand, William F.
A graduate of the Naval Academy class of 1880, he later founded several prestigious engineering schools, 77-79; work in the early part of the 20th century in the Navy's model basin, 170

Edgerton, Dr. Harold
   As a consultant, did important research work on propellers in the early 1940s at the David Taylor Model Basin, 80-81

Education
   In 1935-36 Mumma did postgraduate study in engineering at the Ecole d'Application Génie Maritime school in Paris, 46-49, 55-56; in the late 1800s and early 1900s a number of U.S. naval officers did their postgraduate education in Europe, 46-49; in the 1950s the Chief of the Bureau of Ships monitored the postgraduate education for future members of the engineering duty community, 239-240; John J. McMullen did overseas engineering study in Switzerland, 244-246

Eisenhower, General of the Army Dwight D., USA (USMA, 1915)
   As Supreme Allied Commander in Europe in World War II, agreed to ending a technical exchange with the Soviet Union because of violation of agreements concerning access to Gdynia, Poland, 110; as President in the late 1950s rejected a congressional effort to build an aircraft carrier in a West Coast shipyard, 200-202; when he was President his wife visited the naval officers' wives' club, 285-286

Electric Boat Company, Groton, Connecticut
   Built fine PT boats for the U.S. Navy in World War II, 96; in the 1950s the Navy was concerned that Electric Boat was the only U.S. civilian shipyard building nuclear submarines, 177-178; construction in the late 1950s of the first Polaris ballistic missile submarines, 211-216

Engineering Plants
   See: Propulsion Plants

Enlisted Personnel
   The difficult economy during the Depression of the 1930s resulted in high-quality personnel enlisting in the Navy, 33-34, 62-63; when Mumma left the destroyer Clark (DD-361) in the late 1930s, the ship's engineers presented a clock to him, 271-272

Enterprise, USS (CVAN-65)
   Justification in the late 1950s for construction of this nuclear-powered aircraft carrier, 189-190, 268-269

F-111
   See: TFX

Families of Servicemen
   Living conditions for Navy people and their families in the late 1920s and early 1930s in Long Beach, California, 42-43; in that era the Navy provided little support for families, 43; the son of an Army officer stationed in France in the mid-1930s subsequently became an Air Force officer, 54; in the 1950s the naval officers' wives'

club was formed and had a positive effect, 285-287; role of the Navy Relief Society, 286

Farrin, Rear Admiral James M., Jr., USN (USNA, 1929)
In World War II, while serving in the Bureau of Ships, observed trials for PT boats, 96; in the late 1950s was involved in the design aspects of the Polaris ballistic missile submarine program, 213, 215; in 1959 was a candidate to succeed Mumma as Chief of the Bureau of Ships, 265

Fire
In the late 1920s the captain's gig of the aircraft carrier Saratoga (CV-3) was destroyed as a result of spilled gasoline and a fire when the ship was in Long Beach, 29-30

Fitzsimmons, Ensign John P., USN (USNA, 1926)
In the late 1920s was officer of the deck on board the aircraft carrier Saratoga (CV-3) when an O2U crashed on the flight deck, 28-29

Fletcher (DD-445)-class Destroyers
Design of the propellers for this class in the early 1940s, 227

Fog
In the late 1930s Mumma did a fine job of navigating the destroyer Clark (DD-361) when anchoring in fog in Coronado Roads, California, 68-70

Food
Bill of fare that Mumma served in the late 1930s while serving as mess treasurer in the destroyer Clark (DD-361), 59-60; in the late 1930s the Clark's black messmen were replaced by Filipinos to save on food costs, 59-60; in 1944 U.S. officers of the Alsos Mission to Europe carried rations with them, 103; the British had real shortages of food in the period right after the end of World War II, 121-122; in the late 1950s Congress questioned the Marine Corps about a large supply on hand of canned hamburgers, 193-194

Forrestal, USS (CVA-59)
During construction in the 1950s the aircraft carrier Saratoga (CVA-60) had different main machinery than her near-sister Forrestal (CVA-59), 210

France
In 1935-36 Mumma did postgraduate study in engineering at the Ecole d'Application Génie Maritime school in Paris, 46-50; in the mid-1930s there was a small community of Americans, both military and civilian, in Paris, 54; in the mid-1930s Mumma made a Memorial Day speech about the World War I Battle of Chateau-Thierry, 54-55; in 1944 U.S. officers of the Alsos Mission visited France and Germany to ascertain German technical developments during World War II, 102-104

Franke, William B.
As Secretary of the Navy from 1959 to 1961 did not have the technical vision of his predecessor, Thomas Gates, 191, 280; in the late 1950s, as Under Secretary, constituted a board to study the necessity for engineering duty officers, 191-192, 236, 242-243

French Navy
The battleship Richelieu, after joining the Allies, was completed at the New York Navy Yard in 1943, 153-154; in the 1930s the French designed destroyers that sacrificed firepower and range in order to achieve high speed, 158

Gates, Thomas S.
As Under Secretary of the Navy in 1955 heard Mumma's pitch for an advanced submarine design, 186, 193; as Secretary of the Navy in the late 1950s had a strong involvement in the development of the Polaris ballistic missile submarine program, 212-213; after the Franke Board in the late 1950s recommended doing away with the training of engineering specialists in the Navy, Gates as Secretary opted to retain the status quo, 243; in the late 1950s offered to extend Mumma's tenure as Chief of the Bureau of Ships by four years, 266; served as Secretary of Defense after being Secretary of the Navy, 279; fine understanding of technical issues, 280-281

Gdynia, Poland
In 1945 the Soviets violated agreements made at Yalta concerning the occupation of the port of Gdynia, 108-110

General Dynamics Corporation
In the 1950s the Navy was concerned that the Electric Boat Division was the only U.S. civilian shipyard building nuclear submarines, 177-178; construction in the late 1950s of the first Polaris ballistic missile submarines, 211-216

General Electric, Schenectady, New York
During World War II was involved in a variety of research projects on behalf of the Navy, 98; developmental work on nuclear power plants shortly after World War II, 127-128, 141, 216; in the mid-1950s developed the sodium-cooled nuclear power plant in the submarine Seawolf (SSN-575), 216-217; in the late 1950s tried unsuccessfully to recruit Mumma to work for the company, 288

German Air Force
Used the Messerschmitt ME 163 rocket airplane against the Allies in World War II, 107, 116

German Navy
In World War II Helmuth Walter did experimental work on hydrogen peroxide propulsion plants for submarines, 104, 106, 108, 113-117, 120-121; in 1945 Admiral Otto Backenkohler gave permission for German scientists to talk to Americans about their research work, 115-116; German U-boats were surprised during World War II

by the effectiveness of American airborne radar, 117; some U-boats made voyages to Japan during the war, 117-118; postwar disposition of German assets to the Allies, 123

Germany

During World War II launched V-1 and V-2 rockets against the Allies, 100-101, 106-107; did some developmental work on nuclear weapons in World War II but didn't accomplish much, 104; in 1945, at the end of World War II in Europe, a number of German scientists chose to be captured by Americans rather than Soviets, 108; tour of the defeated country in 1945 by members of the U.S. Naval Technical Mission Europe, 110-113

Gibbs, William Francis

Key figure in the engineering firm of Gibbs & Cox that did design work on the propulsion plants of the new gold-plater destroyers that in the 1930s began entering the U.S. Navy, 64; served in the late 1940s and early 1950s as a consultant on the Navy's experimental destroyer Timmerman (DD-828), which was testing new high-pressure, high-temperature steam propulsion machinery, 134-135; was a curmudgeon in personality, 135, 225-227; in 1956 asked Mumma to ride the liner United States to Europe and give him a technical assessment of the ship, 221-225, 228; had a great interest in high-speed ships, 226-227; some changes to the design of the United States came as a result of Navy requirements, 226, 255, 262

Goudschmidt, Dr. Sam

At the end of World War II took part in the Alsos Mission to France and Germany to assess German technical developments, 97, 101-103

Great Britain

The British had real shortages of food in the period right after the end of World War II, 121-122; amusing anecdote from 1945 when Clement Attlee replaced Winston Churchill as Prime Minister, 122-123

See also: Royal Navy

Greber, Lieutenant Charles F., USN (USNA, 1921)

In the late 1920s was a flight instructor for indoctrination aviation training at North Island Naval Air Station, 25

Groves, Major General Leslie R., USA

In 1944 set up the Alsos Mission, in which U.S. officers visited France and Germany to ascertain German technical developments during World War II, 101; discussions with Bureau of Ships personnel on nuclear power plants, 126-127, in the 1950s worked with computers for Univac, 165

Guantanamo Bay, Cuba
In 1937 was the site of shakedown training for the crew of the recently commissioned destroyer Clark (DD-361), 66; testing in the mid-1950s of missiles fired by Boston (CAG-1)-class cruisers, 258

Gunnery-Naval
Violent effect during the testing of 16-inch guns on board the battleship Iowa (BB-61) in World War II, 253-254

Habitability
Improvements in this area for U.S. warships came after World War II, 229

Halsey, Rear Admiral William F., Jr., USN (USNA, 1904)
In the late 1930s commanded the naval air station at Pensacola, Florida, 66

Hebert, F. Edward
Louisiana Representative to Congress who in the late 1950s raised conflict-of-interest questions with Mumma and other retired flag officers about their civilian employment, 292-294

Higgins Industries
In World War II built PT boats that Mumma considered inferior, 96-97; orders for Higgins boats were not cancelled, despite a Navy recommendation to do so, 97

Hillenkoetter, Rear Admiral Roscoe H., USN (USNA, 1920)
In the early 1930s served as a U.S. military courier in Europe, 50, 52-54; was later first director of the Central Intelligence Agency, 52-53; after World War II commanded the battleship Missouri (BB-63), 53

Holloway, Vice Admiral James L., Jr., USN (USNA, 1919)
In 1955 informed Mumma that he had been selected as the next Chief of the Bureau of Ships, 180

Honsinger, Rear Admiral Leroy V., USN (USNA, 1927)
In the late 1940s served in the hull design section of the Bureau of Ships, 126; in the late 1950s served as Deputy Chief of the Bureau of Ships, 185; in 1959 was a candidate to succeed Mumma as Chief of the Bureau of Ships, 265; later became shipyard commander at Mare Island, 267

Hopwood, Admiral Herbert G., USN (USNA, 1920)
As Commander in Chief Pacific Fleet in the late 1950s, lent his airplane to Mumma to visit various BuShips activities, 273-274

Howard, Rear Admiral William E., Jr., USN (USNA, 1928)
In the late 1950s was the commander of the Boston Naval Shipyard when a group of employees tried unsuccessfully to form a veterans' union, 206-208

Huckins Yacht Company
In World War II built PT boats for the U.S. Navy, 96

Hughes, Admiral Charles F., USN (USNA, 1888)
Used the armored cruiser Seattle as flagship while serving in the mid-1920s as Commander in Chief U.S. Fleet, 16-18

Hull, USS (DD-945)
Destroyer that was christened by Mrs. Mumma at the time of launching in 1957, 276

Hunsaker, Dr. Jerome
After graduating first in the Naval Academy class of 1908, he did important developmental work in aeronautics, 77-78, 169

Hurricanes
In September 1926 a division of U.S. light cruisers ran into an Atlantic hurricane during a voyage to Cuba, 14-16

Implacable, HMS (British Aircraft Carrier)
In 1944 U.S. Navy Bureau of Ships representatives went to Britain to aid the Royal Navy with propeller problems on the Implacable, 99-101

Ingalls Shipbuilding, Pascagoula, Mississippi
In the late 1950s the Bureau of Ships began putting more work here because it was a well-run shipyard, 219

Inspections
In the late 1930s Rear Admiral William Pye, Commander Destroyer Flotilla Two, conducted an annual military inspection of the destroyer Clark (DD-361), 68

Intelligence
Japanese trawlers operated in the vicinity of San Diego in the late 1930s to collect information, 66-67

Iowa, USS (BB-61)
Battleship that was damaged in 1943 when she scraped a rock at Casco Bay, Maine, 83, 254-255; had underwater skegs that impeded turning the ship, 88; in the early 1950s was reactivated from mothballs to take part in the Korean War, 143-144; gunnery trials during World War II, 253-254

Iranian Navy
In the early 1950s the Shah of Iran visited the San Francisco Naval Shipyard to get some ideas for supporting his own navy, 146-147

Italy
    In the years after World War II Italy was one of several European countries that built ships under the aegis of the U.S. Marshall Plan, 221; the Italian passenger ship Andrea Doria sank in July 1956 off Nantucket after colliding with the Swedish liner Stockholm, 222-224

Jackson, Henry M.
    U.S. Senator who in the 1950s was quite interested in nuclear power issues, 176-177; in 1955 was involved in Mumma's confirmation hearing to become Chief of the Bureau of Ships, 184

James, Rear Admiral Ralph K., USN (USNA, 1928)
    In 1959 was selected to succeed Mumma as Chief of the Bureau of Ships, 265, 267

Japan
    Japanese trawlers operated in the vicinity of San Diego in the late 1930s to collect information, 66-67; some German U-boats made voyages to Japan during the World War II, 117-118; operation of U.S. Navy ship repair facilities at Yokosuka and Sasebo in the late 1950s, 274-275; the nation prospered in the years following World War II, 275

Johnson, Lyndon B.
    U.S. Senator from Texas who was involved in the confirmation process in the mid-1950s when Mumma became Chief of the Bureau of Ships, 183-184

Kaiser Shipbuilding Company
    In World War II built Casablanca (CVE-55)-class escort carriers that had problems with "singing" propellers, 86-87

Kaplan, Captain Leonard, USN (USNA, 1922)
    Was subject to prejudice while at the Naval Academy because he was Jewish, 247-248; did a fine job as a naval engineer after being commissioned, 248-250

Kennedy, John F.
    Was involved as a U.S. Senator in the late 1950s when a group of employees at the Boston Naval Shipyard tried unsuccessfully to form a veterans' union, 206-208

Kingdon, Dr. Kenneth
    As technical director of a General Electric laboratory near Schenectady, New York, had a role in the 1940s and 1950s in the development of the Navy's nuclear power program, 141, 216-217

Kniskern, Lieutenant Commander Leslie A., USN (USNA, 1922)
    After postgraduate work in naval engineering, worked in the Bureau of Construction and Repair in the 1930s, 57, 157

Korean War
With the advent of the war in the summer of 1950, the San Francisco Naval Shipyard reactivated a number of ships from mothballs, 143-144

Labor Unions
In the late 1950s a group of employees at the Boston Naval Shipyard tried unsuccessfully to form a veterans' union, 206-208

Land, Rear Admiral Emory S., USN (USNA, 1902)
As Chief of the Bureau of Construction and Repair in the mid-1930s, was interested in the engineering achievements in the French passenger liner Normandie, 44-45, 157

Lash, Captain Frank H., CHC, USN
Chaplain who, near the end of World War II, provided Mumma with a Bible verse for a slightly sacrilegious message concerning the Soviets, 110

Lee, Rear Admiral Paul. F., USN (USNA, 1919)
In the period shortly after World War II was involved in the Bureau of Ships efforts to develop nuclear power plants for ships, 126-127, 129; work with the experimental destroyer Timmerman (DD-828), 133-135

Lee, Lieutenant Commander Willis A. Jr., USN (USNA, 1908)
Top-flight marksman who won medals at the 1920 Olympics as a member of the U.S. rifle team, 10-11

Leggett, Rear Admiral Wilson Durward, Jr., USN (USNA, 1921)
As Chief of the Bureau of Ships in the mid-1950s decided to have the Mare Island Naval Shipyard build nuclear-powered ships, 174; in 1955 completed his tenure as bureau chief and retired, 181-182

Lexington, USS (CV-2)
Aircraft carrier that in the 1920s had a rivalry with her sister ship Saratoga (CV-3), 25-26, 32-35, 209-210, 278-279; the ship's overhang snapped off light poles in the late 1920s when she went through the Panama Canal, 33; in January 1929 took part in a fleet problem that involved an attack on the Panama Canal, 34-35; in 1929-30 provided electrical power to the city of Tacoma, Washington, 36-37

Libbey, Lieutenant Commander Miles A., Jr., USN (USNA, 1939)
Was selected shortly after World War II to be one of the initial participants in the Navy's nuclear power program, 129

London, England
U.S. Bureau of Ships representatives were present in London in 1944 when German V-1 rockets rained down on the city, 100-101; the British had real shortages of food in the period right after the end of World War II, 121-122

Long Beach, California
 In the late 1920s Lieutenant Richard Whitehead crashed an O2U on the deck of the aircraft carrier Saratoga (CV-3) when trying to land with the ship anchored at Long Beach, 28-29; local living conditions for Navy people and their families in the late 1920s and early 1930s, 42-43

ME 163
 German rocket-powered airplane that was used against the Allies in World War II, 107, 116

Manseau, Rear Admiral Bernard E., USN (USNA, 1922)
 In the late 1940s commanded the San Francisco Naval Shipyard, 143, 147-148; from 1950 to 1952 commanded the Mare Island Naval Shipyard, 148; in the mid-1950s served as Deputy Chief of the Bureau of Ships, 182, 184; suffered a heart attack and in 1957 retired from active duty, 185

Mare Island Navy Yard, Vallejo, California
 In 1939, with modest funding support from the type commander, the crew of the destroyer Clark (DD-361) did a ship's force overhaul at Mare Island, 71-72; in the early 1950s was involved in the conversion of destroyers to radar picket ships, 143-145; in the mid-1950s began preparing to build nuclear-powered submarines, 174-177; in 1954 the shipyard celebrated its centennial, 174-175; elements that made Mare Island a fine location for a shipyard, 174-175; involvement with the local community, 179; had a fine set of quarters for the shipyard commander, 178-180

Marine Corps, U.S.
 In the early 1950s, during the Korean War, the San Francisco Naval Shipyard activated and overhauled amphibian vehicles for the Marine Corps, 147; in the 1950s influenced the design of amphibious warfare ships, 155-156; in the late 1950s Congress questioned the Marine Corps about a large supply on hand of canned hamburgers, 193-194

Marksmanship
 In the early years of the 20th century, Morton C. Mumma was one of the top rifle shots in the Army, 1-2, 9-10; his sons followed his example, 10; Navy teams did well in the early 1920s in national and international shooting matches, 10-13, 21-22

Marshall Plan
 As part of the European recovery program in the years after World War II, the United States supported shipbuilding in various overseas shipyards, 221

McCracken, Lieutenant Commander Alan R., USN (USNA, 1922)
 In the late 1930s served as executive officer of the destroyer Clark (DD-361) until he had to leave because of eye problems, 59, 67-68, 70-71

McCrea, Captain John L., USN (USNA, 1915)
   Was commanding officer of the battleship Iowa (BB-61) in 1943 when she ripped a gash in her bottom at Casco Bay, Maine, 254-255

McKee, Rear Admiral Andrew I., USN (Ret.), (USNA, 1917)
   Retired naval officer who worked for Electric Boat in the late 1950s as the Polaris ballistic missile submarines were being developed, 215

McLean, Captain Ridley, USN (USNA, 1894)
   Was a tough taskmaster in the early 1920s while commanding the battleship Arkansas (BB-33), 8-9

McMullen, Commander John J., USN (USNA, 1940)
   Top-notch naval engineer who received specialized training in Switzerland, later left the service in 1954 and founded his own company, 244-246

McNamara, Robert S.
   As Secretary of Defense in the 1960s, instituted total package procurement, which involved buying all ships of a given class from one defense contractor, 197-198, 250

McNeil, Wilfred J.
   In the late 1950s, as Assistant Secretary of the Navy, he steered the nuclear submarine Skipjack (SSN-585) and then agreed to fund another ship of the class, 189

Medical Problems
   In the 1950s Rear Admiral Bernard Manseau, Deputy Chief of the Bureau of Ships, retired after suffering a heart attack, 184-185

Memphis, USS (Armored Cruiser)
   In August 1916 was washed ashore at Santo Domingo by a tidal wave, 16, 18

Mills, Vice Admiral Earle W., USN (USNA, 1918)
   In the late 1930s served as the staff engineer for Commander Destroyer Flotilla Two and directed a study of condenser problems in ships of the flotilla, 60-62 in 1939, with modest funding support from Mills as the type commander's engineer, the crew of the destroyer Clark (DD-361) did a ship's force overhaul at Mare Island Navy Yard, 71-72; around 1940 advised Mumma to transfer from the unrestricted line and become an engineering duty specialist, 73-75, 236; rode the battleship Iowa (BB-61) in 1943 at Casco Bay, Maine, 83; in 1942 cautioned Mumma against speaking about nuclear power plants, 98-99, 128; in 1944 went to Britain to aid the Royal Navy on propeller problems, 99-101; in 1944 selected Bureau of Ships representatives for the Alsos Mission to Europe, 101; involvement shortly after World War II in the Navy's effort to develop shipboard nuclear power plants, 126, 129-132; in the late 1940s steered Mumma into a shipyard job to aid his professional development, 133; in the late 1940s urged testing new high-pressure, high-temperature steam propulsion equipment, 133-134; assessment of as Chief of the Bureau of Ships in the late 1940s,

139-140; involved during World War II in keeping naval engineers informed on new developments, 242

Missiles
Development in the late 1950s of Polaris for use in submarines, 211-214; conversion in the mid-1950s of the Boston (CAG-1)-class cruisers to fire guided missiles, 258-259

Mitscher (DL-2)-class Destroyers
In the early 1950s the propellers in this new class of destroyers were susceptible to cracking in seawater, 138-139

Model Basin, Washington, D.C.
Birthplace early in the 20th century of the National Advisory Committee for Aeronautics, 76; had a valuable wind tunnel for aeronautical testing, 76-78, 170

See also: David Taylor Model Basin, Carderock, Maryland

Moffett, Rear Admiral William A., USN (USNA, 1890)
Contributed a great deal to the development of naval aviation in the early years of the 20th century, 77

Moorer, Rear Admiral Thomas H., USN (USNA, 1933)
In the late 1950s participated in the Franke Board study on the necessity for having engineering specialists in the Navy, 242

Moreell, Lieutenant Commander Ben, CEC, USN
In the early 1930s went to France for postgraduate study in civil engineering, 46

Morgan, Captain Armand M., USN (USNA, 1924)
As a midshipman in the early 1920s, did well in marksmanship, 10; finished first in his class at the Naval Academy, 118-119; at the end of World War II helped in evaluating German submarine development progress, 119; views concerning having multiple propellers on submarines, 119-120, 151-152; shortly after World War II became involved in the program to develop nuclear power for ships, 128; was supportive of Mumma as Chief of the Bureau of Ships, 181; involved in the 1950s in the introduction of nuclear submarines with teardrop-shaped hulls, 189

Motor Torpedo Boats
See: PT Boats

Mountbatten, Admiral of the Fleet, Lord Louis, Royal Navy
In 1956 hosted Mumma during a visit to Britain, 231-232; later visited naval facilities in the United States and reorganized the Royal Navy as a result, 232-233; assessed as a charming, charismatic individual, 233-234

Mumma, Rear Admiral Albert G., USN (USNA, 1926)
Parents of, 1-5, 9-10, 13, 17, 19-20; interest in the Naval Academy, 1, 3-4; siblings, 2-4, 10-13, 19-21; interest in engineering, 4-5; from 1922 to 1926 was a Naval Academy midshipman, 4-14; as a midshipman and junior officer was a member of marksmanship teams, 11-12, 21-22; duty in cruisers shortly after his 1926 graduation from the Naval Academy, 14-19; in late 1926 met his future wife, Carmen Braley, in Iowa and married her in October 1927, 19-21; service from 1927 to 1931 in the aircraft carrier Saratoga (CV-3), 23-37; in the late 1920s underwent aviation indoctrination training, 25-26; from 1931 to 1932 served in the destroyer Waters (DD-115), 37-44; children of, 43-44, 46-48, 145, 149, 237, 294; in 1932-34 attended Postgraduate School in Annapolis, 44-46; in 1934-36 did postgraduate study in France, 46-56, 157-158; duty in the late 1930s in the crew of the destroyer Clark (DD-361), 58-73, 270-272; served in 1939-43 at the David Taylor Model Basin in Carderock, Maryland and subsequently in the Bureau of Ships, 73-100, 253-257; around 1940 decided to transfer from the unrestricted line and become an engineering specialist, 73-75; in the early 1950s commanded the David Taylor Model Basin, 78; in 1944-45 was part of the Alsos Mission and Naval Technical Mission to ascertain German progress during World War II in technical development, 101-126; service following World War II in the ship design section of the Bureau of Ships and involvement with the origins of the Navy's nuclear power program, 126-142; served from 1949 to 1951 as production officer of the San Francisco Naval Shipyard, 143-149; in the early 1950s commanded the David Taylor Model Basin in Carderock, Maryland, 149-156, 162-172; in 1954-55 commanded the Mare Island Naval Shipyard, 174-180; served from 1955 to 1959 as Chief of the Bureau of Ships, 180-252, 257-270, 273-284; post-Navy work for the Worthington Corporation, 287-294; activities following his 1971 retirement from Worthington, 295-297

Mumma, Carmen Braley
In late 1926 met her future husband, Albert Mumma, in Iowa and married him in October 1927, 19-21; learned to fire a pistol, 22; family life in Long Beach in the late 1920s and early 1930s, 42-43; in the mid-1930s went with her husband and children to spend a year in France, 46-48; contributions over many years to her husband's naval career, 237-238, 287; in 1957 served as sponsor during the launching of the destroyer Hull (DD-945) at Bath Iron Works, 276; in the 1950s served as first president of the naval officers' wives' club, 285-286; enjoyed good health while living in New Hampshire in the late 1980s, 296

Mumma, Major Harlan, USA (USMA, 1916)
In 1937, while stationed in Panama, rode the destroyer Clark (DD-361) through the canal, 66; knew Dwight Eisenhower as a cadet, 285

Mumma, Colonel Morton C., USA (Ret.) (USMA, 1900)
Career Army officer who served in the Philippines around 1910 and later served in the ROTC unit at the University of Iowa, 1-3, 5; was one of the top rifle shots in the

Army, 1-2, 10-11; attended the 1926 Army-Navy football game at Chicago with his family, 19-20; served as a football official, 20

Mumma, Commander Morton C., Jr., USN (USNA, 1925)
Around 1918, as a youngster, had his first airplane ride, 2; originally planned to attend the Military Academy at West Point, but in 1921 he took an appointment to the Naval Academy instead, 3; naval duties after he was commissioned, 4; was a top-flight marksman who was involved in shooting matches as a midshipman and junior officer, 11-13, 21; served as executive director of the National Rifle Association, 13; in 1937 was in command of a submarine based in Panama, 66

Mumma, Colonel Morton C. III, USAF (Ret.) (USMA, 1948)
In the 1980s served as executive director of the National Rifle Association, 12-13

NC-4 Flying Boat
The aircraft that made the first transatlantic flight in 1919 was developed at the Navy Model Basin in Washington, D.C., 76-77

National Advisory Committee for Aeronautics
Was founded early in the 20th century at the Navy Model Basin in Washington, D.C., 76, 170

Nautilus, USS (SSN-571)
In the mid-1950s Mumma pushed for submarines with a more hydronamically advanced hull form than that in the Nautilus, 186-188; deliberate melt-down of a prototype nuclear reactor in the early 1950s at Arco, Idaho, 211-212; early tests in 1955 went well, 216

Naval Academy, Annapolis, Maryland
In the early years of the 20th century some Naval Academy graduates went into the Army, 3-4; the class of 1926 was the first to get aviation training, 4-6, 9, 25; summer training cruises in the mid-1920s, 6-9; in the 1920s the academy football was regularly beaten by the one from West Point, 14; classic Army-Navy football game in 1926 ended in a 21-21 tie, 19-20

Naval Technical Mission Europe
Near the end of World War II, U.S. naval officers toured France and Germany to ascertain German technical progress during the war, 104, 106-107, 110-121, 124; postwar disposition of German assets to the Allies, 123

Navigation
In the late 1930s Mumma did a fine job of navigating the destroyer Clark (DD-361) when anchoring in fog in Coronado Roads, California, 68-70

Navy Relief Society
In the late 1950s provided effective help to the families of enlisted men, 286-287

Naymark, Lieutenant Commander Sherman, USN (USNA, 1941)
Was selected shortly after World War II to be one of the initial participants in the Navy's nuclear power program, 132, 140

Newell, John R.
In the mid-1950s, as president of Bath Iron Works, gave back excess profits to the shipbuilding program rather than having them seized by the government, 202; did a fine job for the Navy, 206

New Jersey, USS (BB-62)
Had underwater skegs that impeded turning the ship, 88; in 1943 went on sea trials, 89, 91

Newport News Shipbuilding and Dry Dock Company
In the 1950s did a fine job of aircraft carrier construction, but Mumma was reluctant to have the yard build submarines because it had so much other business, 205; work in the 1950s on the construction of the aircraft carrier Forrestal (CVA-59), 210; construction in the late 1950s and early 1960s of the nuclear-powered aircraft carrier Enterprise (CVAN-65), 268-269

New York Navy Yard/Naval Shipyard
After joining the Allies, the former French battleship Richelieu was completed in 1943 at the New York yard, 153-154; in the late 1950s congressmen objected whenever Mumma tried to impose cuts on this yard, 203-204

New York Shipbuilding Corporation, Camden, New York
Shipyard that got into submarine construction in the 1950s but later ran into problems and went out of business, 178, 205, 217; aircraft carrier work, 205

Niedermair, John C.
Civilian ship designer who worked for many years in the Bureau of Construction and Repair and later the Bureau of Ships, 156-157, 159

Norfolk Naval Shipyard, Portsmouth, Virginia
Repair and design work in the 1940s and 1950s, 218-219

Normandie (French Passenger Ship)
Thanks to the skilled design of the ship, she was able to achieve high speeds in the 1930s during transatlantic crossings, 45, 48-49, 157-158; experienced severe vibration problems that led to several propeller modifications, 49-50, 79; Mumma reported on the ship in 1936 when he returned to the United States, 56

North Carolina (BB-55)-class Battleships
Design of in the mid-1930s, 50, 157-158; inclusion of skegs near the propellers, 81-82, 153; inquiries made by Captain Hyman Rickover on the propeller situation, 176

Nuclear Power
In 1942 Rear Admiral Earle Mills cautioned Mumma against speaking about nuclear power plants, 98-99; after World War II the U.S. Navy moved toward nuclear power for submarines rather than continuing German work on hydrogen peroxide, 120-121; developmental efforts by the Bureau of Ships in the period shortly after World War II, 126-132; in the mid-1950s the Mare Island Naval Shipyard began preparing to build nuclear-powered submarines, 174; justification in the late 1950s for a nuclear-powered aircraft carrier and nuclear-powered escorts, 189-190, 268-270; deliberate melt-down of a prototype nuclear reactor in the early 1950s at Arco, Idaho, 211-212; tests of the submarine Nautilus (SSN-571) in 1955 went well, 216, 216; sodium-cooled plant in the submarine Seawolf (SSN-575), 216-217

Nuclear Weapons
U.S. developmental work in World War II as part of the Manhattan Project, 98-99, 126; concern in 1944 over what the Germans might have accomplished, which proved to be not much, 101, 104; in the period right after World War II, U.S. fissionable material was allocated to nuclear weapons rather than nuclear power applications, 127-128

O2U Corsair
In the late 1920s Lieutenant Richard Whitehead crashed an O2U on the deck of the aircraft carrier Saratoga (CV-3) when his tailhook caught the barrier wire, 28-29

Oak Ridge National Laboratory, Oak Ridge, Tennessee
Site of training shortly after World War II for the early participants in the Navy's nuclear power program, 128-130, 132

Oil Fuel
Requirement in the destroyer Clark (DD-361) in 1937 that water and oil not be mixed in fuel tanks, 64-65

Olmsted, Midshipman Jerauld L., USN (USNA, 1922)
Stood first in his class at the Naval Academy after a rivalry with Midshipman Leonard Kaplan, 247-248

Olongapo, Philippines
Congressional concerns in the late 1950s about the effect of sewer drainage problems in the city of Olongapo on the adjacent U.S. naval base at Subic Bay, 194-195

Olsen, Rear Admiral Clarence E., USN (USNA, 1921)

Served in 1944-45 as a U.S. Navy representative during international negotiations at Yalta in the Crimea, 108-110

PT Boats
Evaluation of the designs developed by various companies in the World War II era, 96-97

Pace, Frank, Jr.
Was a General Dynamics official in the mid-1950s when Electric Boat was the only civilian shipyard building nuclear submarines, 177-178, 211

Panama Canal
In the late 1920s the deck overhang of the aircraft carrier Lexington (CV-2) snapped off light poles when she went through the canal, 33; in January 1929 the aircraft carriers Saratoga (CV-3) and Lexington participated in a fleet problem that involved an attack on the canal, 34-35; in 1937 the recently commissioned destroyer Clark (DD-361) transited the canal en route to West Coast duty, 66

Paris, France
Served in 1944 as headquarters for the Alsos Mission, in which U.S. officers visited France and Germany to ascertain German technical developments during World War II, 102-103

Pasch, Colonel Boris, USA
At the end of World War II took part in the Alsos Mission to France and Germany to assess German technical developments, 102

Pate, General Randolph M., USMC
Commandant who provided a ready answer in the late 1950s when Congress questioned the Marine Corps about a large supply on hand of canned hamburgers, 193-194

Pay and Allowances
In the 1920s naval officers could receive flight pay but midshipmen could not, 9; in the early 1930s, during the Depression, naval personnel took a pay cut, 43-44; in 1959 Congress passed a law that retired pay would no longer be based on active duty pay, 51-52

Pelly, Thomas
Congressional representative from Washington state who tried to get advance word in the late 1950s when the Puget Sound Naval Shipyard would be getting jobs, 208-209

Philadelphia Navy Yard
In the early 1940s solved a problem with "singing" propellers on the light cruiser Denver (CL-58), 84-85; had a shop that could machine large-diameter propellers,

86-87; in the early 1940s did a fine job on the construction of the battleship New Jersey (BB-62), 89

Philippine Islands
Congressional concerns in the late 1950s about the effect of sewer drainage problems in the city of Olongapo on the adjacent U.S. naval base at Subic Bay, 194-195; repair problem with a U.S. destroyer in the late 1950s, 274

Poland
In 1945 the Soviets violated agreements made at Yalta concerning the occupation of the port of Gdynia, 108-110

Polaris Program
In the late 1950s Electric Boat Company built the first submarines to be armed with Polaris missiles, 211; development of the missile, 212-214; congressional support, 282

Pratt, Albert
Assistant Secretary of the Navy who in 1955 accompanied Mumma during his congressional hearings to become Chief of the Bureau of Ships, 183-184

Promotion of Officers
In the mid-1930s U.S. naval officers serving in Europe had trouble getting promoted because examination facilities weren't available, 50-51, 56; as an engineering specialist, Hyman G. Rickover needed congressional support to become a four-star admiral, 75, 283-284

Propellers
In the mid-1930s the French passenger liner Normandie experienced severe vibration problems that led to several propeller modifications, 49-50, 79; propeller research in the early 1940s at the David Taylor Model Basin, 73, 79-80, 159-160; work in the early 1940s to correct vibration problems with the propellers in various battleships, 79, 81-82, 88-89, 91-92, 152-153, 255-256; problems in World War II with "singing" propellers on various types of ships, 83-87; quieting submarine propellers, 93-96; in 1944 U.S. Navy Bureau of Ships representatives went to Britain to aid the Royal Navy with propeller problems on the aircraft carrier Implacable, 99-101; pros and cons of submarines having only one propeller rather than two, 119-120, 150-152; in the early 1950s the propellers in the new Mitscher (DL-2)-class destroyers were susceptible to cracking in seawater, 138-139; propeller shafts on the former French battleship Richelieu, which was completed in 1943 at the New York Navy Yard, 153-154; design and testing of the propellers for the Fletcher (DD-445)-class destroyers in the early 1940s, 227

Propulsion Plants
As fleet flagship in the 1920s, the armored cruiser Seattle had a quadruple-expansion steam plant, 22; in 1928 the aircraft carrier Saratoga (CV-3), which had an electric-

drive system, averaged 33 knots during a speed run off Southern California, 23; fuel consumption in the Saratoga, 26; in the mid-1930s the French passenger liner Normandie experienced severe vibration problems that led to several propeller modifications, 49-50, 79; study conducted in the late 1930s on condenser problems in the engineering plants of the ships of Destroyer Flotilla Two on the West Coast, 60-62; quality of the plant in the destroyer Clark (DD-361), commissioned in 1936, 64-65; requirement in the Clark that water and oil not be mixed in fuel tanks, 64-65 in 1939, with modest funding support from the type commander, the crew of the destroyer Clark (DD-361) did a ship's force overhaul at Mare Island Navy Yard, 71-72; propeller research in the early 1940s at the David Taylor Model Basin, 73, 79-81; work during the early 1940s in correcting vibration problems in battleships, 79, 81-82, 88-89, 91-92, 152-153, 157-160; problems in World War II with "singing" propellers on various types of ships, 83-87; quieting submarine propellers, 93-96; in 1942 Rear Admiral Earle Mills cautioned Mumma against speaking about nuclear power plants, 98-99; in 1944 U.S. Navy Bureau of Ships representatives went to Britain to aid the Royal Navy with propeller problems on the aircraft carrier Implacable, 99-101; in World War II Hellmuth Walter worked on a hydrogen peroxide propulsion plant for German submarines, 104, 106, 108, 113-117, 120-121; pros and cons of submarines having only one propeller rather than two, 119-120, 150-152; nuclear power developmental efforts by the Bureau of Ships in the period shortly after World War II, 126-132, 140-141; in the early 1950s the Bureau of Ships did experiments on a high-pressure, high-temperature steam plant tested in the experimental destroyer Timmerman (DD-828), 133-137; in the early 1950s the propellers in the new Mitscher (DL-2)-class destroyers were susceptible to cracking in seawater, 138-139; propeller shafts on the former French battleship Richelieu, which was completed in 1943 at the New York Navy Yard, 153-154; when the Dealey (DE-1006)-class destroyer escorts were designed in the early 1950s, they were not equipped with enough power, 155; submarines achieved much greater propulsive efficiency when they had teardrop-shaped hulls such as those in the Skipjack (SSN-585) class, 186-188; justification in the late 1950s for a nuclear-powered aircraft carrier and nuclear-powered escorts, 189-190, 268-270; during construction in the 1950s the aircraft carrier Saratoga (CVA-60) had different main machinery than her near-sister Forrestal (CVA-59), 210; deliberate melt-down of a prototype nuclear reactor in the early 1950s at Arco, Idaho, 211-212; tests of the submarine Nautilus (SSN-571) in 1955 went well, 216; sodium-cooled plant in the submarine Seawolf (SSN-575), 216-217

Puget Sound Navy Yard, Bremerton, Washington
In the late 1950s Representative Thomas Pelly from Washington tried to get advance word when the shipyard would be getting jobs, 208-209

Pye, Rear Admiral William S., USN (USNA, 1901)
In the late 1930s served as Commander Destroyers Battle Force and Commander Destroyer Flotilla Two, 60, 68, 70

Raborn, Vice Admiral William F., Jr., USN (USNA, 1928)
In the mid-1950s commanded the aircraft carrier Bennington (CVA-20) and later ran the Polaris program, 180, 212; given authority within BuShips and BuOrd to run Polaris development, 213-215

Racial Issues
In the late 1930s the destroyer Clark (DD-361) replaced black messmen with Filipinos to save on food costs, 59-60; blacks had limited job opportunities on board the Clark, 62-63

Radar
German U-boats were surprised during World War II by the effectiveness of American airborne radar, 117

Radford, Admiral Arthur W., USN (Ret.) (USNA, 1916)
In the early 1920s provided aviation orientation for Naval Academy midshipmen, 5; in the late 1950s, following, his retirement from the Navy, served on the board of the Worthington Corporation, 288-290

Ramsey, Hobart C.
In 1959, as chairman of the Worthington Corporation, recruited Mumma for a post-Navy job, 289-290

Ranger, USS (CVA-61)
Aircraft carrier that was visited by Mumma and other flag officers in the late 1950s during her sea trials, 251-252

Rathburne, USS (DD-113)
In the early 1930s collided with the destroyer Waters (DD-115) and damaged the other ship, 40-41

Rayburn, Samuel T.
Texas Democrat who was an excellent Speaker of the House in the 1950s, 282-283

Read, Commander Albert C., USN (USNA, 1907)
In 1919 commanded the crew of the NC-4 flying boat that flew the Atlantic, later executive officer of the aircraft carrier Saratoga (CV-3), 76-78

Richelieu
Former French battleship that was completed at the New York Navy Yard in 1943, after joining the Allies, 153-154

Richmond, USS (CL-9)
Light cruiser that in September 1926 ran into an Atlantic hurricane during a voyage to Cuba with sister ships, 14-16

Rickover, Admiral Hyman G., USN (Ret.) (USNA, 1922)
In the early 1950s, as an engineering specialist, he needed congressional support to become a four-star admiral, 75, 283-284; favored multiple propellers for nuclear submarines, 120; post-World War II involvement in the development of nuclear power for ships, 128-132, 140, 142; during World War II was involved with the Navy's shipboard electrical requirements, 130, 176; got rid of promising young subordinates, 173-174; recommended Mumma in the mid-1950s to serve as Chief of the Bureau of Ships, 176; had no role in the design of the Skipjack (SSN-585)-class submarine, 188; was stretched by the work in the late 1950s to develop nuclear-powered surface ships, 190-191; because of Rickover's methods, shipbuilding cost overruns increased once Mumma retired in 1959 after being Chief of the Bureau of Ships, 199-200; deliberate melt-down of a prototype nuclear reactor in the early 1950s at Arco, Idaho, 211-212; asked the Bureau of Ships to announce the need in the late 1950s to put a different engine in submarine Seawolf (SSN-575), 217; once he got into the nuclear power program, he was not a broad-gauged flag officer, 240, 249; claimed to be a victim of anti-Semitism within the Navy, 247-249; conflicts with defense contractors, 263; in 1958 attended the keel-laying for the nuclear-powered aircraft carrier Enterprise (CVAN-65), 269

Robinson, Rear Admiral Samuel M., USN (USNA, 1903)
As Chief of the Bureau of Engineering in the mid-1930s, was interested in the engineering achievements in the French passenger liner Normandie, 44-45, 157

Roddis, Lieutenant Commander Louis H., USN (USNA, 1939)
Was selected shortly after World War II as one of the initial participants in the Navy's nuclear power program, 129, 140, 200; consultant work in the 1980s, 173-174

Roop, Commander Wendell P., USN
In the early 1940s was involved with propeller research at the David Taylor Model Basin, 80-81; at the end of World War II took part in the Alsos Mission to France and Germany to assess German technical developments, 97, 101, 105

Roosevelt, President Franklin D.
In World War II decreed that there be no interference by the Navy in the construction of escort aircraft carriers by shipbuilder Henry J. Kaiser, 86

Royal Marines
Contributed manpower to the Naval Technical Mission Europe that was gathering information in Germany at the end of World War II, 113

Royal Navy
When Mumma returned to the United States in 1936 after postgraduate study in France he reported on the armor arrangement in the British battleships Nelson and Rodney, 56, 157-158; in 1944 U.S. Navy Bureau of Ships representatives went to Britain to aid the Royal Navy with propeller problems on the aircraft carrier

Implacable, 99-101; had representatives at the 1945 international conference at Yalta in the Crimea, 109-110; did some developmental work after World War II on hydrogen peroxide propulsion for submarines, 120-121; role of the Royal Corps of Naval Constructors, 192; Mumma told his British counterparts about U.S. shipbuilding practices during a 1956 visit to the United Kingdom, 231-232; Admiral of the Fleet Lord Louis Mountbatten reorganized the Admiralty structure after a visit to the United States, 232-233

Russell, Rear Admiral James S., USN (USNA, 1926)
Served as Chief of the Bureau of Aeronautics from 1955 to 1957, even though he was an unrestricted line officer, 236, 259-260; while serving as a naval aviator in World War II had an interesting dinner with the Aleut Indians, 260-261

Sadler, Captain Frank H., USN (USNA, 1903)
As commanding officer of the Navy's Postgraduate School in the early 1930s suggested that Mumma take a year of education in France, 44-45

Saltonstall, Leverett
Was involved as a U.S. Senator in the late 1950s when a group of employees at the Boston Naval Shipyard tried unsuccessfully to form a veterans' union, 206-208

San Diego, California
In the late 1930s ready destroyers maintained steam pressure so they could intercept and board suspicious-looking ships in the area, 66-67; in the late 1930s Mumma did a fine job of navigating the destroyer Clark (DD-361) when anchoring in fog in Coronado Roads, California, 68-70

San Francisco Naval Shipyard (Hunters Point)
In the early 1950s was involved in destroyer conversions, major combatant overhauls, and reactivation of mothballed ships, 143-145; roles of various officers in the command structure, 146; visit in the early 1950s from the Shah of Iran, who was interested in developing a shipyard for his nation, 146-147; workforce increased during the Korean War, 147-148; activated and overhauled amphibian vehicles for the Marine Corps, 147; concerns of civilian shipyard workers, 148-149

Santo Domingo
In August 1916 the armored cruiser Memphis was washed ashore at Santo Domingo by a tidal wave, and the hulk remained there for years afterward, 16, 18; in 1927 was visited by the Commander in Chief U.S. Fleet in his flagship, the armored cruiser Seattle, 18-19

Saratoga, USS (CV-3)
Aircraft carrier that in 1928 averaged 33 knots during a speed run off Southern California, 23; after going into commission in 1927 had a succession of fine commanding officers, 24; rivalry with her sister ship Lexington (CV-2), 25-26, 30, 32-35, 209-210, 278-279; fuel consumption, 26; ballast tanks on the port side

compensated for the extra weight of the island and guns to starboard, 26-27; the ship was able to turn in a tight circle, 27; incident in which Lieutenant Richard Whitehead crashed an O2U on deck because his tailhook caught barrier, 28-29; the captain's gig was destroyed as a result of spilled gasoline and a fire when the ship was in Long Beach, 29-30; high-quality enlisted men in the ship's crew, 33-34; in January 1929 took part in a fleet problem that involved an attack on the Panama Canal, 34-35; work at the Puget Sound Navy Yard, 35-36

Saratoga, USS (CVA-60)
Aircraft carrier that was commissioned in 1956 with an improved propulsion plant over that in her sister ship Forrestal (CVA-59), 137-138, 210

Saunders, Captain Harold E., USN (USNA, 1912)
Made a substantial contribution to the design and construction of the David Taylor Model Basin, Carderock, Maryland, which opened shortly before World War II, 75-76, 79; great academic achievement as a Naval Academy midshipman, 76; made contributions in the area of propeller research, 80; belief in the value of skegs near the propellers of battleships, 159

Schade, Captain Henry A., USN (USNA, 1923)
In the early 1930s went to Germany for postgraduate work in engineering, 46; at the end of World War II took part in the Alsos Mission to France and Germany to assess German technical developments, 97, 101, 104-105; in 1944 went to Britain to help the Royal Navy solve vibration problems in the aircraft carrier Implacable, 99-101

Scotland
In 1944 representatives of the U.S. Navy's Bureau of Ships went to the Royal Navy dockyard at Rosyth to ride on sea trials of the British aircraft carrier Implacable, 99-101

Sears, Captain Hayden A., USA (USMA, 1920)
In the early 1930s served as a U.S. military courier in Europe, 52-53

Seattle, USS (Armored Cruiser)
In 1927 visited Santo Domingo, 16, 18-19; other operations in the mid-1920s as flagship of the U.S. Fleet, 17-18, 22-23; in 1927 transferred fleet flag to the battleship Texas (BB-35) and was decommissioned, 21; quadruple-expansion steam propulsion plant, 22

Seawolf, USS (SSN-575)
Nuclear submarine built in the mid-1950s with a reactor cooled by liquid sodium, 216-217

Sequoia
Secretary of the Navy's yacht that was used in the late 1950s for conferences of industry leaders to be involved in the Polaris ballistic missile submarine program, 213-214

Shipbuilding
As Secretary of Defense in the 1960s, Robert S. McNamara instituted total package procurement, which involved buying all ships of a given class from one defense contractor, 197-198; in the late 1950s BuShips allocated work among various shipyards, 197-198; the effect of the Vinson-Trammell Act, passed by Congress in 1934, was still felt in the 1950s because it required a certain proportion of Navy shipbuilding be done in naval shipyards, 200-201; in the years after World War II several European shipyards built ships under the aegis of the U.S. Marshall Plan, 221; role of the Navy supervisor of shipbuilding in commercial shipyards, 247, 249

Ship Characteristics Board
Influence in the 1950s on the design of U.S. Navy ships, 155-156, 276-278; justification in the late 1950s for the construction of a nuclear-powered aircraft carrier, 189-190

Ship Design
Work in the 1930s on the French passenger liner Normandie, 45, 48-50; design in the 1930s of the U.S. North Carolina (BB-55)-class battleships, 50, 81-82, 152-153; pros and cons of submarines having only one propeller rather than two, 119-120, 150-152; in the early 1950s the David Taylor Model Basin tested a true hydrodynamic design for submarines, 149-151; design in the early 1950s of the Dealey (DE-1006)-class destroyer escorts, 155; design of amphibious warfare ships, 155-156; in the 1930s the French designed destroyers that sacrificed firepower and range in order to achieve high speed, 158; Mumma's push in the mid-1950s for nuclear submarines to have an advanced hull design, 186; during construction in the 1950s the aircraft carrier Saratoga (CVA-60) had different main machinery than her near-sister Forrestal (CVA-59), 210; use of the Skipjack (SSN-585)-class hull in the late 1950s as the basis for the first Polaris ballistic missile submarines, 211, 214; a longitudinal bulkhead was probably the cause of the capsizing and loss of the Italian passenger liner Andrea Doria in 1956 following a collision, 222-224; some changes to the design of the U.S. passenger liner United States, which was completed in the early 1950s, came as a result of Navy requirements, 226, 255, 262; following World War II the U.S. Navy put an increased emphasis on habitability in its warships, 229; design work in the late 1950s within the Bureau of Ships, 252-253

Skate (SSN-578)-class Submarines
In the mid-1950s Mumma pushed for a more hydronamically advanced hull form than that in the Skate class, 186-187; the last ship planned for the class was redesigned and became the first of the Skipjack (SSN-585) class, 187-188

Skipjack, USS (SSN-585)
The last ship planned for the Skate (SSN-578) class was redesigned and became the Skipjack, 187-188; performed well on trials, 188-189 in the late 1950s, after steering the Skipjack, Assistant Secretary of the Navy Wilfred J. McNeil agreed to fund another ship of the class, 189

Skipjack (SSN-585)-class Submarines
Had efficient propellers without vibration problems, 87; construction of the Scamp (SSN-588) at the Mare Island Naval Shipyard, 176; the last ship planned for the Skate (SSN-578) class was redesigned and became the first of the Skipjack (SSN-585) class, 187-188; use of the Skipjack-class hull in the late 1950s as the basis for the first Polaris ballistic missile submarines, 211, 214

Smith, Margaret Chase
U.S. Senator from Maine who was involved in the confirmation process in the mid-1950s when Mumma became Chief of the Bureau of Ships, 182-183; concern about the Portsmouth Naval Shipyard in Kittery, Maine, 196

Society of Naval Architects and Marine Engineers (SNAME)
Professional society that contributes to the advancement of knowledge in the field, 234-236

Solberg, Commander Thorwald A., USN (USNA, 1916)
In the late 1930s served as head of design in the Bureau of Engineering, 57, 81

Sonar
Impact in the 1950s of large sonar domes on the bows of destroyers, 156-157

South Dakota (BB-57)-class Battleships
Inclusion of skegs near the propellers to enhance water flow, 81, 153

Soviet Union
In 1945, at the end of World War II in Europe, a number of German scientists chose to be captured by Americans rather than Soviets, 108; violations of the 1945 Yalta agreement concerning occupation of Gdynia, Poland, 108-110

Stark, Admiral Harold R., USN (USNA, 1903)
As Commander U.S. Naval Forces Europe in World War II, recommended ending a technical exchange with the Soviet Union because of violation of agreements concerning access to Gdynia, Poland, 110

Stockholm (Passenger Liner)
Swedish ship that was damaged in July 1956 off Nantucket by colliding with the Italian liner Andrea Doria, 222-224

Subic Bay, Philippines
Congressional concerns in the late 1950s about the effect of sewer drainage problems in the city of Olongapo on the adjacent U.S. naval base at Subic Bay, 194-195

Submarines
Developmental work in the early 1940s to quiet the propellers on submarines, 93-96; in World War II Hellmuth Walter worked on a hydrogen peroxide propulsion plant for German submarines, 104, 106, 108, 113-117, 120-121; pros and cons of having only one propeller rather than two, 119-120, 150-152; nuclear power developmental efforts by the Bureau of Ships in the period shortly after World War II, 126-132, 140-142; testing in the early 1950s of a true hydrodynamic design for submarines, 149-151; the last ship planned for the Skate (SSN-578) class was redesigned with a teardrop hull and became the Skipjack, which performed well on trials, 187-189; development in the late 1950s of the Polaris ballistic missile submarines, 211-215

Symington, W. Stuart
U.S. Senator from Missouri who was involved in the confirmation process in the mid-1950s when Mumma became Chief of the Bureau of Ships, 183-184

TFX
Controversial multi-service fighter plane that Robert McNamara tried to inflict on the Navy in the 1960s during his tenure as Secretary of Defense, 198-199

Tacoma, Washington
In the winter of 1929-30 the city was supplied with electrical power by the aircraft carrier Lexington (CV-2), 36-37

Taylor, Rear Admiral David W., USN (USNA, 1885)
Skilled naval constructor who developed the bulbous bow for ships, 48, 157; in the late 1880s did his postgraduate education in Europe, 49; produced a superior academic record as a Naval Academy midshipman, 75-76; involved in the design of the NC-4 aircraft, 76-77, 169-170; in the late 19th century sold the idea of a model basin to Congress, 169-170

Thebaud, Vice Admiral Leo H., USN (Ret.) (USNA, 1913)
In the mid-1930s, as a commander, served as U.S. naval attaché in Paris, 47; author of a book on leadership, 58; in the late 1930s served as commanding officer of the destroyer Clark (DD-361), 58-59, 68; in 1959 invited Mumma to use his home following his retirement from the Navy, 289-290

Thomas, Charles S.
As Secretary of the Navy in 1954, attended the centennial celebration at the Mare Island Naval Shipyard, 175; in 1955 heard Mumma's pitch for an advanced submarine design, 186; assessment of as SecNav, 193; didn't have a ready answer in the late 1950s when Congress questioned the Marine Corps about a large supply on hand of canned hamburgers, 193-194; involved in preventing construction of an

aircraft carrier on the West Coast, 201-202; minimal experience in naval matters before becoming Secretary, 280

Timmerman, USS (DD-828)
Destroyer that in the early 1950s was used as an experimental ship to test new high-temperature, high-pressure steam propulsion equipment, 133-137

Todd Shipyards
Did a good job for the Navy in the late 1950s, later got overextended, 230, 251

Tomlinson, Lieutenant Daniel W. IV, USN (USNA, 1918)
Colorful aviator who served in the late 1920s in the air group of the aircraft carrier Saratoga (CV-3), 28, 31-32; spectacular landing on a street in Coronado, 32

Training
Naval Academy midshipmen made summer training cruises to Europe in the mid-1920s, 6-9; in 1926 members of that year's Naval Academy graduating class were given indoctrinal flight training, 25-26; Lieutenant Commander C. Julian Wheeler, skipper of the destroyer Waters (DD-115) from 1931 to 1934, did an excellent job of teaching his junior officers, 38-39; shakedown at Guantanamo in 1937 for the crew of the recently commissioned destroyer Clark (DD-361), 66

Turnbaugh, Lieutenant Commander Marshall E., USN (USNA, 1939)
Was selected shortly after World War II to be one of the initial participants in the Navy's nuclear power program, 132, 140

Uniforms
When members of the U.S. Naval Technical Mission Europe were traveling in 1945 they wore Army uniforms, 112

Unions
See: Labor Unions

United States, SS (Passenger Liner)
In 1956 William Francis Gibbs asked Mumma to ride this liner to Europe and give him a technical assessment of the ship, 221-225, 228; some changes to the design came as a result of Navy requirements, 226, 255, 262

V-1 Rockets
U.S. Bureau of Ships representatives were present in London in 1944 when these German weapons rained down on the city, 100-101; launching mechanism, 106

V-2 Rockets
Built by the Germans in World War II, 106-107

Vinson, Carl
Georgia congressman who had considerable impact as chairman of the House Armed Services Committee in the late 1950s, 196-197

Vinson-Trammell Act
The effect of this 1934 act of Congress was still felt in the 1950s because it allocated a certain proportion of Navy shipbuilding to naval shipyards, 200-201

Von Braun, Wernher
German rocket scientist who developed V-1 and V-2 weapons during World War II, 106-107; chose to be captured by Americans rather than Soviets, 108

Wallin, Rear Admiral Homer N., USN (USNA, 1917)
As Chief of the Bureau of Ships in the early 1950s was criticized for not supporting Hyman Rickover for selection to flag rank, 283-284

Walter, Hellmuth
German scientist who worked during World War II on a hydrogen peroxide propulsion plant for submarines, 104, 106, 108, 113-117, 120-121; worked on the ME 163 rocket airplane during the war, 107, 116; chose to be captured by Americans rather than Soviets, 108; in the 1950s worked in the United States for the Worthington Corporation, 288-291

War Games
In January 1929 the aircraft carriers Saratoga (CV-3) and Lexington (CV-2) participated in a fleet problem that involved an attack on the Panama Canal, 34-35

Washington, SS (U.S. Passenger Liner)
The flagship of the United States Lines, in 1934 this ship took Mumma and his family to France, 46-47

Washington, USS (BB-56)
When she went into commission in 1941 she had problems with severe propeller vibrations, 81-82, 160-161; sea trials, 90-91, 160-161; inquiries made by Captain Hyman Rickover on the propeller situation, 176

Wasp, USS (CV-7)
Aircraft carrier that went into service in 1940 and ran sea trials off Rockland, Maine, 91

Waters, USS (DD-115)
The ship's design limited her ability to operate in rough seas, 37-38; voyage to Hawaii in 1932 for maneuvers, 38, 40-41; Lieutenant Commander C. Julian Wheeler, the skipper from 1931 to 1934, was an excellent teacher, 38-39; suffered damage during a collision with the destroyer Rathburne (DD-113), 40-41; the ship was in

pretty good material commission even though she had been out of service for a while, 41-42

Weather
In September 1926 a division of U.S. light cruisers ran into an Atlantic hurricane during a voyage to Cuba, 14-16; in August 1916 the armored cruiser Memphis was washed ashore at Santo Domingo by a tidal wave, 16, 18; in the late 1930s Mumma did a fine job of navigating the destroyer Clark (DD-361) when anchoring in fog in Coronado Roads, California, 68-70; unusual phenomenon of very large waves, 168

Westinghouse Corporation
In the period shortly after World War II was involved in developmental work for the Navy's nuclear power program, 132

Wheeler, Lieutenant Commander C. Julian, USN (USNA, 1916)
In the early 1930s was a fine teacher and leader while commanding the destroyer Waters (DD-115) during operations in the Pacific, 38-39

Whitehead, Lieutenant Richard F., USN
In the late 1920s crashed an O2U on the deck of the aircraft carrier Saratoga (CV-3) when his tailhook caught the barrier wire, 28-29

Whiting, Commander Kenneth, USN (USNA, 1905)
In the late 1920s served as the first executive officer of the aircraft carrier Saratoga (CV-3), 24, 31

Wilson, Charles E.
Was Secretary of Defense in the mid-1950s when various issues arose, 193, 201-202

Withington, Rear Admiral Frederic S., USN USNA, 1923)
As Chief of the Bureau of Ordnance in the mid-1950s agreed to give Rear Admiral William Raborn status within the bureau as part of the Polaris ballistic missile submarine development program, 213; involvement in conversion of guided missile cruisers, 258; in the late 1950s served as Commander U.S. Naval Forces Japan, 274

World War I
As Secretary of War during World War I, Newton D. Baker assigned Morton C. Mumma to teach soldiers how to shoot well, 2; in the mid-1930s Mumma made a Memorial Day speech about the World War I Battle of Chateau-Thierry, 54-55

Worthington Corporation
Mumma worked for the corporation in a variety of capacities following his 1959 retirement from the Navy, 287-294

Yalta, Crimea
   In 1945 the Soviets violated agreements made at Yalta concerning the occupation of the port of Gdynia, 108-110

Yarnell, Captain Harry E., USN (USNA, 1897)
   Fine officer who was first skipper when the aircraft carrier Saratoga (CV-3) went into commission in 1927, 24

www.ingramcontent.com/pod-product-compliance
Lightning Source LLC
Chambersburg PA
CBHW080618170426
43209CB00007B/1461